FOR
THALIA MALCOLM

CONTENTS

PREFACE

THIS book is the product of a tenure of the Webb Research Fellowship at the London School of Economics and Political Science. The fellowship is designed to produce studies in fields in which Sidney and Beatrice Webb were interested. The Soviet Union was, of course, one of these. The conclusions of this book are very different from those arrived at by the Webbs in their *Soviet Communism: A New Civilisation*.

The Webbs were writing in the 1930s, when a great many facts which are now known were not available. And if their study was in certain ways misleading, it can hardly be said that this was their fault. Brought up in a tradition in which official documents and statistics more or less automatically corresponded with the real state of affairs, or, if inaccurate, were only so through unintentional errors, they accepted almost without question those of the U.S.S.R., which are in many respects now admitted to have been consciously falsified in varying degrees. Again, they accepted the formal, official structure of society as corresponding, or at least tending to correspond, to what was really going on. For there is a good deal in the Soviet Constitution, and the constitutions of the Communist Party of the Soviet Union, the Soviet Trade Unions and the Soviet Co-operatives, which if put into practice might well produce the society which the Webbs thought they saw.

Soviet internal politics present a field which is very fruitful in the general study of questions of State power. It is so different from what we are used to that it may tend to shake up and freshen our notions. It is also interesting — to the point, on occasion, of being positively hair-raising. Moreover, in the circumstances of the world to-day it is more than ever important that we obtain realistic views of the attitudes, backgrounds and practices of the Soviet political leadership. For it will be agreed that sound opinions on the conduct of our international affairs can scarcely be formed if we are under misapprehensions about one of the most important factors.

The aim here is more to present the study to the general audience of serious students of politics, than to offer — what is in any case impossible — an analysis claiming to be definitive or beyond controversy. It is hoped, nevertheless, that the conditions and general theory of the study have been adequately developed and that the material it so presented as to be of service even to those who may put different interpretations upon it.

R. C.

PART I

THE STUDY OF THE STRUGGLE
FOR POWER

CHAPTER ONE

INTRODUCTION TO THE STUDY

ALTHOUGH this book differs from the Webbs' in its theme, in its approach and in its conclusions, yet it follows them in one respect: it relies on official evidence almost entirely, although this is inadequate. It is not intended as a political history of the U.S.S.R. in recent years. It is not an attempt to provide the whole truth, but to show the evidence: what is known, and what is hypothesis. Further, it strives to show the degree of uncertainty — of how hypotheses range in this sphere from a moral certainty to the most highly tentative sketches of possibilities.

For this is a field in which, to a very large extent, discipline is lacking. Yet, where the evidence is so defective, what discipline is possible? The answer, it seems to me, is simply the establishment of criteria of evidence and of hypothesis.

For the serious student the 'Kremlinologist' has always been a somewhat disreputable figure. He has been seen as someone appearing to speak absolute certainties on the basis of cloudy figures swirling in his crystal ball. For he has had, in the nature of ordinary interest in the matter, not to do as this book does, and restrict the evidence and qualify the conclusions, but to produce for his readers as far as possible an appearance of completeness. This has often led to extrapolations, sometimes inspired indeed, beyond what the traffic will actually stand. More often it has led to the substitution of flat assertion where 'it may reasonably be assumed that' would be more suitable. (In fact this slight grammatical change would make, for example, much of the late Dr. Borkenau's work unexceptionable. I know that as it stands it has put off a number of readers, really rather unfairly, by an air of omniscience which even the non-expert realises cannot be seriously sustained.)

It also leads, in the comparative absence of crucial evidence, to putting, or appearing to put, more weight on individual reports than they can possibly justify. Moreover, again because of the very shortage of good evidence, it leads to an attempt to use *every* piece of evidence in reconstructing events. I shall be finding that a good deal in the course of certain individual careers is quite meaningless with our present knowledge; and that, indeed, though the general outline is plain enough, whole trains of political events (like the Georgian purges) present large areas of incomprehensibility.

It may be asked, if so much suspension of judgment is recommended, what use the method can be. The answer, I think, is that the careful consideration of all facets of an event in the field and of the relevant information about the people concerned at least reduces the possibilities to a limited number, till only some small move may be needed to reduce these to one, and thus provide an illumination to future events, and retrospectively to these too. We are in a realm comparable to that of researchers into fossil man. The odd tooth or even jaw-bone may be susceptible to various explanations, but careful study of it is all that is open to the scientist, and he may at any time be presented with another bone or artefact which will complete the picture. It may even be that all his first ideas are wrong, and the new information may require a complete reversal of the earlier. But (so long as he has not permitted his previous estimate to ossify into dogma) he is still the best prepared to digest the new material. In these sciences of defective information, indeed, no one can be sure of not being hoaxed by a Piltdown skull — or if not by a fake at least by a series of accidental correlations. In neither case does this mean that the studies themselves are either unscientific or unworthwhile.

As I said, I have thought it best to confine myself almost entirely to official evidence, that presented by Soviet statements and admitted events. This is certainly a severe limitation. And it is not one which it would be fair to impose on anyone writing a political history. There are unofficial sources which have been both very reliable and at the same time far more informative than the official ones. For instance the information on the Kirov case given by Alexander Orlov in his book *The Secret History of Stalin's Crimes*, though based only on N.K.V.D. gossip, has since been practically confirmed by Khrushchev's Secret Speech. In later times Mr. Seweryn Bialer's report of the meeting of the Plenum of the Central Committee in July 1955 seems to be quite authentic. But in dealing with this sort of evidence one is instantly in difficulties. How can one test its reliability? If it fits in with all the known facts, that is certainly a point in its favour. Yet many contradictory rumours and reports exist, for example, about the arrest of Beria. All of them fit. And there is no particular reason to choose one rather than another. The historian might be well advised to take this sort of evidence into account, with an eye on possible confirmation from future events. But to provide a criterion for distinguishing between the reliabilities of the more plausible reports for the purpose of this book seemed impossible.

We have recently, indeed, been presented with rather a lot of what one might call quasi-official evidence — interviews with Soviet leaders published later in the Western Press, but never confirmed by the Russians. One cannot treat this as wholly reliable either. It is perfectly possible that some misunderstandings could have taken place — for instance Khrushchev said at the XXIst Congress that the American Senator Humphreys had totally misquoted his views on China (Khrushchev's Secret Speech of February 1956 is another matter, and the question of its authenticity, which has been ambiguously and belatedly denied, has been dealt with in Chapter Three).

However, although this unofficial evidence would provide us with more detail, it is not very often that it would change the essentials of our position. We would still be left with a collection of evidence which, though a little fuller, could only be interpreted by the methods I am examining. Since my main thesis can be demonstrated equally on the basis of the official evidence or of the official evidence plus this unofficial material, it seems sounder to confine myself to the former. At the same time it avoids the doubts which must arise from a broadening which would also be a dilution.

Writings on the subject of questions of power in the U.S.S.R. are often criticised roughly on the grounds that they ignore the existence of large-scale social forces. It should be said at once that though this book is not in principle concerned with these forces it does not for a moment deny or denigrate them. The Soviet leaders do not live in a vacuum, and however much the totalitarian apparatus is designed to enable a few at the centre to manipulate the mass social tendencies, this does not mean that those tendencies do not exist nor, particularly when there is dissension at the centre, that they can fail to be taken into account. But this study is concerned with those large-scale movements only in so far as they are given political expression. And in Soviet circumstances they are not given any direct political expression: they figure simply as influences, competing with other and often more powerful influences, on the moves made in the only area where political change is possible — the central group of politicians.

It is not that this approach lacks a tradition and a background. On the contrary, it is one of the oldest of historical attitudes. The student of this side of Soviet affairs must base himself more on the tradition of Suetonius and Procopius and Tacitus, of Machiavelli and St. Simon and Abulfeda. History written in terms of the lives of princes and the stories of successful usurpation has been denounced as inadequate for many generations now, and rightly so. But in certain respects and in certain matters at least (and these include political history in the U.S.S.R.) this seems to have gone too far. Great social changes, it has been said for a century, progress in much the same way regardless of the particular events of government or war. At its worst this amounts to defining as 'essential' that which happens to suit the thesis. (If a bullet had not struck Stonewall Jackson's left arm on May 2, 1863, the United States might have become two countries. But this would not be 'essential'. Why not? — simply by the circular argument: the result would have depended on accident and not on great sweeping processes, *therefore* it could hardly count.) The worst is not typical, certainly. And clearly there is a sense in which the mass of the world's population might be living in much the same way regardless of any political or military events at all — but this is a point that scarcely seems worth making.

Still, there seems to be a definite feeling among sociologists that the actual events of politics and war are in some way superficial. They believe that deep social tides are more basic to all change in human circumstances and that battles and *coups d'état* are somehow rather petty subjects. And it is true that to concentrate attention on them in such a way as to imply a denial of the existence of the deeper movements would be absolutely wrong. Just the same, it is a little unreal to deal only with the deeper movements and ignore the visible political and military climaxes. It is rather as if a man interested in race-horses should study only their pedigrees, their form and their general condition, without concerning himself with the actual race.

Although military history is a rather despised sideline in most historical faculties, the balance of great social forces may depend on the movements in one day of a brigade of infantry. A similar argument applies to politics, particularly in totalitarian states. It is too early to say what the long-term result of the rise to power of Gomulka in Poland might be. It is certainly conceivable that the whole trend of history may have been altered by it, and in certain very basic ways. Yet, as we now know, its success depended on very minor accidents in the technical details of *coups d'état*. The abortive putsch of the Natolin group against Gomulka had a very good chance of succeeding. And according to the material made public the decisive point seems to have been as small a matter as the fact that their plans were given in error to a member of the Polish Security Police wrongly thought to favour them. In Soviet circumstances details of this sort are very unlikely to be available. But we should at least be able to form a general idea of the forces involved, and the significances of some at least of the moves.

But even if it were held that the facts studied here were of little significance, it would, I hope, be conceded that they deserve study. To the scientist, even the social scientist, no phenomena can be too petty or too vulgar for investigation. I do not think I am wrong in detecting, here and there, a slight feeling that the struggle for power is in some way not academically respectable. A little reflection will no doubt result in the abandonment of what will be seen to be an unreasonable prejudice. Yet it may be worth tracing its causes.

It is only a minor consideration, no doubt, that such a study is 'impure' in that it is bound to imply certain political conclusions: for the mere act of studying the U.S.S.R. at all, rather than accepting official Soviet statements, is itself in a sense a politically controversial act. More important is the speculative nature of the study. This is comparable, in arousing a certain uneasiness, to developments in other fields — for instance, the resistance of early psychologists, to whom their science meant discovering why coins feel larger when placed on the tongue, to this century's techniques of personality study. And this leads us

B

to what is perhaps the basic cause of disturbance — that the type of investigation is not, or is not yet, academically established. But this of course is true, initially, of any study. The chairs and fellowships are never created until the groundwork has been done by amateurs, often quite as eccentric and undomesticated from an academic point of view as any of the 'black art' Kremlinologists.

Moreover, the circumstances of political events in the Soviet Union are, from the point of view of a traditional sober-minded researcher, vulgar and sensational. In the societies which he is used to studying matters are not settled this way. And the general result of all this is that it requires a great effort, even with the best will in the world, for the sociologist to really feel in his heart, as well as to concede intellectually, that the study is a proper one.

The intellectual climate of the various sciences differs for rather obvious reasons. In certain questions of astronomy, for instance, extremely rigorous treatment on the deductive side is possible, but the facts themselves are hard to establish. With sociology it has usually been the other way round. The facts are readily accessible, but general theoretical methods are comparatively vague. This led, perhaps, to a temper inclining to concentrate on matters in which as many facts as possible are available — on such themes as variations in the price of bus tickets in Rochdale, say. This is admirable. But it does, I think, tend to produce a habit of mind which regards areas where the evidence is defective as unsuitable for 'scientific' inquiry.

Further, the greatest amount of sociological research has taken place in countries where the official evidence is more or less objective. The academic researcher has a special respect for official documentation, and it may come as a considerable wrench to realise that studies exist — as they have indeed since long before Napoleon used to manipulate the 'Moniteur' — in which official statements, and even official figures, are highly suspect and at best probably inferior to estimates deduced by roundabout methods.

Unlike social and even political studies in their usual contexts, such studies made of the U.S.S.R. are bound to suffer from a great inaccessibility of knowledge of what really happened in many circumstances. This applies particularly, of course, to the study of power relationships and policy-making at the top levels. There are often gaps in the knowledge of contemporary events at the top political level even in such countries as the United Kingdom. But they are seldom major gaps, while it is difficult for the student of French or English affairs to imagine a situation like that in the U.S.S.R., where, to take one example, it was literally unknown even by report for more than two years (up to 1953) who held the key post of Minister of State Security. It goes without saying that the structure, too, of many of the key state and Party organs, particularly those most closely involved in power struggles — such as the security apparatus — can only be deduced defectively and very occasionally.

In these circumstances two things are clear. First, such indications and items of evidence as do become available must, though possibly small in themselves, by studied with great care. And secondly, the normal method of operation must be hypothesis. This is not to say that a hypothesis may not (as in the natural sciences) reach the stage of a virtual certainty. But if the researcher is not prepared both to entertain the most tentative hypothesis and to be always ready to sacrifice or amend hypotheses for which the evidence has hitherto seemed strong, he will be using the wrong sort of method.

It should also, I think, be pointed out that the study of these top-level relationships in the U.S.S.R. is in a sense not only a political but also a sociological research. The structure of the Soviet State and Party machinery was developed over a period of years, mainly by Stalin, as a means for imposing the decisions of the leading figure or figures in many political and economic matters, on an often refractory social structure. The totalitarian apparatus is, in a sense, a fulcrum designed to give the leading man or group at least as much weight as whole social classes — like that fulcrum given which Archimedes claimed that one man could move the world.

I have said that there is a resemblance between Kremlinology and palaeontology, in the comparative absence of factual evidence. It may be worth referring to a particular case — that of the Chirotheria. These are still only known by their footprints and no bone of any sort has ever been found. Yet their type, appearance and general characteristics, though admittedly long in dispute, were deduced by Professor Sorgel in his *Die Fahrten der Chirotheria* (Jena, 1925) in a way which has met with universal acceptance. Of course, this is not the dubious magic it might at first appear to a non-palaeontologist. Sorgel had studied deeply all the evidence of the bones of creatures conceivably related to the Chirotherium. He had worked out the dynamics of the tread. And he had examined the footprints with a mind trained, as few in the world could be, to understand their characteristics. He examined them, too, for long periods of time and from all angles and magnifications. He had also, naturally, considered a variety of possibilities, however remote, and every objection, however far-fetched. In principle, though 'Kremlinology' is probably easier, this is the sort of ideal which should be set up in the field. And even admitting that an effort of mind of Sorgel's calibre is probably beyond most of us, that does not mean that we cannot try.

Chirotherium footprints were simply there, perfectly visible to anyone who cared to look at them. The layman could see at once that they fairly closely resembled human hands, and when they were discovered the theory immediately went out that they were some sort of ape. In Soviet matters, too, the *facts* — Beria's execution, say — are often readily understandable and a lay theory can be constructed almost instantly. I have read in a French paper a splendid interpretation of that particular matter in terms of rivalry between Malenkov and Beria for the favours of a well-known ballerina. Some English papers produced soberer but no less inadequate reconstructions. Similar things are printed to this day. And, more important, even experts in other fields are only too inclined in cases like these to give their authority to what are in effect the layest of lay opinions, like Sir James Jeans' forays into philosophy. Restraint is as important as willingness to hypothesise.

Prospective students should remember that it is particularly in a study of this sort, with so many variables and so many unknowns, that the maximum intellectual discipline and intellectual effort are required. It would hardly be exaggerating to compare it in this respect to the questions of strategy in the old wars, where information was defective. Napoleon said, 'If I always appear prepared it is because, before entering on an undertaking, I have meditated for long and have foreseen what may occur.' He was not surprised, simply because he had considered all the possibilities. In this field, where similar uncertainties are bound to prevail, attachment to views which only admit of one or two possibilities is to be discouraged. More important is the meditation of which Napoleon speaks. It is only by constant application that the connections and ideas emerge. For instance, one can read the relevant parts of Khrushchev's Secret Speech twenty or thirty times, and still, by pondering each sentence, find some new implication somewhere which one has previously missed.

I am mainly concerned with the issue of power. It will be seen, I think, that this is a big subject in itself. Matters of policy in almost every field are relevant. In fact it is impossible to speak of struggles for power without the context of the issues over which they were, on paper at least, fought. But it is not my primary purpose to deal with policy matters except as they affect the power struggle. Without such a limitation, obviously, this book would become an unwieldy attempt to deal with everything that goes on in the Soviet Union.

A closer consideration than is usually given to the issues of power should be useful to students of the policy side. The assertion that the struggle for power is a permanent feature of Soviet politics is in itself a general theory of their nature. It is one that has sometimes been denied even by Western writers. Soviet political theory implicitly rejects it, preferring to rely on the view that the working class can express a single will through its 'vanguard', the Party; and that the Party is truly represented, through 'democratic centralism', in its Congress, its Central Committee and its Praesidium, in which its various wisdom is concentrated in a 'collective leadership' collaborating in comradely fashion to work out an objectively correct Party line. This view accounts for the frequent upheavals which hamper its smooth working as the result of individuals falling into deviation, or even treachery, to be unanimously denounced on discovery: a thesis which, however implausible, at least enables the troubles to be represented as extraordinary and untypical.

That such a line can be taken is simply a sign of the inadequacy of the Soviet conception, which, unlike those of other political systems, gives no official countenance to the emergence of conflicting views on policy. Yet such opposition is bound to arise in all circumstances, wherever there is a possibility of two

or more courses of action being open to any group. There is
nothing reprehensible about the existence in the Soviet Union
of a struggle between rival groups, urging rival policies. And
there is nothing exceptional in the drive for power being a
motive in the rise of politicians to high posts in the State —
though it might, indeed, be urged that the Soviet conventions
for handling this problem are not those best designed to fit it
into a polity with either constructiveness or humanity.

One sometimes reads the thesis that considerations about the
struggle for power at a given moment are speculative, and that
it is therefore sounder to assume that harmony prevails among
the collective leadership whenever there is no evidence to the
contrary. There seems to be a confusion here. Hypothetical reconstructions of what may be happening, when there is not
much evidence to go on, are indeed speculative. But the speculation is as to details. If we simply oppose the two views — that
a struggle is going on and that a struggle is not going on — the
latter is at least as speculative as the former. If there is no immediate evidence that there is a struggle, neither is there any
evidence that there is not. And we are left with a question not so
much about what is actually happening, as about the nature
of political life in the U.S.S.R. One theory assumes that it is
likely that harmony will on the whole prevail among the leadership; the other that a more or less permanent struggle is taking
place. One must base one's generalisations on the facts of Soviet
political history. In every case when an apparent calm prevailed, with only such minor signs of trouble as could be
explained away by anyone wishing to do so, it always ended
with explosions which showed that behind the façade bitter
contention had ruled over the apparently peaceful interlude. In
fact, this *is* Soviet political life, the real arena in which disputes
on policy such as must inevitably arise in any political system
are solved. All the rest is simply either the echo of what is
decided at the top, or else social pressure which can find political
expression only at the focus of the power struggle.

To assume that harmony now prevails among the Soviet
leadership would be to assume that a very extraordinary change
had taken place in the system. This is not, perhaps, impossible,
but at least one can say the assumption is the most speculative
that could be made. (It would be uncharitable to name the

sources, but I have seen the assumption that stability has been reached at last and that a collective leadership based on mutual restraint has finally emerged, put forward after the death of Stalin; after the fall of Beria; at the time of the XXth Congress; and at almost every other critical point in recent Soviet history. When such an idea gains ground with someone who follows these events, curious results emerge. I have even seen it seriously stated that the trial of Abakumov in 1954 signified only a desire on the part of the then leadership to correct police excesses. Odder still, when obvious signs of dissension appeared in 1957 one commentator argued that this meant nothing, since if dissension had really existed the Soviet authorities would not have permitted the fact to become known to the public!)

That personal rivalries of the most crude type may come before policy considerations proper in a way highly offensive to generalised sociology has been asserted officially, as when Bulganin stated:

These questions were put to the Central Committee by Comrade Khrushchev. Is that not the reason Molotov, Malenkov, Kaganovich and Shepilov came out against these proposals? It is precisely the reason they did not wish to hear of these proposals (*Stenographic Report* of the December 1958, plenum of the Central Committee).

A phrase used about Shepilov in the decision of the Central Committee in June 1957, expelling the Anti-Party Group, and repeated so often afterwards (even in Vol. 50 of the *Large Soviet Encyclopaedia*) that for some time it became stereotyped, was 'Shepilov who joined them'. He was also condemned by Khrushchev as 'a double-dealer'. These expressions are a most definite admission of the extreme, and long persistence, of faction among the Soviet leadership. For they imply that the lines were drawn and that Shepilov's particular fault lay in his breaking not Party discipline, but faction discipline.

In an ancient and famous university some years ago a proposal was put forward that the Professorship of Hebrew should be allowed to lapse, on the ground that no students had been forthcoming for some years. This idea was resisted, with many plausible and educational arguments, by a number of professors and lecturers in the classical languages. A real motive, not mentioned except in private, was that the loss of a vote on the rule-making body of the university might weaken their position if a proposal ever came up to cut down further on Greek, to the advantage of Physics. This is not to say that some of them were not perfectly convinced that the arguments about humanities which they were putting forward were reasonable and righteous; nor, if it comes to that, that almost all did not feel that the interests of the University, Education, the Younger Generation and so on demanded the defence of the classical side even by what they might concede to be tricky and insincere manœuvres. Idealism, conviction, careerism and factiousness formed an inextricable blend.

Anyone who has been connected with a large organisation will recollect similar instances. And it is not difficult to imagine the interweaving feelings and motives of an official of a Soviet economic ministry about the possible dissolution of his own, or even another, ministry in favour of regional Economic Councils. If we think in natural terms, instead of brand-new categories specially created for Soviet conditions, we shall get a sounder picture. From such a foundation of familiar concepts we can go on to what makes the Soviet scene distinctive, after all. And that is a difference of degree; which is not to say a minor difference. At the highest level in the U.S.S.R. are the few survivors who manœuvred adequately in the 'thirties and 'forties and later. Such a process of natural selection means that a hypertrophied type has been bred and trained in which motives that are sufficiently frenetic even in a mild western office or university have become a full-time, consuming passion. It is the intensity rather than the nature of the Soviet power struggle which is so difficult to envisage.

The main temptation in the field is of simplifying too much. Novels of great realism, no doubt founded on fact, have been written, dealing with office politics in big American firms. Though only a handful of characters may be involved, the complexities of alliances, views on policy, careerism and loyalties can stand development and elaboration for hundreds of pages without giving any impression that the barrel is being scraped. Though certain differences between such situations and those of the Soviet power struggle will occur to the reader, yet the comparison is not a very strained one. And when it is considered that in the Soviet case hundreds and thousands of ambitious men are involved (and that the stakes may be supreme power or death), it should be possible to restrain tendencies to too simple a two- or three-sided explanation of every move.

This book does not attempt to be exhaustive. One reason is that exhaustiveness is impossible — there is no knowing in what odd corner of what back number of what provincial newspaper some more or less significant piece of evidence may be found. Common sense alone dictates a limit. And on the whole, although exhaustiveness cannot be obtained, the approach to it is asymptotic: the panning of increased bulk of material produces diminishing returns. In most cases, indeed, the general conclusions emerge clearly enough and it has seldom been felt worthwhile to present every available piece of relevant evidence.

Read purely as history, even as the history of recent events in the struggle for power, the book will appear unevenly documented. I hope, indeed, that all significant moves are adequately covered, but it is true that disproportionate space and documentation are given to certain developments. These are usually matters which have seemed to be capable of providing particular illuminations on the techniques of the actual struggle or the techniques of investigating it.

The bulk of the book consists of an attempt to show these principles in operation. Taken together the chapters form a fairly full political history of the U.S.S.R. in recent years. But this is not their real purpose. Each is intended to demonstrate, in some way, the interplay of the various evidential factors, to be an exercise in the application and development of method.

I have not, except where this way of doing things seems to make it suitable, dealt with the considerable literature published in the United States, Britain and elsewhere on the various aspects of the struggle. After some consideration, I thought it best not to refer much to the bulk of previous investigation — except on one or two points where I have leant heavily on it — but to start again, as far as possible, from the raw material. This is in no way to imply that much useful work in this field has not been done, nor that I am not indebted to the immense amount of work in the field by writers like Nicolaevsky, Rush, Meissner, Brzezinski, Garthoff and many others. In fact, it would be more in order to apologise in advance for points which have undoubtedly been made somewhere in the scattered literature, but which I have missed. Sir Flinders Petrie, who transformed antiquarianism into archaeology, once said: 'When an author collects together the opinions of as many others as he can and fills half of every page with footnotes this is known as "scholarship".' This is not, of course, to suggest that even Petrie's most creative work would not have been made more comprehensive by full consideration of everything everyone else had done or said. And anyone working in a field with a large literature must feel how inadequately he has dealt with the work of other scholars. Yet it may, I hope, be pleaded that there are things more important than this sort of completeness.

Nor is it, of course, that I make any claim at all to have collected *all* the evidence or even all the important evidence in each case, though I believe a number of matters are brought to light here which have not been dealt with before, at least in print. The field is virtually limitless. And any particular hypothesis erected here may conceivably be ruined by some evidence hitherto undetected, at least by the writer; so I have tried to show that certainty is unobtainable on many points. Hypotheses are put forward simply as hypotheses. At least I hope this is adequately done; it is only too easy to start writing of a view that appears convincing as though it were certain, and I have not been absolutely rigorous in putting the reservations into every sentence which requires it. The mere tedium of repeating 'presumably', 'perhaps we may conclude', and so on, forbids. Even as it is readers may well feel that much expressions have clogged things up badly here and there. But their absence should not necessarily be taken as meaning that a statement is categorical. It will often be clear from the context that, though probable, the proposition is at least technically hypothetical.

In a sense this study forms, or should form, a separate discipline — 'dynastics', perhaps. It seems to me to be a pity that no journal exists solely devoted to the matter, and I trust that the foundation of one may be considered. It would, as I see it, cover two explicitly separate fields — the registration of relevant facts, and the setting up of speculative theory. As it is, there are many careful workers and collators in the field, together with others who, though they may play by ear, come across useful information and are the sources of interesting speculation. But the student has to pan an enormous variety of different productions, in which no particular standards prevail. Moreover, the researcher who simply comes across the odd interesting point, and who is not writing an article or book on the particular subject, has nowhere where he can briefly register it: and this, to my knowledge, is not a rare occurrence at all, but one which is happening all the time. A journal which was open to such material, and which also abstracted or re-produced the main material produced elsewhere throughout the world, would do a great service.

It seems not unlikely that in the interval between the writing and the publication of this book sections of it will have been overtaken by events. However, the point on which the author should pique himself is not its up-to-dateness as to facts so much as whether any new facts which have meanwhile emerged are congruent with his scheme. Of this the reader will have to be judge.

CHAPTER TWO

FORCES AND RESULTANTS

If only in broadest perspective, we should consider the pressures under which the tensions of the struggle for power are produced.

In all spheres of Soviet policy, as their own analyses frequently say, 'struggles' are constantly taking place to impose solutions on various refractory situations. We may first consider those which arise within Soviet society. Here, some present particular difficulties to the ruling group. As we shall see, agriculture on the one hand and cultural activities on the other are only kept in harmony with Soviet doctrine by a series of makeshifts, none of which has ever proved satisfactory for very long. Translated into social categories, this is to say that the peasantry and the intellectuals may be thought of as being general and permanent pressures relevant to Soviet politics. The handling of the minority nationalities has been another problem for which the solutions have varied between encouragement of local 'anti-imperialist' traditions and the imposition of an attitude centralised not only in practice but even in theory, as in Stalin's last year. 'Bourgeois nationalism' remains one of the ideologies most frequently attacked by Party spokesmen, and local officials removed are still often accused of falling into one or other aspect of it. In addition to the peasantry, the intellectuals and the nationalities, we may also take the view that the wishes of the population in general are to a certain extent an obstacle, the overcoming of which is part of Soviet politics. The Soviet rate of capital investment has been in the past, and remains (though in a lesser degree) much higher than any population has ever willingly consented to. There seems no doubt that a desire on the part of the citizenry for more consumer goods now, forms a constant force in the social and political field.

These social pressures are best regarded, however, not as part of the Soviet political scene but as external objects needing to be reckoned with, in the same way as the weather or the Ural Mountains. There are other forces outside the control of the

Soviet leadership which intrude into the policy-making sphere: in particular those affecting foreign policy, arising from the conduct of non-Communist states, and those connected with the international Communist movement. An important influence which it has not been possible to take into account here is that of the Chinese Communist leadership. The matter is so obscure that on the whole it has seemed unprofitable to speculate. We know from the 'secret' version of Mao Tse Tung's speech of February 1957 that the Chinese, while approving the attack on Stalin, did not approve the manner of it. We can deduce that in 1956–57 Chinese concern with Eastern Europe was very strong, at first supporting Gomulka, then backing the repression in Hungary while still striving for some political solution, and finally becoming rigorously Stalinist, anti-Yugoslav and even anti-Polish. But that is about all. More or less plausible conjectures have read Chinese influence in postponing a clash within the Soviet Praesidium in December 1956 and later. But the only overt evidence shows that when it came to the point the Chinese were not consulted nor their viewpoint heeded. In the June 1957 crisis they were slow to endorse the outcome. It was not until July 5 that they subscribed to the *fait accompli*, pointedly thanking the Soviet Communist Party 'for having informed us through Comrade Yudin, Soviet Ambassador to China, of the decisions' — a phrase equally pointedly omitted in *Pravda*'s publication of the telegram the following day. And in 1960 Sino-Soviet ideological disputes became virtually overt; but evidence of effective Chinese intervention in the Soviet political struggle is lacking.

The problems presented to the Soviet leadership by circumstances, the manipulation of which constitutes policy, are above all ideological. That is to say, the constant force which drives the political machine into its 'struggle' with things as they are, is the Marxist–Leninist doctrine as interpreted in the Party line. This force, operating in the minds of the thousands of senior officials structured into the apparatus of power, exerts the tensions which produce the struggle for power.

As we have said, there is nothing either odd or reprehensible in there being disputes on policy issues among the top Soviet leadership. However strict, in theory, a guide to political conduct in the form of an ideology or doctrine may be, problems are always bound to arise in which more than one solution is possible. And any ruling group in which the mere existence of alternative solutions is continuously ignored would be on its way to collapse from its sheer rigidity. In fact Soviet teaching is full of warnings against the 'doctrinaire' application of earlier teachings to a new situation. It is natural that various opinions are put forward about what constitutes a flexible interpretation of doctrine and what a departure from it.

We may now treat, in a generalised way, certain basic themes that emerge in detail in Parts II and III. These may be thought of as the conditions of dispute on policy matters, on the one hand, and the political machinery involved in the struggle, on the other.

All policies must be justified to the leading members of the Party aktiv, in terms of their ideological beliefs. While certain areas of our subject are difficult simply because the evidence happens to be defective, or (at first sight at least) contradictory, there are also areas which are refractory in their own right and not through any more or less accidental shortage of information. This is particularly the case where questions of dogma are involved. It is virtually impossible to clarify how far the Communist leaders, or particular ones among them, are motivated by odium theologicum and how far by ambition, even in the struggle for power itself. This is more a psychological question than a political one, and to present it as crudely as this is plainly to over-simplify the matter grotesquely. Yet it may be worth considering those extreme and unreal abstractions: the Communist who is pure ideology and the one who is pure ambition. The devotee cannot but see that the way for him to rise to power and ensure the doom of deviationists is to play the power game. (The aim of Machiavelli was simply to teach the 'good' prince the technique of politics.) On the other hand, the pure cynic in the Soviet Union would see that his rise to supreme power must involve the acceptance, for all practical purposes, of the ruling ideology. Nor, if he once got to the top, would he be in any way free to relax into a sensual sultanate. He would still be ridden to a large extent by the dynamics of the machine which he rode. The difference in practice even between the two extreme types would be likely to be, though not indeed insignificant, not very great. And what is known about the motivation of political and other leaders of all sorts naturally leads one to conclude that such pure types do not exist. It is true that a point Marx, and Lenin too, probably missed was that in a society with political rule power was likely to pass to the politically ambitious, and that this was especially likely in a dictatorship, however proletarian. But it is natural to imagine that the motives of the leaders are mixed and that self-deception plays at least its usual part.

Nevertheless, the long ideological training has its particular effects. I do not mean simply that the acceptance of an ideology (even one which has an apparatus of justification capable of supporting almost any action) results in decisions on practical matters being made at least partly in ideological terms and even from ideological motives. For it is also true that what at least seem at first to be purely ideological controversies suddenly arise for, apparently, no practical immediate reason at all. Since the history of this period is one of sharp political struggles, such matters must become in some way connected with the battle of the moment. Yet what are we to make, for instance, of Stalin's sudden denunciation in 1950 of the linguistics of Marr?

Certain major theoretical considerations are particularly closely connected with policy decisions. The most important of these is 'the construction of Communism'. In principle there is no dispute between Soviet leaders that in the long run a state of affairs will be brought about in which the present 'Socialist' society will be transformed into a 'Communist' one. In Marx's original formulation this could only be done when the whole world was under Socialist control. For 'Communism' implied the stateless society, when the State had withered away. Stalin, however, formulated the view that for economic purposes Communism could be created earlier. That is, he held that the Soviet Union could be Communist except for the fact that it would have to maintain armed forces and a State security organisation. Politically speaking, this would in fact mean that none or almost none of the stateless conditions of affairs previously thought of as characterising 'Communism' would have been attained. 'Communism' has, however, its economic side. It was believed that a truly classless and stateless society could be attained only when production was so advanced that it would be unnecessary any longer to have a system of exchange, and workers could be trusted both to do their work as a matter of social duty and to draw what they wanted from society's stores, without any shortage resulting. It was not, presumably, thought that the Soviet Union was on the immediate verge of attaining Communism (though Stalin in his speech of February 9, 1946, spoke of a period of three Five-Year Plans as sufficient to reach the new phase). But there is one important respect in which progress could be made. The U.S.S.R. at present is officially a society with two classes, the workers and the collectivised peasants, and a third group sometimes differentiated from these, the intelligentsia. The two classes thus exist where in the Communist future, or at the edge of the Communist future, there will be only one. Moreover, there are two forms of ownership: State ownership, which prevails in industry, and the 'co-operative' ownership of collective-farm production. The kolkhozes are operated, in theory at least, by the peasants themselves organised co-operatively. This is not in fact enormously significant, but just the same the day-to-day running of the kolkhoz is not performed by State organs. In addition, of course, the peasants have their private plots, most kolkhozes being on the 'artel' basis, which permits this. Emphasis on 'the construction of Communism' has therefore always gone with, and in practice mainly meant, plans to turn the agricultural worker into a public employee and to proletarianise the countryside.

On the agrarian side Stalin writes: (*Economic Problems of Socialism* — 1952).

In State enterprises, the means of production output are all-national property. In kolkhoz enterprises, on the other hand, although the means of production (land, machinery) belong to the State, production output is the property of the individual kolkhozes since the labour in the kolkhozes, like their seeds, is theirs, while the kolhhozes dispose of the land, which is turned over to them for their eternal use, as actually their own property, despite the fact that they cannot sell, buy, lease or mortgage it. This leads to a state of affairs where the State can dispose of only the output of State enterprises, whereas only the kolkhozes dispose of kolkhoz output since it is their property.

This formulation is accepted by all Soviet polical leaders, and the aim of transforming the U.S.S.R. into a one-class society, in which all the population, urban and rural, is state employed, is acknowledged throughout the Party. On the other hand various methods of securing it have been presented.

Stalin gives the conditions of transition to Communism as:

(a) Expansion of production, and especially production of the means of production.

(b) 'Converting' collective farm property into public property, 'though not necessarily by nationalisation'; 'introducing . . . products-exchange in place of commodity circulation'.

(c) Cultural advance; five-hour day; better houses; and the doubling 'or more' of real wages — particularly by reductions in the price of consumer goods.

In Khrushchev's time the idea that constructing Communism is a task for the fairly near future, as Stalin implied, is also put:

The building of a Communist society in our country is at present no longer a distant aim, but the immediate practical objective of the whole of the present-day activity of the Soviet people and their leading force — the C.P.S.U. The Soviet people are at present facing the majestic task of creating the material–technical foundation of communism, the task of catching up with and overtaking within the shortest possible time the most developed capitalist countries in the per capita production of the population (Party Theses for the Fortieth Anniversary of the Revolution (*Pravda*, September 15, 1957)).

The First Secretary himself said the following year:

One could say we are marching towards communism, but at the same time we are developing commodity relations. Is this not a contradiction? No, it is not. The Party has set the aim of creating an abundance of agricultural products, which is one of the important conditions for the transition to communism; but this can only be achieved if the principle of material interests of collective farms in increasing the output of agricultural products is used correctly. This problem can be solved on the basis of economic relations between the State and collective farms which stimulate increased labour productivity and increased output of farm products. (Khrushchev's *Report* to the December 1958 plenum.)

Hence Khrushchev is justifying the continuance of commodity relations, whose abandonment Stalin had particularly laid

C

down as one of the earliest steps to be taken in constructing Communism. Two opposite policies are thus urged, and justified by the same ideological argument.

The agricultural problem has always been a troublesome one. The various crises reported at the Central Committee plenums in September 1953 to March 1954 indicate that previous methods of obtaining crop increases necessary to the country had not worked. Two policies, in effect, present themselves for solving this. One would be a large-scale application of discipline and organisation to the whole matter — as proposed by Khrushchev in 1950–51 — and this fits in with the notion of proletarianising the peasantry. And the other would be to make concessions to the peasantry and hope to obtain increases in production by the normal method of incentives. To some extent an increase in discipline can be accompanied by an increase in incentives, but clearly there are limits to the degree in which they can be combined. Hence agriculture has always been, for matters of immediate policy, an area in which very different notions have been put forward by different groups. (It may be added, in passing, that failure to have a fairly continuous policy basis itself made all policies less viable. A regular incentive of small profit, if maintained over a longish period, is probably more valuable than a high incentive offered one year and abolished the next.) Thus, in the countryside two different criteria have always to be fulfilled — ideological, to satisfy the party aktiv, and practical, to produce the crops. Failure in either may contribute to a politician's downfall.

In industry something similar applies. Disputes have always occurred on the matter of how much investment should be turned into consumer goods.

The Soviet leaders usually seem to have regarded industry as capable of high production, or sufficiently high production at least, solely on the basis of the 'norm' incentives system. This has always been one which in effect drove the worker rather than lured him. On the other hand, the rigour of the system and the lack of interest on the part of a large section of the population produced a general atmosphere which in its turn made tighter State control and vigilance necessary — a vicious circle. The line for an increase in consumer goods seems to have gone mainly with the thesis that a more satisfied population would be

easier in general to control as well as that it would produce
more. In economics, associated with this, there has been an important policy dispute on 'voluntarism' (see Chapter Five).
That is, how much can be effected by the simple wish of the
Party, and how much depends on economic laws outside its
control?

Foreign policy has been another area in which different views
have been apparent. In general there is the distinction between
a forward policy against the imperialist West, and a more gentle
pressure. Within a forward policy might also be distinguished a
policy based largely on the use of the Communist Parties abroad,
and one in which Soviet power was regarded as the only reliable
weapon. The tactics to be pursued by Soviet supporters abroad
have also varied between revolutionary activity and more
general and shorter-term pressure of the 'peace campaign'
nature. Reflecting this variation in line towards the Communist
Parties in the West, has been a variation in the attitude to the
Communist Parties of Eastern Europe, which at the beginning
of the period were directly or indirectly under strict Soviet
control.

Within the U.S.S.R. a further area of dispute has been the
intellectual front, mainly the arts and sciences. There have been,
over the whole period, discussions of the extent to which the
application of doctrinal decisions made by the Central Committee should be forced upon the artist or scientist. These have
sometimes been politically crucial, as we shall see.

A further point of argument has been the emergence at
certain periods of emphasis on 'vigilance'. This has usually preceded a purge, and has in any case gone with a tightening of
control by the Party organisations and the police. But the theme
of vigilance also had an ideological basis. Stalin propounded in
the 'thirties the thesis that the more thoroughly the class enemy
was defeated (and Socialism established) the sharper the class
struggle became — thus justifying the terror of 1936–38 and
later activities. In 1956 this theory was denounced and for a
while there was, in a number of fields, a certain relaxation of
rigour. Relaxation, that is to say, by Soviet standards: it must
always be remembered that when we use terms like 'relaxation',
'liberal', 'mild' and so on in the political conditions concerned,
they are used comparatively. Failure to bear this in mind leads

to misunderstanding until, say, a *comparatively* unideological leader is thought of as almost entirely free from ideological attachments. This is not really the case.

The present position on the theory of repression in the U.S.S.R. is as follows:

A scientific analysis of the situation which has been created in Soviet society as the result of the victory of socialism and the establishment of the moral-political unity of the people leads to the conclusion that in a socialist society there are no conditions which might lead to an intensification of the class war. Therefore the formula produced by J. V. Stalin in 1937, when a socialist society had already been essentially built in the U.S.S.R., about the inevitable intensification of the class war as socialism became more strongly established and developed in the country, cannot be accepted as correct. . . .

However, the conclusion must not be drawn that there are now no manifestations of class war in Soviet society at the present time. This can only lead to disarming the Soviet people and blunting their vigilance. Agents from the countries of capitalism still penetrate into our country, and they sometimes find accomplices from among individual degenerates inside our country. Our fight against the enemies of the socialist system must continue to be determined and merciless as it always has been. . . .

In spite of the assurances of the opportunists, when the workers secure power the bourgeoisie does not depart from the historical stage voluntarily and without a fight. The overthrown exploiting classes offer every kind of resistance, try to disrupt the building of socialism, to restore their authority and to prevent the collapse of capitalist society. Because of this class war is inevitable. (*Class War in the U.S.S.R. during the Transition Period from Capitalism to Socialism*, by K. Frolov. Pamphlet issued by the 'All-Union Society for the Dissemination of Political and Scientific Knowledge,' and passed for publication August 30, 1957).

In principle there is no reason why a particular agricultural policy should be linked with a particular foreign policy. Nevertheless, taking it very broadly, one may trace in Russia, as in many other countries, a rough-and-ready distinction between a right and a left. The left might be defined as one which favoured the creation of the 'Communist Society' at home and on a world scale by a crash programme; and the right as one more concerned with the immediate problems in hand, and thus more prepared to take them at a slower tempo. The left is thus more ideologically centred. It is inclined to a forward policy in foreign affairs, to a tightening up in collective farms, to no concessions to the consumer, to more rigid control over the intellectuals and to strict centralisation. The right has favoured comparative relaxation in all these matters. There have been various lefts and rights within the Stalinist framework, each with particular characteristics. And the above is only the roughest division. Moreover, 'unprincipled blocs' on the lines of the Fox–North coalition (or the Nazi–Soviet Pact) have occasionally emerged against some particularly dangerous contender with an eclectic policy.

In a sense one may feel that Khrushchev was in 1953–55 virtually forced into a 'left' position by the mere fact that Malenkov took what could most easily be attacked as a right view, so that any alternative contender for power could only rely on the opposite argument. (This point is reinforced by Malenkov's use of 'left' heavy industry arguments during the June 1957 crisis, as against Khrushchev's recent consumer-approach pronouncements.) It will be remembered that Stalin, in the late 'twenties, came to power initially by attacking the 'left' policies of Trotsky and Zinoviev, and later appropriating them. In fact, policies are frequently sponsored less on their merits than on their utility in the struggle — an important conclusion.

Here we must make a major distinction between the types of deviation which have attracted the main condemnation in the U.S.S.R. Until recently these were generally listed as 'leftist' and 'rightist'. Leftist deviations consisted of the urging of policies involving progress too quick for the economy, the opinions of the people and the general objective situation. 'Rightists', who have been much more condemned in recent years, were those who urged policies of concession to the immediate needs and desires of the population as against the over-riding necessity of strengthening the Soviet State economically and otherwise. When Malenkov fell from the premiership in 1955 many accusations of rightism were in the air and the names of Bukharin and Rykov were freely mentioned. For the main accusation against Malenkov was that he proposed to slacken the pace of industrialisation in favour of providing more consumer goods for the population.

It will at once be seen that the distinction here is simply one of what policies the deviationists believe that the leadership should pursue. But since the XXth Congress a new and altogether more radical area of deviationism is denounced. 'Dogmatism' and 'revisionism' are the two poles. The first may still be labelled 'left' and the second 'right', but the issue in dispute is different. The revisionists do not simply urge milder policies on the leadership: in effect they deny the absolute right of the leadership to formulate policy at all.

Within the new field of contest, Khrushchev has left no doubt about his position. He is wholly and entirely committed to the suppression of revisionism. And here it would certainly be true to label him 'leftist'. It has not recently been usual to think of him in this way. But in 1951 he put forward the apparently leftist thesis of the Agrogorod (see Chapter Six). Absence of any sign that he was likely to fall as a result of the Doctor's Plot strengthened this impression. And during his struggle with Malenkov in 1954–55 he clearly took up an anti-rightist position on industrialisation. Yet his other main moves have not been notably consistent with this. The agricultural programme put forward in September 1953 was on the whole a realistic one of concessions. On the Tito issue, his restoration of relations in 1955 might be taken as also a 'rightist' move, as indeed the attack on Stalinism at the XXth Congress also appears to be in some sense. The economic devolution of 1957, on the other hand, could be argued to be a move to strengthen dogmatic Party control at the expense of conservative State control of the economy. The impression gained in general (and reinforced greatly by his foreign policy manœuvres of April–May 1960) is of a flexible tacticism with an inflexible drive to power. But Stalin and Khrushchev are not alone in this tendency to change policies to suit power exigencies, which is, in fact, common to most of the figures we shall deal with. Thus it is probably better not to use the left–right dichotomy, or similar comparisons, except very sparingly.

A point of ideological protocol is of some importance. When a pronouncement is made which is either a relaxation or a tightening of previous policies, it is still usually justified in terms of the last formula in the matter. For instance, the meeting of the Board of the Soviet Union of Writers in October 1953 still

affirmed the principles Zhdanov decrees which they were in fact
revising — a movement to the right accompanied by strong re-
affirmation of left principles. This sort of thing is not, of course,
unknown in other countries. (I have just read a letter in an
English paper urging the suppression of necking in cinemas, but
starting 'I am not a prude'.) And in the Russian case there is
the added point that continuity must be asserted and that (on
the whole and except in special circumstances) the Party line
must be declared to have been always correct.

We may consider shortly the institutional side of the struggle
for power, covering in a generalised way one of the themes that
emerge at length and in detail in Parts II and III.

All those who carry any weight in Soviet politics are naturally
members of the Party, whose highest bodies contain representatives of all important Soviet institutions, and control of the
Party's leading organs has always been essential to the successful
contender for power: the Praesidium and the Central Committee
are the key sites of the struggle. And these bodies may be controlled by men for whom the Party apparatus — the permanent
staff of the Secretariat, the Departments of the Central Committee and the Provincial Secretariats — is not the main or
favourite instrument of rule, as we shall see.

Interpretations of events in the U.S.S.R. are often put forward in terms of a victory for the State over the Party, or vice
versa. And it is frequently represented as if these were two
separate and competing groups, engaged more or less permanently
in a ding-dong struggle, with the teams and rules clearly laid
out. It need hardly be said that matters are not as simple as
that.

The question of relations between the Party organisation and
a government composed of members of the Party is not a purely
Soviet one. In the United Kingdom at the time of the 1945
election Winston Churchill made great play with the notion
that if the Labour Party were returned to power the country
would be dominated by its executive under the chairmanship of
the (to Churchill) sinister Professor Harold Laski. When the
Labour Government took office, these speculations were shown
to be unfounded. Mr. Attlee was, throughout, in complete
control as head of the Government. But this is not to assert
the impossibility of control by a Party group outside the

Government. In Australia, for instance, political caucuses in fact control, or attempt to control, Governments.

In the Soviet Union the spheres of action of the Party and State apparatuses have never been clearly delimited. They overlap in a number of important respects. And it had always clearly been in the interests of a power group controlling one apparatus, but not the other, to give a maximal interpretation to the powers of its own machinery.

During Stalin's rise to power, at the XIIth Party Congress in 1923 (the first at which Lenin played no part) the issues between the two systems of control were fairly freely discussed. The XIIth Congress adopted a resolution put forward by Zinoviev to the effect that 'the dictatorship of the working-class can be guaranteed only in the form of a dictatorship of its vanguard, i.e. the Party'. At the same period an opposition view of the nature of the Party rule was put forward: that 'in the State and leading Party apparatuses the industrialists and economic managers — Party members, of course — should be allowed at least the same share of influence as the journalists, writers and ordinary politicians'.

Stalin's road to power was through his control of the Secretariat. But once he was in full control it gradually came to be accepted that the role of the Party as such was to make basic decisions, look after ideology and conduct the agitational and general campaigning while the Government actually administered the policy side — under the sort of arrangement that roughly speaking exists in all parties and governments. Such an arrangement is, however, open to a number of interpretations. The Party apparatus always tended to try at least to take part in the taking of concrete decisions. Very occasionally the dichotomy shows openly: for example in the autumn of 1954, what amounted to a controversy on policy even took place between the Government's *Izvestia* and the Party's *Pravda*.

It has long since been the case in the U.S.S.R. that decisions are taken by small groups of men at the top. The rank-and-file Party man, even the provincial or republican secretary, played little part except as an instrument, any more than did the junior minister or the director of some economic combine. Since the late 'thirties the Central Committee itself had very little independent role. In Stalin's later years, indeed, it scarcely ever met. And even after Stalin's death its usual function was to accept decisions laid before it in the name of the Party Praesidium. If factions in the Praesidium were deadlocked in an open struggle it might be that the Central Committee would start to operate as laid down in the constitution of the Party. But even in the June 1957 crisis this does not seem to have happened. As was said after Khrushchev's victory, the Anti-Party Group calculated that the Central Committee would vote for a resolution put before it in the name of the Praesidium. It appears that this is what actually occurred, though Khrushchev had by this time undermined and reversed his rivals' majority in the smaller body. Thus, any ruling group which controlled the Praesidium, controlled the Party and might depress or exalt its role.

In the period of Stalin's rule variation is noticeable. On the occasion shortly after the war when he felt that ideological discipline was necessary he strengthened the power of the Party apparatus, and gave Zhdanov, who had no place in the Government, the leading role. But, on the whole, Stalin's later Politburos consisted of figures from the Government apparatus. And Stalin himself, in decrees proceeding from both Government and Party, signed first as representative of the Government, allowing his senior subordinate in the Party Secretariat to sign, second, for the Party. In 1950 all the members of the Politburo held Government posts, with the single exception of Khrushchev. This could be compared with the position in 1958, when nine out of fourteen were members of the Party apparatus only. During the war the subordinate character of both State and Party apparatuses, yet particularly the latter, was illustrated by the supreme powers over both given to the State Defence Committee — all of whose members were members of the Government.

A joint decree of the Praesidium of the Supreme Soviet, the Central Committee of the Party and the Council of People's Commissars of June 30, 1941, created this body 'with full plenitude of power in the State'. It called on all citizens and all Party, Komsomol and Military organs to unfailingly execute the decisions and orders of the State Defence Committee (*Bulletin of the Supreme Soviet*, No. 31 of 1941). The membership was Stalin, Molotov, Voroshilov, Malenkov and Beria. Later Kaganovich, Voznesensky and Mikoyan were added, and

Voroshilov was replaced by Bulganin in November 1944. A Decree of the Praesidium of the Supreme Soviet published on September 5, 1945, abolished the Committee and transferred its powers to the Council of People's Commissars. Thus the Government inherited, and when the People's Commissariats were transformed into Ministries soon afterwards, one of the reasons given for the change was the desirability of strengthening governmental authority.

Thenceforward (apart from the period in 1946 when he was in decline) Malenkov was, except for Stalin, the only man on all the supreme bodies in the country: the State Defence Committee until its dissolution, the Government, the Politburo and the Party Secretariat. He had risen to prominence in 1940 for his denigration of ideological rigour in favour of efficient administration. And his role in the Secretariat may reasonably be interpreted in one respect as that of keeping the Party apparatus, with its particular interests and inclinations, subordinated to the general interests of the State. His decline and removal in 1946 precisely fits with the decision then taken to give the ideologists their head. During Stalin's last years the Central Committee virtually ceased to function. But so, according to Khrushchev's Secret Speech, did the Politburo, leaving the Secretariat as the only Party body in effective existence. This did not mean that it operated more independently: on the contrary, it carried out its functions, always supposed to be purely administrative, simply under the orders of Stalin. In fact the Party had become mainly an administrative machine for assigning personnel and supervising ideology. When purge and ideology were the order of the day, the Party became the favoured instrument, simply for these reasons.

After the war Stalin had created a Government body with wide powers — the Praesidium of the Council of Ministers. In theory at least, the Government now became not simply an administrative machine carrying out orders given it by the Prime Minister on the instructions of the Politburo, but the seat of a small and effective council at which policy could be discussed. The Praesidium of the Council of Ministers as set up in March 1946 included Stalin as Prime Minister, and eight Deputy Premiers, all of them members of the Politburo. This is rather more than the creation of the 'Committees' of the Polit-

buro to which Khrushchev objected in his Secret Speech. For it
was a formally established group with constitutional powers,
from which the Politburo members without Government posts
— primarily Zhdanov and Khrushchev — were excluded.

All this illustrates another point. We will not usually find, at
the highest levels, any sort of team loyalty to the idea of the
Party apparatus, or of the Government, as such. Almost all the
men who rose to power with Stalin and received high posts in
the Government had risen via the Party apparatus, which at
first was all that Stalin controlled.

Apart from the 1946 period there was one other time in
Stalin's post-war regime when the Party began to be emphasised
at the expense of the Government. This was in the second period
of 'vigilance', ideology and purge — the last months of the dictator's lifetime. The old Politburo of eleven full members had
contained one purely Party figure, two holding State and Party
posts and eight in State posts alone. In the new Praesidium of
twenty-five members were nine purely Party figures, two in
both State and Party, twelve State alone and two miscellaneous
— and of the State figures no fewer than four were under attack
and threatened with purge.

In the case of the Party, it is necessary to look at the organisational side as well as to consider general solidarities. In theory
the local organisations of the Party elect delegates to the
Congress, which elects the Central Committee, which elects a
Praesidium (and a Secretariat). The role of the Praesidium is
simply to ensure the continuity of policy and leadership between
meetings of the Central Committee which gives it instructions
and to which all disputes must be referred. The Central Committee in turn is similarly subordinate to the Congress. This
theoretical position bore some relation to reality during Stalin's
rise to power, and he was able to secure majorities in the
Congresses by using his control of the Secretariat to appoint
the local secretaries, who greatly influence the make-up of
delegations to the Congress, and thus in turn to pick the
Central Committee and the Politburo — then a body of,
theoretically, a more informal nature than the present-day
Praesidium.

Since the establishment of Stalin's rule, however, all vestiges
of independence of the Congress have disappeared. No vote has

lately been taken there, either in Stalin's time or under his successors, and its decisions have clearly all been worked out and agreed beforehand by the smaller bodies. (There were, indeed, some slight signs of disputes being hinted at on the floor of the Congress at the XXIth Congress in January–February 1959, but these were not pressed.) The difficulty of controlling a small permanent body through a large one meeting only occasionally is an old one. The Councils could never manage the Popes. And the Central Committee, too, became, as we have said, a rubber stamp for the leadership under Stalin. Under the present Party Constitution it must meet once in six months, and it in fact met more often than this in 1958. Yet a body of over a hundred and thirty full members alone, or two hundred and fifty if candidates are included, cannot be expected to exercise much control over a small picked group firmly in power at the centre, except in very unusual circumstances.

The publication of the Stenographic Report of a Central Committee plenum took place for the first (and only) time in this period with the plenum of December 1958. Certain interesting procedural points emerge.

The plenum started with an announcement that 'The Praesidium of the Central Committee introduces for discussion by the Plenum of the Central Committee the question of Results of the Development of Agriculture during the past Five Years and the Task of Further Increasing the Production of Agricultural Products. The Praesidium of the Central Committee has confirmed Khrushchev N. S. as rapporteur on this question.'

Khrushchev's report followed, then the debate, during which Aristov, in the chair, proposed an editorial Commission of sixty-six names (to which three more were later added), under Khrushchev's chairmanship, to draft the Central Committee resolution. This, as it finally appeared, was little more than a formalised and boiled-down version of his speech.

These arrangements indicate strongly that the Praesidium virtually presents the Central Committee with a *fait accompli*. It names the rapporteur and has presumably discussed and approved the proposals he will present. These are then put. Any serious opposition could only be made with the greatest difficulty, even assuming that 'factional' methods were used. The Anti-Party Group's alleged calculation in June 1957 that the

Central Committee would carry a resolution presented to them in the name of the Praesidium seems well-founded.

An analysis of the composition of the Central Committee at the time of its election in 1956 is of significance. (A number of the members have since died, or been expelled, or changed posts.) It was:

	Full Members	Candidate Members
Central Party Organisation . .	11	7
Union Republican Secretaries . .	17	3
Moscow and Leningrad Secretaries .	5 *	2
Provincial Secretaries . . .	38	26
Total Party apparatus	71	38
Central Government . . .	31	31
Regional Government . . .	13	16
Total Governmental	44	47
Military	6	13
Police	2	1
Foreign Ministry and Diplomatic .	5	6
'Unofficial' bodies	1	7
Miscelleneous and unidentified .	4	10
	18	37
	133	122

The new organs elected in February 1956 (including the insignificant Revision Commission, whose members are present on certain occasions at C.C. plenums, and membership of which is a sort of minor accolade), had the following members:

Central Committee	133
Central Committee Candidates . .	122
Central Revision Commission . .	63
	318

* Not including Furtseva, Secretary of the C.C. as well as of the Moscow Party Committee.

At the June 1957 plenum *Party Life* (No. 13, July 1957) states that 309 attended. During 1957 five members were publicly expelled from the Committee, and by the end of 1958 four members and five candidates had died and two more candidates seem to have retired through illness. At the December 1958 plenum the total *membership* (of whom not all attended) is given as:

Central Committee	124
Central Committee Candidates	115
Central Revision Commission	61
	300

which seems to imply that the lost members had not been replaced, even to the extent of promoting candidates to full membership.

Why this is so is not clear, unless a deadlock of some sort had been reached. On previous occasions it had been stated that members of the C.C. have even been removed between Congresses for wrong behaviour (see p. 257), while in 1953 promotions had been carried out: the plenum of March 14, 1953 (*Pravda*, March 21, 1953), raised Shatalin from candidate member to full member of the Central Committee under Article 32 of the Party Statutes. This article, after providing for the election of the Central Committee and the Central Revision Commission by the Party Congress, goes on: 'In case of the removal (vybytiya) of members of the Central Committee, its establishment is made up from the ranks of the candidates elected by Congress'. Perhaps Shatalin took Stalin's place — though several other members of the Central Committee had died or disappeared since the XIXth Party Congress, e.g. Mekhlis and Poskrebyshev. Again, the raising of Zhukov to full membership of the Central Committee took place in July 1953, perhaps replacing Beria.

Khrushchev, in his speech to the XIXth Congress on the New Party Statutes, said: 'A person expelled from the Central Committee, is automatically replaced by a candidate for membership in the Central Committee in the order established by the Congress in electing candidates to the Central Committee' (*Pravda*, October 13, 1952). But no such procedure has taken place, and the Statutes themselves are not so explicit. The presumption is that the Central Committee itself votes on the matter. If so, it is plain that a group with a small but certain majority on that body can, if it thinks it tactically desirable, fairly rapidly increase its strength.

That the Praesidium is the true seat of power in the U.S.S.R. is undoubted. It may be that in certain circumstances of factional deadlock some effective power might fall into the hands of the Central Committee, as it did in critical circumstances in Poland and Hungary in 1956. Because this has not yet happened in the U.S.S.R. does not prove that it never can.

Most commentators see the permanent apparatus of the Party as the main contender for power with the Praesidium. In fact this became an issue discussed almost openly in 1955 (see Chapter Eleven). We have considered the Secretariat's role. The question of the relation between the size of the Secretariat and its power is of interest. At the XIXth Congress Khrushchev's speech on organisational matters dealt with the Secretariat–Bureau relationship at provincial and republican level. 'In order to prevent the secretariats supplanting the bureaux . . . the number of secretaries should be reduced to three, and the secretaries should be directed to report decisions adopted by them to the bureau'. This was incorporated into Article 42 of the new Party Statutes. But when Khrushchev became powerful in 1953–54, the numbers in the secretariats were generally increased to four or five — at the republican congresses held in the early months of 1954.

The situation at the centre is not quite identical, since local secretaries are almost invariably all members of the bureaux, while the secretaries of the C.C., C.P.S.U. may not be so. When Khrushchev came to full power in 1957 he produced a situation in which all the Secretariat was on the Praesidium as well — all except one as full members. The significance of this can be read from Khrushchev's own words five years previously.

An increase in the number of secretaries, even without their promotion to the Praesidium, may not strengthen the Secretariat. But at the very least it promotes more apparatchiks to positions of great public prestige and weight. As soon as Khrushchev was able, he enlarged the Secretariat, which had come almost completely under his domination with the removal

of Shatalin, by Aristov, Belyaev and Shepilov's promotion in
July 1955, accompanied by the promotion of Suslov and
Kirichenko, both of the Party apparatus, to the Praesidium.

Under the Secretariat operate the permanent Departments
'of the Central Committee', the great bastion of the
apparatchiks. There seems to be an allocation of departments
among the various Secretaries. For example, an analysis of the
main theme of the speeches by the then Secretaries (apart from
Khrushchev) at the XXIst Congress gives the following results,
which may be significant of the spheres covered by the speakers
in their secretarial work:

Kirichenko: Cadres and policy in general.
Suslov: General theory.
Furtseva: Cultural development.
Mukhitdinov: Central Asia and Transcausia; Free Asia.
Brezhnev: Metallurgy.
Pospelov: Ideological controversies.
Aristov: R.S.F.S.R. (C.N.E.s, machine building, etc.).
Ignatov: Agriculture.
Kuusinen: International Communist Relations.

That certain Party Secretaries are associated with certain
Departments is clearly established. For some years Suslov
always appeared with Ponomarev in negotiations with foreign
Communist delegations. For a time the Party representative at
police functions was Mukhitdinov. And so on.

The Departments of the Central Committee are presumed to
be those mentioned to the Italian Communist delegation (see
Appendix VIII). This listing, however, does not distinguish
between the parallel Departments for Union Republics and the
R.S.F.S.R. *The Handbook of the Party Worker* (Moscow, 1957)
gives an announcement of the Central Committee dated March
14, 1956, in which the R.S.F.S.R. Departments are named in a
paragraph not published at the time with the rest of the
announcement. These are: Party Organs; Agitation and Propaganda; Science, Schools and Higher Education; Agriculture;
Industry and Transport; Administrative and Trade-Financial
Organs. The heads of Departments named in *Pravda, Izvestia,
The Bulletin of the Supreme Soviet, Verchernaya Moskva* and elsewhere in 1956–57 were: Administrative Organs; Agriculture–
Union Republics; Agriculture — R.S.F.S.R.; Construction;

Culture; Heavy Industry; Machine Building; Party Organs — Union Republics; Party Organs — R.S.F.S.R.; Agitation and Propaganda–Union Republics; Agitation and Propaganda R.S.F.S.R.; Science and Schools; Science and Schools R.S.F.S.R.; Administrative and Trade Financial Organs — R.S.F.S.R. With some of these departments we need not greatly concern ourselves.

Considerable secrecy envelops much of the staffing of the departments. There are certain heads of Departments who are always mentioned simply as such, without the name of their Department being given. For instance, at the Supreme Soviet Election in 1958 in the list of successful candidates five Department heads were named with their Departments, but Malin, Zheltov and Ponomarev were simply spoken of as heads of (unspecified) Departments. In *Pravda* of November 13, 1957, November 21, 1957, August 8, 1957 and June 19, 1957, respectively, Andropov, Kidin, Orlov and Ponomarev are named simply as heads of Departments.

It might be taken that there is some implication of those not fully identified occupying posts of particular sensitivity. Ponomarev has appeared very frequently in discussions with foreign Communist delegations and has also spoken on ideological themes. Andropov was sent, for a time, as ambassador to Hungary. In general, less has been stated about the Foreign Department of the apparatus than any other and it has been suggested that it has been divided up into Soviet bloc and non-Communist world Departments.

The relative importance of the Departments of the Central Committee may be seen from noting those whose heads figure in the highest Party bodies. In those elected at the XXth Congress, Candidate membership of the Central Committee was held by:

1. The Head of the Department of Agitation and Propaganda.
2. The Head of the Department of Party Organs for the R.S.F.S.R.
3. The Head of the Department of Party Organs for Union Republics.
4. The Head of the Department of Agriculture for the R.S.F.S.R.

D

The next ranking body, the Revision Commission, included:

1. The Head of the Department for Agriculture for Union Republics.
2. The Head of the Department of Culture.
3. An official of one of the Departments of Party Organs.

The Party Organs Department remains the key power organisation. And it may also be noted that in the Bureaux of the Central Committees of the Union Republics elected in January 1956, just before the XXth Congress, the Head of the local Party Organs Department figures as full member in four and as candidate member in two out of the fifteen. The only other Department represented (apart from the special Petroleum Department in Azerbaidzhan) was *one* Agitation and Propaganda Department (in Estonia).

Formerly there was a single Party Organs Department, and even now they must work in the very closest union. They direct and control cadres in the Party, the Trade Unions and the Komsomol. This machinery, under its present name or its earlier one of the Administration of Cadres, has been one of the most effective levers of power in the U.S.S.R. Among those who have risen through it are Yezhov, Malenkov, who headed it for many years, Patolichev, Pegov, Ignatiev, Shatalin, Andrianov and Aristov.

The Agitation and Propaganda Department is seen to be the other key one. Its spokesmen cover all issues of deviation and correction on ideological and political issues, and are in a position to present the charges and define the official line. Its alumni include Suslov and Shepilov. The associated Culture and Science Departments had a similar, though lesser, prestige, which seems to have diminished lately.

The Agricultural and Industrial Departments carry some weight in the struggle, in a more indirect way. And the Administrative Organs Department, which covers the Party's links in the Government machinery, has a certain significance. Its 'control' of the Police Ministries has been read as giving it great importance in power matters, but this control does not seem to go very far, and it is noteworthy that appointees to these Ministries from the Party positions have always come from the Party Organs Departments (Yezhov, Ignatiev and Shelepin).

A further important body, though an agency of the Central Committee and not elected by the Congress, is the Party Control Committee. It has the main tasks of 'checking discipline' and 'calling to account' all offenders. It no longer possesses its original power of having representatives at a local level, and its role in the 1957 crisis seems merely to have been the accumulation of evidence for use against the losers. Under Shvernik it is said (see p. 368) to have intervened with particular sharpness against Malenkov, Bulganin and the others, and we may conclude that Khrushchev had succeeded in filling it with his own supporters. Of its seven members, four or five are full members of the Central Committee. Although in early Soviet times it was given wide theoretical powers to prevent abuses in the Party, its activity and power grew less and less, and it may be regarded simply, for most purposes, as an instrument.

The permanent Party officials have always constituted, up to a point, a group differentiated from other Party workers in certain respects. Just as the Party member in a day-to-day administrative post in a government office, or the director's chair in a factory, is likely to develop short-term attitudes of a practical routine, so the apparatchik charged with overseeing the political and ideological purity of developments tends to concentrate on the doctrine. It is even more true that a faction with strong ideological preoccupations is likely to put more stress on operating through the Party machine.

It may well be argued that Malenkov, though rising through the Party apparatus, sympathised with the administrative and short-term approach natural to the economic managers. A good deal of allowance must be made for the idea that rival policy and power groups use the apparatus through which they happen to have risen, or which they happen to control, simply as the instrument to hand, and are quite capable of reducing its power to suit events when and if both the apparatuses have fallen into their hands. This is not to deny that, on the whole, a tendency of men whose career has been in the Party to dogma, ideology and 'Left' views is tenable: but it should not be exaggerated into a complete interpretation.

After the few days in March 1953 when Malenkov held both the premiership and the leading secretaryship of the Party, it seems that pressure was put on him collectively (that is, presumably by a majority of the Party Praesidium) to relinquish one post or the other. The solution that he found acceptable was to retain the premiership. And it seems natural to suppose that, being a not unskilled operator, he had good reason to imagine that this would secure his leading position. Regarded solely from the point of view of a hold on the essentials of power, there seems no *a priori* reason why the controllers of the State apparatus cannot rule the Party too, even against rivals in control of the Secretariat. All that is required is a firm majority on the Party Praesidium, and the enforcement of that majority's views in all subjects, including major Party appointments. And this method can be carried out all the way down the Party machine. In the republics and provinces the Party bureaux are in a position, theoretically at least, to control the secretaries. (It was almost certainly to combat this possibility that, as we have said, from about 1954 the republican secretariats began to be increased from the three permitted by statute to four and five, all members of the bureaux.)

The difficulty is obvious. It is easier for one man (and for the permanent official) to keep up pressure than it is for a group to maintain its unity. On the other hand, Malenkov retained a foothold in the Party apparatus in the form of Shatalin's presence in the Secretariat. And in spite of the increase in Khrushchev's prestige and power it was not until a majority of the Praesidium was found against Malenkov early in 1955 that the First Secretary was able to rid himself of Shatalin, too, and begin to pack the local secretariats on a large scale.

During Malenkov's ascendancy the Government continued to sign joint decrees first, as in Stalin's time. As Khrushchev gained influence this began to be changed. For instance, a decree of the Central Committee and the Council of Ministers (*Pravda* of March 9, 1955) is signed by Khrushchev and Bulganin, in that order, for the two bodies.

During the June 1957 crisis, as we shall see, the opposition was accused of minimising the role of the Party. Afterwards Khrushchev was praised for increasing the Party's power and prestige, until the point could be made as part of the proposal to give him direct control of the Government too:

Dear Comrades Deputies: In tabling the proposal for the appointment of Comrade Khrushchev as Chairman of the U.S.S.R. Council of Ministers I wish at the same time to refer to his highly productive work in the post of First Secretary of the C.C. of our C.P.

Our Party has restored the Leninist norms of Party life and Party structure. Over the past few years the guiding, directing and organising role of the C.P. and its Central Committee, of the Central Committee Praesidium, has particularly increased. The authority of our Party has risen even higher; the unity of the Party and people has grown strong to an extent never known before. And the Central Committee of the Party has decided that Comrade Khrushchev should remain in the post of First Secretary of the C.C. of the C.P.S.U. (Voroshilov's Speech to the Supreme Soviet nominating Khrushchev for Chairman of the Council of Ministers. *Tass*, March 27, 1958).

In late years, in particular, it has been common for the Central Committee to issue direct 'instructions' to the Government, as in May 1958, when:

The Plenary Session of the C.P.S.U. Central Committee instructs the U.S.S.R. Council of Ministers, the Councils of Ministers of the Union Republics and the C.N.E.s of the Economic Areas to make provision in the plan for the Economic Development of the U.S.S.R. during 1959–65 for the following. (Resolution of the May 1958 Plenum of the Central Committee on the Chemical Industry. *Tass*, May 8, 1958.)

The extent to which the Party, especially after Khrushchev's victory in June 1957, became involved in administrative detail, rather than simply providing political guidance, may be seen in the 'Resolution of the C.C. of the C.P.S.U. and the U.S.S.R. Council of Ministers on Preparations for the Harvesting and Processing of Sugar Beet of the 1958 Harvest' (*Tass*, July 1, 1958), whose basic theme, elaborated under a series of subheadings, is:

In order to avoid premature harvesting of the beet, its deterioration and loss of sugar content, it is essential for the C.C.s of Republican C.P.s and Councils of Ministers, Territorial and Provincial Party Committees and Territorial and Provincial Soviet Executive Committees to work out measures for the organisation of the storage of the beet in clamps so that the long refining period should not lead to loss of beet or a reduction in its sugar content during storage.

This, and the whole economic reorganisation of 1957, can, as we shall see in Chapter Twelve, be interpreted in one aspect at least as a usurpation by the Party of powers hitherto reserved for the Government.

While we have so far looked at the higher-level picture, it is possible also to see solidarities on a rather broader scale — Marx was not the first sociologist to note that groups with similar economic interests tend to act together politically. He even noted that this applied to collections of people far more fortuitous than the 'economic classes', like the members of the bureaucratic machine under Napoleon III.

In explaining events in the U.S.S.R. it has been common to see them as involving struggles between various groups acting more or less corporately. The economic Managers (khozaistvenniki), the Police, the members of the Party apparatus, the Generals, are all seen in this light. In addition, much smaller groupings whose members are all in key spots are seen if not as apparatuses with their own economic interest, at least as personal groups with the common interests of clients of a given political leader, disciplined to acting in unison on given issues — for example, the political machinery in the armed forces is treated by Mr. Nicolaevsky as a special group long under Bulganin's control.

In such cases as the Army and the Police there is indeed a formal organisational connection. And, although there is no doubt that rivalries take place within these apparatuses, the temptation to regard them as, on the whole, corporate political entities is a strong one. The Army and the Police certainly play an important part on the Soviet political scene, as we shall see. But there is a sense in which their interests are limited as compared with State and Party.

On the Police apparatus, seen as an independent contender in the struggle for power in this period, we need only say that it was throughout divided into a Ministry (and later Committee) of State Security (M.G.B.–K.G.B.) and a Ministry of the Interior (M.V.D.), except during the period from Stalin's death to the fall of Beria, when the M.V.D. covered both spheres. (That Beria, though no longer Minister, also had general responsibility for the M.G.B. in the immediate post-war period seems to be shown by Khrushchev's assertions in the Secret

Speech about his collaboration with the M.G.B. Minister, Aba-kumov, in preparing the Leningrad Case (see Appendix IV.))

When Beria fell, the purge of his followers struck mainly at those who had served the security side, and the old M.V.D. officials were not directly involved. The right way of looking at it seems to be to regard the M.V.D. as concerned solely with the regulation and repression of the population, while the M.G.B.–K.G.B. covers also the repression of losers among the leadership by the winners. In particular, the Section for In-vestigating Specially Important Cases may be regarded as a weapon solely directed against high-level Party figures. The fact that three successive heads of this section were shot — in December 1953, July 1954 and December 1954 — for having killed or tortured what turned out retrospectively to be the wrong people, is indicative.

That the K.G.B. carries more weight than the M.V.D. can be seen from the fact that two K.G.B. officials were in the 1956 Central Committee as against one from the M.V.D., while in the Union Republic bureaux elected that year eight local K.G.B. chiefs figure, as against three M.V.D. Under the Khrushchev régime, some of the M.V.D.'s powers — such as control of the border troops — were transferred to the K.G.B., and finally the U.S.S.R. M.V.D. ministry was abolished; this did not, of course, affect its operational network, but removed its representatives from the centre.

To break the ruling apparatus up into these divisions does not mean that they in their turn are not racked by internal faction. Nor does it mean that the groups do not have direct methods of influencing or controlling each other. The Party Secretariat is in charge, to some degree at least, of the Police. So is the State, through the Council of Ministers. The Party has very powerful direct control in the Army, through the Army Political Administration. And in Stalin's time, the dicta-tor's personal secretariat had direct control in all key areas.

Party relations with the Police are particularly significant. That the local Party Secretary was directly involved in purge activities and arrests is shown by a curious passage in Khrush-chev's Secret Speech:

A second declaration by Eikhe has been preserved which he sent to Stalin on October 27, 1939. In it he cited facts very convincingly

and countered the slanderous accusations made against him, arguing that this provocative accusation was on the one hand the work of
real Trotskyites whose arrests he had sanctioned as First Secretary
of the West Siberian Krai party committee and who conspired in
order to take revenge on him, and, on the other hand, the result of
the base falsification of material by the investigative judges.

Thus Khrushchev, too, in Kiev, had his responsibilities. The
Party control of the Police at the centre is or was formally
exercised by the Administrative Organs Department of the
Central Committee. The Party Secretary dealing with this department was presumably assigned the Police link with particular emphasis, as when Khrushchev tells us:

> Kuznetsov was elected Secretary of the Central Committee. The
> very fact that Stalin entrusted Kuznetsov with the supervision of the
> State security organs shows the trust which he enjoyed.

Except for the few months after the death of Stalin (dealt
with in Chapter Nine), the Police were never in a position to
make any sort of bid to control the State and Party. It is conceivable that the Army, in certain circumstances, might do so, and it
was evidently suspected of tendencies that way in the autumn
of 1957: if so, its defeat was complete. The case is otherwise in
hypotheses put forward about the role of the apparatchiks and
the khozaistvenniks. It has been strongly urged that these two
groupings have formed, as it were, the two possible 'mass'
bases for rival Soviet factions over the last twenty years or so.
It is argued, for instance, that Khrushchev's 1957 reorganisation of industry was intended to destroy the Managers' control
of the economy. What significance are we really to attach to
this idea? There is no need to over-simplify. Nobody would
maintain that there are not individual and clique rivalries
within such groups. Nor would anyone urge that a faction
victorious with the support of the Managers would not be able
to take control of the Party machinery. But it is worth examining
the whole question of the supposed managerial class. Such
people are, indeed (or were until recently), a large group with
technical training — members of the Party who have directed
the main branches of Soviet industry, the planning centres and
that large section of the State apparatus devoted to economic
matters (in effect practically the whole State apparatus except

for the administrative machinery, foreign affairs and the armed forces). These men, who number about a third of the Party membership, have certainly been of enormous importance in the Soviet Union. They are not linked organisationally to form one body. And in speaking of them as a single effective group we are manufacturing a hypothetical entity.

This is perfectly legitimate practice. In such a case it is quite insufficient to make the assumption that because on theoretical, economic and other grounds they have interests in common they *must* therefore act (on the whole and with the obvious reservations) as a group. That would be mere scholasticism, and it is necessary to examine events of Part III to see how far the use of this hypothesis justifies itself.

The evidence will be seen to be extremely strong that contenders for power in the U.S.S.R. have treated the Managers as a genuine political entity. And there is no apparent reason to reject this estimate. It is sociologically most interesting and should appeal to Marxists as, perhaps, an instance of the emergence of something like a new and unforeseen economic class. Moreover, the loyalties of this group seem to have been to a particular set of policies — less adventurous, less ideologically motivated, in certain ways more 'liberal' and more peaceful in foreign policies than those of the various factions which had opposed them. It can be and has been argued persuasively that this is natural in view of their economic and social position. That is not the concern of this book. I am taking that hypothetical group whose unity was the least demonstrable and most questionable. And it seems to me that it is at least established that if done carefully, it is legitimate to utilise these hypothetical entities in any calculus of Soviet political affairs.

Two things may indeed be urged. The first is that the Soviet State machinery is constructed so that the will of the man in control can be imposed on subordinate groups without taking their views much into consideration. This is certainly true. But where there is any disunity at the top the feelings of important subordinate groups are bound to have some influence. Where the disunity at the top becomes great the tendency is to appeal to other and even larger circles, as Beria seems to have appealed to the nationalities and Malenkov later to the consumers. And, on the contrary, it is in the interests of those who cannot or do not wish to appeal to a given group to do their best to destroy its corporate power. The Doctors' Plot seemed intended in part to destroy the conservatism of the managerial class. In 1957 Khrushchev seems to have attempted to disrupt the class as a whole.

Secondly, there is the perennial question of who should be taken as effectively constituting this group. It can hardly be held that the hundreds of thousands of managers and directors who are Party members have any immediate effect at all. The top twenty or thirty ministers and members of the Central Committee, whom one might associate with this stratum, obviously have to be taken very much into account. Perhaps it is reasonable to think for most purposes in terms of a few tens of thousands — the immediate subordinates of the Managerial Ministers, the central cadres of the economic administrative machine. This group Khrushchev attempted to break up. The rank-and-file directors of factories were not, in principle at least, affected by his reorganisation, but simply put under the effective control of the Party organisation.

A like position would probably be found in all the groupings of the U.S.S.R. A few thousand policemen, a few thousand officers, a few thousand Party Secretaries constitute the utmost limits of the section of the population which has any active political influence whatever. Or such is the impression given by Soviet evidence. Nevertheless, it might not be too speculative to say, as has often been done, that they represent the interests of the larger groups below them with whom they are in constant contact and from whom promotion is made to their ranks. This would, at least, be in accord with general sociological principles and with what is known of the U.S.S.R.

It is in this penumbra, in any case, that we may see the present limits of the Soviet political community. At some future date it may expand to embrace the mass of the population. But at present the influence even of the élite thousands is fairly small and may be countered by the vigorous action of half a dozen leaders.

In this chapter we have considered, in broad outline, certain general matters relevant to the power struggle. We have sketched the types of social stress and of ideological considerations affecting Soviet policy decisions; we have considered the conflicting corporate loyalties (apart from mere personal feelings) which emerge within a supposedly united ruling élite; and we have noted the layout of the actual machinery of power.

Without some such preliminaries it would be less easy to follow the substantive account of the struggle given in Parts II and III. But until the detail is reached, which will give body to what has been said above, it should be regarded as a framework only, and not an exhaustive discussion.

CHAPTER THREE

QUESTIONS OF EVIDENCE

THE problem of studying changes in policy and in possession of the instruments of power in a totalitarian state is a complicated and, to some extent, novel one. Usually, the subjects of sociologists and political writers have not suffered for lack of reliable data — if anything, the contrary. But the Soviet Union adds considerably to their difficulties. Before any interpretation of changes in the political leadership, or in the policies involved, can be made, preliminary work, unnecessary in most other circumstances, must be done. For the unknowns usually include the rather basic ones: what exactly is being done? and with what motives?

A good deal of excellent work on Soviet affairs has been accomplished. But, even at its best, it has often had the air of intelligent intuition. One is reminded of the elder St. Simon watching the movements of the Bourbon Court. The writers often seem to be playing, very well, indeed, but by ear and not according to system. It is my purpose to examine what has happened over recent years and to see to what extent it can be correlated with evidence available at the time and later. It is thus hoped to establish a general method for the interpretation of Soviet events, which may prove useful in future. It is certainly the case that trends in the U.S.S.R. can, to some extent, be predicted from small pieces of assembled evidence. It is also true that startling and abrupt political changes, which have surprised even well-informed students throughout the world, have been accurately foreseen on occasion by certain experts. But it would be unscientific not to investigate equally whether important switches have occurred *without* any of the slight signs which a forecaster could pick on; and, if so, whether this signifies that no method is reliable.

It may be asked why any indications at all of impending change or current conflict are allowed to appear. The short answer seems to be that, when the proponents of two policies are secretly at grips, if either of them is able to give the leading Party members an indication that it is the winning side, it is advisable for it to do so in order to induce defections from the hostile group and to secure the support of neutrals. It can thus combine, for many purposes, the advantages of secrecy and of publicity.

That information is deducible at all is due to such factors, which make it desirable for the ruling faction both to preserve some appearance of secrecy and at the same time to make the position clear to the mass of their supporters and enemies. (Mr. Myron Rush covers this admirably in his 'The Role of Esoteric Communication in Soviet Politics', which figures as Appendix 2 in his *The Rise of Khrushchev*.)

A common expression used in Soviet parlance is 'it is not accidental'. It occurs, for instance, in the accusation against the Anti-Party Group in June 1957, with the implication that every part of their activity for years back formed part of a concerted plot. With this in mind we may at least tend to assume that those in power do everything they can to preserve a political objective in all that *they* say and do. This is not to exclude the possibility of an occasional blurting out of a fact for no particular reason or for the occasional slip in the censorship. But on the whole it is a powerful argument for devoting to quite minor hints and formulations an attention which in a less highly organised society would be quite out of place.

A Polish columnist, J. Kisielewski, writes:

In our public, political and intellectual life, in our organisations and newspapers, there exists a special figurative speech. It consists of the usage of certain turns of phrase . . . All that is needed is a clue. Those who have guessed that clue are able to read public utterances as if they were an open book and thus learn a lot of things. It goes without saying that one has to read between the lines, to follow hidden ideas. And this reading between the lines is not illegitimate: on the contrary, the texts are construed in such a way that reading between the lines is the only way to grasp their meaning. To be able to follow the figurative speech one has to possess many years' training in reading it, one must have lived for years in milieus indulging in this form of speech, one must have lived for many years in our country. Those who cannot read our special language are as naive as little children. . . . (*Tygodnik Powszechny*, July 6, 1958.)

This is to make it sound rather more recondite than is strictly necessary. A few common-sense principles can be adequately established. In the first place, there is so much political writing in the Soviet Union that some principle of selectivity is necessary.

In one of the campaigns of the American Civil War Robert E. Lee was faced by Pope, a commander who, whatever his other faults, was very energetic in reconnaissance, in seeking information. Lee's recourse was to swamp his patrols with a mass of information, some true, some false and much irrelevant. The result was that Lee beat him just as badly as generals who failed to reconnoitre at all. In something of the same way, the significant formulation revealing an important policy difference in the U.S.S.R. is frequently hidden in a page of ideological generalities, and sometimes surrounded by assurances of unexampled unity and solidarity.

Moreover, signs may be sought in almost any field. It is in the nature of the totalitarian State that when factions become involved in struggles with each other, even sections of public life which are not normally regarded as political in the West may produce symptoms (e.g. the literary struggle in Zhdanov's time). In the same way, long-term ideological problems which may seem to have no immediate significance are often linked with present developments. For example, as we have seen, the dispute on whether 'Communism' can be 'constructed' in the near future has important *immediate* applications.

There is no shortage, as far as quantity is concerned, of Soviet documents. And though their quality leaves a good amount to be desired from the point of view of providing the student with genuine information, one frequently finds that more than might be supposed can be seen from material which does not at first appear very revealing. There are two problems. First, material that is relevant has to be separated from the vast mass that is absolutely useless. And then the chosen material has to be made to yield results, care being taken not to fall into the temptation of reading too much into them. A useful book might be compiled solely of the documents quoted here, together with others which I have not referred to. Such a compilation would, in its way, be something like the excellent productions of the Russian Institute and the Programme on

Eastern Europe, at Columbia University — the *Anti-Stalin Campaign and International Communism* and *National Communism and Popular Revolt in Eastern Europe* respectively — which are quite indispensable to any students of Communism. It would be less revealing than these compilations, which deal with periods when the Communist authorities in the countries concerned were writing and speaking very much more freely than is usual. Still, a volume of the sort would be a splendid exercise book for students, rather in the manner of documentary collections like Stubbs' *Charters*. Even the documents quoted in the present book should prove useful in this way. The writer believes that a careful study of them by fresh minds would almost certainly yield more information and further plausible speculations which have evaded him.

There are a few signs that a number of documents may be made available to Soviet researchers on the history of the Communist Party, though that would not indeed, with present censorship arrangements, guarantee freedom of selection from them as far as publication is concerned. Still it must be considered some advance, if put into effect as stated in *Voprosy Istorii*, No. 2, 1957, in an article 'Scientific Research Work in the Central Party Archives':

Until quite recently there was an almost complete absence in the archives of documents dealing with the plenums of the C.C. C.P.S.U., the Secretariat and the Politburo for the 1920's and 1930's, which hampered the development of the history of the C.P.S.U. in the Soviet period. In June–July 1957 there arrived from the C.C. C.P.S.U. about 13,000 of the most valuable documents including verbatim reports and minutes of the XVth, XVIth, XVIIth and XVIIIth Party congresses and conferences, and also the minutes of the plenums of the C.C. for 1924–41. Minutes of the City Committees, the Provincial Committees and the Central Committees of the Communist Parties of the Union Republics for 1946–49 have been received. As soon as the technical arrangements can be completed, these documents will be put into scientific circulation.

However, even assuming that the 'technical arrangements' do not involve a lot of work with the scissors, there is no reason to believe that clearance for foreigners to perpetrate bourgeois objectivism upon the documents will be available. And meanwhile we must make do with the public material.

The public indications of what is going on include:

The removal of persons previously associated with certain leaders. Where single individuals are concerned this is by no means a reliable method, for individuals may change sides. But where three or four or more men are involved it tends to become virtually unassailable.

Then there are public pronouncements on matters of policy in which the policies most closely associated with given leaders are often attacked directly — or by implication (when omissions and emphasis require study).

The arrest and trial of police officials for shooting past leaders can normally be interpreted as an attack on the factions which benefited from such executions; and in addition the phrasing of the accusations is often significant; much the same can be said of the denunciation of persons for the murder or attempted murder of members of one faction.

There are, too, matters of protocol, such as the listing of leaders (when in non-alphabetical order), the credit given for victories in the war and so on.

One must, particularly in matters directly relating to the struggle for power, distinguish between words and real intentions. Stalin defended Zinoviev and Kamenev against Trotsky on the grounds that the Party needed them. And he later defended the Rightists against Zinoviev and Kamenev, saying, 'How could the Party be run without Bukharin, Rykov and Tomsky?' In fact, in principle, evidence cannot necessarily be taken at its face value. But commonsense methods of interpretation frequently give adequate service. For example, if Voznesensky was attacked in December 1952 as 'anti-Marxist', it does not necessarily show that he was in disagreement with the formulations of *Capital* or *The Eighteenth Brumaire of Louis Bonaparte*, but it does show that he was in disgrace, almost certainly expelled from the Party and possibly executed. It is also likely to signify that policy disagreements had occurred.

In general, too, accuracy varies with the passage of time. The original accusations against the Anti-Party Group in June 1957 are, of course, angled from the point of view of the victors. Nevertheless, when they state that Molotov had opposed the Virgin Lands scheme, but do not mention the others in that connection, there is some presumption of an accurate distinction. The fact that later and wilder attacks give all three as hostile to the scheme must then be discounted somewhat. In the same way, the failure to blame Beria for the Doctors' Plot for a number of years enables one to be sceptical about belated and rather general remarks listing it among his crimes (in *Pravda* of July 8, 1956, which says that Beria's 'rotten band' had 'fabricated the Leningrad Affair, the Doctors' Affair' and other things).

I am confining myself in principle to official Soviet evidence. Khrushchev's Secret Speech is not precisely in this category. But I propose to treat it as such for the following reasons:

That Khrushchev made a secret speech is of course not denied. The Stenographic Record of the XXth Congress states that on February 25, 1956, 'In closed session the Congress heard a report of the First Secretary of the Central Committee of the Communist Party of the Soviet Union, N. S. Khrushchev, on the cult of personality and its consequences and adopted a decision on the question' (Vol. 2, Moscow, 1956). And something of its contents were widely rumoured shortly after the Speech was delivered (though for our purposes we must ignore this point). In June 1956 the American State Department published a text which had come into its hands, without guaranteeing its authenticity. This was, however, accepted as authentic by Communist Parties and newspapers everywhere. An article in the New York *Daily Worker* of June 18, 1956, by the Secretary of the American Communist Party, Mr. Eugene Dennis, which takes this point for granted, was republished in *Pravda*, of June 27, 1956. The Speech's general points (though not references to particular crimes) were given at length in a resolution of the Central Committee published in *Pravda* on July 2, 1956.

It was only a few of the smaller Communist Parties, and that only at the beginning, which accused the Americans of (in the words of the Dutch Communist paper *De Waarheid* of June 7, 1956), 'broadcasting falsified statements . . . merely for the purpose of creating confusion and distrust'. This line was soon dropped, for it received no encouragement from Moscow, and the major Communist Parties and their leaders, who were presumably in possession of the facts, made no attempt to deny the authenticity. In his article of June 16, 1956, in *Nuovi Argomenti* ('Nine Questions on Stalinism'), Togliatti actually quoted

E

from the speech sentences which occur in the American version — on Stalin that 'he did a great deal for the Soviet Union' and that 'he was the most convinced of Marxists and had the strongest faith in the people'.

In *l'Humanité* of June 19 a statement of the Political Bureau of the French Communist Party said:

The bourgeois Press has published a report attributed to Comrade Khrushchev. This report, which adds to Stalin's already known errors statements of other grave mistakes committed by him, justifiably provokes high feelings among the members of the French Communist Party. The French Communists, as do the Communists of all countries, denounce the arbitrary acts of which Stalin is accused and which are contrary to the principles of Marxism–Leninism. The creditable effort of the leaders of the C.P.S.U. to undertake the correction of the errors and faults connected with the cult of the individual emphasises the strength and unity of the great Party of Lenin, the confidence which it enjoys among the Soviet peoples and its authority in the international labour movement.

However, the Politburo regrets that because of the conditions under which Comrade Khrushchev's report was presented and divulged, the bourgeois Press was in a position to publish facts of which the French Communists had been unaware. Such a situation is not favourable to normal discussion of these problems within the Party. It facilitates, on the contrary, speculations and manœuvres on the part of the enemies of Communism.

The British Communist Party in a statement published in the *Daily Worker* on June 22, 1956, said: 'In the light of the unofficial text now published, which in the absence of official denial may be regarded as more or less authentic . . .'

The American version was generally believed to have come from Poland. Nor was there any difficulty in understanding how a copy could have become available in that country. The delegate from the 'Paris Commune' shipyards, speaking over Radio Szeczecin-Gdansk Regional at 16.45 on October 25, 1956, gave an account of the events in Warsaw leading to Gomulka's triumph. In this he stated that 'the materials of the XXth Congress were only obtainable if they were signed for and then the demand for their return was always made'. In Zeran, however, the materials were made available 'not only for Party Comrades but for all workers'. (This in his view accounted for the leading role played by the workers at the Zeran Car Factory on the side of Gomulka some months later.) From this it is plain that the Speech circulated fairly widely in Warsaw. (It is certainly true that the version circulated to the Poles may have been amended somewhat not only from the Speech as originally delivered but from the version originally circulated in the Soviet Union.)

More evidence on the general authenticity of the State Department version can be obtained from a study of the text. For instance, Khrushchev speaks of the deportations of the Karachai, Kalmyk, Chechen, Ingush and Balkars, and condemns them. This list omits two further deported nations — the Volga Germans and Crimean Tartars. In January 1957 a Decree of the Supreme Soviet was announced restoring to their homelands precisely those nations mentioned by Khrushchev and omitting precisely those not referred to by him. The odds against this being coincidence are obviously high and it goes far to verify at least this section of the Speech as published in the West.

Again, the dates of death of various purged figures such as Eikhe were confirmed as the same as in the Speech, when the *Large Soviet Encyclopaedia*, Vol. 51, came out two years later.

Though the Russians never overtly accepted the American version of the Speech as authentic they did not actually deny it for some time, but in 1958 Khrushchev, answering correspondents' questions, began vaguely to refer to fabrications by Allan Dulles. Even now the way Khrushchev put it could at a pinch mean no more than that the translation he had seen of the American version, which would have been rendered from language to language at least three times, was not identical with the original. But Khrushchev's statement was not only ambiguous: it was also too late. The authenticity of the text had been established by default. Certainly other versions had circulated. But these varied only in a few minor respects, mainly extra material.

We must in any case examine the whole question of the precise reliability of official Soviet evidence if taken literally, and not subjected to a process of interpretation. For official accounts of events are sometimes hard to credit. And in recent years there have been so many contradictory stories put out about identical matters that there is no longer any serious reason for it even to be claimed that any special credence should attach to official statements simply because they are official. We may take a few examples. Khrushchev in his Secret Speech says, quite rightly, 'Could Yezhov have arrested Kossior, for instance, without the knowledge of Stalin? Could Yezhov have decided such important matters as the fate of such eminent Party figures? No, it would be a display of naivety to consider this the work of Yezhov alone. It is clear that these matters were decided by Stalin and that without his orders and his sanction Yezhov could not have done this.' It would indeed be a display of naivety to imagine that Politburo members could have been executed simply on the word of police officials without the complicity of Stalin. Yet for several years the official post-Stalin account of the fate of Voznesensky demanded just this naivety. The execution of Voznesensky and his colleagues was, at the Abakumov trial in December 1954, blamed entirely on Abakumov and Beria. It was over a year before this version was amended (in the Secret Speech) to concede that Stalin was really implicated. Later speeches, made in July 1957, attributed the responsibility to Malenkov too. (The Doctors' Plot also was attributed solely to Ryumin's 'careerist' ambitions when he was executed in July 1954.)

That even moderately important Party members, such as some at least of the delegates to the Party Congresses, do not have access even to political documents of a more or less 'agitational' nature may be seen from the Secret Speech, where Khrushchev says:

The indictment in the Beria case contains a discussion of his crimes. Some things should, however, be recalled, *especially since it is possible that not all delegates to the congress have read this document.* . . . As a result of the particularly detailed legal proceedings it was established that Beria had committed monstrous crimes and Beria was shot. [My italics.]

The 'detailed' proceedings have never been published, and the only material available to the general public, and apparently to any except a small circle, is that given in Appendix VI. On the other hand, we may certainly regard the full indictment, and similar documents circulating among the upper level, as being drafted with a view to their political effect on their recipients. If we had access to *all* this material the whole study would be transformed. It is precisely because we do not that it shows its present characteristics.

That we are likely to obtain early official information of even reasonable completeness and accuracy about important changes is highly unlikely. The key to Stalin's success in breaking the opposition to the Yezhovshchina at the February–March plenum of 1937 was the elimination of Ordzhonikidze. Many unofficial rumours circulated almost from the beginning, that Ordzhonikidze had been killed, or forced to commit suicide, on Stalin's order. But it was only nineteen years later, in Khrushchev's Secret Speech of February 1956, that this was confirmed. Yet the documentation of Ordzhonikidze's natural death, signed by four leading doctors, including the Minister of Health, is about as good as a documentation can be. Its falsehood casts a doubt on other documents.

Some of the difficulties in these matters of evidence may be seen in a relatively straightforward point. In the last volumes of the *Large Soviet Encyclopaedia*, second edition, there are biographies of certain victims of Stalin, now rehabilitated. Among these are five members or candidate members of the Politburo in the 1930s — Kossior, Postyshev, Eikhe, Chubar and Rudzutak. The dates of death are given in each case.

Mr. Boris Nicolaevsky is probably as well-informed a student of these matters as anyone in the Western world. In his edition of Khrushchev's Secret Speech, published by the American *New Leader* under the title *Crimes of the Stalin Era*, he had footnotes on these men, also giving their death dates. That he was not just guessing is shown by his putting '?' in the case of Kosarev, the Komsomol secretary (whom the *Encyclopaedia* now gives as dying in 1939).

Khrushchev actually states the date of death of one of the five in the body of his Speech — Eikhe, who was executed in 1940. The dates of the deaths of every one of the other four is given differently by Nicolaevsky and the *Encyclopaedia*. (Kossior: E. 1939, N. 1938; Postyshev E. 1940, N. 1938; Rudzutak E. 1938, N. 1940; Chubar E. 1939, N. 1938.)

This is no reflection on Mr. Nicolaevsky. It may simply show how much things can be kept secret, and how the indirect and unofficial evidence is inadequate. On the other hand, I would not be taken as saying flatly that the dates now given officially are correct. Two different dates have been given for the death of Krylenko in the past few years, for example: In a collection of *Memories of Lenin*, published in Moscow in 1956, it is stated that he died in 1938. The *Large Soviet Encyclopaedia* (Vol. 51, 1958) gives 1940. Orakhelashvili's case illustrates even more strikingly how precarious any of our deductions must be if we base them on official Soviet statements. The same volume of the *Encyclopaedia* has an article on him which gives his date of death as 1940. *Pravda* of December 20, 1937, stated definitely that he had been sentenced, on December 16, 'to the supreme punishment of shooting' and that 'the sentence has been carried out'. It is hardly worth going into what this particular contradiction means. (There must be a presumption in favour of the later story, though a possible motivation might be a desire to implicate Beria even further.) But it will be plain that the proven possibility of such announcements being false must shake with a temblor of uncertainty many a structure of speculation founded on them.

Khrushchev states in the Secret Speech that in Stalin's last years the Central Committee Plenary Sessions were not convened. It is difficult to trace sessions of the plenum. One was announced in February 1947 (to which Andreyev reported on agriculture). In the article 'Bulganin' in the second edition of the *Large Soviet Encyclopaedia* there is mention of a plenum in February 1948. A plenum was announed in August 1952 — which called the XIXth Congress. And Khrushchev himself mentions the plenum of the newly elected Central Committee in October 1952, which elected the new large Praesidium and heard a speech from Stalin denouncing Mikoyan and Molotov. Again, Khrushchev states that 'during all the years of the patriotic war not a single Central Committee plenum took place', adding that the Central Committee members did indeed assemble in October 1941, but were then dispersed. Yet a report of a plenum on January 27, 1944, is given in the official collection *The Communist Party of the Soviet Union in Resolutions and Decisions of Congresses, Conferences and Central Committee Plenums* (Marx–Engels–Lenin–Stalin Institute, 1954). Thus we are in the position of not knowing whether Khrushchev fails to refer to plenums which in fact took place or, alternatively, whether plenums officially announced did not take place at all.

Examples of the unsatisfactory nature of Soviet evidence could be culled from almost every sphere. For example, when Khrushchev, at the December 1958 plenum of the Central Committee, accused Malenkov of giving falsified figures on the grain crop in his Report to the XIXth Party Congress in October 1952, he is denouncing what had figured as a major official statistic for six years. The denunciation of trials as frame-ups is frequent in the period we are covering. And faults of omission are even more extraordinary — extending in some cases to the total cessation during, and for some time after, the Stalin epoch, of the naming of deported and disgraced national minorities, like the Kalmyks, even in the historical accounts of the area they had inhabited for centuries. The rewriting of history, and particularly Party history, to suit the line of the moment has been continuous, and it has actually been claimed that history is 'politics projected back into the past'. This produced curious results, as in the Burdzhalov controversy of 1956–57, when historians tried to take advantage of the relaxation to discover what Stalin and Zinoviev had actually said and done in March 1917.

The evidence, then, is not necessarily accurate in any ordinary sense. But it may still be indicative. We may now consider a quite different point about these indications. There is a particular type of Soviet evidence which might be described as protocol evidence. This is the sort perhaps most familiar to, and most reprobated by, occasional readers of the Kremlinological literature: it concerns the formal orders of appearance, positions in photographs and so on which come out in the Soviet Press.

Kulski in his *The Soviet Regime* (Syracuse University Press, 1954, p. 692) takes a couple of particular photographs — those published in connection with the meeting of the Supreme Soviet in August 1953. He says, rightly, that the precedence apparent in such groups 'may be misleading'. And it is 'more sensible' not to draw hasty conclusions. In particular he argues against anyone holding that such a thing 'faithfully reflects the respective political importance of those concerned'.

It is certainly clear that no simply mechanical formula can be applied. But this does not deprive such groups of all significance. The lay-out of the photograph in question is as follows:

Mikoyan   Bulganin

Kaganovich, Khrushchev, Malenkov, Voroshilov, Molotov

and to the side:

Saburov, Pervukhin, Shvernik, Ponomarenko

As Kulski points out, this 'would be most easily interpreted': Malenkov, Khrushchev, Voroshilov, Kaganovich, Molotov, Bulganin, Mikoyan, Saburov, Pervukhin, Shvernik, Ponomarenko. It is, to be sure, a lay-out which lays less emphasis on the seniority as between the couples Khrushchev and Voroshilov, Molotov and Kaganovich, etc., than does a straight line, as on the saluting base on November 7. Nevertheless it does plainly represent something like the order of precedence, and is intended to do so. Where Kulski seems to be a little schematic is in identifying an order of precedence with an order of power. It seems certain that some additional assumptions must be made. For example, Voroshilov's position as President of the Praesidium of the Supreme Soviet was plainly more decorative than powerful, and it has, almost certainly rightly, been assumed by everybody that Voroshilov's power over the last seven years has not been very great. On certain occasions, particularly State ones, he was (right up to 1960) given higher precedence than Khrushchev himself. And thus honorary or quasi-honorary factors certainly affect the simpler picture. On the other hand, Khrushchev's position close to the top at this stage at least goes with an increase in his power since the announcement of the new Praesidium in March 1953, as was shortly to be seen.

In the second photograph of the same proceedings the box on the right had (in addition to the two junior members of the Party Praesidium and the two candidate members) Suslov, Pegov, Pospelov, Shatalin and Shkiryatov. Kulski suggests that this might signify their eventual possible promotion to the Praesidium. But in the case of Suslov, Pospelov and Shatalin their presence is presumably merely that of non-Praesidial members of the Secretariat, in a case where there is room for them. Pegov, as Secretary of the Praesidium of the Supreme

Soviet, no doubt figures, on this particular occasion, in an honorary position similar to that of Voroshilov — though there is perhaps a minor demonstration of the temporary ascendancy of the leader he was most closely associated with, Malenkov. Shkiryatov, as Chairman of the Party Control Commission, was in theory the next most important Party figure, and had appeared as such on similar occasions. Thus, in principle there seems to be nothing wrong with a seniority interpretation, suitably modified.

We shall see certain significant uses of the photographs and of the listings given in the Press. The introduction of alphabetical order in 1954 might at first sight appear to benefit no one, especially not Khrushchev, who happened to come last. But reflection shows that this is not so. So long as a non-alphabetical listing existed, the First Secretary had no particular claim to the first spot. (In fact in other Communist countries, e.g. Bulgaria, where order of precedence was maintained, and the post of First Secretary introduced also, that official ranked after several others.) As soon as alphabetical listing came in, Khrushchev was the only member of the Praesidium to stand out from an apparent equality by virtue of a leading Party post. And, after this, in 1958, a listing in which Khrushchev appeared first began to compete with the alphabetical one.

The listing of war services in another major variable. The *Large Soviet Encyclopaedia* article on the Communist Party of the Soviet Union (September 1953) lists all the senior members of the Praesidium for their war services in the order then correct: Malenkov, Molotov, Khrushchev, Voroshilov, Bulganin, Kaganovich, Mikoyan. A more exclusively Khrushchevite method was devised, and first used in *Trud* of March 5, 1954, as follows:

'Stalin was placed at the head of the armed forces of the Soviet State. The Central Committee of the Party assigned N. A. Bulganin, A. Zhdanov, A. S. Shcherbakov, S. Khrushchev and other members of the C.C. directly to military work.' This was repeated frequently.

During the summer of 1954, a period of Malenkov's revival, these listings ceased, but the Khrushchevite 'war service' list reappeared on the eve of Khrushchev's victory, in December 1954. An anti-Khrushchev device was soon brought into play, particularly during the period immediately after Malenkov's ouster, which saw a certain hardening against Khrushchev: this was the listing of members of the State Defence Committee — in which only Khrushchev, of the senior Praesidium members, had not figured.

In the 'historical sketch' of the U.S.S.R. in Volume 50 of the *Large Soviet Encyclopaedia*, published in 1957, after the purge of the Anti-Party Group, we get, instead of an interim demonstration, a victory summary: 'Those given important assignments' during the War were the 'leading Party workers — Andreyev, Bulganin, Voznesensky, Voroshilov, Zhdanov, Kalinin, Kosygin, Mikoyan, Stalin, Khrushchev, Shvernik and many other members of the Central Committee'.

These considerations are shown in other types of descriptive material on the leaders, for instance in the *Encyclopaedic Dictionary* (Vol. III, 1955) Khrushchev is called 'one of the closest comrades in arms of J. V. Stalin'. Molotov, Voroshilov, Mikoyan and Kaganovich are called simply 'close comrades in arms'.

The applause given to various Praesidial speakers at the XXth Congress is listed in a non-egalitarian manner: Khrushchev: 'stormy, prolonged applause transforming itself into an ovation. All rise.' Bulganin: 'continued, lasting applause. All rise.' Mikoyan: 'stormy, long-lasting applause'. Molotov, Voroshilov, Malenkov, Suslov: 'stormy continued applause'. Kaganovich, Pervukhin: 'stormy applause'. Kirichenko: 'continued applause'. Saburov: 'applause'.

In the Khrushchev Secret Speech it is mildly interesting to compare his ways of referring to his colleagues. Voroshilov, Mikoyan, Molotov, Marshal Vasilevsky and Andreyev are referred to by their Christian names as well as their surnames and patronymics. In fact Voroshilov is once called 'our dear friend Kliment Yefremovich'. Kaganovich and Malenkov are simply named. The best Malenkov gets is 'Comrade Malenkov' in a passage immediately following one in which Khrushchev has ostentatiously spoken of Marshal Vasilevsky as Alexander Mikhailovich.

In an article in *World Politics* of April 1958 ('Ten Theories in Search of Reality'), Mr. Daniel Bell puts this sort of speculative Kreminology into interesting perspective. With all the pitfalls in analyses of this type, whoever abjures them altogether is likely to fall into the worse trap which caught the *New York Post* in 1953. That newspaper, as Mr. Bell points out, 'scoffed at the speculations arising from the fact that all the Bolshevik leaders but Beria had appeared *en masse* at the Bolshoi Ballet. "Perhaps Beria does not like ballet," it stated archly. Perhaps he did not, but we never had the opportunity to find out, for two days later came the announcement that Beria had been arrested as a traitor.'

Mr. Bell has also reviewed Mr. Myron Rush's *The Rise of Khrushchev* (in *Problems of Communism*, March–April 1958). He comments on Mr. Rush's noting that on May 25, 1955, *Pravda* printed Khrushchev's title of First Secretary with the first letters of each word in capitals; Mr. Rush said that this change was 'so subtle and so elusive as virtually to have escaped notice in the West'. The following day the capital S of Secretary was replaced by a lower-case letter, but the capital was retained at the beginning of the title. The clue, as Mr. Bell points out, was 'slim', and Mr. Rush's deduction from this and similar (sometimes even more tenuous) points was that Khrushchev would make a bid for supreme power. (Mr. Rush correctly predicted early in 1957 that Khrushchev would get rid of Malenkov, Kaganovich and Molotov.)

It is a little unfair to view pieces of evidence of this sort, just because note is made of them, as decisive in forming an opinion like Mr. Rush's. For even if the change in lettering may be taken as significant (and it is not an unreasonable hypothesis to take it as possibly so), it would only be so in connection with two major propositions accepted as already established: that a struggle for power was already proceeding, and that Khrushchev was one of the major contenders.

Yet it does seem to be a very extreme case of what can be regarded as evidence at all. It happens to fit the general trend, and it cannot be excluded in Soviet circumstances that it was consciously used to forward that trend. But if an entire case is built on even quite a number of points as small as this, as sometimes happens, it must be regarded as feeble to the point of non-existence. In non-quantised branches of learning, in their early stages, there have been extra-scientific theories built up with a very similar basis (and these are often the most popular with the general public — as with the Atlantis myth).

A minor point of Soviet protocol is the use or omission of the prefix 'Comrade'. Technically the prefix indicates Party membership, and its omission would ordinarily imply that the man named had been expelled from the Party. In the article by Khrushchev in *Kommunist*, No. 12, 1957, published in August (as also in *Pravda* on August 28) he still refers to Malenkov as 'Comrade Malenkov', in spite of very strong words about how he used to be a tool in Beria's hands. In early Soviet documents 'comrade' is occasionally omitted — e.g. when Rykov was removed from membership of the Politburo in 1930 he was not referred to as Comrade, while his replacements were, although in fact he remained a member of the Party. But though references omitting the title are occasionally met with, we can at least be certain that where one man is referred to as 'Comrade' and another one not in the same announcement, the one without the title had lost favour. For example, an announcement of the plenum of the Central Committee held in January 1938 states 'the plenum freed Postyshev P. P. from candidate membership of the Political Bureau of the Central Committee of the All-Union Communist Party (Bolsheviks). The plenum elected to candidate membership of the Political Bureau of the Central Committee of the All-Union Communist Party (Bolsheviks) the Secretary of the Moscow Provincial Committee of the All-Union Communist Party, Comrade Khrushchev N. S., and to membership of the Orgburo of the Central Committee of the All-Union Communist Party Comrade Mekhlis L. Z.'

The degree to which definite formulae in referring to individuals become stereotypes was, as we have seen, demonstrated in the expression 'Shepilov-who-joined-them', used of the fallen ideologist for eighteen months after his fall. The phrase was occasionally omitted, but its correctness as part of the formula is emphasised by the following exchange at the December 1958 plenum:

Z. T. Serdyuk. '. . . the political bankruptcy of the anti-Party group of Malenkov, Kaganovich, Molotov, Bulganin and Shepilov.'

N. S. Khrushchev. 'And Shepilov who joined them.'

Z. T. Serdyuk. 'It becomes very long like that.'

This was the time when Bulganin's name was being inserted into the list, and it was evidently considered too much of a mouthful. So thenceforth the epithet was usually dropped and the five names listed as Serdyuk gives them.

An example of a similar sort of evidence was the business of places (and other institutions) named for prominent politicians. As Khrushchev said in his Secret Speech, it was only when Radio Kiev one day ceased to call itself Radio Kossior that the population deduced the latter's fall. Nothing was publicly said against the N.K.V.D. chief Yezhov for many years, but the town of Yezhovo-Cherkessk dropped its prefix, confirming that he had not simply retired for reasons of health.

Usually the loss of name follows a public degrading, and is thus of no importance as evidence — as in the changes of name of the various Molotov and Molotov-derivative towns, starting with Perm, in 1957, and the Kaganovich and Beria equivalents in 1957 and 1953. In the case of Stalin's own ambiguous demotion few of the myriad Stalin towns and institutions lost their title in the U.S.S.R. except in a roundabout way. (Of the satellites' Stalin towns, the Polish was changed permanently, the Hungarian temporarily, the Bulgarian simply reverted quietly to its old name, and the others remained as they were.) But there are occasions when such changes precede open denunciation and are often signs of concealed tensions — as when the Moscow Metro was withdrawn from Kaganovich's collection in the autumn of 1955.

There is one peculiar case, revealing in its way. Sergo Ordzhonikidze, as Khrushchev finally confirmed in 1956 in his Secret Speech, had perished on Stalin's orders. But until 1956 the pretence had been kept up that he was Stalin's closest friend and supporter. Yet in 1944 the various towns named after him were mostly quietly renamed: Ordzhonikidzegrad (formerly Bezhitsa), Ordzhonikidze (formerly Yenakiyevo) and Sergo (formerly Kadiyevka) reverted to their earlier names, while Ordzhonikidze in the Caucasus, formerly Vladikavkaz, was given a new Ossetian name, Dzaudzhikau.

The sensitivity of the leadership to minor points of precedence and so on thus seems clear enough. Another, and absurd, example may be seen in an excerpt from a speech by Matskevich at the December 1958 plenum:

In addition to the known facts about the active fractionist activities of Bulganin, I consider it my duty to recall an event of which I was witness. At the opening of the All-Union Agricultural Exhibition in 1957, Bulganin arranged an obstruction to Comrade Khrushchev and at the head of a fractionist group demonstratively left the Exhibition.

This was long before the Central Committee plenum which unmasked the fractionist group. Why then do you say that during the June events you fortuitously became a member of this group? This is dishonest.

(Voices) — Shame!

The reflection of the struggle in the status of individuals does not apply only to the leaders, but also to a wide range of subordinate officials.

The main categories of men whose careers are significant are:

(a) Politicians—
    (1) Members of the Praesidium and Secretariat.
    (2) Secretaries of local parties — especially of the Ukraine, Leningrad, Moscow, Georgia and Kazakhstan.
    (3) Other members of the Central Committee.
    (4) Apparatchiks of the Central Committee Departments.
(b) Top Police officials — especially those of the M.G.B./ K.G.B.
(c) Military figures.
(d) Ideologists and experts.

These categories overlap; for instance under (d) there is a spectrum from more or less full-time academics like Ostrovityanov to full-time politicians with a special interest in ideology, like Suslov, or apparatchiks like Ponomarev who are also 'Professors' of Marxism–Leninism.

The existence of groups of clients attached to important figures is not in doubt. Indeed, it was openly asserted of Beria that he had formed a 'gang', and the list of those who followed him from Georgia into important posts in the State apparatus, and later fell with him, is formidable (see Chapters Seven and Nine). In the same way Khrushchev's rise to power at the centre was accompanied by the occupation of a whole series of key posts by members of his old Ukrainian Party apparatus. In 1954–56 alone, for example, ten members of the Ukrainian

Central Committee got important appointments outside the Republic (not to mention others of lesser significance): these included five provincial First Secretaryships in the R.S.F.S.R. and Kazakhstan, two U.S.S.R. Ministries and one deputy Ministry, the Ministry of State Farms in Kazakhstan, and the Headship of the Agricultural Department of the C.P.S.U. Central Committee.

Yet care is needed in considering the significance of the individual career, particularly of minor figures, in the power struggle. It is the commonest thing in interpretative pieces to see someone referred to as a 'Molotov man' or a 'Khrushchev man'. Yet there are obvious difficulties in handling such material. Up to the time of the June 1957 purge in the U.S.S.R., for instance, I believe that every Soviet expert would have called Shepilov a 'Khrushchev man'. Not, indeed, as someone who had owed his entire career to Khrushchev, but a Khrushchev man as against any opponents of Khrushchev in the post-Stalin era. We can go further — Khrushchev thought so too! The regularity with which Shepilov has been referred to as a 'turncoat' and — in connection with the other deviationists — as 'Shepilov who joined them' seems to show that Shepilov was in this sense a 'Khrushchev man' who changed sides. At any given moment, in the secretive periods between public outbursts, we cannot regard the promotion of any single character as *proving* that the power of the leader of the faction he has so far been associated with is being increased.

Yet I am not urging that the possibility of changed allegiances should mean that we must dismiss evidence of promotion of this kind. They can always be taken as *prima facie* indications that there is some probability of the natural deduction being true. Simply, the possibility that a given promotion may signify the opposite cannot be excluded and must always be borne in mind. As Anatole France's characters say in *Penguin Island*, when allocating prospective Cabinet posts: 'Loyalty must be rewarded,' 'Yes, and treachery too.'

And this is only one of the difficulties. It is not often possible to assume, even to this extent, a definite allegiance. The careers of many, though not of all officials — particularly those who came up before the death of Stalin — must have depended on a complexity of relationships which we simply cannot penetrate.

While affiliations like those of Shatalin to Malenkov and Bagirov to Beria are absolutely clear, there are a number of others which, as will come out in Parts II and III, present what appear at first sight, and sometimes later, to be anomalies.

To take for the moment a single case: Among those who sank after Stalin's death, Army General Shtemenko is peculiar. This political General was removed from the post of Chief of Staff on February 21, 1953 — that is, before Stalin's death. Thenceforward little was heard of him for some years. He was not re-elected as a member of the Central Committee in February 1956, and he finally appeared, with the rank of Lieutenant-General (two grades lower), in October 1956. Then *Pravda* (March 30, 1957), reported the award to him, in the intermediate rank of Colonel-General, of a military award for good service. It will be seen that this cannot lend itself to simplified solutions.

It cannot normally be possible for any leader to build up a large enough 'tail' (khvost) of truly devoted clients to man every post which he may wish to secure. Frequently posts must be given simply to the man against whom the patron has no particular objection; or to the uncommitted man whose adherence he wishes to secure; or to the follower of a rival whom he wishes to bribe away from his allegiance. Again, it is important to remember that while a Kirichenko or Shatalin or A. A. Kuznetsov may be wholly dependent on a powerful patron, there are others who seem to be more or less acceptable to faction after faction — occasionally made examples of as executives of a rejected policy, but even then frequently forgiven after a short period. Examples are Patolichev and, to some extent, Aristov. Of course, even such careers may eventually become irrevocably caught up in the struggle.

Once the general thesis of continual struggle is accepted, the greatest remaining danger is over-simplification. It is only too easy to accept, often half consciously, a view in which every important figure is finally lined up on one side or another. Then, after an open clash, those who fall are the members of the defeated faction, and those who remain in power are the members of the victorious faction.

Yet in the June 1957 purge, while the four main culprits were removed from the Central Committee, there were two less drastic demotions — of Saburov to simple membership of that

Committee and Pervukhin to be a junior candidate member of the Praesidium, and one of those later to be denounced as a major accomplice, Bulganin, kept *all* his posts. This sort of thing can be seen even more clearly in the provinces — in Georgia for example. The normal process was for a local leader whose protector at the centre had fallen to denounce him heartily, and then to fall himself. Moreover, one local client might be removed at once and others replaced gradually. In fact, the next wave of purges had often started before an earlier one was complete, so that judged solely by time of removal it might seem (wrongly) that complete confusion prevailed.

A posting much used to remove from the seat of power men who are unwanted, but still employable, is the ambassadorship. G. M. Popov, on his way to oblivion from being Moscow and C.C. Secretary, went first to Poland. He was succeeded there in March 1954 by Mikhailov, and he in turn in May 1955 by Ponomarenko. Benediktov was briefly, in the summer of 1953, sent off to India, to return on Beria's fall. Tevosyan, a prominent supporter of Malenkov, was sent to be ambassador in Japan in 1956. More recently, Ponomarenko was sent to India, Pegov to Iran and Pervukhin to East Berlin.

Certain of these posts are of considerable importance. Even so, they would hardly appear to rate the services of a member of the Central Committee, let alone of the Party Praesidium, except in very particular circumstances. Yet Ponomarenko remained a candidate member of the Praesidium until February 1956; and Pervukhin continued to be (junior) candidate member while at Pankow. In the first case, at least, demotion was evidently intended from the start, and, pending final arrangements, the position abroad saved face and adequately removed the new ambassador from effective participation in the Praesidium's deliberations.

The durability of alliances need be emphasised no more than the durability of allegiances. The core of the Anti-Party Group consisted of:

(*a*) Molotov and Kaganovich (and even they had been by no means united on a number of issues).

(*b*) Malenkov (whom the first two had helped bring down from the Premiership and who had himself led the attack on their clients in 1941).

F

(c) Shepilov (who had replaced Molotov at the Ministry of
Foreign Affairs, and had been the spokesman of the
attack on Malenkov in 1955).

They seem to have acted with very great unity in June 1957.
But still the alliance was of fairly recent date, and it is natural
to think that if it had emerged victorious it would have broken
up pretty rapidly. Indeed, the actual victors (the Khrushchev–
Zhukov alliance) did so. And we need go no further than the
old Khrushchev–Bulganin grouping to see how unstable
alliances are in a crisis.

None of this is to say that groupings do not arise, and often
persist for a considerable time. It is simply that they cannot be
regarded as indestructible. They tend to break up when the
stresses become extreme if, at the same time, changes of alliance
or allegiance can be made to appear profitable.

Individual careers can, if the staff and energy are available,
often be traced back for many years. But allegiances and
alliances change. This sort of Realpolitik applies even more to
secondary figures, most of whom are practically compelled to
live in a world of complicated reinsurances. Thus, it is seldom
worth tracing their histories back more than a few years.

There are exceptions to this. These are usually men who have
become so closely dependent on some leader that virtually no
reinsurance is possible. Certain of Beria's men come into this
category. And there are figures like Shatalin whose link with
Malenkov appears to be absolute. On the whole such men are
those who have been promoted fairly rapidly from a low post
solely as the result of an individual's patronage, rather than
those who have risen at a fairly natural pace, even though
with the assistance and general support of some leader. The
moves of these highly identified small fry are of great evidential
value.

It is difficult, just the same, to draw a definite line between
these two categories. In some cases allegiance is absolutely clear
and certain. In others it is impossible to make head or tail of the
reasons for the vagaries of the careers in question. Even in these
cases, however, it must be worth while to keep them in view.
Even a few further pieces of information might render them
suddenly intelligible. And there are many cases of general

allegiance over a sufficient period to be worth taking into account.

Nor does the difficulty of interpreting the role of junior officials make research into them fruitless. For they may be dealt with not singly, but in groups. And there may be enough of them to be an adequate statistical sample. For instance, a high proportion of local Party Secretaries were appointed in 1949, 1950 and 1951, when Malenkov was at the height of his influence, and were removed in 1955, at the same time as and after Malenkov's removal from the Premiership. In any given case it would be impossible to say that the individual concerned was not an odd exception who owed his appointment to some quite different reason — pleasing Stalin by an article, perhaps — and owed his removal to being stricken with galloping consumption. When a whole series of cases appear, however, we can certainly start to draw political conclusions, as from the following table:

R.S.F.S.R. Provincial Party Secretaries
Of the appointees who remained until 1953:

Year of appointment	Number appointed	Removed in:		Number still in position (or transferred or promoted within the Party machine) in 1956	Number transferred to non-apparat posts
		1954	1955		
1949	12	0	3	6	3
1950	8	1	3	3	1
1951	11	2	3	6	0
1952	19	2	2	15	0

It will be seen that 1955 saw a far higher rate of removal than 1954, and also that the proportion of removals was very much higher for those promoted in 1949, 1950 and 1951 than for those promoted in 1952. The interpretation is that appointees of Malenkov's greatest ascendancy were falling in large numbers after his defeat in January 1955.

An analysis of the thirty-one announced or deduced dismissals from Party or Government posts (and of four names no longer traceable) in the period between 1952 and shortly before the XXth Congress in 1956, enabled a prediction to be made that they would no longer figure in the new Central Committee. This proved true in all but two cases. One of these seems meanwhile to have regained his old post, and the other, who, though replaced, had not been announced as 'relieved' of his, had moved to another of equal standing. As showing the severity of the treatment of the thirty-three actually dropped, it is interesting that only two of them were demoted to candidate membership or to the Revision Commission, and the rest were removed entirely. What proves the deduction useful is that the thirty-one purgees thus deduced constituted the whole of the list of those of the 1952 Committee who did not figure in that of 1956, except for five. Three of these were removed from their offices between the date of the estimate and the XXth Congress. This left only two exceptions, which fuller information might have accounted for. (The total number of removals was thirty-six in all, and of demotions seven.)

There are various subsidiary reasons why it is difficult to be absolutely rigorous about officials at the level of provincial secretaries. In particular, a common name and initial may reappear later in another post, but with nothing to identify him with, or distinguish him from, the earlier mention.

Allowing for this, certain trends are traceable. To take another case: the number of U.S.S.R. Provincial First Secretaries who seem to have been removed in the period 1946–51 without promotion or transfer (and who had not been traceable over a period at least up to the death of Stalin), works out at just over sixty. There are a few doubtful cases, but we can certainly say that about fifty appointees at this level faded right out. Far the highest fall-rate was in 1949, when nineteen seem to have been demoted. Of these, ten could not be traced in any way (even in adverse comment) over the period to 1953.

It is natural to associate this with the Leningrad purge. It is true that many of the demoted were in Siberia and elsewhere far from the Zhdanovist capital, but that is not a real objection. By chance we have an account of what happened to I. N. Turko, First Secretary of the Yaroslavl Provincial Party Committee. He survived, though it seems possible that he was imprisoned. In July 1957 he held a minor economic post in Leningrad, presumably as part of the Zhdanovite rehabilitation Khrushchev had long been embarked on. At the Leningrad

Provincial Party aktiv meeting called to denounce Malenkov and the Anti-Party Group on July 2, 1957, he said:

In February 1949 it fell to my personal lot to know the 'style and methods' of Malenkov's work with Party cadres. I was then secretary of the Yaroslavl Party organisation. During the conference I received an urgent summons to place myself at the disposal of the Central Committee. I was 'received', if one can use such a word, by Malenkov. I had thought that here was a real man. But I was utterly mistaken. In him I met a man harsh and cruel, without honour or conscience. They tried persistently to force me to sign a palpable forgery, accused me of every kind of sin, threatened me (*Leningradskaya Pravda*, July 3, 1957).

Turko had been a secretary of the Leningrad Provincial Committee under Kuznetsov in 1945. It seems certain that the 'urgent summons' was in connection with the decision to proceed with the Leningrad Case, and that Turko was ordered to provide evidence, inculpating others and possibly himself. The Yaroslavl Provincial Committee was one of those censured by the Central Committee at this time. Turko's replacement came from Sverdlovsk, and it may be significant that Andrianov, who took over the Leningrad First Secretaryship, was also from Sverdlovsk. We seem to get a picture — from this and other cases — of a scattering of rival groups of provincial committees dominated by one or other faction.

It is possibly in this aspect that we can see a certain time lag, in ordinary circumstances, in the destruction of all the support of a given ruler, even after he has lost some power. Except in a period of admitted mass purge, the removal of local Party secretaries requires time, excuses and formalities. And if a leader can hang on for a year, or a few months, he may find that if circumstances have changed he is still able to take advantage of it in this respect.

This is one of the types of evidence on which it is necessary to rely, and it will be seen that care is required in its handling. The points gone into here in a general way are illustrated at length in the text. The evidence is going to be incomplete, but that does not mean that it is impossible to deduce a good deal from it if approached with reasonable restraint.

PART II

THE STRUGGLE FOR POWER
IN CONDITIONS OF ONE-MAN RULE,
1949-53

CHAPTER FOUR

A SKETCH OF THE POST-WAR
BACKGROUND, 1945–48

THOUGH the main theme of this book is Soviet politics in the decade just past, it is necessary to sketch the context rather generally for a little farther back.

Before the war Zhdanov, with a vigorously Party-and-ideology attitude, had figured as Stalin's most trusted spokesman.

At the XVIIIth Conference of the Party in February 1941, Malenkov, till then a little-known figure, delivered a speech which was to mark a whole future crux of controversy:

It is time to put an end to the biological approach in the selection of cadres and to test people in action, to judge them by their own work, and not be guided by questionnaires.

To this day, in spite of the instruction of the Party to the contrary, many Party and business bodies, when selecting personnel are more concerned in ascertaining their genealogy, who their grandfathers and grandmothers were, than in studying their personal, business and political qualities, and abilities.

Windbags, people incapable of handling a live job, should be relieved of their posts and placed on less responsible work, irrespective of whether they are Party members or not.

There is another type of business leader, comrades — the ignoramus. We have some of that kind too. The ignoramus is the type who knows nothing and does not want to know anything. He does not study technique, has no use for improved methods, does not know the least thing about technology, and does not understand or wish to understand the economics of his enterprise. But, on the other hand, the ignoramus is as conceited as they make them. He doesn't need advice, he will tell you; he knows exactly what is wanted. What is more, he usually prides himself on his proletarian origin (*Moscow News*, February 22, 1941).

The emphasis on practical, commonsense handling of affairs, with a certain contempt for theoretical principles, was to be notable in Malenkov's periods of ascendancy from then on. Mr.

Boris Nicolaevsky has interestingly distinguished between the early post-Stalin period during which Malenkov was in the leading position, and the later Khrushchev period — the first being rational and the second mythopoeic (*Sotsialistichesky Vestnik*, February–March 1959). Something similar applies to the distinction between the Zhdanov and Malenkov policies during the period of their ascendancies in the forties.

At the XVIIIth Conference a number of Governmental and Party demotions were decided on, on the basis of Malenkov's new line. Demotions from the Central Committee included Zhemchuzhina, Molotov's wife. Kaganovich's brother (M. M. Kaganovich) was removed from his Ministry. Of those who were thus downgraded, only one, N. G. Ignatov, was to rise to power again, and show himself a determined opponent of Malenkov.

Though Malenkov was not formally a full member of the Politburo until 1946, he was often given powers indicating that he was regarded as of adequate seniority, as when the important Committee for the Restoration of the Economy of the Liberated Regions was appointed in 1943, consisting of Malenkov as President and Mikoyan and Andreyev as members (*Pravda*, August 22, 1943).

At the end of the war there came a period in which the regime devoted most of its energies to the practical tasks of reorganisation. Malenkov was at the centre of power and Zhdanov was mainly concerned with parochial chores like the Allied Control Commission in Finland. There was then some relaxation in certain fields from the strictest Party criteria. In 1946–47 Zhdanov made his way back to power on these issues.

The controversies of the period are facets of a single fight for ideological purity and party enthusiasm. But they may be considered under several heads: ideological discipline, expressed in the Zhdanov decrees on the arts; the possibility of capitalist economic recovery, expressed by Varga and other Soviet economists and denied by Zhdanov's ally, Voznesensky; the strategy of Soviet foreign policy — centred on a revolutionary offensive by Zhdanov's Cominform; and later a dispute about the possibilities of the Soviet economic system, conducted between Stalin and Voznesensky.

Even in 1944 a number of articles had appeared on

strengthening ideology. Some of these were general, others were connected with Party cadres (for example, *Bolshevik*, Nos. 17–18, 1944), and others were on the indoctrination of students, and so on (e.g. Voznesensky in *Bolshevik*, No. 22, 1944).

In August 1946 Zhdanov launched a series of attacks in the cultural field. He started with a blast at literary failings in Leningrad, where he had served until 1944 at First Secretary, and where his *locus standi* was indisputable. But in fact the decree he put through, with Stalin's support, was a strong *general* call for ideological strictness in literature, and for no concession to any of the 'rotten' moods of the bourgeois enemy. By implication, it was violent criticism of those previously in control who had allowed this state of affairs to come to pass.

Literature is a peculiar field in the Soviet world. For it is virtually the only area in which Party members employed in it have been, up to a point, allowed to dispute Party rulings more or less publicly and even to disobey them. Yet the principles of 'Democratic Centralism' state that Party members must in all circumstances obey the rulings of the Party — that is, between Congresses, of the Central Committee. (It will at once be seen how extraordinary and exceptional it is that, for example, the poet, Evtushenko, should have been expelled from the Young Communist League following the appearance of a poem of his in the first number of *Literaturnaya Moskva*, in the autumn of 1956, and *then* to have a poem justifying his position published in the second number of that anthology, edited by Party members.)

To some extent the reasons for this anomaly are understandable. Literature is a border-line area in which the Party has never defined to its own satisfaction the extent of its powers to control. It was recognised as early as the Rapp deviation in the early 'thirties that simple Party fiat cannot produce literature. And this naturally gave a foothold to writers interested in as much freedom from control as possible. It was in their interests to define their area of liberty as widely as possible, and they have consistently done so or tried to do so whenever the opportunity arose. On the other hand, the laws of literature were laid down before the war by Zhdanov, basing himself on some general ideas of Gorki, in the principles of 'Socialist Realism'. The Party was thus early committed to enough control at least to be able to arrange that certain types of literary production (those outside the Zhdanov definition) should be excluded and suppressed. But in the long run this only meant that the struggle for greater freedom had to be conducted within the Zhdanov terminology. The authors simply went as far as possible in defining socialist realism to include anything they wanted to write.

This pressure from the creative writers may be regarded as a constant. The variable has been the attitude of the Party. At times under Stalin the pressure was resisted by all methods up to and including full-blown terrorism. But more usually the Party has oscillated between two positions, neither of which has proved satisfactory to it in practice. The first approaches the Rapp deviation, that great Soviet literature can simply be ordered from above. This has invariably resulted in literature of high orthodoxy and low quality. After a few years of this the Party decides that some attempt must be made to produce better standards, and that these can be obtained by a relaxation. The result has invariably been a raising of the quality and a proportional lowering of the orthodoxy.

The large volume *The C.P.S.U. in Resolutions and Decisions of Congresses, etc.* (Moscow, 1954) contains only five documents between the end of the war and the summoning of the XIXth Congress in the summer of 1952. These are:

(a) A decision of the Central Committee of August 2, 1946 (concerned with the education of leading Party workers and with tightening up ideological discipline).

(b) *On the magazines Zvezda and Leningrad*, August 14, 1946 (the Zhdanov cultural assault).

(c) A similar decision of August 26, 1946, *On the Repertoire of the Dramatic Theatre*.

(d) A decision of the Council of Ministers and of the Central Committee of September 19, 1946, 'on measures for the liquidation of breaches in the constitutions of rural-economic artels in kolkhozes' signed by Stalin as President of the Council of Ministers and Zhdanov as Secretary of the Central Committee.

(e) Decisions of a plenum of the Central Committee of February 1947, taken on a report by Andreyev on measures for improving the rural economy in the post-war period.

This selection shows the importance attached to cultural questions (and to agricultural issues with which we shall deal later).

Andrianov, in his speech at the XIXth Party Congress, mentioned the resolution of the Central Committee on the Leningrad magazines as having been 'adopted on the initiative of Comrade Stalin' (*Pravda*, October 8, 1952). But in any case by the middle of 1946 Zhdanov was firmly in the saddle with a campaign implying fault in those previously responsible. The Leningrad resolution directly criticises 'the directorate of propaganda of the Central Committee', which is to say G. F. Aleksandrov, a past and future associate of Malenkov's. Malenkov himself seems to have been removed from the secretariat at this time.

Zhdanov later also personally attacked G. F. Aleksandrov's *History of Western European Philosophy* (in *Party Life*, No. 16, August 1947) because of its failure to show 'passion and lack of compromise' in its description of bourgeois philosophies. Aleksandrov, 'perhaps without suspecting it himself', had fallen into 'servility' towards his opponents, whereas 'Marxist–Leninists assail their enemies in this struggle with crushing criticism'. Zhdanov took it as a bad sign that this book had been 'praised by the majority of our leading philosophers, presented with the Stalin Prize, recommended as a text-book'. For this reason 'it was necessary for the Central Committee and for Comrade Stalin personally to intervene'. This article of Zhdanov's was regarded as of such importance that it also appeared in both *Voprosy Filosofii* (No. 1 of 1947) and in *Bolshevik* (No. 16, August 1947).

The Party line in music is expressed in a resolution of the Central Committee denouncing Muradeli and others (*Bolshevik*, No. 3, February 1948). Muradeli's opera 'The Great Friendship' failed to provide the listener with one melody or aria to be remembered. 'The composer simply forgot the past traditions and experience of classical opera in particular . . . the genre of music beloved by and accessible to the large popular masses.' The resolution attacked the theory that 'the people' were simply not sufficiently educated in music to appreciate complicated new forms and 'the Central Committee resolves to declare the formalistic trend in Soviet music to be anti-popular'.

The adoption of the resolution had been preceded by a meeting in January 1948 between Soviet composers and representatives of the Central Committee — Zhdanov, V. V. Kuznetsov and Suslov (*Bolshevik*, No. 6, March 1948).

As this campaign proceeded, Zhdanov's position in the Party apparatus became very strong (see page 395), though Stalin does not seem to have let him gain direct control of the critical Cadres Administration. Malenkov was soon reinstated in the Secretariat, though he seems to have had little influence in the ensuing year.

Stalin now also contrived a more tortuous method of easing those not in favour from active power. Khrushchev in his Secret Speech complains that Stalin disorganised the Political Bureau by creating committees of it to deal with particular subjects. He then quotes a resolution of the Politburo of October 3, 1946:

Stalin's Proposal:

1. The Political Bureau Commission for Foreign Affairs ('Sextet') is to concern itself in the future, in addition to foreign affairs, also with matters of internal construction and domestic policy.

2. The Sextet is to add to its roster the Chairman of the State Commission for Economic Planning of the U.S.S.R., Comrade Voznesensky, and is to be known as the Septet.

Signed: Secretary of the Central Committee, J. Stalin.

Khrushchev had already referred to several other committees with unspecified duties — from 'quintets' to 'novenaries'. The new 'septet', however, seems to have had power in every sphere, thus in effect replacing the Politburo as a whole. The implication is that Stalin could have selected any of the irregular committees for this purpose and chose the foreign affairs commission because (with the addition of one name only) it already happened to contain those men he wanted to use, and to exclude those who were not then in favour. As Khrushchev says, 'The result of this was that some members of the Political Bureau were in this way kept away from participation in reaching decisions on the most important State matters'. The Foreign Affairs commission must almost certainly have included Molotov, Zhdanov, Beria, Bulganin and Mikoyan, all of whom had duties in that field, besides Stalin himself.

This certainly gives the impression that Malenkov in particular was, in the second half of 1946, on his way out, but that Stalin changed his mind, as he did also in the following case.

One of the most curious episodes of the immediate post-war period was Kaganovich's brief tenure of office as First Secretary of the Ukrainian Communist Party. He was sent there on March 3, 1947, and Khrushchev, who had hitherto combined the offices of First Secretary and Prime Minister, retained the latter and lower post only. Kaganovich returned to Moscow on December 28, 1947, and Khrushchev resumed the First Secretaryship, while handing over the Premiership to Korotchenko. This incident has never been fully explained. Kaganovich was accompanied by other officials from Moscow and in particular Patolichev, who was made member of the Ukrainian Politburo, and Ukrainian Secretary in charge of agriculture. In August 1947, however, Patolichev was degraded to be Party secretary at Rostov.

A natural assumption would be that Khrushchev's regime in Kiev had not been found satisfactory by Stalin. Soviet rule in the Ukraine certainly faced considerable difficulties at this time, including agricultural troubles, the persistence of nationalist partisans and general resistance to Soviet authority in the western regions annexed from Poland in 1939. It had always appeared previously that Khrushchev had been a protégé of Kaganovich's, and the arrangement might conceivably have been a fairly amicable one. For instance, it might have been held that the presence of two of the central leadership was necessary in the area. The removal of Patolichev was a sign of some sort of dispute, no doubt. But in any case we were here in the presence of an affair involving Politburo members which did not lead to any purge or other public culmination, so we could not tell whether Stalin changed his mind or whether a solution was worked out.

In 1957, however, Khrushchev finally made a definite statement casting considerable light on the matter. In *Kommunist* of August 1957, in a speech printed as 'Towards close contact between literature and art and the life of the people', he took the opportunity to attack the fallen Kaganovich. He described how he himself 'was able with great difficulty to protect from devastating criticism such a worthy writer as Maxim Rylsky'.

'Unfounded accusations against Rylsky' had been based on his omitting to mention Stalin in a patriotic poem about the Ukraine. Khrushchev went on to say that 'Comrade Kaganovich, who toadied and did everything to encourage the Stalin personality cult', described Maxim Rylsky as a 'Ukrainian bourgeois nationalist'. Khrushchev goes out of his way to add, 'This could have led to drastic consequences not for literature alone'. In a speech in Kiev (reported in *Pravda* of July 3, 1957), Kalchenko was to say that in the Ukraine at this time Kaganovich had 'discredited many honest people devoted to the Party, degraded them. Without proof he made grave accusations against many leading workers . . . if he had not been recalled from the Ukraine in time, he would have done immense harm to the Ukrainian Party and people'.

What these passages appear to indicate is that Kaganovich's mission involved a vigilance campaign and rigid purge against Ukrainian 'nationalism'. We know from Khrushchev's Secret Speech that Stalin had become extremely hostile to the Ukrainians at the end of the war. There is no doubt that Khrushchev had been putting into effect a policy of repressing any tendencies which looked in the least nationalist. This passage seems to indicate that his efforts had not been regarded as sufficiently thorough; that Kaganovich had urged and presumably to some extent practised a considerably tougher policy; but that Khrushchev had attempted to save at least his own protégés and was finally successful in doing so. It also makes it at least highly probable that he and Kaganovich were thenceforward, or at least for some time, on terms of rivalry.

There is a parallel with contemporary events in Moscow. The attack on Ukrainian nationalism was carried out very largely in cultural terms. *Literaturnaya Gazeta* of September 3, 1946, attacked the Institute for Language and Literature in the Ukrainian Academy of Sciences on the grounds that it had produced material on Ukrainian literature praising Western and concealing Russian influence. *Bolshevik* (1947, No. 7) strongly attacked the main historical writings lately printed in the Ukraine, on the grounds that they had not overcome the influence of the 'bourgeois nationalists'. The editorial boards of the major Ukrainian literary journals were replaced and the Ukrainian Union of Soviet Writers had its leading officers (including Maxim Rylsky, who was then its president) dismissed in November 1946. Rylsky was described as being a 'prisoner of bourgeois nationalism' together with a number of other Ukrainian writers (*Literaturnaya Gazeta*, November 24, 1947).

These are now clearly seen to be attacks on the policy of the First Secretary of the Ukrainian Party over the period in question, Khrushchev, who was thus replaced shortly after the campaign really got going. It was in 1947 that Zhdanov was at the height of his power, and one might very tentatively suggest that Kaganovich and Zhdanov, using similar methods and asserting similar cultural disciplines, were working in accord. In that case the recall of Kaganovich in December 1947 and Khrushchev's reassumption of the Ukrainian First Secretary-ship might perhaps represent the beginning of the success of those opposed to Zhdanov and Zhdanovism.*

This matter, a highly important one, was not understood in the West, even as to its major point, until the turns of politics happened, ten years later, to lead to a brief official reference to it. This is instructive.

We may also perhaps read a weakening of Beria's position in 1946, in some of the moves of the period. The replacement of Merkulov by Abakumov in the M.G.B. was at best the removal of one of Beria's oldest and closest associates in favour of one whose connection with him was at any rate rather slighter. In Georgia, too, several of Beria's firmest supporters were de-moted. Bakradze slipped from Premier to Deputy Premier, to be restored to the senior post only in Beria's moment of com-plete power in Georgia in April 1953 — though admittedly the reason given at the time for his down-grading was illness; Sturua was dropped from Presidency of the Georgian Supreme Soviet and later from the Party Bureau — to which he was only restored in April 1953; Shariya was removed (and was de-nounced in July 1953, after Beria's fall, as 'devoted' to him). And Rapava was moved from the local M.G.B. to the Ministry of Justice (see Chapter Seven). These are not decisive indica-tions, but it may still be true that, as Khrushchev says in his

* The Ukrainian cultural purge was linked with the Zhdanov decrees, as in the *Large Soviet Encyclopaedia* (first edition Vol. 55; April 25, 1947), which says, 'Basing itself on the decisions of the Central Committee, and the Ukrainian Central Com-mittee, of 1946 on literature and art, criticism revealed in Soviet Ukrainian litera-ture a series of serious distortions and inadequacies.'

G

Secret Speech, Beria had reason to fear a threat to his position in the police ministries, through A. A. Kuznetsov (see Appendix IV).

A further sign of the tensions of this period, in which Zhdanov, Voznesensky, Andreyev and Kaganovich were evidently aligned against Malenkov, Khrushchev and Beria, was the demotion, precisely parallel to Khrushchev's in the Ukraine, of Ponomarenko in Byelorussia — to be Prime Minister from being First Secretary. The intruder was N. L. Gusarev, from the C.C. apparat; he was accompanied, as Secretary in charge of agriculture, by S. D. Ignatiev. But in 1948, on Zhdanov's defeat, Ponomarenko was doubly promoted — to be Secretary of the Central Committee.

Meanwhile a campaign parallel to those conducted by Zhdanov himself, and one forming an essential part of the congeries of uncompromising policies we know as Zhdanovism, was being waged by Voznesensky against the views that capitalism had a chance of avoiding crisis and that it had made concessions to the working class. To admit these theses would have been to abandon or modify both the appreciation that a revolutionary forward foreign policy was viable and the most rigorous notion of the irreconcilable hostility of the two systems.

Voznesensky, who had been Chairman of the City Planning Commission in Leningrad during Zhdanov's first years as Party Secretary there (1935–37), and from 1938 to 1941 Chairman of the U.S.S.R. State Planning Commission (Gosplan), rose with Zhdanov's return to power. In 1946 he was reappointed Chairman of Gosplan in place of Malenkov's associate Saburov, and in 1947 was promoted to full member of the Politburo.

Academician E. S. Varga had long been closely connected with Stalin. His book *Changes in the Economy of Capitalism as a Result of the Second World War*, a series of lectures delivered in 1946, now came under fire from Voznesensky. Its fault was that it was inclined to admit the possibility of a softening of the harsher features of capitalist economy. On May 7, 14 and 21, 1947, a meeting of economists and political experts was organised under the presidency of Ostrovityanov (who was to be the economic spokesman of the 'left' throughout this dispute and has lately figured as a supporter of Khrushchev). The discussion was referred to and Varga was criticised in *Bolshevik* of

September 1947. And in the following months *Pravda* and other papers made a full-scale attack on the moderates. But the stenographic report of the discussion itself only became available at the beginning of 1948 in the form of a supplement to *World Economy and World Politics* (No. 12 of 1947). In January 1948 this periodical, which had hitherto been Varga's organ, was suppressed and the institute he had headed was merged into a single Institute of Economics coming under the control of the State Planning Commission headed by Voznesensky. Ostrovityanov was appointed its director, and editor-in-chief of the new organ, *Voprosy Ekonomiki*.

In the first issue Ostrovityanov summarised Varga's views in terms reminiscent of the Zhdanov cultural decrees:

This tendency is characterised by the following features: The questions of the Leninist–Stalinist theories of imperialism, of the general crisis of capitalism and of the conflict of the two systems are ignored; a concrete description predominates over Marxist theoretical analysis; there is a narrowly technical approach to the clarification of the economies of foreign countries; neutrality in the conflict against 'bourgeois' theory; an underestimation of the importance and role of the countries of the new democracy; the presence of a non-political and objectivist approach to the problems under study; an uncritical attitude towards bourgeois statistics; and deference to the achievements of bourgeois science and technology (*Questions of Economics*, No. 1, March 1948).

Ostrovityanov continued:

In his introductory and concluding remarks at the discussion, Comrade Varga not only failed to admit his mistakes, but in large measure made them even worse. . . . He reaffirmed his thesis (as stated in his book) that 'the question of greater or less participation in the management of the State will constitute the main conflict between the two main classes of capitalist society — the bourgeoisie and the proletariat.' But from this there emerges the conclusion that the bourgeois State is above classes . . . that the functions and prospects of the revolutionary struggle of the working class are a struggle for the influence of the working class in the apparatus of the 'bourgeois' State — a reformist conclusion (ibid).

Varga and his associates were also accused of scholasticism, lack of self-criticism, mutual flattery, isolation from Soviet reality, nepotism and a lack of understanding of Marxist–Leninist theory.

The most important refutation of the Varga school, however, was made in Voznesensky's own book, *The War Economy of the U.S.S.R. during the Patriotic War*. This was printed in 1947 and became available to the public at the beginning of 1948. He writes that 'the opinions of certain theoreticians, who consider themselves Marxists', about the 'decisive role of the State in the war economy of capitalist countries' are 'empty opinions which deserve no consideration' (pp. 30–31).

The next published attack on the Varga school was in Ostrovityanov's further report to the Learned Council of the Institute of Economics in October 1948. Ostrovityanov repeated the charges of 'bourgeois objectivism', 'uncritical approach to bourgeois statistics' and 'subservience to bourgeois science'. He again complained that Varga and his followers had not admitted their errors. 'Nor had they shown by means of positive work any effort to take the path of correcting these errors. Such a non-Party approach to criticism led to fresh theoretical and political errors.' However, in the debate which followed, the criticism was very lukewarm, and again Varga stubbornly defended his opinions.

For his behaviour at this debate Varga was attacked in the November–December 1948 number of *Planned Economy*, the organ of Voznesensky's Gosplan. This was the most violent denunciation which had yet appeared, and seemed to put Varga right outside the Party pale.

Yet, meanwhile, Varga continued to defend himself. He had lost his most important post — that of Director of the Institute of World Economics — but he held all his other appointments and was even elected to new ones. For example, he became a member of the Praesidium of the Society for the Dissemination of Political and Scientific Knowledge. On the board of *Voprosy Ekonomiki* he was made assistant editor — a colleague, therefore, of his critic, Ostrovityanov.

In Soviet circumstances Varga's continued self-defence, and the fact that even so he was not finally denounced and removed from all posts, indicate that he had protectors. Moreover, it was clearly a question of protectors who, though perhaps in disagreement with Varga on certain points, were prepared to fight — while in the cultural decrees proper no defence had been made. One reason is almost certainly that Varga's analysis had a *direct* bearing on urgent matters of policy. The other is that the forces opposed to Zhdanovism were strong at the crisis of the dispute and gradually grew stronger.

It is of interest that *Pravda* of March 15, 1949, just two days after Voznesensky's fall, published a letter from Varga, making some concessions, but on the whole defending himself strongly from the more extreme and indirect charges which had been made.

Voznesensky's attack on Varga is the best confirmation that Zhdanov and Voznesensky were closely associated. For he is attacking him, in effect, for an inadequately doctrinaire view of foreign policy — for failing to insist that American imperialism was conducting a dangerous offensive against Communism, and for stating that the social orders of Western Europe could not be seen as black and white and that their colonial policies were not entirely imperialist.

That the Cominform was intended as an instrument of the Zhdanov conception of foreign policy is generally admitted. Here we may deviate momentarily from strict adherence to Soviet evidence, to mention that according to Dedijer (*Tito Speaks*, p. 202) it was first discussed by Stalin with foreign Communists in June 1946, and may of course have been considered in Soviet ruling circles rather earlier. The first meeting of the Cominform in September 1947 was very much under Zhdanov's control. Malenkov was present as the other Soviet delegate, but spoke only on internal affairs and preparations for the next Soviet Party Congress. (Incidentally, if such a congress was in contemplation as early as 1947 the fact that it did not take place until 1952 needs some explanation. A possibility is that Stalin, having managed since 1939 without a congress, was caught up in the political crises and purges of 1948–50 before a congress could be properly arranged, and then called the XIXth Congress in 1952, after a period of comparative calm, as a set-piece with which to inaugurate his own controlled crisis and purge.)

The resolution of the first Cominform conference, published on September 30, 1947, had two main points. The first was that the world was now divided into 'two camps'. That is, it was a formal declaration of political war. The second was that 'the greatest danger of the working classes to-day lies in under-rating their own powers and in over-rating the powers of the imperialist camp': that is, a call for aggressive forward tactics in that war. This tallied with such things as the Civil War in Greece and the attempts at revolutionary strikes in Western Europe. The policy was not a success as far as the efforts of these foreign Communist Parties were concerned. When Zhdanov lost influence a forward policy was continued — in Berlin and Korea, for example — but the reliance was no longer on foreign Communists but on established State power and armies. The Cominform went into disuse as a major strategic weapon.

On the question of when the Zhdanov international policies were abandoned there is some relevant factual material in the semi-official Yugoslav book, *Tito Speaks*, by Vladimir Dedijer, mentioned above. This book gives some fascinating insights into the methods of control used by Stalin and his associates in more or less confidential circumstances, but here I only want to note the names of those present on the Soviet side in the various negotiations with the Yugoslavs, which may be regarded as fact pure and simple. On May 27, 1946, Tito had an official meeting with Stalin, Molotov and the Soviet Ambassador in Belgrade, Lavrentiyev. At the supper following this, those present were Stalin, Molotov, Zhdanov, Beria and Bulganin. At a later supper Beria is again mentioned. In March 1947 a delegation headed by Kardelj met Stalin and Molotov.

In January 1948 a delegation headed by Djilas had its official meeting with Stalin and Molotov and supper with Stalin, Molotov, Zhdanov, Voznesensky and Beria.

On January 22, 1948, *Pravda* printed a statement by Dimitrov enthusiastically advocating an East European Federation. On January 28 it strongly denounced Dimitrov's statement. On February 10, 1948, a meeting of the Bulgarian leaders headed by Dimitrov and the Yugoslavs headed by Kardelj had as the Russians present Stalin, Molotov, Malenkov, Zhdanov, Suslov and — presumably as a technical foreign affairs adviser — Zorin. The names are given in that order in Dedijer with some implication that they were seated that way. If the composition of this meeting is compared with that of previous suppers and meetings there seems in any case to be a presumption that it was at this moment that Malenkov and Suslov were being brought into the international field to counter Zhdanov. Attacks on Tito began immediately after this meeting, in Bucharest, and on February 21 the Soviet Ambassador in Tirana was giving toasts openly insulting to the Yugoslavs.

At the second meeting of the Cominform held in Bucharest in June 1948 Zhdanov was still the official spokesman of the Soviet Union, but with him were Malenkov and Suslov, who had been brought into foreign Communist matters at precisely the time when Stalin turned against the Yugoslavs. It seems certain that Zhdanov was required to put through the demolition of his own policy, as sometimes happens in the U.S.S.R.

Zhdanov died on August 31. A month previously Malenkov was signing messages in the name of the Central Committee.

Zhdanov's death took place at a time when Stalin evidently had no more use for him. It was later to be alleged, in the Doctors' Plot, that he was actually murdered by those supposed to be treating him. It is certainly true that Stalin rid himself of opponents not only by 'official' methods, as we have seen in the Ordzhonikidze case, for example. So the possibility that Zhdanov was liquidated cannot be dismissed entirely even now.

There seems no doubt that the main issue on which Zhdanovism failed in Stalin's eyes was that of foreign policy. The ideological pronouncements proper were not abandoned: in fact, it was in this very month that the most extraordinary of all such decrees — that condemning orthodox genetics in favour of Lysenko's pseudo-biology — was put through. During Malenkov's period of greatest influence in 1950–52 the totems erected in Zhdanov's time continued to stand. The impression given is not that Malenkov was opposed in principle to any of these things, but that he did not care enough about them to bother much with them. Except in economics, the only theoretical event of the period was Stalin's denunciation of Marr's linguistic theories in 1950. This may possibly be read, at least in part, as an argument against the Voznesensky–Zhdanov attitude that revolutionary enthusiasm and big changes were inevitable in the U.S.S.R. *Pravda* of October 5, 1949, commenting on Stalin's criticism of Marr, says:

Comrade Stalin's formulation . . . of the law of transition from an old qualitative state to a new qualitative state without a 'break' has tremendous importance for the concept of the special features in the development of a socialist base and its superstructure. Comrade Stalin showed for the first time in Marxist literature that in socialist society, where there are no hostile classes, one of the basic laws of the dialectic comes into operation, the law of transition from the old quality to the new. Comrade Stalin annihilated the vulgar proposition that qualitative changes can be effected always and in all cases only by means of a 'break'. Comrade Stalin showed that the law of transition from the old qualitative situation to the new by means of a 'break' is obligatory in a society which is divided into hostile classes. But it is not at all necessary for a society which does not have hostile classes.*

Zhdanov continued to be praised and the anniversary of his death was celebrated in the ensuing years. It may be noteworthy that *Literaturnaya Gazeta* was attacked by *Pravda* of August 16, 1950, for failing to celebrate the anniversary of the Zhdanov literary decrees and on August 21, 1950, started an apologetic article on them: 'Four years ago on the initiative of Comrade J. V. Stalin the Party Central Committee adopted the decree. . . .' This episode gives the impression that literature was under the control of people who disliked the decrees, and possibly imagined that the purge of Zhdanov's followers meant that they could be forgotten.

Meanwhile we have given, briefly enough, an account (which should be supplemented by a look at Appendix I) of how things stood by the end of 1948, when we enter on the period substantively covered in this book. Even what has been mentioned shows already a number of the points which it was desired to demonstrate.

* And see pp. 105–111.

CHAPTER FIVE

THE LENINGRAD CASE, 1949–50

THE Tito issue had ruined the Zhdanovists. And as Stalin turned from denouncing the Yugoslavs for heresy to the old technique of calling them spies and criminals too, the controversy in the U.S.S.R. itself took a darker turn. At the same time, basic disputes about internal economic policy took place.

Zhdanov had been succeeded as First Secretary in Leningrad in 1944 by A. A. Kuznetsov, and he in turn in 1946 by Popkov. V. M. Andrianov was sent to Leningrad on February 24, 1949, to take Popkov's place as First Secretary. He had been in the Orgburo as a member of the central apparatus and had lately served as First Secretary of the Sverdlovsk Provisional Committee. That Sverdlovsk was a Malenkov stronghold may be shown by the fact that, as we have seen, the Leningrader, I. N. Turko, First Secretary in Yaroslavl from 1946 to February 1949, was replaced there by Sitnikov, who had served under Andrianov at Sverdlovsk. This is an example of the sort of evidence that must be sorted out and interpreted at a provincial level. If it is seldom entirely satisfactory, it yet gives plausible leads. That Andrianov was a Malenkov associate seems very highly probable for other reasons — as will be seen when we reach his dismissal in 1953.

Pravda of March 13, 1949, printed a Supreme Soviet decision on the 'release of Comrade N. A. Voznesensky' from his ministerial and State planning posts, and his replacement in the latter by Malenkov's associate Saburov. On the same date *Pravda* printed a decree on the release of 'Comrade P. S. Popkov' from the Praesidium of the U.S.S.R. Supreme Soviet and the election of V. M. Andrianov to that body, and *Izvestia* published a decision by the Praesidium of the Supreme Soviet of the R.S.F.S.R. to release 'Comrade M. I. Rodionov' from his post as Chairman of the Committee of Ministers of the R.S.F.S.R. and his replacement by B. N. Chernousov. (*Pravda and Izvestia* of May 29, 1949, published a decree of the Supreme

Soviet of the R.S.F.S.R. confirming the removal of Rodionov, and two of his subordinates.

These formal State decisions can be taken as having come later than the decisions about Party posts. Most of these last were not published at all, but just left to be noticed. Thus the names of Voznesensky and of A. A. Kuznetsov (last mentioned as Secretary of the Central Committee in *Pravda* of December 16, 1948) simply no longer appear in the list of leaders from the Politburo and Secretariat mentioned at the Komsomol Congress on March 24, 1949, or on subsequent occasions.

It was much later stated (*Leningradskaya Pravda*, July 5, 1957) that Malenkov was bullying Party officials to produce 'palpable forgeries' in connection with Party cadres in February 1949. There is no indication of how long before this the purge had been planned. In his Secret Speech Khrushchev says: 'It is a characteristic thing that the decision to remove [Voznesensky] from the Political Bureau was never discussed, but was reached in a devious fashion. In the same way the decision concerning the removal of Kuznetsov and Rodionov from their posts. . . .'

Meanwhile, as a sign that Voznesensky had not yet become an unperson, *Pravda* and *Izvestia* of April 15, 1949, reporting various medals given to workers in institutions, included the Voznesensky Seed Culture Station. And that, although the major figures had already fallen, the purge had not yet reached all who were to perish in it is shown by the report of a speech by A. A. Voznesensky at the Supreme Soviet, in *Izvestia* of May 31, 1949. We are also told by the *Leningrad Encyclopaedia* (1958) that Kuznetsov was sent in 1949, on losing his post as Secretary of the Central Committee, to be 'Secretary of the Far Eastern Bureau of the C.C., C.P.S.U.'.

By July 1949 dismissals in Leningrad and district included all five Secretaries of the Leningrad City Committee (Popkov, Kapustin, Nikolayev, Sintsov and Levin), all five Secretaries of Leningrad Provincial Committee, the top four officials of the Executive Committee of the Town Soviet (including the Chairman, Lazutin), leading officials of the Executive Committee of the Provincial Soviet (including the Chairman, Kharitonov), leading officials of the Leningrad Provincial Trade Union Council, including its Chairman, and its Deputy Chairman. All disappeared without trace.

The disappearances at the centre included, in addition to Voznesensky, M. I. Rodionov, Chairman of the R.S.F.S.R. Council of Ministers; Colonel-General I. V. Shikin, Head of the Chief Political Directorate of the Red Army; Voznesensky's brother, A. A. Voznesensky, Rector of Leningrad University 1944–48, and later Minister of Education of the R.S.F.S.R. Only Shikin remained alive to be rehabilitated at a later date (being awarded a medal 'for length of service in the Soviet Army' in December 1954 — a week after the execution of Abakumov). By this time (July 1949) Voznesensky had lost his title of 'Comrade' in confidential Party documents later made public (see page 104), and had therefore been expelled from the Party, which almost certainly, in Stalin's era, meant that he was under arrest.

Most of the victims in the Leningrad Case can be pretty certainly regarded as Zhdanov's men, who were or had been officials of the Leningrad Party organisation under him. And it is interesting incidentally to note a parallel: Zhdanov himself died full of honours, if not years, though it is true that the subsequent allegation, still more subsequently withdrawn, that he had been murdered by his doctors (presumably on the orders of someone in authority), must cast a certain doubt over the affair. Like Zhdanov, his predecessor as Party Secretary in Leningrad, Kirov, died while apparently in highest favour with Stalin and continued after death to receive all honour. Yet within three years all *his* main appointments in Leningrad (Ugarov, Chudov and Pozern, all secretaries of the Leningrad Provincial Committee, and others) were shot in connection with an earlier Leningrad Affair — the case of the 'Leningrad Centre', referred to by Khrushchev in his Secret Speech. Khrushchev implies very strongly indeed that Stalin was in fact responsible for Kirov's assassination. (He asserts definitely, as in the case of Ordzhonikidze, that Stalin did procure the death of his colleagues who were afterwards held in public honour, so that his long-suspected responsibility for Kirov's death is at least perfectly possible.) One cannot press the parallel between the fates of Kirov and the Kirovites and Zhdanov and the Zhdanovites too far, striking though it certainly is. Yet the precedent is revealing.

Voznesensky, the leading victim in the Leningrad Affair,

cannot so certainly be regarded as falling solely because of his connection with Zhdanov. To try even disparate elements together is an old Soviet method employed even in the open trials of the 'thirties — where the appearance of right and left wingers together in the dock was made a further point against them on the grounds that this represented an 'unprincipled bloc'. But the whole basis of the later political attack on Voznesensky was on matters of economic theory, not linked directly, at least, as we shall see, with the Zhdanov issue. The fall of Zhdanov and his friends was certainly, as is alleged now, mainly to the political benefit of Malenkov. Stalin himself seems to have been particularly concerned with Voznesensky and his economics. And the major policy document of Stalin's last years is in effect devoted to repudiating them.

Whether Vosnesensky was actually in a different category from the others or not, he was certainly disgraced with them. Not only does Khrushchev list him as one of the victims of the Leningrad Case, but he was dismissed from his offices at precisely the same moment as the other major accused.

Pravda and *Izvestia*, of January 13, 1950, published on page 1 a decree dated January 12 of the Praesidium of the Supreme Soviet 'on the application of capital punishment to traitors to the motherland, spies and subversive diversionists':

In view of petitions from National Republic, Trade Unions, peasant organisations and cultural representatives urging amendment of the decree on the abolition of capital punishment to make the decree inapplicable to traitors to the motherland, spies and subversive diversionists, the Praesidium of the U.S.S.R. Supreme Soviet decrees: (1) that the death penalty, as the highest form of punishment, may apply to traitors to the motherland, spies and subversive diversionists, as an exception to the May 26, 1947, decree of the Praesidium of the U.S.S.R. Supreme Soviet on the abolition of capital punishment; (2) that the present decree becomes effective from the date of its publication.

I used to regard this as possibly indicating the time of the execution of the Leningraders — for no official date of their deaths was given for eight years, and indeed no official confirmation that they were dead, or even tried, appeared for five years.

Since then it has been officially stated that Voznesensky's

death did indeed take place in 1950. For instance, the index of names to Vol. 50 of the second edition of the *Large Soviet Encyclopaedia* follows almost all entries, including Voznesensky's, with the years of birth and death. (It also gives, for the first time, the dates of death of a number of other rehabilitated political figures; e.g. Kossior, 1939; Postyshev, 1940; Bubnov, 1939; Antonov-Ovseenko, 1938; Blyukher, 1938. And cultural figures: e.g. Meyerhold, 1940; Babel, 1941; Koltsov, 1942; N. I. Vavilov, 1943 — with a suggestion in the chronology section that his work ceased to be published in 1940; and Kvitko and other Jewish writers, 1952. A curious point is that dates are not given with the names of any people's enemies — e.g. Zinoviev, Bukharin, Yezhov, Beria: they also, unlike other entries, only rate initials and not Christian names.)

But later again the whole argument had to be adjusted to fit yet another published fact. In the *Leningrad Encyclopaedia* published in 1958, the dates of death are given of Kuznetsov (1949) and Popkov (1949) as well of Voznesensky (again 1950). Unless the two first died during the course of the investigation, as has happened to certain accused in trials from that of Zinoviev to that of Nagy (and the Leningrad Case is said to have been conducted with particular brutality), there are perhaps two separate trials involved. In any case, the date of the restoration of the death penalty would no longer be relevant — though its restoration may still have been motivated retrospectively by the case. If there were two trials, Kuznetsov and Popkov were presumably tried together, although Kuznetsov was no longer connected with Leningrad.

It seems to have been regular practice (as indeed it has been in the post-Stalin era too) for death sentences to be carried out almost immediately — in the case both of the 'public' trials and of those more comparable to the Leningrad Affair, like that of Eikhe, whose execution in 1940 followed two days after his trial, according to Khrushchev's Secret Speech. There is no doubt that Voznesensky and the other accused were linked. If they were tried separately it would tend to confirm the idea that Stalin's hostility to Voznesensky was, at least in part, differently motivated from his grudge against Zhdanov's old apparatus proper.

Vol. 51 — the supplementary volume — of the second edition

of the *Large Soviet Encyclopaedia*, appeared in 1958, with articles on Voznesensky and A. A. Kuznetsov. The date of death of the former is again given as 1950 and of the latter as 1949. Kuznetsov's tenure of a secretaryship of the Central Committee is stated to be 1945 to February 1949. Finally, later still, the *Small Soviet Encyclopaedia*, which began to come out in 1958, gives certain exact dates of death, some of them of great interest to the student. Vol. II (October 1958) states that Voznesensky died on September 30, 1950. This is such a long time later than those of Kuznetsov and Popkov in 1949 that it strongly suggests a second trial. (The extent of the Leningrad purge may be judged by a remark of F. Kozlov's in his speech to the XIXth Congress, that in that city, 'Recently more than 2,000 persons . . . have been promoted to executive positions' (*Pravda*, October 14, 1952).)

Some rather less close associates of Zhdanov's, through his ally Shcherbakov, remained in the Moscow Party machine. In December 1949 Khrushchev took over G. M. Popov's post as City and Provincial First Secretary of Moscow. Within a few months all the other four Moscow Provincial secretaries, who had served under Popov, had been removed and did not re-appear in other public posts. A number of other officials were also removed, but the changes were not on the same scale as the Leningrad purge, just as Popov fell no lower than a minor government post, while his Leningrad opposite number was being shot.

Whatever the real moves behind the milder treatment of Moscow, Khrushchev was in a good position to attack the organisers of the Leningrad Case later on. (Meanwhile it may be noted that his own replacement in the Ukraine, L. G. Melnikov, was not one of those who had served with him in Kiev, but a Russian intruded from outside in late 1947.)

Official information about the purge was slow in appearing. It was not until December 1952 that any reference whatever was again made to Voznesensky, in the attack on his economic theories quoted on page 103–105. In December 1954 the first reference to the Leningrad Case was made. Abakumov, Minister of State Security 1946–(?)51, was shot with several subordinates for fabricating the case with the result that State and party officials had perished: even now no names of victims appeared.

Beria was also named as responsible, though at his own trial in December 1953 nothing had been said of it (see Appendix VI). In February 1956 Khrushchev stated in his Secret Speech that Stalin personally ordered the affair, on the basis of slanderous material from Beria and Abakumov (see Appendix IV).

It was not until July 1957, after the showdown with the 'Anti-Party Group', that Khrushchev asserted flatly: 'Malenkov . . . was one of the chief organisers of the so-called Leningrad Case', Shvernik also said that 'the Leningrad Case, in the organisation of which Malenkov took part, was falsified' (*Pravda*, June 7, 1957).

It will be seen that information was totally lacking from 1949 to 1954, and apportioned the blame variously in 1954-56, 1956-57 and 1957 on. The story as it now stands is compatible with the evidence, and is roughly as students have always believed. (But there are still cases where political developments subsequent to obscure events have not ensured that all those responsible could be publicly named.)

One major piece of information about the Leningrad Affair has still not been provided. What was the charge? This is a point of some political significance. We can make certain tentative deductions.

There are two points which suggest a Titoist component in the accusations against the Leningrad purgees. When, in January 1948, the Yugoslav delegation in Moscow began to be cold-shouldered by the Soviet leaders in what was evidently the critical weeks in Stalin's decision to break Tito and Zhdanov, Djilas paid a visit to Leningrad, where he was warmly received. In Dedijer's *Tito Speaks* he is quoted as being delighted with his welcome and with the revolutionary atmosphere, superior to that of Moscow. He mentions the Party secretary 'Popov' (evidently Popkov) as most helpful, and adds that he expressed his pleasure to the escort provided by Moscow. This would seem to mean at least that the Yugoslavs were regarded with particular friendliness by the Zhdanov faction — which seems in any case to be established. That the visit itself cannot have pleased Stalin and that he inflated it to a charge of contact between Popkov and Djilas in his later role as imperialist spy would seem natural.

In his communications to the Yugoslavs at the time of the

break, Stalin refers to this sourly in his letter of May 4, 1949:

It must be emphasised that Yugoslav comrades visiting Moscow frequently visit other cities in the U.S.S.R., meet our people and freely talk with them. In no case did the Soviet Government place any restrictions upon them. During his last visit to Moscow, Djilas went to Leningrad for a few days to talk with Soviet comrades.

According to the Yugoslav scheme, information about Party and State work can only be obtained from leading organs of the C.C. of the C.P.Y. or from the Government. Comrade Djilas did not obtain information from these organs of the U.S.S.R. but from the local organs of the Leningrad organisations. We did not consider it necessary to enquire into what he did there, and what facts he picked up. We think he did not collect material for the Anglo-American or French intelligence service but for the leading organs of Yugoslavia. Since this was correct we did not see any harm in it because this information might have contained instructive material for the Yugoslav comrades. Comrade Djilas cannot say that he met with restrictions (*The Soviet–Yugoslav Dispute*, Royal Institute of International Affairs, November 1948).

Thus the Leningraders are said to have given Djilas material which would have been harmful to that State if handed over to imperialist secret services. But within a year it was said that the Yugoslavs *were* agents of these secret services. The way was at least open to accusing the Leningraders of harmful leakages and wrong contacts. And it might easily have taken on a more sinister significance. This is particularly likely in view of the Soviet practice of accusing those on trial of anything that could possibly be sustained by any fact at all.

Another hypothetical imputation, which seems particularly possible in view of the coincidence of dates, may link the accused with a statement in *Pravda* and *Izvestia* of February 15, 1949, announcing the arrest of the 'well-known secret agent, the American journalist, Anna Louise Strong', though it blamed her presence in the U.S.S.R. on 'the negligence of certain foreign relations officials'. The same papers on February 24, 1949, announced her expulsion from the country.

Miss Strong, who had always been an extremely pro-Soviet writer, had lately been to Yugoslavia, and seems to have nourished some idea of bringing about a Soviet–Yugoslav *rapprochement.* In any case her sympathies with Tito had not abated, as they should have. There is no particular reason to believe that she had any connection with the Leningraders. But, if Miss Strong was really trying to influence anyone, it seems very probable that she might have tried to get in contact with higher officials, and might possibly have tried to approach those known to her as previous sympathisers of Tito. If the accusation of espionage had any basis whatever it would scarcely have been anything other than that.*

After 1949 the first open reference to Voznesensky was made in a strong attack on his anti-Marxist views in an article by Suslov in *Pravda* of December 24, 1952.

Ostensibly Suslov is concerned with taking to task P. N. Fedoseyev for two articles he had contributed to *Izvestia* of December 12 and 21, 1952, dealing with subjects drawn from Stalin's recent *Economic Problems of Socialism in the U.S.S.R.* Suslov does not object to the content of these articles — he says that they are unexceptionable — but to the fact that Fedoseyev omits to mention that he once made the mistakes which, in line with Stalin, he now hastens to condemn.

Suslov goes on to say what these mistakes are. For years there has been in the Soviet Union a 'group of philosophers and economists' who do not believe in the objective nature of economic laws and who hold that the Party and the State can order the economy at will, can create or change economic laws to suit their taste. Stalin condemned these views in his *Economic Problems* as 'erroneous', 'dangerous', 'utterly anti-Marxist', 'subjective' and 'idealist'. Fedoseyev had been guilty of these views when he was chief editor of *Bolshevik*, the Party's top ideological journal, from 1947 to 1949. And then his chief sin was that:

'In this journal the anti-Marxist booklet by N. Voznesensky *The War Economy of the U.S.S.R. During the Great Patriotic War* was praised almost to the skies and presented as the last word

---

* Some rumours about the actual origins and accusations in the Leningrad Case are perhaps worth registering, if only with a view to their future confirmation or otherwise if the full story is ever officially told. These are that (originally in connection with an attempt by the Leningrad authorities to hold an international fair in that city) Stalin began to hear of alleged plans to make Leningrad the capital of the R.S.F.S.R. and to strengthen the R.S.F.S.R. Government (which latter has of course been done recently — in 1957 — under Khrushchev). These vague notions could not, indeed, have formed the substance of the alleged plot.

H

in science, as a "valuable contribution to Soviet economic science". . .'

This was in *Bolshevik* No. 1 of 1948. At once the whole un-fairness of the charge against Fedoseyev is apparent. For at this time Voznesensky was still Deputy Premier and Head of the Planning Commission. Moreover the book in question, pub-lished in 1947, had just received a Stalin prize.

Suslov continues:

In actual fact this booklet of Voznesensky's confused the solution of problems of the political economy of Socialism, represented a hotch-potch of voluntarist views on the part to be played by plans and the state in Soviet society and fetishism of the law of value, which was allegedly the governor of the distribution of labour between the sections of national economy of the U.S.S.R.

This is plainly to pin down Voznesensky as the main target of Stalin's *Economic Problems of Socialism*, and *still* the major theor-etical enemy more than two years after his execution. (The fact that the first public attack took place at this stage is another matter, and certainly indicates that the Doctors' Plot purge was going to be linked to economic deviationism, and presumably linked up with the Leningrad Case 'plotters' on a criminal level too.)

On the pretence of reminding Fedoseyev of his former errors, Suslov finds it 'appropriate to recall' the whole of a decree passed by the Central Committee of the Communist Party as long ago as July 13, 1949, 'On the Journal *Bolshevik*'. This decree had never been published before. It runs in part:

In their activities the editorial collegium of the journal *Bolshevik* are not linked with party organisations, and rely on a narrow group of authors who have occupied a monopolistic position in the journal. The editors employ inadmissible methods of work. In articles received by the journal there are interpolated new texts which radically alter the contents of the article. Such actions are a gross distortion of the traditions of the Bolshevik press.

The editors of the journal *Bolshevik* permitted a serious mistake when it opened its columns to sycophantic praise of the booklet by N. Voznesensky *The War Economy of the U.S.S.R. During the Great Patriotic War*, advertising it without any grounds as a text-book and as a 'profound scientific investigation'. In their sycophancy the workers in the editorial department of the journal *Bolshevik* have

gone so far that, against the wishes of the authors, they have interpolated in their articles quotations from the booklet by N.
Voznesensky.

By July 1949, then, Voznesensky had already lost his 'Comrade', and he had already been obliquely denounced to the
Party aktiv. The Central Committee goes on to hand out reprimands to a mixed collection of theorists, including Fedoseyev,
G. F. Aleksandrov and M. T. Yovchuk, and also Shepilov, then
head of Agitprop, who committed 'the grave mistake' of recom-
mending Voznesensky's work as a text-book. And it decrees a
new editorial board. (The Central Committee was simply being
used as a rubber stamp on this occasion. For the new editorial
board was already listed on the back page of *Bolshevik*, No. 11,
June 15, 1949, as being in office, i.e. at least one month before
it was supposedly appointed by the Committee.)

The one definite economic policy with which Voznesensky
was associated, and which was dropped after his death, was an
attempt to see that producer goods were sold at a price based
on the cost of manufacture. In January 1949 an overhaul of the
price system went into effect, to establish a factory price reflecting the cost of production plus a small profit. As a result
the prices of many basic materials and freight charges increased
to double or more. In 1950, after Voznesensky's fall, this policy
was reversed and the prices of producer goods were again
reduced — to be cut yet again in 1952.

Stalin's *Economic Problems of Socialism*, a work to which he
attached great importance, consists of a series of 'remarks' and
comments dated from February 1952 to September 1952, and
basing themselves on an economic discussion held in November
1951. But he is evidently attacking the Voznesensky price policy
when he writes:

Can means of production be regarded as commodities in our
socialist system? In my opinion they certainly cannot.

A commodity is a product which may be sold to any purchaser,
and when its owner sells it, he loses ownership of it and the purchaser
becomes the owner of the commodity, which he may resell, pledge or
allow to rot. Do means of production come within this category?
They obviously do not. In the first place, means of production are
not 'sold' to any purchaser, they are not 'sold' even to collective
farms; they are only allocated by the state to its enterprises. In the

second place, when transferring means of production to any enterprise, their owner — the state — does not at all lose the ownership of them; on the contrary, it retains it fully. In the third place, directors of enterprises who receive means of production from the Soviet state, far from becoming their owners, are deemed to be the agents of the state in the utilisation of the means of production in accordance with the plans established by the state.

It will be seen, then, that under our system means of production can certainly not be classed in the category of commodities.

Why, in that case, do we speak of the value of means of production, their cost of production, their price, etc. ?

For two reasons.

Firstly, this is needed for purposes of calculation and settlement, for determining whether enterprises are paying or running at a loss, for checking and controlling the enterprises. But that is only the formal aspect of the matter.

Secondly, it is needed in order, in the interests of our foreign trade, to conduct sales of means of production to foreign countries. Here, in the sphere of foreign trade, but only in this sphere, our means of production really are commodities, and really are sold (in the direct meaning of the term) (*Economic Problems of Socialism*).

And again:

Consumer goods, which are needed to compensate the labour power expended in the process of production, are produced and realised in our country as commodities coming under the operation of the law of value. It is precisely here that the law of value exercises its influence on production. The effect of all this, taken together, is that the sphere of operation of the law of value in our country is strictly limited, and that the law of value cannot under our system function as the regulator of production (ibid.).

But it appears that the Voznesensky heresy did not refer only to pricing, but extended to labour distribution too (as also stated by Suslov):

Totally incorrect, too, is the assertion that under our present economic system, in the first phase of development of communist society, the law of value regulates the 'proportions' of labour distributed among the various branches of production.

If this were true, it would be incomprehensible why our light industries, which are the most profitable, are not being developed to the utmost, and why preference is given to our heavy industries, which are often less profitable, and sometimes altogether unprofitable.

If this were true, it would be incomprehensible why a number of our heavy industry plants which are still unprofitable and where the labour of the worker does not yield the 'proper returns', are not closed down, and why new light industry plants, which would certainly be profitable and where the labour of the workers might yield 'big returns', are not opened.

If this were true, it would be incomprehensible why workers are not transferred from plants that are less profitable, but very necessary to our national economy, to plants which are more profitable — in accordance with the law of value, which supposedly regulates the 'proportions' of labour distributed among the branches of production.

Obviously, if we were to follow the lead of these comrades, we should have to cease giving primacy to the production of means of production in favour of the production of articles of consumption. And what would be the effect of ceasing to give primacy to the production of the means of production? The effect would be to destroy the possibility of the continuous expansion of our national economy because the national economy cannot be continuously expanded without giving primacy to the production of means of production (ibid.).

This implies that Voznesensky's plans would have led to a 'rightist' consumer-goods policy. But it is not actually stated that this was intended, and it may equally well read as an attack via *reductio ad absurdum*, not really relevant except as polemic.

On the other hand, during the whole Stalin and post-Stalin period theoretical attacks on economic policies of those purged in the 'thirties have almost invariably been made against rightists (Bukharin, Rykov, etc.). Trotsky, Zinoviev and Co. were simply treated as traitors and nothing more, and there was little inclination to bother more formally about their economic heresies (cf. Khrushchev's references to Bukharin in January 1955, Stalin's letters to Tito in 1948, etc.). The reason is fairly obvious. The policies of the Right exert an endless attraction upon the population, and upon the Party members, and even upon Party leaders who see the dangers, or at least the difficulties, of the continual pressure of the straight Stalinist policies. The ideas of the Left exert no such attraction.

On the main issue on which Suslov publicly attacks Voznesensky — the theory that the Soviet State can 'create' economic laws — Stalin writes:

Reference is made to the specific role of the Soviet government in building socialism, which allegedly enables it to abolish existing laws of economic development and to 'form' new ones. That also is untrue.

It is said that the necessity for balanced (proportionate) development of the national economy in our country enables the Soviet government to abolish existing economic laws and to create new ones. That is absolutely untrue. Our yearly and five-yearly plans must not be confused with the objective economic law of balanced, proportionate development of the national economy. The law of balanced development of the national economy arose in opposition to the law of competition and anarchy of production under capitalism. It arose from the socialisation of the means of production, after the law of competition and anarchy of production had lost its validity. It became operative because a socialist economy can be conducted only on the basis of the economic law of balanced development of the national economy. That means that the law of balanced development of the national economy makes it possible for our planning bodies to plan social production correctly. But possibility must not be confused with actuality. They are two different things (ibid.).

This farcical set of truisms cannot be a genuine representation of Voznesensky's case: it is scarcely possible that he maintained that *anything* done by a planning body was bound to be all right under Socialism. Conceivably it may mean that he urged something slightly different — that a 'socialised' economy could be relied on to balance itself reliably under market conditions, with the planners accepting a market verdict on whether or not a project was uneconomic. It is not likely that Voznesensky held that this should always be decisive. Perhaps he believed that disproportions of a vast and uncontrollable nature might arise if no genuine method of checking were available. Some such idea seems to be required if we are to reconcile his price theory with his planning ideology.

This is to some extent supported by another passage from Stalin:

Is there a basic economic law of socialism? Yes, there is. What are the essential features and requirements of this law? The essential features and requirements of the basic law of socialism might be formulated roughly in this way: the securing of the maximum satisfaction of the constantly rising material and cultural requirements of the whole of society through the continuous expansion and per-fection of socialist production on the basis of higher techniques.

It is said that the law of the balanced, proportionate development of the national economy is the basic economic law of socialism. That is not true. Balanced development of the national economy, and, hence, economic planning, which is a more or less faithful reflection of this law, can yield nothing by themselves, if it is not known for what purpose economic development is planned, or if that purpose is not clear. The law of balanced development of the national economy can yield the desired result only if there is a purpose for the sake of which economic development is planned (ibid.).

Stalin concludes:

Suppose for a moment that we accepted this incorrect theory which denies the existence of objective laws of economic activity under socialism, and which proclaims the possibility of 'creating' and 'transforming' economic laws. Where would it lead us? In the end we should find ourselves at the mercy of 'economic' adventurers (ibid.).

At the XIXth Congress, Malenkov was to say:

'Denial of the objective character of economic laws is the ideological basis of adventurism in economic policy, of complete arbitrariness in economic leadership.'

'Adventurism' is a vague term, but at least it seems to imply that Voznesensky was urging some striking project of consider-able novelty. It seems certain that he was criticising the actual layout of the Soviet economy as full of dangerous disproportions.

Would it be sounder to conclude that the point at issue was one of economic projects as such rather than of political and ideo-logical control? It might be argued that the link is certainly a little tenuous, that though Zhdanov insisted on rigid ideological discipline he nevertheless relied in foreign policy on the dynam-ism of the Communist Parties, Soviet and foreign. It seems possible that he and Voznesensky might have been associated in a view which, though rigidly ideological, yet looked to the initiative of the properly trained faithful rather than to the power of the administrative machine as the *primum mobile* of the next period of Soviet development. That Voznesensky's views have been partially rehabilitated, and that Stalin's *Economic Problems of Socialism* has been partly condemned since the XXth Congress, may indicate an affinity with Khrushchev's recent demolition of large sections of the economic State machine in favour (in theory at least) of more initiative on the spot, and mainly from the Party cadres.

Thus there are a number of curious features about this whole economic controversy. Voznesensky was not, except confidentially, denounced for his errors until two years after his execution. Nor is it clear, whatever the theoretical arguments, that any major change in Soviet economic methods took place at any stage. More difficult still, the precise significance of the attacks on Voznesensky remains uncertain.

Voznesensky's execution is of course not explicable purely in terms of economic controversy. In his book Stalin strongly attacks economists like Yaroshenko, who in his view needed refuting, and Yaroshenko's views appear to be at least as bad as, if not worse than, those of Voznesensky. Yet Yaroshenko survived to be censured by Khrushchev after the XXth Party Congress.

But it is plain that Stalin attached enormous importance to the controversy. His *Economic Problems of Socialism* was clearly intended as the great seminal classic for the next period of Soviet development, and indeed was made the grand theme of the XIXth Congress. This was far more than was necessary to counter the views of an executed and refuted economist. But it is practically impossible to draw from Stalin's book any economic ideas whatever. It seems entirely, or almost entirely, concerned with verbal definitions, Marxist scholasticism (and on a rather petty level at that).

On the face of it Zhdanov and Stalin had been doctrinally at one. Zhdanov's views may quite legitimately be regarded as Stalinism at its purest and most explicit. But it is precisely this, no doubt, that made it in the long run unacceptable to Stalin. However dogmatic the old dictator was, it is notable that in most of his later political and economic moves he proceeded with caution, testing every step as he went forward, and thus never committing himself completely to a clear-cut programme in advance. And, again, in spite of Stalin's pronounced tendency (compared with Malenkov or Khrushchev) to give elaborate scholastic interpretations of his moves, there is little doubt that the objective situation was always a most important factor with him in deciding what moves were possible or desirable. We may, basically, read this in the attack on Voznesensky for the view alleged to have been held by him that the Soviet State was in a position to do what it liked economically and could ignore the 'economic laws', i.e. objective factors.

Thus, even if we concede (as seems possible) that the practical application of Voznesensky's view might be an increase in consumer goods rather than in industrialisation, we may perhaps regard this side of it as not the point at issue. For Stalin might regard *any* major planning change as 'adventurism', committing the C.P.S.U. to the ignoring of objective difficulties — a typical ideological crux.

In the later denunciations of Voznesensky by (directly) Suslov and (by implication) Stalin the points in dispute seem to be more on matters of economic theory related in some way to economic practice in the U.S.S.R. But their practical implications are nowhere stated, and though we have considered what these may have been, this point remains obscure. This is not to deny that it is highly probable that Zhdanov, with his clear-cut and well-organised system of ideas, may have had a definite thesis about the economic and political future of the U.S.S.R. as much as of its foreign policy. And the balance of probability is that his ideas would have involved (*a*) a greater emphasis on Party activism as against State organisation as the main moving force in Soviet affairs, and (*b*) the use of radically new methods to procure higher-pressure mobilisation of the economy on a war footing with a view to supporting a completely uncompromising foreign policy. This second point seems to conflict, formally at least, with the consequences Stalin claimed to see in Voznesensky's price policy. But if that is regarded simply as a method of increasing efficiency (whether or not *via* consumer-goods advocacy), they can be reconciled. It will, in any case, be seen that when controversies are conducted in this fashion, difficulties of interpretation arise, and certainty is unobtainable. Meanwhile this episode may serve to show the ways in which essential disputes are woven into the political struggle.

CHAPTER SIX

AGRICULTURAL DISPUTES, 1950–53

IN the period 1950–53 agricultural questions became a centre of controversy within the leadership, as they were also to do in the following years. The disputes grew intense enough to gain public expression and crucially affected the position of several members of the leadership.

As we have said, agriculture is one of the spheres in which the Soviet regime has found its most intractable problem. The aim of securing maximum production is often in conflict with the aim of increasing the proletarianisation of the peasantry. Oscillations, compromises and sudden drastic changes in policy are frequent.

Moreover, it is a sphere, above all others, where results depend in a large measure on an uncontrollable phenomenon — the weather. A bad crop is a major factor in the struggle for power, for it is usual to blame it, in part at least, on the incompetence of those in control. A good crop makes the *status quo* easier to maintain.

Without over-stating the parallel we may compare the two spheres (as far as internal policy is concerned) in which the Soviet Government have found it particularly difficult to obtain at the same time good results on the one hand and doctrinal orthodoxy and political discipline on the other — the arts and agriculture. It was disarray in these two fields to which the Party turned the major part of its attention during the post-war tightening up of doctrine and discipline. In agriculture the collective-farm system, as existing over the last thirty years, has failed to produce a solution of the agricultural problem in accord with Party theory. In every period of comparative relaxation — both immediately after the war and in the first years of the 'fifties — it has begun to be stated, almost in so many words, that the system has, in certain areas, virtually disintegrated. In 1945 this was said not only of the liberated areas, but also of the lower Volga.

In this period the disintegration of the collective-farm system was on a colossal scale. *Collective Farm Law*, by N. D. Kazantsev and others (Moscow, 1947), stated that 2,255,000 cases of illegal misappropriation of land had been discovered in just over 200,000 collective farms investigated, involving 4,700,000 hectares. Another Soviet source gives 5,900,000 hectares as the amount of land misappropriated up to May 7, 1949, in addition to the 4·7 million hectares restored to the collective farms by the beginning of 1947 (*Land Law*, I. L. Braude and others, Moscow, 1949).

How continuous and cunning supervision had to be can be seen from *Vestnik Statistiki*, No. 6 of 1951, which quotes a decree for the branding of all collectively-owned animals in order to prevent illegal exchange between private and public herds, and a decree that no animal death be registered as from natural causes until official inspections by the veterinary and administrative officials; a widespread practice of exchanging dead or incapable private animals for good ones from the collective herd had grown up.

The disintegration of the collective-farm system owing to lack of Party discipline became intense in Georgia some years later. *Pravda* of June 14, 1952, reporting the session of the Georgian Central Committee, names a number of secretaries of District Party Committees and other officials who 'tolerated' the 'pilfering of collective lands', and similar charges were made at the September 1952 Congress of the Georgian Communist Party, where Mgeladze, the local First Secretary, spoke of the return, between May and September 1952, of 7,779 hectares of land, 6,926 head of cattle, nearly 93,000,000 roubles and a whole list of other embezzled kolkhoz property. He quoted other malpractices, such as a number of districts where nearly half the peasants failed to complete their minimum collective labour — in some cases doing none at all (*Zarya Vostoka*, September 15, 1952). There had of course been no formal change in the organisation of agriculture. What had happened was that in many farms the forms of collectivisation were preserved, but with the connivance of local Party and Soviet officials they were to a great extent run in practice on a private-property basis. The implication, clearly stated at the time, was that in the absence of continuous pressure of discipline from above the natural tendencies on the spot in the village could not be contained.

On the other hand, the fact that the Party never felt able to do away with that temporary concession to petty bourgeois moods made in the 'thirties — the peasants' private plot and cattle — is a flaw from the point of view of both doctrine and discipline in the whole Soviet agricultural approach. Yet the reason it cannot easily be eliminated is plain: even in 1957 the private animals produced about 55 per cent. of the milk and meat of the U.S.S.R. And here in a nutshell is the whole dilemma: higher production can only be obtained by further concessions. But each concession, generally speaking, weakens Party control. The present position is a pragmatic compromise, in which the balance can only be maintained by continuous effort. Every time a policy-maker wants either more food or more political relaxation, he is likely to urge larger concessions to the peasant. Yet this soon produces a situation in which another faction in the leadership can point out that the peasantry are getting out of hand. Or, alternatively, the dog-matists can urge tighter and tighter controls, and a faster progress towards the proletarianisation of the peasantry, and State operation rather than co-operative operation of agriculture (which is admitted by all leaders to be the final aim). Yet such plans can at once be denounced as 'adventurist'. (Khrushchev's method of fighting this dilemma in 1954 was an interesting one. In devoting a huge effort to the Virgin Lands which had not previously been owned by an agricultural peasantry, he was able to start from scratch and operate largely through State farms manned chiefly by people drafted from the cities. If there had been enough, and sufficiently good, virgin land in the U.S.S.R. this might conceivably have gone some way to solving the Party problem, though opposition even on this point was to be offered in the highest circles — see p. 241.)

The aims of Soviet agricultural policy are thus threefold: productive, administrative and ideological. It is desired to increase output, to ensure maximum immediate control over the peasantry, and to go forward in the direction of 'eliminating the differences between town and country' by turning the peasants into wage-earning employees of large-scale agricultural production units.

These aims are largely irreconcilable. The private plot and cattle left to the peasants as a result of their strenuous resistance to the initial collectivisation have ever since been the most productive section of Soviet agriculture. All ideology calls for the abolition of this private sector: all realism postpones such a revolution. (The vast centralised farm, employing hundreds and thousands of people, has never proved economic in spite of advantages that may appear on paper: otherwise other countries would have used it, in 'capitalist' form.)

Agricultural disputes are therefore certain to arise all the time. They have centred on two main issues: production and ideology. Ideological considerations greatly narrow the solutions open to the leadership in purely productive questions. But the ideological arguments have often been mainly verbal: does handing the previously independent Machine Tractor Stations over to the kolkhozes strengthen the latter and make them less amenable to eventual conversion into State farms, as Stalin held, or the opposite, as maintained by Khrushchev? — and similar points which are not susceptible of any real proof, but simply require certificates of orthodoxy. On the other hand, real production policies, while also having their ideological aspects, are susceptible to empirical tests, at least in the long run.

The basic difficulty of the kolkhoz system was given particularly clearly, as late as the December 1958 plenum, in the following exchange:

Mustafaev, I. D. (Secretary of the Azerbaidzhan Central Committee): 'Nevertheless an enormous quantity of cattle in the private sector consumes a great deal of people's time; a great deal of the fodder resources of the kolkhozes is expended.'

Khrushchev: 'The kolkhoz cattle is being embezzled.'

Mustafaev: 'We have checked in the kolkhozes. In individual kolkhozes payment has been levied for pasturing cattle. . . . It is true that when this question was discussed in many kolkhozes they did not agree with this and decided to pasture the cattle free.'

Khrushchev: 'Comrade Mustafaev, we do not object to reorganisation of the countryside. But you are introducing an incorrect proposal. In essence you are proposing to lay down a tribute. But the countryside must be reconstructed on socialist principles. What you are talking about is a tax; this is a policy of fines; it does not suit us. Educative work must be carried on among the population. In the first place, Communists who work in the countryside must set a real example. Attention must be paid to this. Otherwise cattle owners will pay a tax, buy themselves off and develop private livestock rearing, and it will be difficult to improve the collective side. The facts of which you speak are evidence of weakness in education of the kolkhozniks and even of Communists.'

Mustafaev: 'True, Nikita Sergeevich; time is needed to make use of the opportunity.'

Khrushchev: 'What time is needed? Forty-one years of Soviet power, a sufficient period, has passed.'

Mustafaev: 'We have not made use of our opportunity yet. I agree with your reply. . . .' (*Stenographic Record* of the December 1958 plenum of the Central Committee.)

Officials of the Soviet Ministry of Agriculture told a Polish correspondent in 1957 that agricultural output was about eight quintals per hectare (*Polityka*, No. 41, 1957). This is about the same as in Tsarist times, and as in the late 'twenties. In the meantime extraordinarily triumphant claims have been made, without figures.

The critical situation in Soviet agriculture in 1949 was to be gone into by Khrushchev at the December 1958 plenum. Khrushchev spoke of the period as follows:

Comrades, the C.C. of the Party, at the September [1953] Plenary Session, openly and directly admitted that stock-breeding was the most neglected branch of agriculture, that implementation of the long overdue measures for the upsurge of stock-breeding had become one of the most urgent tasks of Party and Government. It cannot be said that the backwardness of stock-breeding was noticed only in the autumn of 1953, when the September Plenary Session was held. Our stock-breeding had been lagging behind for a long time. In spite of the fact that this was obvious, the backwardness of stock-breeding was kept quiet by many workers, including those who occupied high Party and Government jobs. Among them there were also workers who, in their public speeches, often declared that our stock-breeding was on the upsurge.

This bragging could not further the successful development of communal stock-breeding; and this was felt more acutely every year. In 1949 when the lagging became quite intolerable, a three-year plan for the development of communal collective and State farm productive stock-breeding was adopted. As will be recalled, the fate of this plan proved an unenviable one; it was not fulfilled and the backwardness of stock-breeding continued to become more acute.

The makers of the plan base themselves on the assumption that it was sufficient to decree the tasks required for the development of stock-breeding, and matters would improve. As a result of this, communal cattle-breeding on collective farms proved to be economically unprofitable. The collective farm workers concerned themselves with it less and less, and the tasks set by the plan remained unfulfilled. (*Stenographic Record* of the December 1958 plenum of the Central Committee.)

In the other themes covered by this report Khrushchev openly attacks the 'Anti-Party Group' by name. Here (except to the extent that Saburov, who became head of Gosplan in 1949, may be under fire) the anonymity of 'makers of the plan' seems to cover Andreyev, then the Politburo member responsible for agriculture.

Pravda, on February 19, 1950, printed an article 'Against Distortions in Collective Farm Labour Organisation'. This concerns itself mainly with the fact that 'the Party and Government recommended the permanent *work brigade* to collective farms as the *basic* and *principal* form of labour organisation', and it also criticises the Kursk Provincial Party Committee for weakening the work brigade and in general weakening organisation and thus 'splitting large-scale production'. The main assault is on 'the incorrect views expressed in this matter by Comrade A. A. Andreyev'. He is accused of attacking, with the accusation that it amounted to 'depersonalisation of the collective farmers', the principle of labour in large brigades. (Andreyev had as recently as 1949 preferred the 'small-team system'.)

Pravda of February 28 — in a letter dated February 25 — gives Andreyev's recantation (and on March 2 that of his leading economist). Andreyev's letter is quite short and amounts to saying that his statements were wrong, though he had not intended to imply that the team should replace the brigade. He promised to check his practical results more carefully in future.

This accusation against Andreyev is of so minimal a character that it must stand for something else. This moment of public humiliation probably coincides with Stalin's practical expulsion of Andreyev from the Politburo, mentioned by Khrushchev in his Secret Speech, when he said: 'Stalin separated one other man from the work of the Political Bureau, Andrei Andreyevich Andreyev'. It is also clear that henceforward Andreyev had no say in agriculture. Yet, apart from this incident and a few other signs that Andreyev was no longer very well regarded, there was no public indication of actual removal from power. On the contrary, he continued to appear on platforms as a Politburo member, until his removal from all high offices as a result of the praesidial election of October 1952, following the XIXth Party Congress. His deputy in the Party Control Commission, Shkiryatov, had already been appearing on platforms since the time of the Leningrad Case as if ranking with C.C. Secretaries, and this may indicate that he was already *de facto* in charge of the Commission, though Andreyev remained its nominal Chairman until 1952. (Shkiryatov did *not* become a member of the Secretariat — replacing Kuznetsov —as has sometimes been supposed. This can be seen from *Vechernaya Moskva* of September 17, 1952, which lists: 'Molotov, Malenkov, Beria, Voroshilov, Mikoyan, Bulganin, Kaganovich, Andreyev, Khrushchev, Kosygin and Shvernik; Suslov and Ponomarenko, Secretaries of the Central Committee; and M. F. Shkiryatov, Deputy Chairman of the Party Control Commission'.)

This may indicate that Andreyev was already under a cloud in 1949, and that his open censure on the agricultural issue in 1950 was merely the formal recording of earlier resentment. On the face of it, at least, Shkiryatov's post as Deputy Chairman of the P.C.C. was not of major public importance. It is true that the fact that A. A. Kuznetsov was not replaced when he fell from the Secretariat might possibly have meant that certain of his duties — particularly the Party supervision of the police ministries — were transferred from the Secretariat to a sector of the Control Commission under Shkiryatov. Shkiryatov had been one of the key operators under Stalin in the great purge of the 'thirties, and his promotion to actual Chairman of the Party Control Committee, as it was then renamed, in October 1952 strongly implies that use was to be made of that body in the new purge intended by Stalin. He was also, unlike Andreyev, elected to the 1952 'large' Praesidium. After Stalin's death Shkiryatov did not lose his P.C.C. post, though he did not figure in the new Praesidium.

Not much more was heard of him, though he continued to appear with high precedence, though only on the more formal occasions. That he was not well regarded is indicated by the absence of any article on him in the relevant volume of the *Large Soviet Encyclopaedia* (Vol. 48). But if he had been a *direct* agent in the Doctors' Plot, or even a fairly direct one like Aristov or Ignatiev, one might have expected him to fall as they did. The informality and moderation of his downgrading are more in accord with the drop in status of such people as Mikhailov, and it may be more reasonable to think that this was just the relegation of those members of the big Praesidium being groomed by Stalin as replacements of the old leaders, yet not themselves directly responsible for his plans. In that case we can assume that, at least after the XIXth Congress, Shkiryatov did *not* directly link with the M.G.B.

Meanwhile various other minor signs of Andreyev's loss of prestige appeared. The formal list of acceptance of nomination as candidates for the Soviet of the Union elections is given in *Pravda* and *Izvestia* of February 5, 1950, in the following order: Stalin, Molotov, Malenkov, Beria, Voroshilov, Kaganovich, Khrushchev, Andreyev (Mikoyan, Shvernik, Bulganin and Kosygin stood for the Soviet of Nationalities).

Pravda and *Izvestia* for March 8 to 11, 1950, printed electoral speeches by members of the Politburo; Andreyev is only given 500 words, compared with, for example, Malenkov and Molotov 6,000 words; Beria, Voroshilov and Khrushchev 5,000 words; Mikoyan 7,000 words; and Kaganovich 5,500 words.

The direct links between culture and politics may again be seen in the echoes of the denunciation of Andreyev of his small-team theory. When he retracted, the playwrights Bondareva and Ovechkin, who had written plays to his thesis, were sharply criticised (*Sovietskoye Izkustvo*, No. 4, 1950).

Pravda, on April 25, 1950, published a 5,500-word article by Khrushchev on 'Some Questions of the Further Organisation and Economic Strengthening of the Collective Farm'. In it he urged the fusion of small collective farms with larger ones, and strongly supported the criticism made of Andreyev, without naming him. This may indicate that Khrushchev had now taken over Andreyev's responsibilities for agriculture: he was to produce a number of similar articles and speeches.

I

In his article Khrushchev spoke on the need for amalaga-mating the large number of collective farms in the U.S.S.R. into a smaller number of large farms, in the interests of increasing agricultural efficiency. One reason given was that the advance towards full Communism required the gradual elimination of the technical and cultural discrepancy between town and countryside. In this connection the amalgamation of the collective farms was planned to be accompanied by the construction of 'large, well-appointed villages to which the collective farmers would move from small, badly-equipped villages'.

After this important policy statement, a number of reports appeared in the Soviet Press about its gradual implementation. A great many collective farms were reported to have undergone amalgamation, and references were made to the construction of new and improved villages. Some of the new villages — existing then in project form only — had been given the imposing title of 'agrotowns'.

On January 6, 1951, *Moskovskaya Pravda* (Khrushchev's paper) said that 'a radical reorganisation of the village is . . . not a distant project', and on January 18, 1951, Khrushchev spoke on 'Construction and Planning in the Collective Farms', to a conference in the Moscow province. The speech was printed in *Pravda* on March 4, and thus seemed to be intended as an official guide to all concerned in the amalgamation process. The same day it was also carried by *Moskovskaya Pravda* and *Socialist Agriculture*.

Khrushchev began by pointing out that peasant labour in the collective farms was becoming to an ever increasing degree a variant of industrial labour, being carried on with the help of modern machinery. In short, the 'process of the liquidation of the discrepancy between town and countryside' was 'gradually proceeding'. The amalgamation of collective farms already carried out had made possible a great new increase in agricultural productivity, which in turn would raise the cultural level of the countryside. In order to derive every advantage from amalgamation, however, the farms would have to be strengthened organisationally. One of the most important problems in this connection was the evacuation of small villages and the construction of new collective farm settlements.

Khrushchev went on to detail at considerable length the

great advantages the peasants could expect, in the way of amenities, from such a change: better schools and houses, hospitals, clubs, cinemas, parks, public baths, shops, piped water, pavements, street lamps and so on.

Next, Khrushchev dealt with the peasants' private allotments. Clearly it was in the interests of economy to restrict the overall area of the settlements as far as possible. Many leading collective farmers understood this and had correctly observed that it would be inexpedient to attach a large private allotment to every house — the normal practice in collective farms. However, Khrushchev continued, 'Proposals have been made to limit the private allotment within the settlement to the small size of ten or fifteen hundredths of a hectare' — (the collective-farm statute allowed an area of from one quarter to one half of a hectare for each private allotment). The reduced size, said Khrushchev, 'is quite sufficient to contain the house, essential agricultural buildings, a small orchard of fifteen to twenty trees and a small vegetable garden'. The rest of the allotment area allowed by the collective-farm statute was to be located outside the settlement boundary, not in fields under collective cultivation, but in a specially assigned portion of land entirely devoted to private allotments. This can certainly be regarded as a first step to the elimination of the private plot.

Finally, Khrushchev had a few words to say about the name to be given to the new collective-farm communities. He observed that the name of 'village' no longer satisfied the collective farmers, and that in the Ukraine certain new villages under construction had been called 'agrotowns'. This term, however, seemed too pretentious, as 'the name of "town" carries a number of obligations. A town must satisfy the high demands of urban culture.' He preferred the term 'collective farm settlement', but added that it was up to the farmers themselves to choose a name.

On March 5, the day after it was published, each of the newspapers printed the following correction:

Correction by the editors: In publishing the article by Comrade N. S. Khrushchev 'On Construction and Public Welfare in the Kolkhozes' in yesterday's issue a note from the editors was inadvertently omitted. This note stated that the article by Comrade N. S. Khrushchev was published only as a basis for discussion.

The timing of this repudiation is remarkable. The speech had been made in January and was published in leisurely enough fashion without attracting attention in the meanwhile. Then the disavowal of its official status came in a day. This rather implies a quick decision, without much discussion, by Stalin personally. That he had not much faith in Khrushchev's attitude to agriculture, when allowed his head, can be seen from a conversation reported years later by Khrushchev:

Why did our agriculture lag so considerably for so long? Because nobody in the centre really wanted to disentangle the state of affairs on the spot. Stalin, as is known, never went anywhere, did not consult workers of agriculture, did not listen to the voice of local workers, while the people in the centre whom he delegated to watch over agriculture concealed great drawbacks from him and indulged in whitewashing. The principle of material incentive of the collective farmers and all agricultural workers in increasing the output of agricultural produce was grossly violated.

I shall quote, for instance, the following example. Soon after the end of the war I went to the village where I was born. There I went to see my cousin. She has an orchard. I told her, 'You have wonderful apple-trees.' She replied, 'I shall cut them down in the autumn.' I asked her, 'Why?' 'Heavy taxes have to be paid,' she said; 'it is not profitable to have an orchard.' I mentioned this conversation to Stalin and reported that the collective farmers were cutting down orchards, to which he replied that I was a narodnik, that I had a narodnik attitude, and that I was losing the proletarian class sense (*Kommunist*, No. 12, August 1957).

During March Khrushchev failed to appear at a number of local conferences, State funerals and so on. He had been at similar occasions in the previous two months.

We shall try to be sparing with order-of-listing analyses (the use of which has already been demonstrated for Andreyev), except where they contribute a notable clue or possible clue. But we may note one here. The Secretariat is seldom listed separately in the Soviet Press, as the Politburo membership given before it includes the senior members of the Secretariat. But the handbook *Aid to Students of Political Schools* in its 1951 edition gives the Secretariat as consisting of Stalin, Malenkov, Ponomarenko, Suslov and Khrushchev. It can scarcely be that

Khrushchev was in any sense junior to the two before him; but the order could represent Stalin as First and Malenkov as Second Secretary, with the remaining three in alphabetical order. The fact that the third of the Secretaries who also ranked as Politburo members had to sit below the salt, among his juniors, may be a sign of a certain decline.

From this point Khrushchev ceased to speak and write a great deal on agriculture, though he was still among those consulted on the subject (see p. 127). In January 1955 criticism of Malenkov was to include his errors as Party Secretary in charge of agriculture, and the presumption is that this refers to the period 1951–53.

Apart from the immediate disavowal there were a few attacks on 'fantastic plans for peasant resettlement' from Beria's associates Arutinov, First Secretary in Armenia (*Kommunist* (Erevan), March 20, 1951) and Bagirov at the Azerbaidzhan Party Congress in May 1951 (*Bakinsky Rabochy*, May 25, 1951). Then the idea was hardly referred to again until attacked openly by Malenkov at the XIXth Congress in the following terms:

It must be noted that some of our leading workers, especially in connection with the amalgamation of the small collective farms, displayed a wrong, consumer, approach to questions of collective-farm development. What they suggested was that the population of the villages be congregated en masse and in a brief space of time, in large collective-farm townships, that all the old collective-farm buildings and the homes of the collective farmers be demolished and that big 'collective-farm settlements', 'collective-farm towns' and 'agrotowns' be built on new sites. This they regarded as the key task in the organisational and economic consolidation of the collective farms. The mistake these comrades made was to forget the major production tasks of the collective farms, and give prominence to tasks that derive from them, to consumer tasks connected with welfare amenities in the collective farms. These tasks are, undoubtedly, important, but all the same they are derivative, subordinate, and not major tasks, and they can be carried out successfully only if collective production is further developed. Forgetting, or belittling, the major production tasks may place all our practical work in the rural areas on a wrong track, may hinder the further development of the collective farms and injure those very welfare amenities as well as the whole of our work of socialist construction.

The party took timely measures to correct these mistaken tendencies in collective-farm development (Malenkov's *Report* on the Work of the Central Committee to the XIXth Party Congress, 1952).

A good deal has been made by some commentators of the revolutionary nature of Khrushchev's 'agrogorod' proposals. But basically they seem to have amounted to little more than a dramatisation of the fusion of collective farms into larger units, and this fusion continued and was still treated as orthodox. This is not to say that the differences are not of importance. First, the construction of much larger settlements, though in line with general Marxist theory, could not have been other than a long-term project, and was perhaps regarded as exaggerated, and upsetting to the peasant at the given moment. Secondly, the division of the private plot into local and distant sections was again only likely to annoy the peasant — though this point was not raised in the criticism of the project. Thirdly — and this bore the brunt of the official repudiation — the great emphasis put by Khrushchev on the superior amenities of the system was regarded as a 'consumer' approach. Thus the scheme was fiercely attacked as a right deviation, rather than for the 'left' aspects it seems to present at first sight. As in the Voznesensky case, there appears to be reason to suppose that denigration of a policy as 'rightist' is the best way to secure its repudiation by those who bother themselves with theory — in fact with the Party aktiv; and thus that any aspect of a condemned policy that can be held up as 'right' is the one picked on, regardless of other aspects.

It also seems likely that Khrushchev was already at this time urging the fusion of State-controlled Machine Tractor Stations with the collective farms (a policy he finally put into effect in 1958), and that Stalin was attacking his views when he wrote:

What, in view of this, would be the effect of selling the M.T.S.'s to the collective farms as their property? The effect would be to involve the collective farms in heavy loss and to ruin them, to undermine the mechanisation of agriculture, and to slow-up the development of collective-farm production. The collective farms would become the owners of the basic instruments of production; that is, their status would be an exceptional one, such as is not shared by any other enterprise in our country, for, as we know, even the nationalised enterprises do not own their instruments of production. How, by what considerations of progress and advancement, could this exceptional status of the collective farms be justified? Can it be said that such a status would facilitate the elevation of collective-farm property to the level of public property, that it would expedite the transition of our society from socialism to communism? Would it not be truer to say that such a status could only dig a deeper gulf between collective-farm property, and public property, and would not bring us any nearer to communism, but, on the contrary, remove us farther from it?

The outcome would be, secondly, an extension of the sphere of operation of commodity circulation, because a gigantic quantity of instruments of agricultural production would come within its orbit. What do Comrades Sanina and Venzher think — is the extension of the sphere of commodity circulation calculated to promote our advance towards communism? Would it not be truer to say that our advance towards communism would only be retarded by it? (*Economic Problems of Socialism.*)

The kolkhoz amalgamation campaign as such was not affected by the condemnation of Khrushchev's particular approach. An article by Benediktov, Minister of Agriculture, in *Socialist Agriculture* of March 3, 1951, just the day before the printing of the condemned Khrushchev article, strongly supported the campaign, and said that already consolidation had affected more than two-thirds of the former 254,000 kolkhozes. This article attracted no hostile attention and the process continued.

At the XIXth Party Congress, Malenkov reported that the number of kolkhozes had been reduced from 254,000 on January 1, 1950, to 97,000 in October 1952. (At the September 1953 plenum of the Central Committee Khrushchev gave the figure of 94,000.)

Malenkov added that:

The amalgamation of small collective farms into large ones was an important step in increasing the productive forces of agriculture, since collective husbandry can be more successfully enlarged and improved on big farms . . . (Malenkov's *Report* on the Work of the Central Committee to the XIXth Party Congress, October 5, 1952).

Stalin's solution to the agricultural problem was the great irrigation and afforestation plan of the time. This was connected with an extension of grazing land, through ley-farming (a method Khrushchev was to show himself hostile to in the years after Stalin's death). As Malenkov said at the XIXth Congress:

The task now is to complete the irrigation, shelter-belt and drainage projects in the appointed time, and Party, Soviet and economic organisations must concentrate special attention on this . . . (Malenkov's *Report* to the XIXth Party Congress).

On the organisational and ideological side Stalin's solution, as given in *Economic Problems of Socialism*, was to take the next step in 'the process of the liquidation of the discrepancy between town and countryside', by the introduction of a direct barter system (Tovaro-obmen) instead of trade for money. This, too, was condemned later, as in *Kommunist* No. 14 (September 1953), as far as its being an 'urgent practical task' was concerned.

Malenkov's criticism of the Khrushchev 'agrogorod' project had been a sharp one. Now he gave a hostage to fortune in the statement:

'The grain problem, which in the past was regarded as our most acute and gravest problem, has thus been solved, solved definitely and finally . . .' (Malenkov's *Report* to the XIXth Party Congress, October 5, 1952).

Khrushchev was to attack this formulation strongly when his open assault on the 'Anti-Party Group' was in progress. He also attacked Malenkov personally for using the 'biological yield' crop-estimate method of the Stalin period to inflate the harvest figures (though it was Malenkov himself who was first to repudiate this, in August 1953). In his speech to the December 1958 plenum Khrushchev said:

Did the people who were responsible for the position of agriculture — Malenkov specifically — know about the shortage of bread in the country? There is no doubt that they did. But, in spite of facts, Malenkov declared in 1952 from the rostrum of the Party Congress that the gross harvest of grain in the country amounted to 8,000,000,000 puds and that now the grain problem was allegedly solved finally and for all times.

Malenkov acted dishonestly, juggling with the data on so-called 'biological crop-yielding capacity', since everyone knows that the 'biological crop yield' is far from being the same as real grain in corn-bins. For one cannot bake bread out of the concept of 'bio-logical crop-yielding capacity'. Bread is baked out of the grain which has been gathered.

The actual state of affairs in grain production was different. The collective and State farms, even in the year of the best harvest in that period — the year 1952 — gathered not 8,000,000,000 but only 5,600,000,000 puds of grain.

Despite the fact that the collective and State farms delivered to the State even some of their seed grain, only 2,100,000,000 puds of bread-grain was procured in the country. This did not meet the current needs of the State — not to mention the need to accumulate necessary reserves.

The statement on the 8,000,000,000 puds harvest of bread grain was nothing but eyewash, was deceiving the Party and the people and was intended to conceal major failures in agriculture, the management of which had been put into the hands of Malenkov. Such was the state of affairs as regards bread-grain production. (*Stenographic Report* of the December 1958 plenum of the Central Committee.)

This allocation of blame, while inequitable, seems to show that the whole thing rankled with Khrushchev. Of course, it is plain that Malenkov's statement was not a private forgery. The 'biological yield' method was obviously a grotesque one, and the fact was certainly known to all members of the leadership, including Khrushchev.

That Khrushchev was still consulted on agriculture in Stalin's last years, in spite of the censure, is shown by a passage in the Secret Speech:

And when he [Stalin] was once told during a discussion that our situation on the land was a difficult one and that the situation of cattle-breeding and meat production was especially bad, a com-mission was formed which was charged with the preparation of a resolution called 'Means toward Further Development of Animal Breeding in Kolkhozes and Sovkhozes'. We worked out this project.

Of course, our proposals of that time did not contain all possi-bilities, but we did chart ways in which animal breeding on kolk-hozes and sovkhozes would be raised. We had proposed then to raise the prices of such products in order to create material incentives for the kolkhoz, M.T.S. and sovkoz workers in the development of cattle-breeding. But our project was not accepted and in *February 1953* was laid aside entirely [my italics: R. C.].

It will be noted that Khrushchev emphasises his own participation in this Commission, and that the Commission's proposals were concerned with incentives (and not, or at least not as a major point, with anything in the agrogorod line). In fact, they seem to have a great deal in common with the proposals actually announced by Khrushchev in September 1953.

Why Khrushchev mentions that Stalin set this plan aside in February 1953 is not clear. It may seem to be an attempt to connect agricultural matters with Stalin's proposed purge in some way. Certainly if agriculture was in a bad condition it seems likely that Stalin would have used the purge to provide a scapegoat, as in 1938, when Chernov, People's Commissar for Agriculture, was publicly held responsible for sabotaging the food supply and was tried and shot. The general measures of social tightening up which the Soviet Press was urging in the winter of 1952–53 included mass appeals for stricter discipline in agriculture. The tendency of the whole campaign was against material incentives and in favour of discipline, and it may be that this was Stalin's substitute.

CHAPTER SEVEN

GEORGIA, 1951–53

IN this period a series of major changes took place in the political leadership in the Georgian S.S.R. A study of these is instructive for several reasons. In the first place, the local leadership can be regarded, without introducing any important inaccuracy, as having no influence at all in the major policy decisions of the country as a whole. The individuals involved can therefore be looked upon as taking part in a power struggle pure and simple. On the other hand, combats of this sort cannot take place in areas as important as Georgia purely on their own. They must reflect, and have evidential value in interpreting, more essential struggles in Moscow.

The changes in Georgia were so frequent and so far-reaching that as mere demonstrations of the political mechanics of Soviet rule they are especially striking and illuminating. At the same time, as will be seen, there are anomalies in the roles of key individuals which show very clearly that however soundly a general theory may be constructed, the information available is insufficient to give a plausible explanation of important particulars. Georgian affairs are thus most useful illustrations of both the known and the unknown in the struggle for power in the U.S.S.R.

It also happens that changes in the Georgian leadership were especially crucial to the main struggle in the U.S.S.R., owing to the extent to which they figured in the career of Beria, which was central to Soviet politics in the period concerned. The Georgian purge of November 1951 was the first step in the wave of purges which marked Stalin's last year. The counter-purge of April 1953 indicated Beria's return to power. And the purges following Beria's fall destroyed his remaining associates. Georgia is thus important evidence at each stage of developments at the centre. At the same time it can be treated, as I propose to treat it, as a single narrative, a sort of microcosm of

the whole. This will mean a certain chronological and factual
overlap between chapters.

The Georgian purges went very much further than the
equivalent events in Moscow. The 'Mingrelian' plotters
already included political leaders like Baramiya, and Beria's
police cadres (against which, in the Doctors' Plot, only the
preliminary manœuvre of condemning the 'former officials of
the M.G.B.' for laxity had been reached by the time of Stalin's
death) were directly implicated, in the person of Rapava. In
Moscow, Khrushchev tells us in the Secret Speech, Stalin had
only started to *say* that the old Politburo members should be
replaced and to make 'charges' against some of them. In
Georgia, Charkviani, who had headed the Party Bureau there
since the 'thirties, was already actually removed. His successor,
Mgeladze, may be seen as the prototype of the new leaders
Stalin was preparing to instal at the centre as well. In a sense
Georgia may be regarded as an almost completed pilot project
for a larger central scheme which was only roughly and tentatively sketched and finally abandoned. The complexities re-
mind one sharply not to over-simplify in these matters. But
though the mass of detail seems overwhelming at first sight,
both patterns and loose ends can be readily detected. (It would
be a most valuable exercise for students to construct their own
hypotheses to cover these.) They will find that although
Occam's Razor, the principle '*entia non sunt multiplicanda*', is sound
basically, yet to reduce everything to two or three clear-cut
factions is to leave out of account cross-currents of a dozen
sorts, and the often omitted qualification '*praeter necessitatem*'
needs due attention.

A look at the composition of the Bureau of the Georgian
Central Committee for the period will give a superficial idea
of the problem:

THE BUREAU OF THE GEORGIAN CENTRAL COMMITTEE

JUNE 1938

Beria *First Secretary*
Kochlamazashvili *Second Secretary*
Charkviani *Third Secretary*
Bakradze

Makharadze (d. 1941)
Ishkanov
Sturua (till 1948)
Mamulov
Goglidze
Dekanozov
Merkulov

Candidates:
Grigoryan
Topuridze
Mirtskhulava
Shariya

JAN. 1949–NOV. 1951

Date of
entry.

1938	Charkviani
1943	Baramiya
1939	Topuridze (d. Feb. 1951)
1949	Tskhovrebashvili
1948	Shaduri
1944	Chkhubianishvili
1937	Bakradze
1938	Ishkanov
1947	Ketskhoveli
1948	Zambakhidze
1948	V. B. Gogua

Secretaries } (Charkviani, Baramiya, Topuridze (d. Feb. 1951), Tskhovrebashvili, Shaduri)

Candidates:
Kochlamazashvili
Lelashvili
Rukhadze
Tsimakuridze

DEC. 1951

Charkviani
Tskhovrebashvili   } *Secretaries*
Kvirkveliya
M. K. Balavadze
Ketskhoveli
Chkhubianishvili
Ishkanov

Bakradze
Lelashvili
Rukhadze
V. B. Gogua
Mgeladze

Candidates:

  Tsimakuridze
  Kochlamazashvili

MAY 1952

Mgeladze ⎫
Tskhovrebashvili ⎪
V. D. Budzhiashvili ⎬ *Secretaries*
Melkadze ⎭
Ketskhoveli
M. K. Balavadze
Chkhubianishvili
Ishkanov (out by July)
Bakradze
Lelashvili
Rukhadze (out by July)

Candidates:

  Tsimakuridze
  Kochlamazashvili

SEPT. 1952

Mgeladze ⎫
Tskhovrebashvili ⎬ *Secretaries*
V. D. Budzhiashvili ⎭
Ketskhoveli
Chkhubianishvili
Bakradze
Kochlavashvili
Kochlamazashvili
K. D. Budzhiashvili
M. K. Balavadze
Getiya

Candidates:

  V. K. Balavadze
  Dzhavakhishvili
  Kandelaki

APRIL 1953

Mirtskhulava ⎫
Romelashvili ⎬ *Secretaries*
Chkhikvadze ⎭
Bakradze
Tskhovrebashvili
Zodelava
Dzhavakhishvili
Dekanozov
Mamulov
Sturua
Baramiya

Candidate:

  Kochlamazashvili

JULY 1953

As above, *less* Dekanozov and Mamulov and *plus*
Efimov.

SEPT. 1953

Mzhavanadze ⎫
Romelashvili ⎬ *Secretaries*
Chkhikvadze ⎭
Dzhavakhishvili
Chubinidze
Inauri
Kuchava
Antonov
Gotsiridze

Candidates:

  Georgadze
  Guniya

FEB. 1954

Mzhavanadze ⎫
Georgadze ⎬ *Secretaries*
Mchedlishvili ⎭
Antonov
Dzhavakhishvili
Inauri
Kuchava

Lelashvili
Chubinidze
Gotsiridze
Guniya

Candidates:

Sekhniashvili
Dzhanelidze

JAN. 1956

Mzhavanadze ⎤
Georgadze   ⎟
Mchedlishvili ⎬ *Secretaries*
Kadagidze   ⎟
Kvachadze   ⎦
Fedyuninsky
Dzhavakhishvili
Inauri
Kuchava
Lelashvili
Chubinidze

Candidates:

Sekhniashvili
Dzhanelidze

JAN. 1958

Mzhavanadze   ⎤
Kovanov (Aug. 1956) ⎟
Kadagidze   ⎬ *Secretaries*
Dolidze   ⎟
Dumbadze   ⎦
Galitsky
Dzhavakhishvili
Inauri
Kuchava
Lelashvili
Chubinidze

Candidates:

Gegeshidze
Rtveliashvili
Chogovadze
Shevarnadze

This lay-out of names does indeed make a confusing first impression. It gives some idea of the complexities involved. Every change at this level must certainly be taken as the result of carefully calculated political decision regarded, probably even in the Party Organs Department in Moscow, as of definite importance. There are many of them. And when it is realised that every name in this list is (or was) an individual, pursuing his career amid a tense and complicated political situation, motivated by a variety of considerations, and seeking to secure himself (at least in many cases) by a system of reinsurances and ambiguity of position, something of the difficulty of the investigator becomes apparent. And this is but one republic.

On the other hand, in a sense, this table makes excellent practice. For it is doubtful if there is any single student in the free world who would pretend to understand it, or even to have gone into it very thoroughly. Thus, in a way, it presents a fairly fresh field for an exercise in the sense in which the much-gone-into Moscow variations do not.

These tables can be referred back to in considering the events now described.

That Stalin took a close personal interest in his native Georgia is undoubted. During the 1951-52 purge such things were frequently stated as 'Comrade Stalin found deficiencies in the leadership of the Communist Party and Komsomol organisation of Georgia . . . and showed ways to correct mistakes' (Mgeladze at the XIXth Congress of the Georgian Komsomol, May 15, 1952). And, as we shall see, in 1956 Khrushchev said in his Secret Speech that 'Stalin had personally dictated' the Central Committee resolutions on Georgia made at this time.

Beria was 'directed by the Party to Chekist work' in April 1921, and 'from 1921 to 1931 he held leading posts in the organs of Soviet Intelligence and Counter-intelligence' (according to his biography in the *Large Soviet Encyclopaedia*, second edition). These posts included Deputy Chairman of the Cheka in Georgia and again in Azerbaidzhan, Chairman of the Georgian G.P.U. and Chairman of the Transcaucasian G.P.U. He became First Secretary of the Georgian Communist Party and Secretary of the Transcaucasian Party Committee in November 1931; and in 1932 First Secretary of the latter and

K

Secretary of the former. In 1934 he was a full member of the All-Union Central Committee. In 1938 he gave up his Party posts and returned to the State Security organs first as Deputy People's Commissar and then, in December 1938, as People's Commissar for Internal Affairs in Moscow, becoming a candidate members of the Politburo in 1939.

In the public indictment of Beria in *Pravda* on December 17, 1953 (see Appendix VI), he and his accomplices are accused of 'having elbowed their way to responsible posts by means of these criminal methods in the Transcaucasus and Georgia and later in the U.S.S.R. Ministry of Internal Affairs'. And the careers of his co-accused, even as stated in brief in the indictment, show the way in which Beria's adherents were shifted to and fro between positions in Georgia and the central apparatus of the M.V.D. Dekanozov, Kobulov and Goglidze are all mentioned as having held posts in both centres. The same, though this is not there stated, is true of Merkulov.

Beria's double career in the Party and the security organs in Transcaucasia clearly gave him a very powerful position there, and, while he brought many of his Caucasian adherents to the centre to replace those N.K.V.D. officials who fell with Yezhov, he left enough to make a good effort at keeping the area solid — and indeed sometimes sent people back from the centre, as in the case of Dekanozov, who became Minister of Internal Affairs in Georgia in April 1953, having for the previous fourteen years worked in the Ministry of Foreign Affairs and the Chief Administration for Soviet Property Abroad.

Beria's special interest in Georgia — and to a lesser extent in Transcaucasia as a whole — was publicly recognised long after he had left the republic. He reassumed control of the area for the purposes of the war. The Georgian C.P. always made a point of sending special greetings to him, even at the Republican Party Congress of September 1952. He was sent down, as in April 1952, to represent the Moscow Politburo when local changes had to be put through. He seized control with great ease and completeness in April 1953. And on his fall, his nominees fell too (as well as the First Secretaries in Armenia and Azerbaidzhan, also linked with him for years).

The other chief figures in the period under review are Baramiya — Second Secretary until his fall in November 1951, and restored to the Bureau in April 1953; Charkviani, First Secretary until he 'left the republic' on being removed in March 1952; and Mgeladze, First Secretary from Charkviani's dismissal until he was himself removed under grave charges in April 1953.

The situation in the leadership of the Georgian Party was reasonably stable from Beria's departure in 1938 till 1947–49, when there were a number of not very startling changes. These are, however, of possible significance as implying that Charkviani's ruling apparatus was becoming increasingly manned by persons without as direct links with Beria as their predecessors had had. Those of the 1949 Bureau who had come up in the past year or two were: Tskhovrebashvili, 1949; Shaduri, 1948; Gogua, 1948; Ketskhoveli, 1947; Zambakhidze, 1948. The Bureau elected in January 1949 then settled down without change (except for the death of one member in February 1951) until November 1951.

In that month there commenced a series of catastrophic changes. But first came the announcement of an administrative reorganisation. This was contained in a decree of the Praesidium of the Supreme Soviet of November 1951 'On the formation of the Tbilisi and Kutaisi provinces within the Georgian Republic' (*Bulletin of the Supreme Soviet*, No. 47, 1951).

This is relevant to the great accusation made in the period 1951–52 — of 'sheftsvo', which may be translated 'patronage', and referred to the practice of little chiefdoms forming in which everything depended on the influence of a local boss, more or less immune to Party orders. Already in the September 1950 issue of the Georgian organ *Komunisti*, Mgeladze had an article on this theme which was later stated (in *Zarya Vostoka* of September 19, 1952) to have been a warning to the Charkviani regime. There is at least an implication that he was put up to it, or at least that his point, like himself, was rapidly taken up by Stalin.

As the setting up of the new Georgian provinces was said to be a help in overcoming 'sheftstvo', and as Stalin was personally praised for the decision, it must be seen as in some way providing a direct link with Moscow, enabling the ordinary channels through the Republican Secretariat to be by-passed.

(Provinces were set up at the same time in certain other Union republics, so it seems to have been adopted as a general measure of security against too much power falling into the hands of the Republican Party authorities; but it was only in Georgia that anything was said of the reasons.) Evidently not only the appointments to the Kutaisi and Tbilisi posts but the direct control, too, in important matters at least, lay in the hands of the Party Organs Department of the Central Committee of the C.P.S.U.

This illustrates some of the mechanics of the struggle for power. Actual power is no doubt more important than the machinery of its operation (it is clear enough, for instance, that in April 1953 the new appointments in Georgia were simply Beria's nominees, and not those desired by the Secretariat, or even the majority of his colleagues, but only acquiesced in). But even Stalin could not fully control the emergence of local power groups without a definite effort, so long as instructions went through the leaders of the group itself, and reports came back, in the main, from them too. The new provincial secretaries formed a counterbalance which could be relied on in its own interests to show great keenness and activity in doing the job, without much further effort from the centre — an interesting example of the system of checks and balances through which the operation of power in the U.S.S.R. is maintained.

The natural assumption is that Moscow was able to deal directly with the new provincial secretaries (either formally or informally), and in any case that the direct power of the Georgian Bureau was weakened. That the appointees to the new provincial posts were hostile to Beria (and to those disgraced in November 1951 and rehabilitated by Beria himself in 1953) may be deduced from the fact that both of them were removed from the Bureau by Beria after Stalin's death and never reappeared even as members of the Georgian Central Committee. That the greater powers and status given to the provincial secretaries were not in accord with Beria's ideas is shown, too, by the fact that the provinces were liquidated at the same time as his purge of his opponents, by a decree of the Praesidium of the Supreme Soviet of April 23, 1953 (*Collection of Laws of the U.S.S.R. and Decrees of the Praesidium of the Supreme Soviet, 1938–58*).

The November 1951 announcement of the Central Committee of the Georgian Party stated:

Recently it has become known that the Second Secretary of the Central Committee of the C.P. (b) of Georgia, Baramiya, M. I., Minister of Justice, Rapava, A. N., and the Prosecutor of the Republic, Shoniya, B. Ya., have been extending protection to certain officials who have committed crimes and have been shielding them in every possible way.

Subsequently reference was made, among other things, to failure to implement Soviet laws regarding the struggle with thieves of State and public property; to the undue mildness of sentences imposed; to the condonation by officials in the Prosecutor's Office of anti-State activities; to signs of a liberal attitude in the cases of bribery; to an inadequate struggle against speculation and hooliganism. The Georgian Press produced ample evidence of cases of officials who had committed these very offences. It emphasised the need to deal appropriately with leading officials who thought that Party and State regulations did not refer to them, 'and must be removed from leading posts without hesitation regardless of their services in the past. Another type which must be removed is that of the prattlers who are unable to lead and organise; a third is of the officials who are contemptuous of the masses and do not listen to warnings from below.'

Baramiya had become a member of the Bureau fairly early, in 1943, when Beria's influence was strong. Indeed, this was when Beria was in the Caucasus, with general control of the area during the war.

All those named were dismissed from their posts, to be arrested later. The purge was accompanied by a strong attack on a wide range of economic, party and administrative malpractices. Changes in the leading body included the entry of the secretaries of the new provinces of Kutaisi and Tbilisi, Mgeladze and Lelashvili, and the promotion of the Minister of State Security, Rukhadze, to full membership.

On December 22, 1951, a plenum of the Georgian Central Committee was held at which further changes took place. Shaduri was removed from the Bureau and Secretariat and Zambakhidze from the Bureau, and two new secretaries were brought in — M. K. Balavadze and Kvirkveliya.

In January 1951 Zodelava was removed from his post as leader of the Georgian Komsomol, together with all the other secretaries of that body. It was later stated that Baramiya, Rapava and he had been the victims of a case fabricated by Rukhadze, and this appears to have been what, as Khrushchev later revealed in the Secret Speech, was known as the Mingrelian conspiracy. The allegation was that a treacherous nationalist organisation had been formed. No more was heard of Shoniya, but the other three were rehabilitated alive in April 1953, so they may not have been charged with major guilt in the matter: but more probably they simply had not yet come to trial. (Rapava was shot in 1955 on other charges.)

What Khrushchev said in 1956 was:

> Instructive in the same way is the case of the Mingrelian nationalist organisation which supposedly existed in Georgia. As is known, resolutions by the Central Committee of the Communist Party of the Soviet Union were made concerning this case in November 1951, and March 1952. These resolutions were made without prior discussion with the Political Bureau. Stalin had personally dictated them. They made serious accusations against many loyal Communists. On the basis of falsified documents, it was proven that there existed in Georgia a supposedly nationalistic organisation whose objective was the liquidation of the Soviet power in that republic with the help of imperialist powers.

Mingrelia is the wedge of Georgia between Abkhazia and the River Rion, and fell into the new Kutaisi province. But it seems plain that the 'Mingrelian' conspiracy refers not to this rather small area, but to a group of Mingrelians powerful in Georgia as a whole. Otherwise they would scarcely have been accused of having as their objective 'the liquidation of the Soviet power in that republic'. In fact Baramiya, Rapava, Shoniya and Zodelava, all those of whom it has publicly been stated that they were victimised at this time, were all Mingrelians, as was Beria himself. And, in Georgian conditions, it seems that such local affiliations are extremely persistent.

On April 6, 1952, the Georgian Supreme Soviet passed a decree 'on expelling M. I. Baramiya', unpublished until rescinded a year later (see *Zarya Vostoka*, April 16, 1953). The omission of 'Comrade' from Baramiya's name is probably significant.

Meanwhile, in March 1952 further decisions had been taken by Stalin (as stated in Khrushchev's Secret Speech), and the First Secretary, Charkviani, now fell and was replaced by Mgeladze. Another Secretary, Kvirkveliya, was also dismissed.

Mgeladze, in his speech to the Tbilisi Party Conference on April 13, 1952, said:

We have to re-create a single, and genuinely Bolshevik will within the Georgian Communist Party. We have to make redoubled efforts to rally it and to unite it in an indivisible whole. We will allow no one, whether he was on the old Committee or is on the new, to attempt to exercise the kind of *shefstvo* which for the last few years has prevented the Party from possessing a single will. For this period there have existed only the wills of separate bosses who have gathered round themselves groups of loyal followers: these un-Bolshevik practices we must eradicate. Unfortunately we still have with us members who seek to arrange appointments and promotions behind the closed doors of the Central Committee and who drop hints about the chance of being appointed to this post or that. An uncompromising campaign will be prosecuted against these abuses of the former Central Committee and every attempt of this kind will be nipped in the bud.

By virtue of uncovering and expelling elements inimical to the Party and State and removing from positions of responsibility members who are apolitical and spineless, the Georgian Communist Party has gained added strength and toughness and has become an impregnable fortress to its enemies and an indestructible bastion of communism.

The former Central Committee did great harm to Georgia and the Georgian people by disregarding the political side of things. We should have achieved considerably more in the economic and cultural fields had the right political guidance been forthcoming. The Central Committee of the All-Union Communist Party and Comrade Stalin have rendered Georgia a great service by the establishment of the Tiflis and Kutaisi Oblasts, which has brought the administration into closer touch with the country and made it more concrete (*Zarya Vostoka*, April 14, 1952).

At the Georgian Komsomol Conference on May 15, 1952, Mgeladze again introduces Stalin's direct control of the purge (resulting, in this case, in Zodelava's fall):

Comrade Stalin found deficiencies in the leadership of the Communist Party and Komsomol Organisation of Georgia, which threatened to have serious consequences, and showed ways to correct mistakes (*Zarya Vostoka*, May 16, 1952).

He added:

There have been instances of intimidation of persons exposing shortcomings in the work of the Central Committee of the Georgian Komsomol. The complacency and conceit prevalent in the Central Committee of the Georgian Komsomol have engendered political blindness and lack of political watchfulness. Taking advantage of this, persons capable of causing us injury have, through ingratiation, manœuvred themselves into positions of confidence and filtered into positions of authority. (Ibid.)

Associated with this was, significantly anticipating the tone of the ensuing year in the whole U.S.S.R., a charge of insufficient political enthusiasm throughout the organisation.

In July 1952 Rukhadze, who, as Minister of State Security, was responsible for the Baramiya purge, was removed. Some reason to think that Rukhadze's removal may have been a partial victory for Beria — perhaps granted as part of a Stalin deception plan — is that his replacement, Kochlavashvili, though dropped from the Bureau in April 1953, only reverted to the position of Deputy Minister under Dekanozov, and was not removed until Beria's fall. (Whereas Loladze, the M.V.D. minister, appointed from the local Party Organs department in April 1952, was dismissed in April 1953, and regained a minor post on Beria's fall, while the man he had replaced, Karavadze, regained a post as Deputy Minister in April 1953, and fell with Beria.)

In September 1952, at the Georgian Party Congress, a Bureau based on the year's charges was elected.

There is some evidence that the struggle in Georgia was strongly contested. Presumably, with Beria still in the seat of power, and Stalin's intentions not yet made explicit, the factions opposed to Mgeladze still had some hope. The Georgian press, and political speeches, of late 1952 are full of references to resistance to Party directives and threats against obstreperous officials. Gogua, who had been demoted in April 1952 from Chairman of the Praesidium of the Georgian Supreme Soviet, was attacked in September 1952 for failing to make any self-criticism, and speeches and an article he finally produced were strongly censured. He was removed from his lesser post in February 1953. It is also notable that among the many criticisms of 'bourgeois nationalism' made at this period there seem to be none from men later proved to be in Beria's favour. And Kvirkveliya, who became a member of the Georgian Secretariat in December 1951, during the removal of those later rehabilitated by Beria, seems to have calculated that a change of sides was desirable soon afterwards, and was removed in May 1952: he was attacked at the September 1952 Republican Congress for 'political dishonesty'.

'Those who are seeking to divide Georgia and exercise chieftainship over separate provinces or to set one province against another, will be crushed in Stalin's manner' (*Report* of the Georgian C.C. to the Georgian Party Congress, September 1952). This implies a live issue. Its use of the expression 'will be crushed' seems to mean that a trial was to be staged later.

At this Congress, Mgeladze spoke of the troubles faced by

the Georgian Communist Party . . . Central Committee at two of its plenary sessions (November 1951 and April 1952). These plenary sessions adopted resolutions based upon the decision of the Central Committee of the All-Union Communist Party and upon Comrade Stalin's personal instructions. This political blindness of the former heads of the Central Committee enabled persons hostile to us to worm their way into confidence and to harm the Party and State. Comrade Charkviani, former Secretary of the Georgian Communist Party Central Committee, committed a major error when he entrusted all the organisational work, the selection of personnel and check-up on fulfilment, to persons alien to us, to people who had penetrated into the apparatus of the Central Committee and pursued aims hostile to the Party.

It has now become obvious to everyone that the boastful speeches by former Secretary of the Georgian Communist Party Central Committee Charkviani and the numerous boastful press and radio reports about unprecedented gains in the development of Tbilisi were false and intended to deceive our public. (*Stir in the hall*.) . . .

If this anti-Party principle of 'precedence' and 'patronage' had not received a proper rebuff from the Party, then 'patrons' (shefy) would have emerged who would have liked to have taken under their 'lofty hand' 'their' provinces and protect people who had been found guilty of some offence, trying thereby to strengthen the authority of their patronage among the 'masses'. If this had happened, Georgia would have disintegrated into a number of 'province princedoms' which would have had 'real' power, and of the Communist Party of Georgia and the Government of the Georgian S.S.R. there would have remained only emptiness. . . . This was the danger which was created in the Communist Party of Georgia by the mistakes, political blindness, major political failure in the work of the old leadership of the Central Committee of Georgia and, in the first place, of its former First Secretary, Charkviani (*Report* of Mgeladze, September 15, 1952, to the XVth Congress of the Georgian C.P., *Zarya Vostoka*, September 16–17 and 18, 1952).

The extent of the purge in Georgia was very great, and quite comparable (that is, in dismissals rather than deaths) with what had occurred in the time of the Great Purge under Yezhov. *Pravda* of January 30, 1953, states that the number of changes in secretaries and heads of departments in provincial, city and district Party Committees in Georgia was already 427 — and two major purges were yet to come. Dzhashi's report to the XVIIIth Congress of the C.P.S.U. in 1939 had spoken of 500 such changes in Georgia in the comparable period.

Stalin's death produced a complete revolution. The context will be seen in Chapter Nine.

A plenary session of the Central Committee in Georgia was announced on April 21, 1953, as having established that 'the former secretary of the Central Committee, Mgeladze, took an active part in the arrest of completely innocent workers in the creation of a provocational case concerning non-existent nationalism fabricated by the enemy of the Party and the people, Rukhadze . . . who placed their hopes on stirring up feelings of national enmity, creating dissatisfaction among the Soviet people, smashing honest cadres of loyal people, getting rid of active workers of the Communist party and government of Georgia.' Mgeladze admitted that he was one of the instigators of 'a stupid and provocational story' about the existence in Georgia of a nationalist group (*Zarya Vostoka*, April 21, 1953).

The same issue announced the expulsion of Mgeladze from the Tbilisi City Party Committee. It also reported that he had 'admitted' the falsification of charges for 'personal careerist purposes'. Others criticised included Getiya, secretary of the Abkhaz provincial party committee, and the two Balavadzes, secretaries of the Kutaisi provincial committee and the Tbilisi city committee respectively, for 'intimidation'.

During the ensuing period a series of Party and government changes were announced piecemeal, amounting to a very complete turnover. The details are hardly worth listing.

On April 15, 1953, Bakradze, newly appointed Prime Minister of Georgia, submitted a Government to the Georgian Supreme Soviet. He said:

> I want in a few words to give you explanations concerning candi-
> dates to the body of the government of Georgia, Comrades Baramiya,
> Rapava and Zodelava. It has now been fully established by the
> organs concerned that, against these comrades and some other
> workers loyal to the Party and Soviet people, the enemy of the
> people and Party, former Minister of State Security . . . N. M.
> Rukhadze had cooked up an entirely false and provocative affair
> concerning a non-existent nationalism whose victims were eminent
> workers of our republic. . . . Rukhadze and his accomplices have
> been arrested and will be severely punished.

Baramiya, Rapava and Zodelava were made Minister of Agriculture, Minister of State Control and First Deputy Chairman of the Council of Ministers, respectively. Bakradze said of them:

> Each candidate was a member of the Communist Party, educated
> and hardened by the Georgian organisation of the Lenin–Stalin
> Party, that organisation which over a period of many years was
> directed by the best son of Georgia, the talented pupil of Lenin,
> comrade-in-arms of Stalin, outstanding worker of the Communist
> Party and the great Soviet State, Comrade Lavrenti Pavlovich
> Beria [loud and long applause].

In his speech Bakradze also said:

> Former Secretaries of the Georgian Communist Party Central
> Committee Charkviani and Mgeladze not only failed to manifest the
> elementary ability to make a critical assessment of the provocational
> 'materials' fabricated by Rukhadze, but, on the contrary, fostered
> his dastardly actions. What is more Mgeladze himself took an active
> part in the arrest of completely innocent officials (*Zarya Vostoka*,
> April 16, 1953).

The story, at this stage, carried two implications: that Mgeladze was more responsible than Charkviani for the 1951–

52 purge, as seems likely enough; and that Mgeladze was in
the greatest possible disfavour with those now in authority —
i.e. Beria.

Zarya Vostoka of May 30, 1953, reports a meeting of the
Tbilisi committtee at which Mgeladze, S. Getiya, M. Balavadze and V. Balavadze were attacked and a call was made for
them to be severely disciplined. These four were accused of
'crude administrative pressure, terrorism, and even beating
people up'. On the 'cultural' side there were accusations of
wrong behaviour in connection with museums, and the secretary of the South Ossetian Provincial Party Committee,
Imnadze, was alleged to have taken the initiative in publishing
adulatory verses to Mgeladze (*Zarya Vostoka*, April 29, 1953).

Beria's fall in June 1953 resulted in another revolution in
Tbilisi. This was conducted in two phases: at plenums of the
Georgian Central Committee held in mid-July and mid-
September respectively. First the police, or former police,
adherents of Beria were removed at high speed, while Beria's
own political appointees violently attacked their late patron.
Afterwards they, too, were removed — not merely from their
posts, but from the Central Committee as well.

Zarya Vostoka of July 15, 1953, gives a speech by Bakradze at
a Georgian C.C. plenum just held. He now, of course, condemns
Beria, and makes the point that Charkviani and Mgeladze had
acted 'under Beria's protection'. Bakradze himself was shortly
to fall, but at present the main action taken was the expulsion
of Dekanozov and Mamulov from the Party.

A number of 'accomplices' of Beria's in the M.V.D. in
Georgia were referred to by Tbilisi Radio on July 15,
1953, including Rapava, Rukhadze, Mamulov, Shariya and
Milshtein.

The Georgian Supreme Soviet met on August 18, 1953, and
confirmed decrees of July 12 and July 17, dismissing Dekanozov
and Rapava from their State posts. Bakradze spoke condemning Beria and significantly saying that some of the rehabilitations had been unjustifiable. He himself (together with
Mirtskhulava and Baramiya) was removed at a plenum of the
Georgian C.C. attended by Shatalin on September 20, 1953.
Mzhavanadze was appointed First Secretary. Other changes
followed.

Mzhavanadze seems never to have worked in Georgia since he left military school there in 1927. His work since the early 'thirties had been as a political commissar in the Army. Since the war he had served in Ukrainian military districts — from 1950 to 1953 as a member of the Military Council of the Carpathian Military District, and member of the Ukranian Central Committee and Orgburo (*Large Soviet Encyclopaedia*, Vol. 51, article 'Mzhavanadze'), presumably being as much a transfer from the Khrushchev machine in the Ukraine as the various 'enkos' who now began to appear in R.S.F.S.R. posts.

Purge and counter-purge had discredited (or shot) so many of the experienced that in September 1953 no less than four Georgians whose careers had been outside the republic had to be brought in: Mzhavanadze (the new First Secretary), Georgadze (shortly to become Second Secretary), Inauri (M.V.D.) and Gotsiridze (Head of the local Party Organs Department). In addition, it now became the practice for the Russian C.-in-C. to take his place on the Bureau, starting with Efimov in July 1953. And though right up to Beria's fall the Bureau had included several members of some years' experience, that elected on September 22, 1953, included only one man (Dzhavakhishvili) who had served even one year.

A number of Stalin's September 1952 selections re-emerged in minor posts: Ketskhoveli, Chkhubianishvili, V. D. Budzhia-shvili (who became Deputy Minister of State Control of Georgia). On the other hand, none of the Beria nominees has reappeared in office.

The mass effect of the double purge conducted for Beria in April 1953 and against him in July–September 1953 can be seen by a comparison between the Central Committee of the Georgian Communist Party elected at its congresses of 1952 and 1954. Of the seventy-four full members of the C.C. elected in 1952 no fewer than fifty did not appear in 1954, even as candidate members or members of the Revision Commission. Only one was demoted (to candidate member) rather than removed entirely. And only twenty-three remained. Of the thirty-seven 1952 candidate members, twenty-three were nowhere listed in 1954, one was demoted to the Revision Commission, and eight were promoted to full membership.

Even these figures do not tell the whole story, for they do not take into account the members co-opted in April 1953 and removed later. These certainly included Baramiya, Zodelava, Dekanozov and Mamulov, since they became members of the Bureau of the C.C., and almost certainly Rapava as well, from his Ministerial position. And a number of those named as replacements in provincial and other posts and not previously members of the Georgian Central Committee most probably obtained the Central Committee status of their predecessors. If these could be taken into account the turnover would appear greater still.

In Armenia, too, the purge had been intense. Of the eleven full members of the Republican Party Bureau elected in 1952, ten had been removed by the Congress of February 1954. Seven of these had already gone by May 1953. Casualties in the Central Committee were also very high.

We may also note the fall of the Georgians who had been members of the C.P.S.U. Central Committee elected in October 1952. In the new C.C. elected in February 1956 the following no longer had places (apart from the dead Stalin and the executed Beria, Goglidze and Kobulov): Ketskhoveli and Mgeladze (full members in 1952) and Bakradze and Tskovrebashvili (candidate members in 1952) — a clean sweep. The three representatives from Armenia and Azerbaidzhan had also been replaced.

Rapava and Rukhadze were shot together as accomplices of Beria in September 1955. (See Chapter Eleven and Appendix VI.) In brief, the difficulties associated with this Rapava–Rukhadze question alone may be summarised as follows:

(1) Rapava was dismissed in November 1951 and arrested soon afterwards.
(2) Rukhadze was dismissed in July 1952.
(3) Rukhadze (with Mgeladze, who had meanwhile remained in power unaffected by Rukhadze's dismissal) was blamed for arresting, beating and fabricating a case against Rapava. He was dismissed and arrested and Rapava reinstated in April 1953.
(4) Both Rapava and Rukhadze were denounced as devoted to Beria in July 1953.

(5) Both were shot as accomplices of Beria in September
1955.

An interesting point is that the allegations in their trial avoid
the Mingrelian Case, for fabricating which Rukhadze had been
under arrest since at least April 1953, and which Khrushchev
was again to refer to as an absurd frame-up in his Secret Speech
of February 1956. Indeed, no definite allegation of recent
actions was made, unlike in the Beria case proper. (In fact, as
far as Rapava is concerned, he is by implication not accused of
any action since the war, by being described only in connection
with posts he had held in the old People's Commissariat for
Internal Affairs — i.e. prior to the change in that organisation's
title.)

An important conclusion from the Georgian events is that
the official 'facts', without interpretation, are meaningless.
This is not just because they do not speak for themselves, but
because they contradict each other. It is impossible that Beria
'protected' Charkviani *and* Mgeladze *and* the April 1953
regime's collection of Mgeladze victims and future co-defendants in the Beria Case itself. It is impossible that Rapava,
arrested in 1951–52 by Rukhadze, and Rukhadze, himself
arrested in April 1953, on Rapava's release, for framing him,
were at the time conspirators equally 'devoted' to Beria.

To approach a general understanding of these Georgian
events it will be sufficient to consider only a few of these names:
Charkviani, Baramiya, Mgeladze, Rapava and Rukhadze, let
us say. If we recapitulate, we have the following main events as
announced to account for:

(*a*) The removal and later arrest of Baramiya and Rapava
    in connection with a 'nationalist' conspiracy
    (November 1951 to April 1952).

(*b*) The removal of Charkviani for allowing these alien ele-
    ments to gain control of vital posts (April 1952).

(*c*) Beria's presence at the April plenum at which all this was
    formalised.

(*d*) Rukhadze's direct fabrication of the evidence and carry-
    ing out of the arrests.

(*e*) Rukhadze's removal (June 1952).

(*f*) Denunciation and arrest of Rukhadze for the frame-up; attack on Charkviani for passive, and Mgeladze for active complicity. Release of Baramiya and Rapava and their promotion (April 1953).

(*g*) Denunciation of Charkviani and Mgeladze for having committed their errors and crimes with Beria's encouragement (July 1953).

(*h*) Denunciation of Rapava and Rukhadze as among those devoted to Beria (July 1953). Presumed arrest of the former. Removal of Baramiya by September 1953.

(*i*) Trial and execution of Rapava and Rukhadze as fellow conspirators of Beria's (September 1955).

There seems to be an excellent case for regarding these complexities as due to the interaction of three rather than two main factions. On this view Beria's allies, and Stalin's new men of 1951, should be complemented by a group built up by Charkviani, no doubt with Stalin's consent, over the years since Beria left the republic. The evidence is as follows: Bakradze can be definitely labelled a sympathiser of Beria. He was Prime Minister under Beria in 1938, was restored to that post in Beria's period of complete ascendancy in 1953, and was expelled even from the Georgian Central Committee after Beria's fall. In 1946 he was replaced as Premier by a new arrival on the Buro, Chkhubianishvili, and demoted to Deputy Premier. Similarly with G. F. Sturua, a member of the 1938 Bureau who became President of the Praesidium of the Georgian Supreme Soviet on Makharadze's death in 1941 and was replaced by the new man Gogua and removed from the Bureau in 1948. Sturua, too, was restored to the Bureau in April 1953, and expelled from the C.C. on Beria's fall. When Charkviani fell in April 1952 both Chkhubianishvili and Gogua were demoted: Chkhubianishvili giving up the Premiership to Ketskhoveli and dropping to President of the Praesidium of the Supreme Soviet, and Gogua being dropped from the Buro entirely.

That Beria in April 1953 rehabilitated the purgees of November 1951, but *not* those who had fallen or lost ground in April 1952 (indeed he expelled the last survivor of these from the Bureau), indicates that he regarded Charkviani's group as enemies: in fact he had Charkviani publicly attacked for complicity with Rukhadze. We may take it, then, that Charkviani was prepared to compete with the Mgeladze group for Stalin's favours and to throw Beria's protégés to the wolves.

The categories arrived at under this conception may themselves be divided up. Beria's adherents consist of

(a) Those who had followed him closely, from Georgia through the M.V.D.; Dekanozov and Mamulov, both arrested immediately after his fall.

(b) The rehabilitees of the Mingrelian case: Baramiya and Zodelava.

(c) Georgian politicians who had remained in the republic — like Bakradze, Sturua and Mirtskhulava.

(b) and (c) were only expelled from the C.C. in September 1953.

Beria had also promoted the new men Romelashvili and Chkhikvadze, and these seem to have had no long faction record to annoy the victors. They lost their posts in the Bureau and Secretariat in February 1954, but Romelashvili only left the C.C. in 1956, while Chkhikvadze's name still appeared.

Stalin's 'new' group can be divided into two.

(a) Veterans of an earlier period like V. D. Budzhiashvili (who had briefly held a secretaryship in the late 'forties) and Ketskhoveli, who lost their posts in April 1953, but reappeared in minor positions after Beria's fall,

(b) truly new men like Mgeladze, the Balavadzes and Getiya, who bore the brunt of the attack in April 1953 and have never surfaced since.

In the first place, Beria's own position is clear. As soon as he was in a position to enforce his own views he filled the Georgian Bureau with his own nominees. Mgeladze he treated as an enemy pure and simple; and Rukhadze, too, whom he had arrested.

That Charkviani was also, though more mildly, denounced in April 1953 seems to indicate that he went along with the first phase of Stalin's purge in an attempt to preserve his own position, and that Beria did not forgive this.

As to the, rather vague, attack on Beria for 'protecting' Charkviani and Mgeladze, all that can be said in its favour is

L

purely formal. Beria did preside at the Georgian plenum which removed Baramiya, and received devoted telegrams even from Mgeladze's plenums and congress. But these can only be explained as simple protocol. Beria was in no position to oppose policies undermining his own power, nor had he yet sunk low enough to be openly excluded from verbal assurances of support. The words are refuted by the actions. And it seems plain that we must lay down one important principle to account for the *ex post facto* blame laid on Beria for the actions against himself of both Charkviani and Mgeladze. This is that, as far as possible, the public enemy of the moment be blamed for the actions of all those in his purview who are regarded as too compromised, or too expendable, for rehabilitation. Such a principle allows us to account for certain paradoxes. At the same time it gives special significance to cases where it is *not* found possible to attribute a given crime to a fallen enemy — as in the failure to link Beria with the Doctors' Plot.

In spite of the high turnover, it seems probable that even in Georgia the final stages in planned purges were never quite reached before some new coup made them abortive. (The possible exception is the Beria Bureau of April 1953.) There were still a few lukewarm-looking characters in Stalin's September 1952 bureau, and it might be expected that when and if the Moscow purge had really got moving, Bakradze and others would have gone.

The Georgian cases show also, as indeed can be seen from other material, that the steps may be gradual. No interpretation of Stalin's moves in Georgia in 1951 and 1952 seems reasonable except on the view that Stalin was *gradually* lessening Beria's influence — even perhaps allowing him an occasional apparent concession, as in the removal of Rukhadze in June 1952.

The case of Dzhavakishvili shows that it was possible for one person at least to be completely acceptable to all factions, remaining in the Bureau during Stalin's anti-Beria period, during Beria's purge of his enemies and right through the next anti-Beria purge. Those who were simply demoted to the Central Committee show that there is a continuous gradation between those acceptable to all parties, through those only deserving mild censureship and demotion, and those who are quietly removed, down to those who are shot. These facts emerge most clearly in the Georgian affair, partly because so many people are involved. But in any case it shows that even though a broad theory about a struggle between factions is undoubtedly correct it does not do to have too *simpliste* a conception of the detail. The struggle for power in the U.S.S.R. should not be viewed as taking place *mutatis mutandis* as in the British Parliament, with the whole body of those concerned divided into two or three clear-cut groups. If a comparison of this sort were to be made it would be better to think in terms of the Palais Bourbon. Moreover, it is clear from the whole Rapava–Rukhadze incident that it is sometimes, if not impossible, at least of doubtful utility to construct a theory to reconcile the contradictory elements in the official evidence.

A further example of these difficulties may be seen in *A History of the U.S.S.R. in the Epoch of Socialism* (Moscow 1957), which says, 'In 1951–1952 the so-called Mingrelian Case was created, as a result of which many honest Party and Soviet workers were repressed'. It then accuses Beria 'and his myrmidons, who for a protracted period held the leadership of the C.C. of the C.P. of Georgia', of 'activising bourgeois-nationalist elements in the Union Republics' and in Georgia in particular. Thus it is belatedly implied, though *not* explicitly asserted, that the Case was Beria's responsibility.

Mzhavanadze, at a plenum of the Georgian Central Committee in August 1956, had listed the policies of Beria and his agents, ruling the republic over a long period. He 'promoted the activisation of nationalist elements'; he 'pursued an essentially anti-kolkhoz policy'; and he 'tried in every way to create an active barrier between the republic's leading Party and Soviet organs and the Central Committee of the C.P.S.U.' (*Zarya Vostoka*, August 23, 1956). These accusations fit well with the main issues in Georgia over the whole period. They also raise the more general question of Beria's bid for power, which is dealt with later, in Chapter Nine.

CHAPTER EIGHT

THE XIXTH CONGRESS AND THE DOCTORS' PLOT, 1951–53

WE may date the last phase of the struggle for power during Stalin's lifetime as beginning towards the end of 1951. At this time we find the Mingrelian purge in Georgia, almost certainly aimed at Beria's supporters, and the best estimate of a date for the accession of a new Minister of State Security, Ignatiev, not from Beria's entourage. It was also in November 1951 that the purges in Eastern Europe, which had hitherto struck at the 'Titoist' revolutionaries associated with Zhdanov, turned against the international M.V.D. connection with the arrest of Slansky in Prague. With this arrest came the introduction of the new anti-Semitic note.

At the same time a turn took place in the propaganda line. Once again, as after the war, calls for greater discipline and vigilance, and for a more rigorous attitude to State property and to the kolkhoz system began to become frequent.

On August 20, 1952, *Pravda* announced that 'there has recently taken place in Moscow a plenum of the Central Committee of the C.P.S.U.(b)'. This called the XIXth Congress of the Party for October 5. And it listed the rapporteurs. The agenda was:

(1) Report of the Central Committee — Secretary of the Central Committee Comrade Malenkov.

(2) Report of the Central Revision Commission — President of the Revision Commission Comrade Moskatov.

(3) Directives on the Fifth Five-year Plan 1951–55 — Chairman of Gosplan Comrade Saburov.

(4) Changes in the Constitution of the C.P.S.U.(b) — Secretary of the Central Committee Comrade Khrushchev.

(5) Election of the central organs of the Party.

The XVIIIth Congress had been called by a plenum of the Central Committee announced in *Pravda* on January 27, 1939, for March 10, 1939. (As in 1952, the decision is signed by Stalin as Secretary of the Central Committee.) The agenda of the XVIIIth Congress was: Central Committee report — Stalin; report of the Central Revision Commission — Vladimirsky; report of the Delegate to the Executive Committee of the Comintern — Manuilsky; report on the Five-Year Plan — Molotov; report on changes in the Constitution of the Party — Zhdanov. At the XVIIth Congress of 1934 also, Stalin had made the report on the work of the Central Committee; Molotov and Kuibyshev had reported on the Five-Year Plan; and Kaganovich had spoken on organisational questions, including the changes in the constitution of the Party.

Moskatov's report is perfectly ordinary and does not indicate any special importance on his part. The others are obviously significant. They seem to indicate that in August Malenkov was in favour, as well as Khrushchev. And they give at least some negative support to the idea that Molotov was not. A further note on the date of this plenum is that it must have taken place (if it did) at the time of the execution of Lozovsky, etc., in the 'Crimean Affair' (see Appendix V). In this a group of Jewish politicians and writers were shot.

When the Congress met, its main themes were two: *Economic Problems of Socialism* was taken as the banner of the new phase of economic and ideological policy. And a very strong line was laid down for greater economic and State discipline and vigilance against enemies.

In his Report of the Central Committee on October 5, 1952 Malenkov said:

A spirit of negligence has penetrated our Party organisations. There are cases of Party, economic, Soviet and other executives relaxing their vigilance and failing to see what is going on around them; there are cases of divulgence of Party and state secrets. Some responsible workers get absorbed in economic affairs; they allow their heads to be turned by successes, and begin to forget that we are still in a capitalist encirclement, that the enemies of the Soviet state are working persistently to smuggle their agents into our country and to utilise unstable elements in Soviet society for their own malignant ends.

Khrushchev spoke equally strongly:

Manifestations of political carelessness and gullibility and instances of disclosing Party and state secrets have become fairly widespread among Communists. Many persons, carried away by
economic successes, forget the Party's instruction on the necessity of
taking every measure to increase vigilance. We must always remember the capitalist encirclement, remember that the enemies of
the socialist state have tried and will try to send their agents into our
country for subversive work. In order to achieve their foul purposes,
hostile elements try to make their way into offices in the Party, state
and economic organisations and to take advantage of careless,
talkative individuals who do not know how to keep Party and state
secrets.

It is the duty of Party organisations to put a decisive end to
political carelessness, to train Communists in the strictest guarding
of Party and state secrets. Greater political vigilance on the part of
Communists, an implacable struggle against any intrigues whatsoever by hostile elements, are important requisites for further
strengthening our party and the Soviet state. Every Communist
must remember that vigilance is necessary on every sector and under
all circumstances.

Poskrebyshev, the man most closely and directly associated
with Stalin (later described in Khrushchev's Secret Speech as
Stalin's 'shield-bearer'), was given unwonted prominence. He
linked economic offences with espionage in a manner which was
to be typical in the following months:

Comrade Stalin teaches that the safeguarding of socialist property
is one of the basic functions of our state. Soviet law strictly punishes
pilferers of public property. The Stalin Constitution states that
persons who infringe on socialist property are enemies of the people.

This is why every Party and Soviet official, every honest Soviet
citizen must regard pilferers of socialist property not only as enemies
of the state but as their own personal enemies as well.

Comrade Stalin has pointed out that 'a thief who pilfers public
property and undermines the interests of the national economy is
the same as a spy and a traitor, if not worse'.

Nevertheless events indicate that many local Party organisations
obviously underestimate the full danger of the pilfering of public
property. Such events occurred, for example, in the Kiev and
Zaporozhe Party organisations in the Ukraine. . . .

Lenin and Stalin teach that the slightest lawlessness is a crack
which our enemies use to undermine our social and state system.

And we have enemies: capitalist encirclement continues to exist. It is not a coincidence that the brazen U.S. imperialists are allocating tremendous sums for subversive work in the U.S.S.R. and the people's democracies. We must not forget this.

The Party member is required to keep Party and state secrets and to display political vigilance, remembering that the vigilance of Communists is essential on all sectors and under all circumstances, as is stated in the new Statutes.

It may be said without any exaggeration that many negative phenomena in our public life are the result of the incorrect attitude toward Party and state discipline and toward our Soviet laws which has taken root in the minds of certain of our officials (*Pravda*, October 13, 1952).

Shkiryatov, the first speaker in the discussion on Khrushchev's report, while attacking embezzlement, also associated it with the divulging of Party and state secrets (*Pravda*, October 13, 1952).

And the duties of a Party member given under Article 3 of the Revised Party Statutes adopted at the Congress (*Pravda* of October 14, 1952) put much more emphasis on discipline and on Soviet property, and on the reporting of wrong-doings. There was also added a special section on 'Party and state secrets and the display of political vigilance'.

The composition of the Congress praesidium is interesting. As against, for example, that of the XXth Congress, which included the names of all the outgoing and incoming members and candidate members of the Praesidium of the Central Committee, in addition to a number of more honorary local figures, that elected on October 5, 1952, omits three of the old Politburo: Andreyev, Kosygin and Mikoyan. It includes four of the Praesidium about to be elected: Aristov, Andrianov, Korotchenko and Kuusinen.

Other figures given formal honours include: Melnikov (proposer of this praesidium); Brezhnev (proposer of the Congress secretariat); Poskrebyshev (Head of the Congress secretariat); Mgeladze (proposer of the Editorial Commission); Pospelov (head of the Editorial Commission); Patolichev (proposer of the Credentials Commission) and Pegov (Head of the Credentials Commission, and hence presumptively identified as the outgoing Head of the Party Organs Department of the Central Committee).

The Central Committee elected at the Congress in turn elected a new body, the Praesidium of the Central Committee, and a Secretariat (see Appendix I). Meanwhile it listened to the first attack made in this period against members of the leadership. Khrushchev tells us in the Secret Speech:

> Let us consider the first Central Committee plenum held after the Nineteenth Party Congress when Stalin, in his talk at the plenum, characterised Vyacheslav Mikhailovich Molotov and Anastas Ivanovich Mikoyan and suggested that these old workers of our party were guilty on some baseless charges. It is not excluded that had Stalin remained at the helm for another several months Comrades Molotov and Mikoyan would probably have not delivered any speeches at this Congress.
> Stalin evidently had plans to finish off the old members of the Political Bureau. He often stated that Political Bureau members should be replaced by new ones.
> His proposal after the Nineteenth Congress concerning the election of twenty-five persons to the Central Committee Praesidium was aimed at the removal of the old Political Bureau members and the bringing in of less experienced persons so that these would extol him in all sorts of ways.
> We can assume that this was also a design for the future annihilation of the old Political Bureau members.

The new Party Praesidium 'elected' by the Central Committee, after the Congress had, as its very name implies, a more important status than the Politburo — no doubt only a formal point, but even formality is significant in this context. The new Secretariat was greatly enlarged — to ten members. And all its members were also members or candidate members of the Praesidium, which included other members of the Party apparatus, such as Andrianov, the Leningrad First Secretary, and Melnikov, First Secretary in the Ukraine. Moreover, it was exclusively members of the Council of Ministers whom Stalin has been definitely stated as, or can reasonably be deduced as, intending to purge — Molotov, Mikoyan, Voroshilov, Beria as a minimum.

(Apart from Andreyev, the only member of the old Politburo to be dropped from the new Praesidium was Kosygin, who became a candidate member. Kosygin seems originally to have been associated with Zhdanov. He served in Zhdanov's Leningrad fief from 1935 to 1939. He became a candidate member of the Politburo in March 1946, and a full member in 1948. His later service had been entirely in the Ministries of the consumer-goods industries, apart from a period before 1946 when he was Chairman of the Council of Ministers of the R.S.F.S.R. And over the years his links with Zhdanov and his associates had doubtless become less incriminating. His work as an economic technician seems to have been adequate, and though neither in 1952 nor in 1953 were any protectors to emerge willing to restore him to major rank, he retained posts just below the highest level throughout, having presumably given little offence either. In later crises he was to play a significant part.)

For the moment the personnel of neither the Central Committee nor the Praesidium gave a clear-cut view of Stalin's plans. Even given the evident intention of Stalin to rid himself of at least some of the more senior members of the new Praesidium, it is clear that the newly-promoted themselves did not form a coherent body, simply opposed to their predecessors. To compare the careers, both previous and subsequent, of Andrianov, Melnikov, Ignatov, Aristov, Mikhailov and Suslov, for example, makes this obvious. A suggestion has several times been made that the new arrangement, in the Secretariat at least, represents a balance between Khrushchev and Malenkov protégés, and was so intended by Stalin. It is certainly reasonable to associate Ponomarenko, Pegov, and Mikhailov with Malenkov. Brezhnev can be seen as already a connection of Khrushchev's, but though Ignatov and Aristov were later to be closely associated with him against Malenkov, there is little to connect them at this time, and it may be preferable to regard them quite simply as Stalin's appointees.

In the reorganisation following Stalin's death reference is also made to the existence of a 'Bureau of the Praesidium' as a body not provided for in the Party statute.

The question of the composition of the Bureau of the Praesidium is an interesting and important one, and it is typical that it has never been named. Two separate theories at once present themselves: that it was formed of the senior members of the new Praesidium, and that, on the contrary, it was a body selected by Stalin from his new nominees, thus excluding senior members whom he in any case planned, according to Khrushchev, to get rid of. On the face of it the second supposition seems plausible. But there are a number of reasons why it is almost certainly incorrect.

In the first place, it will be noted that in the Secret Speech Khrushchev, who had been making several critical remarks about Stalin's habit of forming small unconstitutional committees within the old Politburo, has nothing to say against the Bureau of the Praesidium. On the contrary, he attacks the large Praesidium itself as being part of a design of Stalin's to overthrow the old Politburo members. The Decree of March 1953 refers to the Bureau as unconstitutional, and sets up in place of the Bureau (and of the large Praesidium itself) a new, small Praesidium. This is perfectly compatible with, in practice, giving the old Bureau the title and powers of the Praesidium.

As we shall see, it is fairly reasonably established that the doctors were arrested not earlier than the beginning of November 1952, and anyhow after the election of the Party Praesidium. In his Secret Speech Khrushchev says that Stalin circulated the doctors' confessions to the 'Political Bureau', which, from all other accounts, had ceased to exist. But Khrushchev's remark may not have been a slip of the tongue for 'Praesidium': he may well have been referring to the 'Bureau of the Praesidium', and indeed the unofficial title may still have been Politburo. If so, there is an implication that the full membership of the Praesidium was not normally assembled or consulted, but simply remained a reserve from which Stalin could replenish his Bureau. That he was (unless prepared actually to arrest a Political Bureau member, as in the case of Voznesensky) a little pernickety on these constitutional forms was shown by his retention of Andreyev on all formal occasions when the Politburo appeared, though he had actually 'excluded him' from the work of that body.

The precise membership of the Bureau still remains obscure. But there are a number of indications.

In the first place, those who appeared on the platform in the Red Square on November 7, 1952, were not the whole Praesidium. With Bulganin on his right as Minister of Defence, on his left Stalin had Malenkov, Beria, Khrushchev, Kaganovitch, Molotov, Shvernik, Pervukhin, Saburov, Mikoyan, Ponomarenko, Suslov, Shkiryatov, Aristov, Pegov, Brezhnev. The six names following Mikoyan are of members of the Secretariat (except Shkiryatov, Chairman of the Party Control Committee, as it was now rechristened). Pegov and Brezhnev were not full members of the Praesidium: if the intention had been to have simply a group of senior members of the Praesidium, there would be no excuse for their presence. If the intention was to have the Bureau of the Praesidium, plus the Secretariat, their presence (as members of the Secretariat) becomes explicable. It is true that two Secretaries, Ignatov and Mikhailov, are missing, but it is easier to account for the absence of two of the Secretariat than of ten of the Praesidium. If we assume that the order is that of the old protocol, by which the Political Bureau appeared on the platform, followed by those members of the Secretariat not on it, we must assume that on this occasion the Bureau membership (or candidate membership) went down at least as far as Mikoyan, since he is not a member of the Secretariat. Whether it went any further cannot be decided.

With Ponomarenko we are perhaps on a border-line case. There is no way of telling if his presence is due only to his membership of the Secretariat or to hypothetical membership of the Bureau. Nevertheless, there is an argument for the latter. After Stalin's death Ponomarenko became the candidate member of the new, 'small' Praesidium, ranking immediately below Shvernik, and it may reasonably be supposed that this represents roughly his seniority in the 'large' Praesidium. If the 'small' Praesidium was in principle based on the Bureau of the old 'large' Praesidium, as seems probable, Ponomarenko may have been a member of the Bureau. (Whether that body had candidate members is, of course, quite unknown.) The other candidate members of the small post-Stalin Praesidium of March 1953 were Melnikov and Bagirov. Melnikov was absent at his post in Kiev during both listings relevant to seniority, on November 7 and February 13. It seems quite possible that he, too, was a member, or candidate member, of Stalin's Bureau of the Praesidium. This view would be based not merely on the general ranking of the Ukrainian First Secretary, but also on the fact that Melnikov was shown at the time of his fall in June 1953 to have been very closely associated with Stalin's own particular Russifying policies, and there are reasons, as we shall see, to believe that few members of the post-Stalin Praesidium were willing to defend him.

If this were the case, the new 'small' Praesidium of March 1953 would quite simply be the old Bureau of the Praesidium renamed, with the promotions back to their natural places of those in disfavour in Stalin's last months: the only exception would be Bagirov, the junior candidate member. His association with Beria is one of the few really uncontroversial facts, and his promotion to that position when he had not figured even as a candidate in Stalin's 'large' Praesidium is one very definite indication both that Beria had been isolated in the large Praesidium and that his position was greatly strengthened on Stalin's death.

The guard of honour over Mekhlis's body (*Pravda*, February 16, 1953) was listed in the following order: Bulganin; Kaganovich; Khrushchev; Saburov; Pervukhin; Shvernik; Suslov; Shkiryatov; Mikhailov; Malyshev; Aristov; V. V. Kuznetsov; Pegov.

This is clearly in an order of seniority, and one adequately similar to that of November 7. Twelve of the full members of the Praesidium are listed (down to V. V. Kuznetzov). Of those absent, apart from Stalin himself, there were four men with posts outside Moscow: Andrianov, Korotchenko, Melnikov and Kuusinen. This leaves Malenkov, Mikoyan, Molotov, Voroshilov, Beria, Ponomarenko, Chesnokov and Ignatiev. From this incomplete list it appears that the old members of the Politburo ranked top, but that Saburov and Pervukhin had been intruded above Shvernik, a candidate member of the old body. If we make this assumption, and put the missing men in their relevant places, it will be seen that a line drawn under Pervukhin now has above it exactly those who became full members of the 'small' Praesidium nominated in March, after Stalin's death, with Shvernik in his correct place.

The presumption therefore is that Stalin had created the new 'large' Praesidium with rather more subtle tactics in view than might at first appear. For the 'Bureau', unlike its earlier equivalent, the Politburo, now became an informal committee whose membership was not announced and replacements within which could be handled unceremoniously. And if any difficulties arose with the old members who now knew themselves to be on the point of political, and possibly personal extinction, their votes had no significance and could be swamped by those of the new men. It may therefore be looked upon as a transitional stage. At the same time the existence of the Bureau might be seen as not merely an operational convenience, in view of the over-large size of the Praesidium itself, but also as a form of apparent concession to the old Politburo, one of Stalin's rather devious manœuvres.

It will now be convenient to deal with the Doctors' Plot itself, as, although publicity was not given to it until January 13, we shall see good reason to believe that the arrests were made early in November. First we may take the official announcements.

ARREST OF GROUP OF SABOTEUR-DOCTORS

Some time ago agencies of state security discovered a terrorist group of doctors who had made it their aim to cut short the lives of active public figures of the Soviet Union through sabotage medical treatment.

Among the participants in this terrorist group there proved to be: Prof. M. S. Vovsi, therapeutist; Prof. V. N. Vinogradov, therapeutist; Prof. P. I. Yegorov, therapeutist; Prof. A. I. Feldman, otolaryngologist; Prof. Ya. G. Etinger, therapeutist; Prof. A. M. Grinshteyn, neuropathologist; G. I. Mayorov, therapeutist.

Documentary evidence, investigations, the conclusions of medical experts and the confessions of the arrested have established that the criminals, who were secret enemies of the people, sabotaged the treatment of patients and undermined their health.

Investigation established that the participants in the terrorist group, taking advantage of their positions as doctors and abusing the trust of patients, by deliberate evil intent undermined patients' health, deliberately ignoring the data of objective examination of the patients, made incorrect diagnoses which did not correspond to the true nature of their illnesses, and then doomed them by wrong treatment.

The criminals confessed that, taking advantage of Comrade A. A. Zhdanov's ailment, incorrectly diagnosing his illness and concealing an infarct of his myocardium, they prescribed a regime counterindicated for this serious ailment and thereby killed Comrade A. A. Zhdanov. Investigations established that the criminals likewise cut short the life of Comrade A. S. Shcherbakov by incorrectly employing strong drugs in his treatment, prescribed a regime which was mortal to him and thus brought him to his death.

The criminal doctors sought above all to undermine the health of leading Soviet military personnel, to put them out of action and to weaken the defence of the country. They sought to put out of action Marshal A. M. Vasilevsky, Marshal L. A. Govorov, Marshal I. S. Konev, General of the Army S. M. Shtemenko, Admiral G. I. Levchenko and others, but arrest disrupted their evil plans and the criminals did not succeed in attaining their aim.

It has been established that all the murderer-doctors who had become monsters in human form, trampling the sacred banner of science and desecrating the honour of scientists, were enrolled by foreign intelligence services as hired agents.

Most of the participants in the terrorist group (M. S. Vovsi, B. B. Kogan, A. I. Feldman, A. M. Grinshteyn, Ya. G. Etinger and others) were connected with the international Jewish bourgeois nationalist organisation 'Joint', established by American intelligence for the alleged purpose of providing material aid to Jews in other countries. In actual fact this organisation, under direction of American intelligence, conducts extensive espionage, terrorist and other subversive work in many countries, including the Soviet Union. The arrested Vovsi told investigators that he had received orders 'to wipe out the leading cadres of the U.S.S.R.' — received them from the U.S.A. through the 'Joint' organisation, via the Moscow doctor, Shimeliovich, and the well-known Jewish bourgeois nationalist Mikhoels.

Other participants in the terrorist group (V. N. Vinogradov, M. B. Kogan, P. I. Yegorov) proved to be old agents of British intelligence.

The investigation will soon be concluded. (Tass.) (*Pravda*, January 13, 1953.)

Etinger's name seems to have last appeared in the medical journals in 1949. He would have been well over eighty, and it seems probable that he was dead by 1953. M. B. Kogan had died on November 26, 1951 (obituary in *Klinicheskaya Meditsina*, No. 2 of 1952).*

Zhdanov's death certificate on August 31, 1948, is signed by Drs. Yegorov, Director of the Kremlin Medical Administration,

---

* Such at least is the argument against the common view that these two died under torture during the investigation. On the other hand, the announcement of April 4, 1953, repudiating the case, speaks of the two as having been arrested, though not released. Perhaps Etinger was still alive, and there *may* have been two Dr. M. B. Kogans (see p. 206).

Vinogradov, Vasilenko, Fedorov and Mayorov. (Exactly the same doctors signed Georgi Dimitrov's death certificate on July 2, 1949.)

The timing of the arrest of the doctors is important. The XIXth Congress ended on October 14, 1952. On the following day the plenum of the new Central Committee elected the Party Praesidium and Stalin made his 'grave accusations' against Molotov and Mikoyan — and possibly others Khrushchev did not find it suitable to name in 1956. The arrest of the doctors, as will be seen below, can be very probably pinned down to between November 4 and 9.

It seems reasonable to imagine that the decision to take immediate action to look for some sort of plot involving those Stalin wished to destroy may have been made immediately after the Congress. Even that only leaves a fortnight to cook up a plan for a *prima facie* case.

The evidence for the dates of the doctors' arrest is as follows: Professor Vovsi spoke at a meeting of the Moscow Medical Society on October 29, 1952, with Professor Vinogradov in the chair (*Terapevticheski Arkhiv*, No. 3, June 30, 1953). Vinogradov's seventieth birthday on November 3 produced congratulatory articles not only in the medical Press but also in *Vechernaya Moskva* of that date. These two doctors were those named first in the accusation as published in *Pravda* on January 13, 1953. Vovsi is given as the leading American agent and Vinogradov as the leading British agent. Moreover, Vovsi has the same name as and seems to be a relation of the actor Mikhoels (this being a stage name only), announced as one of the doctors' fellow-plotters in the published announcement. He had also been a prominent member of the Jewish Anti-Fascist Committee. Most of its surviving members had been shot already, in August 1952. And it seems natural that the links in the Jewish plot that was gradually being invented would lead first to Vovsi and through him to the other doctors. There is no real reason to believe that the doctors, or most of them, were not arrested all at once. But if some were pulled in later than others it seems natural to think that Vovsi, and probably Vinogradov, were among the first to be arrested. Khrushchev in the Secret Speech speaks of Stalin coming to 'an immediate conclusion' that a Doctors' Plot existed, so that 'he issued orders to arrest a group of eminent medical specialists'. For what it is worth, this seems to imply a simultaneous arrest of the main body.

Thus on November 3 not only were the doctors almost certainly not under arrest, but no hint that they were in the slightest disfavour had penetrated to Party journalistic circles. The next date is the appearance of the magazine *Klinicheskaya Meditsina* on November 10. Vinogradov and Vasilenko had been on its editorial board and had been shown there in the journal's issue of October 3, 1952. Their names no longer appeared. A further point of interest in this issue is that it contained an article by Dr. Lydia Timashuk, later awarded the Order of Lenin for denouncing the doctors. Since she was otherwise an unknown medical worker, who does not seem to have had any other articles in the medical Press, and since the subject of the article was myocardial infarcts, concealment of which condition by the specialists in the case of Zhdanov was later alleged to have led to his death, we may perhaps regard this as evidential. It seems likely that the production of a scientific magazine cannot be held up for changes as easily as a daily paper; that at least the changes in the editorial board could hardly have been available to the printers less than a day or two before, while if Timashuk's article was a hurried insertion, the delay was probably longer. At any rate, we would probably not be too far wrong in taking November 8 as the latest reasonable date for the arrest.

Other evidence in general fits with the above. The names of Doctors Feldman and Preobrazhensky appear in the November 4 issue of the bimonthly *Vestnik Oto-Rino-Laringologii* but not in the following issue. In the case of Grinshteyn his name *is* included on the editorial board of *Sovetskaya Meditsina* as late as December 2: but as his name and a paper he had written, which would in ordinary circumstances automatically have been included in the yearly index issued at the same time, are *not* there, this may conceivably have been a slip. The name of Zelenin does appear in *Klinicheskaya Meditsina* of December 6, although not in the January issue, and in the absence of anything to the contrary one must believe that he was a later arrest.

The only other published fact that may be relevant concerns

Marshal Govorov, who, when the announcement was made in *Pravda* of January 13, was one of five living officers against whose health the doctors were allegedly working. Admiral Levchenko was comparatively junior, but all the military figures except Govorov were named as members or candidate members of the Central Committee elected at the XIXth Party Congress, in the list published in *Pravda* of October 15. By a very curious-looking circumstance, *Pravda* of October 30, 1952 — that is, over a fortnight later — published an announcement that owing to an error by the Accounting Commission the name of Marshal Govorov had been omitted from the listing of members of the Committee as published. That this should be literally the case is plainly incredible, for it would certainly have been noticed the following day. It seems certain either that Govorov *was* 'elected' at the Congress but at once removed or suspended by some underhand business, the suspension being reversed as the result of a struggle presumably connected with the decision to proceed with the Doctors' Plot investigation: or, more likely, his name was simply added by Stalin's order on October 30, also in connection with the building up of his cadres for the purge to be launched in connection with the Plot. For what it is worth, this date fits in reasonably well with the evidence from the medical literature. (It is of some incidental interest that on Govorov's death two years later *Pravda* (March 21, 1955) published an extremely long medical certificate signed by six doctors, including Vasilenko, which described how he had long suffered from 'hypertonic illness and general arterosclerosis' troubles leading to myocardial infarcts, of which he is described as having had three in 1954–55.)

The fact that the doctors, though receiving 'a directive on destroying the leading cadres of the U.S.S.R.' (*Tass*, February 15, 1953), are only accused of plotting against military men, apart from the long-dead Zhdanov and Shcherbakov, is significant.

Khrushchev says in the Secret Speech that some of the arrested doctors had 'once treated us' — i.e. the 'members of the Political Bureau'. If they had treated the old Politburo members, and were yet not accused of having attempted at least some of their lives, the presumption that the exclusion

M

was not accidental, and was ill-meant, is practically unavoidable.

We should not, with this victims' list, fall into the error of thinking that all those mentioned together must be taken as being in the same category. To look at an obvious parallel, the doctors themselves: the animus of the case was anti-Semitic, yet a number of Gentiles were publicly accused (and others secretly arrested) as well. Stalin's manœuvres were usually of a highly roundabout and complicated nature, and we might perhaps interpret the list of military men as designed to attract support from the various rather different military circles. From later developments it is possible to guess that Konev and Govorov represent the most loyal of the fighting Marshals, Vasilevsky a professional rather under the thumb of the politicians — a sort of Communist Keitel — and Shtemenko the political general proper. The most obvious military men missing from the list were Zhukov, Sokolovsky and Admiral Kuznetsov.

Yet the military aspect of the Doctors' Plot presents some curious features. The replacement of Shtemenko by Sokolovsky as Chief of Staff was announced on February 21, 1953, though it may have taken place rather earlier. This is only a month after the singling out of Shtemenko for distinction in the Plot accusation.

If this were definitely an isolated incident it might have an isolated explanation — such as something coming up that proved to Stalin Shtemenko's unsuitability for such a key post. But Admiral Kuznetsov, who had been demoted in 1947 after being war-time C.-in-C. of the Navy, had already been made Minister of the Navy. And Zhukov, who had been expelled from the Central Committee in 1946, was re-elected, if only as a candidate member, in 1952. There is also some rather indirect evidence for supposing that Zhukov had been recalled to the centre at, or before, this time (the main thing being that his appointment as Deputy Minister of War on Stalin's death does not seem to have been followed by any reappointment in the commands of Military Districts). Even if this is not so, the natural reason for appointing Sokolovsky, omitted from the Doctors' Plot list, would seem to be a wish on Stalin's part to strengthen his military machine. Shtemenko, though his military record was creditable, hardly seems of the right stature for the post. (He was not at once demoted, and even paid an inspection visit to Berlin in May 1953, after Stalin's death, in his old rank, but he later fell two grades, at a time when the army was reassessing the dead-end of 'Stalinist military science'. (See Chapter Thirteen.))

The whole of Soviet military doctrine was dangerously fossilised in 1952–53, and it may be that Stalin began to realise this, at least in part, and not necessarily (as has sometimes been suggested) because of any intention of launching an immediate war.

The question is whether the Sokolovsky appointment, and any other moves of the same sort, are to be thought of as contradicting the original intentions of the Doctors' Plot purge. If this were the case it would seem that Stalin must have changed his mind about the purge sometime in February. There is absolutely no evidence of this, and everything points to it not being true — the tardy reversal of the plot, the removal of Poskrebyshev, Khrushchev's statement that if Stalin had lived Mikoyan and Molotov might have perished.

We may therefore seek to reconcile the Sokolovsky appointment with the main themes of the plot. Party and police control of the army seems to have been unshakable at this point. And moreover most key military posts were held by officers devoted to the political leadership or, at least, totally unassociated with dangerous ideas. This contrasted with the position in 1937 very markedly. It is true that the selection of officers as potential Doctors' Plot victims was to some extent partial, and may be taken as the equivalent of a high award, from which pointed omission could be considered a mild rebuke or warning. Yet it has never been suggested, even by Khrushchev in the Secret Speech, when he was doing his utmost to emphasise Stalin's hostility to Zhukov and others, that the purge was to involve the army. Indeed, we may think that the 'army factions' aspect, though present, was minor, and the main aim of the inclusion of the military 'victims' was to reassure the army leadership as a whole. And it is, after all, possible that Sokolovsky had never been ill while Zhukov had anyhow not for years been stationed in Moscow, where the accused worked (while it is barely conceivable, apart from the fact that Khrushchev states the opposite, that *none* of the old Politburo had been ill and not treated by the Doctors).

As to the question of whether Stalin intended (or feared) immediate war, it can only be discussed at all if we at least assume that he was not by now raving mad. Ordinarily, he can scarcely be imagined to have intended war to coincide with a major political purge. This is not to say that he may not have been planning war, after a year or two of political terror, and have been beginning the military preparations. But if, on the contrary, he was fearing war, he may well have had some such thought as that the imperialists would choose the internal political crisis he was about to create, as an opportunity to attack, and that they could best be blocked by a powerful and ostentatious solidarity and reorganisation in the Soviet Army.

It is true that a *mass* purge on 1937–38 lines might sooner or later be expected to hit the army. But it is at least possible that the new terror was meant to be more selective — more on the lines of the Leningrad Case, where a populous city was brought to heel at the cost of a few thousand Party members. It is also true that Tukhachevsky and his followers were struck at in a more dangerous international situation, in the face of the enemy, as it were. But all that is known of that case implies that there was no original intention of downing the Marshals at that stage, and that they were shot as the result of a genuine fear of their next move. The *propaganda* of the Doctors' Plot was aimed at non-military institutions and persons, and there is no real reason to think that the true intentions were otherwise. Indeed, Sokolovsky's appointment may be read as a calculatedly belated admission that, of the military men, not only the supposed victims of the plot were to be well regarded, and as a further means of rallying military opinion behind Stalin. It has to be conceded, nonetheless, that that incident remains potentially obscure, and that a very broad general estimate of Stalin's policies has had to be made, to cover the point. I believe it is reasonably satisfactory, but such extrapolations always carry a weight of uncertainty.

One of the most substantial unknowns of this period is, how far was Stalin really, as Khrushchev implies, the victim of persecution mania? That his attitude was in some sense paranoid will hardly be denied. Indeed, a good case could be made out to show that the ideology and attitude taken up by the Communist Party as a result of his influence is in one aspect a paranoid rationalisation, with the typical refrain of its propaganda 'it is not accidental'. But the immediate question is how far Stalin really believed in the accusations he made.

Did he really 'reach an immediate conclusion' that there were 'doctor poisoners', simply on the basis of a letter from Dr. Timashuk? It seems rather unlikely, not only in general, but also because of Khrushchev's other hints about the 'plot', which seem to connect it with definite plans, and because Stalin was (according to the same source) already seeking ways of purging the leadership. He had used the doctor-prisoner method in his previous great purge. In the 'thirties, as Khrushchev mentions, one of the leading N.K.V.D. officials, Zakovsky, frankly told Rozenblum that his confessions would be invented for him by the N.K.V.D. In the Eikhe case, also according to Khrushchev, changes in the staffing of the alleged plot were made by the N.K.V.D., and only then communicated to the accused. It seems fairly plain that the security interrogators did not even go through the motions of believing the accusations, where this could be dispensed with. And it is, of course, clear that Stalin could not really have believed that Zinoviev and Kamenev planned the murder of Kirov if he had, as Khrushchev implies, organised it himself.

In fact, during the early purges he showed himself capable of carrying out liquidation on a colossal scale without really believing the charges as made public. This is not to say that he did not think that the victims were his enemies, or at least stood in his way, or were inconvenient to him. But that is rather a different point.

In particular one feels that Khrushchev is exaggerating in maintaining that Stalin half-believed Voroshilov to be an English spy. If there had been the slightest real suspicion he would scarcely have contented himself with expressing discontent when Voroshilov turned up to Politburo meetings. (But it is hard to see why the idea that Voroshilov was an English spy is any more absurd than the idea that Beria was — a view to which Khrushchev is committed!)

We may write off part of Khrushchev's accusation against Stalin. The motive of maintaining that the Doctors' Plot, e.g., was due to an accidental personal caprice, rather than to the nature of politics at the time is obvious. It fits in with what

Togliatti was to condemn as a non-Marxist analysis of the Stalinist errors — the blaming of all evil on the 'exceptional and even astonishing faults' of one man (*Nuovi Argomenti*, June 16, 1956). This acquits the system, or rather avoids even consideration of the possibility that it is at fault. And this was the essence of the whole Secret Speech — to blame the horrors of the past on Stalin and claim the credit for its achievements for the Party.

It is difficult to follow Khrushchev's line that Stalin became particularly suspicious after the war, when we consider that the real blood-bath was in the 'thirties. Nevertheless when all is said we cannot exclude the possibility that in his last years the old dictator may have become specially capricious, and that in the last months of the Doctors' Plot he had lost control in some quite unpredictable way. If this is even partially true it complicates our estimates with an unknown.

Yet we are not really so much concerned with why Stalin picked on certain of his colleagues as enemies, as with the fact that he did so and with his methods in dealing with them. So although we must bear this point in mind, it may not affect our estimate of events too much. It would, however, give a strong additional motive for many of the leaders to act against Stalin if they could, and hence rather increase the (quite unknown) possibilities that he was killed by a prospective victim.

Meanwhile, even before the public announcement of the Doctors' Plot itself, very great publicity was given to the trial of the leaders of a large gang of criminals operating 'over a prolonged period', before a Military Tribunal sitting in Kiev at the end of November 1952. H. A. Khain, Ya. E. Yaroshetski and D. I. Gerzon — Jews — were sentenced to death by shooting for 'counter-revolutionary wrecking in the provinces of trade and goods turnover', while two others got twenty-five years' imprisonment each. Khain had been the manager of the Kiev Trading Base of the Ministry of Light Industry's Chief Directorate of Sales. They were accused of embezzling socialist property and other crimes, and the heads of several Ukrainian Ministries (Trade, Food, Meat, Light Industry and Milk Production) were subsequently criticised for their lack of vigilance, which had 'cost the Republic dear'. Two secretaries of the Kiev Party committee were also accused of connections with the Khain gang.

A very large number of other cases of embezzlement, espionage, bad security and so on — crimes usually linked together — were reported, and exhortations to the public became extremely menacing in tone.

Meanwhile relevant events had taken place in Prague. The trials and arrests in Eastern Europe in the period 1949–51 had all been of Party leaders with a 'nationalist' complexion. They included both 'Zhdanovite' leftist revolutionaries and rightist deviationists, but in any case were men largely not in the cadres of the international apparat. The Czechoslovak purge had started in orthodox fashion — with the arrest of Clementis, Sling and others, whose affiliations were local. The accusations against them included plotting against the life of Slansky. In November 1951 matters took another turn. Slansky and Geminder were arrested and accused of complicity in the plot.

These two men, and especially Geminder, were certainly of the international apparatchik type, associated with the M.G.B. Although they were now accused of nationalism and Titoism, and the usual run of crimes, the reversal of the original story itself shows that a decision had been taken to extend the purge from those who might genuinely be considered centres of resistance to Soviet control, to those on whom no such suspicion could rest. Moreover, the case soon took on the new anti-Semitism which was to mark Stalin's last phase — not merely as a subsidiary tinge, but as one of the main themes.

Now, in November 1952, Slansky and his co-accused were brought to trial. As in the Doctors' Plot, a majority of those publicly accused were Jews, while a number of arrested gentiles were not put in dock. The trial may be considered a blow at Beria's international apparatus: and it is notable that Slansky and his associates were the only major purge victims not to be rehabilitated in 1955–56 (though the charge of Titoism was withdrawn). On the contrary, Slansky himself is now blamed for the police excesses of the purge period. (It is also noticeable that Eastern European purges ceased in 1953, but were resumed immediately after Beria's execution.)

Just as the Slansky arrest may be considered, with the simultaneous Mingrelian purge in Georgia, as part of a first blow at Beria, the trial itself a year later may perhaps be thought of as a pilot model for Stalin's intended top-level purge in Moscow.

Various types of charge, a variegated group of defendants, a strong anti-Semitic flavour, a concentration against right-deviationism *and* the international police machine, give some idea of what might have occurred in the U.S.S.R. At the same time a number of Czech leaders were removed, and evidently shot, without any public trial. We can perhaps envisage in Russia, too, as in 1938, public trials and mere disappearances going together, until Stalin had rid himself of those he regarded as superfluous.

As a final parallel, many commentators have noted that immediately after Stalin's death, Gottwald — the beneficiary of the Slansky purge — also became ill while attending Stalin's funeral in Moscow, and died a few days later; and they have cast doubt on the naturalness of Gottwald's illness. We may at least say that *if* Stalin was done away with (and it cannot be called impossible), then those who took such action might not have felt any reluctance to pursue the matter in the Czechoslovak case also: many deaths have taken place at moments particularly convenient to political adversaries or immediately following the death of a patron — Zhdanov's, Dimitrov's, Stalin's, Bierut's and Gottwald's. Yet people do die naturally, even within a few days of each other.

On January 13, as we have seen, the Doctors' Plot was made public. *Pravda*'s leading article on January 13 reminds readers that Stalin had issued a warning against the 'opportunist theory' of 'extinguishing' the class struggle as a result of Soviet successes. It quoted Stalin as having said:

This is not only a rotten theory but also a dangerous theory, because it lulls our people to sleep, leads them into a trap, whilst giving the enemy the opportunity to rally for struggle against the Soviet regime. In the U.S.S.R. the exploiting classes have long since been routed and liquidated, but remnants of bourgeois ideology, remnants of private property, psychology and morality, have been preserved. There have also been preserved carriers of bourgeois opinions and bourgeois morality — *live people*, hidden enemies, supported by the imperialist world, who will continue to do harm also in the future. [*Pravda*'s italics: the phrase 'live people' was to become commonly used throughout the campaign.]

Pravda concludes that the cure for all this is greater vigilance and harder work, for apart from all these external and internal

enemies there is another 'enemy' that Soviet man must individually overcome, namely laziness or 'slackness':

There can be no doubt that as long as slacking exists in our
country, so will wrecking. Consequently, in order to liquidate
wrecking, one must put an end to slackness in our ranks.

The youth newspaper *Komsomolskaya Pravda* makes the same
point in its leader that day:

Comrade Stalin has frequently warned that our successes also
have a bad side to them. They produce complacency and self-
contentment among many of our workers, and this in turn blunts
vigilance and produces laziness. We still have many slackers who
present everything in a good light and who see nothing beyond their
own noses. One must not forget that it is precisely laziness that
produces a breeding ground for diversion, wrecking, espionage and
other hostile actions against the U.S.S.R.

The entire Soviet Press was filled with vigilance material.
Apart from many articles on the Doctors, there were also a
whole series of cases of embezzlement, lack of vigilance and so
on brought up — some of them apparently quite old ones.
The Slansky case, too, was frequently referred to (and it is
perhaps significant that at Slansky's trial in November 1952 a
doctor linked to both the Zionists and the Party plotters was
brought in — Dr. Haskovitz, who was accused of having
'shortened the life of Gottwald').

We may give a few examples of the general theme. The
Agitators' Notebook of January 1953 linked doctors and spies,
and *Sotsialistichesky Donbas* of January 18 attacked 'Ukrainian
and Jewish nationalists' as agents of U.S. imperialism. On
January 25 *Pravda* celebrated the eighteenth anniversary of the
death of Kuibyshev — also a victim of doctor-poisoners, a fact
which, the paper pointed out, should be a reminder to the
Soviet people.*

Trud of February 14 mentioned the Khain group again, and
also attacked a Jewish railway doctor called Izrailit. *Pravda
Ukrainy* of February 17 carried an attack on Zionists who,
before the war, had penetrated the Communist Party in
'Czechoslovakia and Transcarpathia', and named local rabbis

* By a curious irony, the Dr. Vinogradov now under arrest had been an expert
witness against the earlier doctor-poisoners.

and others in Uzhgorod as enemy agents — an interesting case
of a direct link with the satellite traitors. *Izvestia* of February 18,
1953, had a leader linking the 'Rajk, Kostov, Slansky, Xoxe
and Gomulka-Spychalski plotters' with the Doctors' Plot, and
going on from these to denounce various minor Soviet saboteurs
and spies — with Jewish names. And there were dozens of
similar articles, all in terms of extreme menace.

The Doctors' Plot, as far as it went, seems to have served
mainly as a creator of the purge-atmosphere, and not yet to
have approached the long-term objects of the purge. It is
possible that further charges would have been made against the
doctors had they come to trial. It was several times said that 'the
arrested Vovsi testified at the investigation that he had received
a directive on "destroying the leading cadres of the U.S.S.R."
from the U.S.A., from the Zionist organisation Joint' (*Medit-
sinski Rabotnik*, March 3, 1953, *Trud* of February 15, 1953, etc.).

The Doctors' Plot was the only high-level aspect of the purge
to be made public. But it seems virtually certain that other
arrests had been made. The announcement of the Doctors'
guilt was made about ten weeks after their arrest; and if we
take this as a rough guide we may consider that arrests as early
as the last days of December might not have matured into a
publicisable case by the time of Stalin's death. (It is also
possible, of course, that other cases had already come to secret
trial, as with the Crimean Affair, whose victims were shot in
August 1952; it is true that Stalin seems to have decided to
give his new purge wide publicity, partly for reasons of public
discipline, but even in the Yezhovshchina, secret trials went
with public ones.)

In any case the impression that other victims were awaiting
the death-blow can be documented. There is, of course, the
statement of Khrushchev that Stalin intended to finish off the
old Politburo, and that Molotov and Mikoyan in particular had
been in danger of their lives since October 1952. (Mikoyan's
danger was confirmed personally by him when in conversation with the American journalist Louis Fischer.) Beria's
Georgian allies, and perhaps the Abakumov group of police
officials, were already under arrest. But apart from that there
is a group of facts of broader significance. The attacks on the
various economic ministries was accompanied by the dis-

appearance, at least from public life, of a number of the chiefs named.

The Ministries criticised in *Pravda* for inadequate vigilance include:

(*a*) Ministry of Non-Ferrous Metallurgy — whose 'former' Deputy Minister, Petrov, was accused personally of negligence.

(*b*) The State Supply organisation (Gossnab.). The Deputy Minister, Tsyren, a candidate member of the Central Committee, has not been heard of since January 1953.

(*c*) The Ministry of Geology. The Minister, P. A. Zakharov, a candidate member of the Central Committee, has not been heard of since early 1953.

(*d*) The Ministry of Health. When Stalin died it was learnt that the former Minister, Smirnov, had been replaced. He has not been mentioned since.

These are reasonably senior officials comparatively easily traceable. A number of junior officials were criticised by name, and it may be that their superiors were also involved. Other economic figures not heard of since January–March 1953 include V. P. Pronin, Minister of Labour Reserves, a member of the Central Committee, and G. V. Alekseenko, Minister of the Communications Equipment Industry, a candidate member of the Central Committee. It is even more significant that these two, and (*b*) and (*c*) above, are the only complete disappearances from the Central Committee which seem to be dated about this time. Moreover, among the eighty-three members and candidate members of the 1952 Central Committee who were not re-elected in 1956 only three (apart from the four mentioned) were in the economic ministries — that is, more of these fell in a couple of months than in the remaining three years.

Whether they, or any of them, were arrested or executed is unknown. But it is worth noting that when Ryumin came to trial in July 1954 he was accused of 'provocative cases' (plural) and 'unjustified arrests of a number of Soviet citizens, *including* prominent medical workers' (my italics). Moreover, he was charged only under Article 58–7 (see Appendix VI) of the

Criminal Code of the R.S.F.S.R., dealing with sabotage of the economy.

Thus it seems clear that the economic chiefs were being got at. What this signified is less obvious. The ministries concerned seem to have come under the direct supervision of Malyshev and Tevosyan, who were, later at least, close associates of Malenkov. But it would be pointless to draw any definite conclusions from this chain of command, if only because any given member of it might be the man specifically entrusted with conducting the administrative side of the purge! What is to the point is to consider the policy aspect.

The purge was specifically aimed at the 'rightist' deviation (*Pravda*, January 13, 1953). In the economic field it struck fairly widely at those actually in possession, and at the dispensation which had produced indiscipline. On the face of it, it may be taken as reversion, in substance, to the rigours of Zhdanov's time. (And it might be relevant that Zhdanov's line against 'rootless cosmopolitans', i.e. Jews, had been vigorous.)

At this stage it may be well to list those figures who, for one reason or another, were certainly, or practically certainly, in Stalin's good books at the time of the Doctors' Plot, and may be presumed to have favoured the abortive great purge.

These seem to be:

(1) *Suslov*. His article in *Pravda* on December 24, 1952, attacking Voznesensky included a decree of the Central Committee on the matter which had remained secret for the previous three years (see Chapter Five). This cannot possibly have been published without a decision of the Central Committee, and in fact of Stalin. The fact that he commissioned Suslov to write it, or at least to sign it, is a probable indication that Suslov was in favour at this late stage.

The most extremely minor error of Fedoseyev's which Suslov purported to be attacking cannot have been more than a convenient peg for producing the set-piece with its revelations about the 1949 purge. As soon as it is asked why such revelations should be made at that particular time, December 1952, it is difficult not to connect it in some way with the new purge surrounding the Doctors' Plot. It seems reasonable to speculate that Stalin had some intention of linking the prospective purges of 1953 with those of 1949. It is perfectly true that the new victims were to be accused of murdering Zhdanov. But a study of the complexities of the purges of the 'thirties shows several relevant facts: and in particular that Stalin preferred to link together successive waves of purges, even when the victims of one wave had actually been prominent in destroying their predecessors (for example, compare the relations of Yagoda and Zinoviev). There also arises, though as no more than a possibility, the idea that those named in the Suslov article, headed by Fedoseyev, Aleksandrov and Shepilov, might have been destined to be an alleged link between the two alleged conspiracies.

(2) *F. R. Kozlov.* Selected to write the article in *Pravda*, February 6, 1953, which was in effect the key policy statement on the purge. His demotion from Second to Third Secretary in Leningrad after Stalin's death is probably relevant, as is his later rise under Khrushchev.

(3) *Mikhailov*, selected to deliver the Lenin birthday address — largely about the plot.

(4) *Ryumin.*

(5) *Poskrebyshev.*

(6) *Ignatiev*, although evidently to a lesser degree.

(7) *Shkiryatov* on the basis of his nomination to head the Control Committee, a good post in purges.

(8) *Aristov.* Head of the Party Organs Department of the Central Committee and demoted in March 1953.

(9) The military and naval figures against whom the plotters had allegedly worked: *Konev, Vasilevsky, Shtemenko, Govorov* and *Admiral Levchenko.*

(10 *Mgeladze* and his new Georgian apparatus.

(11) *Chesnokov*, the ideologist raised to the Praesidium at the time of the eclipse of all the others — Shepilov, Pospelov, Fedoseyev, Aleksandrov, etc. — himself to fall in complete obscurity after Stalin's death until 1957, when he emerged in a radio post.

(12) *Yuri Zhdanov*, Head of the Science and Culture Department of the Central Committee, also writer of a key article and demoted in April.

Two other men, candidate members of the Central Committee, who seem not to have been heard of since Stalin's death (and were not re-elected in 1956) are M. T. Pomaznev, who was 'administrator' in the Council of Ministers; and V. N. Pavlov, head of a department in the Ministry of Foreign Affairs, who acted as Stalin's interpreter.

Yuri Zhdanov was given big space in *Pravda* of January 16, 1953, for a theoretical article attacking anti-Pavlov trends in science. This was almost the only major piece of neo-Zhdanovism. It bitterly criticised certain scientific institutions for laxity in their Marxism, with the possible implication that those responsible for ideological discipline had not been equal to their responsibilities. The author might well be expected to be seeking revenge for his father, and the prominence given him may be read in that light, rather than for the article's actual contents. His immediate and extreme demotion on Stalin's death seems to confirm that his role was ill-regarded by the new rulers. We need not take it that Stalin was about to throw his whole weight behind a Zhdanovist revival. But it certainly appears that he was toying with a weapon which could most naturally be used as a threat, or at least a hindrance, to Malenkov. The key article in *Pravda* on February 6 by Frol Kozlov, also to prove a strong anti-Malenkov man in future crises, makes all the vigilance points very strongly, and contains an interesting sentence: 'One of the causes of the continued lack of alertness in our ranks are certain rotten theories unfortunately current among a section of our comrades, providing a spiritual soil in which it can flourish.' *Pravda* of January 13 also makes an ideological, intra-Party, point of considerable weight, in attacking 'Right opportunists standing on the anti-Marxist point of view of the "damping down" of the class struggle', the danger of whose attitude had been shown by the exposure of the doctors. This seems to imply an attack on Party figures, and it is, of course, a regular component of trials of Party men that they are accused of deviation, as well as crime.

Mr. Nicolaevsky's interpretation of the period culminating in Stalin's death is an interesting and plausible one. He maintains that the original objectives of the purge plan by Stalin did not include Malenkov or the industrial managers as such, and that Malenkov was in good standing roughly until the end of 1952. (This last appears to be confirmed by his being chosen to deliver the main speech at the XIXth Congress, while

Beria, for example, was given an excessively minor role.) Then (it is argued) Malenkov, too, lost influence.

In bringing in Aristov, later to prove a determined opponent of Malenkov's, to be Party Secretary and Head of the crucial Party Organs Department of the Central Committee, Stalin had removed from the control of Malenkov all access to the power apparatus of the Party.*

As a long shot we might even guess that Aristov was destined to be Stalin's new police viceroy. A certain discontent with Ignatiev had been shown by Stalin, according to Khrushchev's Secret Speech. And Aristov would have been following in the path of Yezhov and of Ignatiev himself who had gone to security police from the Central Committee cadres side.

That Ignatiev, as well as Aristov, came under Khrushchev's protection later, whatever may have been the case during the Doctors' Plot period, is indicated less by his re-emergence in his provincial secretaryship after Beria's fall, than by his retention of his post, and his membership of the Central Committee, in 1955–56, at a time when Malenkov's allies were being removed in dozens. Moreover, he was the spokesman who launched the attack on Bulganin in the Central Committee plenum of December 1958 — a charge of trust, from Khrushchev's point of view.

What was the organisation of the purge? We know from Khrushchev's Secret Speech that Stalin gave direct instructions to Ignatiev, Minister of State Security. But Ryumin, the Deputy Minister, was arrested in April 1953, and shot the following year for direct responsibility, and this (with the comparatively minor censure received by Ignatiev) makes it probable that he was the main confidant of Stalin in the police side.

A. A. Kuznetsov, who Khrushchev states was the Party Secretary in charge of State Security, was not replaced when he was removed. This meant that control over the police apparatus (through the Administrative Organs Department) reverted to another secretary — who must have been Malenkov,

* We should note here that the often repeated statement that Aristov came under Khrushchev's patronage some time before the Congress is based on a misreading of *Moskovskaya Pravda* of September 25, 1952. This shows a different Aristov (A. P.) as a member of Khrushchev's Moscow Party Committee. Our Aristov in any case spoke at the Congress as Secretary of the Chelyabinsk Provincial Party Committee.

Khrushchev or (more likely) Stalin himself. In any case, after the XIXth Congress we can most reasonably conclude that Stalin exercised direct control, presumably through the Special Sector headed by Poskrebyshev. A consideration of those members of the Central Committee, and others, who lost status at Stalin's death confirms this.

The first reshuffle, on March 7, seems mainly a reassertion of power by the old Politburo, and especially Malenkov and Beria, as we shall see. For instance, Ignatiev had to cede his Ministry to Beria, but was compensated by being made a Party Secretary. The biggest drop seems to be Brezhnev from Party Secretary to head of the Navy's Political Department, and this may perhaps simply be the downgrading of the one undoubted Khrushchev Client in the Secretariat.

But with the mid-March plenum and the official reversal of the Doctors' Plot in April the full demolition of Stalin's agents took place. The final losers were:

(a) Ryumin: arrested.
(b) Ignatiev: removed from all central posts, and later to appear as Provincial Secretary in Bashkiria.
(c) Aristov: Secretary and Head of the Party Organs Department, demoted to the very low (and not even Party) post of Chairman of the Executive Committee in the Khabarovsk Territory.
(d) Chesnokov: as full member of the large Praesidium, very much established as Stalin's top ideologist. He now went into obscurity.
(e) Yuri Zhdanov: Head of the Science and Culture Department of the Central Committee. Removed to a minor Party post at Rostov.
(f) Poskrebyshev: not heard of again until briefly sneered at in Khrushchev's Secret Speech in February 1956.

If Aristov, as Secretary in charge of the Party side of the purge, suffered so radical a demotion, we can take it for granted that all those connected with the police aspect suffered as badly or worse. That Ignatiev's demotion was less than Aristov's probably confirms that his role was not a decisive one, in spite of his official position. That no other Party secretaries were so deeply affected shows that none of them formed part of the central apparatus of the purge. (The fall of even the ideologists of the purge makes this very much *a fortiori*.) We are again left with the strong presumption that Poskrebyshev was the key man.

From this we may conclude that though Khrushchev, and possibly Malenkov, were parts of the *status quo* on whose general support or neutrality Stalin relied (for the time being at least), the old dictator had built up a new power apparatus of his own to which they were not admitted. By the same token it seems that those new men brought in by Stalin, and only lightly demoted by his successors (i.e. those not on the above list), were intended as potential replacements of the old Politburo, but had not themselves been admitted to his confidence nor had any direct complicity in the project for a purge.

Thus by 1953 Stalin had practically cut off all the old members of the Politburo from direct access to the main machinery of power — the Security organs on the one hand and the cadre administration of the Party on the other. This might not, in any particular case, mean that complete destruction of the individual was intended. Molotov, Kaganovich, Mikoyan and others had had no real power for years, while remaining high in favour.

On the main public references to individuals in *Pravda* over the months of 1953 before Stalin's death, in the first place references to Stalin himself almost crowd out the others. In particular, *Economic Problems of Socialism* is referred to in extravagant terms in almost every editorial. The only other leader quoted is Malenkov. 'As Comrade Malenkov said in his report to the XIXth Congresss' is fairly frequent right up to the last.

The others are mentioned as making appearances only. Khrushchev's presence is noted at one or two Moscow functions — the latest on February 27. The order given at the Mekhlis ceremony on February 13 has already been noted. Other appearances of names, for the record, are:

(*a*) in the same issue of *Pravda* (January 13) in which the Doctors' Plot is announced there is a report of the presence at the Bolshoi Theatre for an exhibition of the art of the Polish People's Republic of 'Stalin, Molotov,

N

Malenkov, Beria, Voroshilov, Khrushchev and others'.
It is hard to believe that this announcement is an
accidental coincidence, but it is difficult to make
sense of it unless we do it in terms of some devious
deception of Stalin's. This is quite plausible, but it
naturally makes nonsense of any attempt to create a
rigorous system of rules of deduction from the presence
and order of names. This is as it should be, but at the
same time it remains hard to lay down any definite
method of coping with apparent anomalies except to
say that if they occur they must be due to causes at
present unknown to us. This may sound like the
application of what engineers call Finagle's Constant,
being the figure which when added to a wrong result
makes it right. Yet the alternative is to abandon the
names method altogether, and it is plainly of too
much use for that, if treated critically.

(b) It is at least noteworthy that several of these names are
not again mentioned. In *Pravda* of January 22 the
ceremonial meeting of the twenty-ninth anniversary
of Lenin's death is attended simply by 'leaders of the
Party and Government', a rare piece of anonymity.
Shvernik is mentioned as in the Chair, Mikhailov
(who had a photograph) made the speech — with
references to 'live persons', hidden enemies of the
Party, which was the catch-phrase of the period.

(c) *Pravda*, January 27, gives the signatures of Kaganovich,
Pervukhin and Tevosyan to an obituary of B. N.
Arutyunov, Assistant Minister of Ferrous Metal-
lurgy.

(d) *Pravda*, February 14, gives the commission for Mekhlis'
funeral, headed by Suslov.

(e) *Pravda*, February 15, mentions the presence at a reception at the Chinese Embassy of Bulganin, Tarasov,
Vyshinski, Marshal Vasilevski, Admiral N. G. Kuznetsov and others — a very low level contingent.

(f) Though not relevant to the immediate point, it may be
worth recording here the award of orders to various
second-line party officials such as Snechkus and
Belyaev (on their fiftieth birthdays).

Between the Party Congress and the announcement of the Doctors' Plot (October 1952 to January 1953) the constant references to Stalin's *Economic Problems of Socialism* seem to show that apart from the intended purge, this aspect of things was regarded as most important. Suslov's article in *Pravda* of December 24, 1952, linked opposition to Stalin's economic views with criminal activity. Conversely, the rise of the economic leaders who had replaced Voznesensky and spoken for years favourably of Stalin's view is notable. Saburov, as head of Gosplan, delivered the economic report at the Party Congress. Pervukhin made the November 6 report at the usual ceremonial meeting at the Moscow Soviet. Both men were not only taken into the big Praesidium, but, as shown by the *Pravda* listings of November 7 and February 13, were promoted even above former Politburo members.

Both, particularly Saburov, have always been taken as linked with Malenkov. And it certainly seems as if they, and as far as can be seen he, were not to be the ones who would suffer from the predicted Doctors' Plot purge. But of course Stalin had in the 'thirties promoted men like Eikhe and turned on them almost immediately. And the attacks on industrial ministries which followed the Doctors' Plot announcement may, as has sometimes been stated, be thought to have undermined the position of Malenkov and his friends. In the crisis of the 1930s those who were not prepared to support the purges to the limit were soon themselves included in them. And if Malenkov and the industrial managers felt that matters were developing dangerously for their own friends, it is quite conceivable that they made some attempt to slow up the process. Moreover, in the unbalanced state Stalin may have been in in the last few months of his life, as reported by Khrushchev, sudden switches of target were by no means impossible.

Just the same, present information does not exclude the idea that Malenkov, Saburov and Pervukhin were in favour with Stalin right up to the end. The assumption of power by Malenkov, the inclusion of Saburov and Pervukhin in the Post-Stalin Praesidium — identical (if my view is correct) with the old Bureau — show a striking continuity which was only interrupted at the plenum of March 12. Even the Doctors' Plot seems still to have been gone on with at least until that date. It is equally possible that Stalin was beginning to transfer Malenkov and his supporters to the victims' list.

Thus whether the purge in any way threatened Malenkov is a most important point, but one on which it seems impossible to form a definite opinion. The arguments favouring the view that Malenkov was indeed threatened are strong ones and may be summarised:

(1) The whole tone of the propaganda of the period was in terms of Party enthusiasm and vigilance and of strict ideology. The emphasis at all times of Malenkov's ascendancy had been on administrative efficiency. In 1941 his first rise to prominence had been on the basis of criticism of Party orthodoxy as the main criterion for leadership. His eclipse in 1946 had been as the result of implied allegations that ideological discipline become slack under his auspices. And in 1953–55 he was to defend the administrative apparatus and sound government against opposition charges of slackness and heresy.

(2) The economic minstries controlled by his apparent allies were under attack.

(3) He had at least been edged out of control of the main machinery of power.

These are powerful arguments. As against them:

(1) Malenkov had recently been nominated, for practical purposes, Stalin's successor.

(2) His allies Pervukhin and Saburov had just been promoted to the highest rank.

(3) There were no overt signs of any attacks on him.

That Malenkov was not deeply implicated in fabricating the Doctors' Plot, or at least no more so than Khrushchev himself, is shown by the fact that while Khrushchev has continually raised the Leningrad Case against his defeated rival, he has steered clear of doing the same with the Doctors' Plot. On the contrary, the only time the Doctors' Plot was given publicity after Beria's fall was in the Ryumin trial, mounted during a period of Malenkov's ascendancy, and evidently directed against his rivals, possibly including Khrushchev.

An easier thing to estimate is the position of Beria; we have seen how the purges in Georgia and Czechoslovakia seem to have been directed against his nominees.

It only became known after Stalin's death, with the repudiation of the Doctors' Plot by the M.V.D. (then under Beria), that Ignatiev had been Minister of State Security in the plot period. (The first public mention of Ignatiev in connection with the M.G.B. seems to be a reference in Moscow papers on January 28 of his being elected by employees of the M.G.B. to the City Soviet.)

Ignatiev's predecessor, Abakumov, appears to have been removed late in 1951, though direct evidence of this is lacking. Ignatiev, who had been working in the Party Organ's Department of the Central Committee, was the first holder of the Ministry not to have served under Beria. That Abakumov's removal was not simply a matter of personal corruption (as Moscow rumour of the period had it) is shown by the fact that his subordinate as head of the Section for Investigating Specially Important Cases had also been replaced by 1952, when Ryumin had the job.

If the Secret Speech is at all accurate, it confirms the impression of a conflict between Stalin and Beria in 1951–53. It states that Beria was involved in fabricating the 1949–50 Leningrad Case, but omits his name when it comes to dealing with the 1951–52 'Mingrelian' conspiracy and the 1952–53 Doctors' Plot. This could hardly be due to any desire to spare Beria's reputation and is best accounted for by his audience's possession of positive knowledge incompatible with such an allegation. This implies that Ignatiev's appointment meant the severing of Beria's direct connections with the Ministry of State Security.

But the mere fact that Beria was not consulted about the Doctors' case is a sign that his position was very shaky. It virtually proves that Stalin no longer permitted him a say in the field which had been his Politburo speciality for more than a decade — in fact that he had lost Stalin's confidence and was, at best, superfluous.

Khrushchev's description of the Doctors' Plot in the Secret Speech is peculiar (see Appendix IV). He states that Dr. Timashuk's denunciation was the cause of the affair but that she was 'probably influenced or ordered by someone (after all, she was an unofficial collaborator of the organs of State Security) to write Stalin a letter' telling him of the matter. Stalin then 'issued orders to arrest' the doctors and 'personally' instructed the investigative judge and ordered 'the former Minister of State Security, Comrade Ignatiev', to obtain confessions unless he himself wished to be 'shortened by a head'.

Ryumin, who was after all publicly accused and officially executed for having played a major part in the plot for reasons of 'careerism', is not mentioned. Yet it was presumably he, if anyone, in the State Security Ministry, who 'influenced' Dr. Timashuk. The fact that Beria is nowhere mentioned even in this connection is also significant: it seems likely that if it had been in the least plausible Khrushchev would have brought his name in. Moreover it is interesting that Dr. Timashuk is represented as writing direct to Stalin — rather as if she did not feel that either Beria or the Ministry of State Security as a whole were suitable and secure channels. A letter to Stalin might be expected to go through his personal Secretariat headed by Poskrebyshev.

A notable point was the direct criticism of the State Security organs. *Pravda* (January 13, 1953) said: 'The State Security organs did not uncover in good time the wrecking terrorist organisation among the doctors. However, these organs should have been especially vigilant.' (Presumably because of the experience of the earlier doctor-prisoners in the Kuibyshev case.) *Izvestia* (January 13, 1953), said:

> The wrecker-doctors were able to function over a considerable period because some of our Soviet organs and their executive officials lost their vigilance and were infected with gullibility. . . . The State Security organs must be specially vigilant. However, these organs did not promptly discover the terrorist organisation of wrecker-doctors.

This was an overt attack on the controllers of State Security from the period of the first alleged crime of the doctors — the death of Shcherbakov in May 1945. The Ministers responsible over the ensuing years were Merkulov and Abakumov, under Beria's supervision. Moreover, the charge of lack of vigilance is one which is easily convertible into actual complicity, as it had been in the case of the Leningrad N.K.V.D. officials originally tried for insufficient vigilance in guarding Kirov, and retried in 1938 as accomplices in his murder. The then People's Commissar, Yagoda himself, was tried and executed on the same charge, and the reference in *Pravda* to the need for the M.G.B. to have borne in mind the case of the earlier doctor-poisoners may perhaps be considered a rather sinister warning, as *those* doctors were alleged to have acted under the instructions of Beria's predecessor. Even if Abakumov may possibly have become detached from Beria, the inclusion of the murder of Shcherbakov among the doctors' crimes involves the security officials at a time when Merkulov, whose affiliations with Beria are complete, was Minister of State Security.

Other indications of a decline in Beria's influence were the demotion at the XIXth Party Congress of some of those associated with him. Merkulov, later shot with Beria, had been a member of the Central Committee from 1939, and was reduced to candidate member in 1952. Dekanozov (also shot with Beria) had been candidate member in 1939 and a full member in 1941, but was not re-elected at all in 1952. Another of Beria's associates to be excluded from the new Central Committee was M. M. Gvishiani, a Georgian who had served in various M.V.D. posts, and who had been a candidate member since 1939.

Apart from the actual evidence, it may not seem too far-fetched to argue *a priori* that Beria must have been a destined victim of Stalin's new purge. No one has been removed from control of the State Security apparatus and survived. Each new wave of purges, whoever its other victims, has always struck at the police leaders. Perhaps men who have actually held positions of such real power may not be trusted in lower or other posts. Moreover, it is a natural thought that the only agency capable of organising and concealing the murder (by doctors or otherwise) of political leaders is the Security Police. Indeed, this argument had already been applied in the case of the previous 'doctors'-prisoners', who had allegedly acted on the instructions of the then Police Minister.

We may summarise the evidence that the Doctors' Plot purge was directed against Beria, among others:

(a) The accusation was made that the former State Security authorities had shown insufficient vigilance.

(b) Stalin dealt directly with Ignatiev in the matter (Khrushchev's Secret Speech).

(c) Beria was not accused of the frame-up at his trial, or in the Secret Speech, or (until much later) elsewhere.

(d) No reference was made at the trial of Ryumin to Beria's complicity.

(e) In April 1953 it was Beria's newly organised Ministry of the Interior that issued the repudiation of the plot. At the same time Beria's nominees in Georgia were repudiating similar but more developed plots there, which had definitely implicated Beria's protégés.

(f) Beria's position was shown to be greatly strengthened on Stalin's death, by his gaining control of the new joint Police Ministry, by the elevation of Bagirov and by his own definite emergence as No. 2.

It seems almost certain, therefore, that Stalin had removed Beria from control of the security apparatus, that Beria's protégés were being victimised and that the Doctors' Plot frame-up was highly distasteful to him. The conclusion seems practically unavoidable that he was an intended victim.

The argument associating Khrushchev with Stalin's purge plan is not entirely conclusive. The fact that the police side of it seems to have been directly under the old dictator's control implies that Khrushchev was at least not privy to that. On the other hand, figures who were in high favour with Stalin and occupied posts which would have been key ones had the matter gone any further — such as Aristov, Ignatiev and Kozlov — all came under Khrushchev's protection in the ensuing years. Brezhnev and Ignatov, the other Party Secretaries to decline in power after Stalin's death, were also to be keen supporters of Khrushchev in the later crises. Brezhnev had certainly come up in his Ukrainian apparatus.

Then again, the trial of Ryumin in 1954 came at a point in which Malenkov was in the ascendancy and is best interpreted as a blow at Malenkov's opponents — that is, presumably, Khrushchev. But this is to say that the raising of the Doctors'

Plot issue was in some sense a threat to Khrushchev, or at least to his supporters.

The final argument is a negative one, though none the less not without point. That is, that there is no sign whatever of Khrushchev having been out of favour with Stalin and nothing that can even be interpreted that way. In fact, Khrushchev does not even claim in the Secret Speech that he was himself in trouble. It is true that he says that the old Politburo as a whole was menaced by Stalin, but that is a general enough proposition, and it is difficult to take it too seriously. There were several of the pre-1930 Politburo who survived right through the extremely thorough purges of the 'thirties, and there is little reason to believe that Stalin could have exceeded the ruthlessness of that time.

But it is reasonable to think that even those among the old leadership aimed at by the incipient purge — and perhaps even those compelled to co-operate in it — might have regarded it without enthusiasm. As they knew from experience, once these things get started the chances of survival are low. Yet their position must have been difficult. For they would remember that it was precisely those who had attempted to prevent the Yezhovshchina who had been quickest to follow its first victims. Thus while they might have taken some hesitant steps unostentatiously to slow down the course of events, they may well have felt that there was no way of stopping it — apart from the dead-stop of assassination. Just as in the 'thirties, Stalin was operating directly through the Security Police, and simply presented the leadership with the 'protocols' of the doctors' guilt, which, as Khrushchev complains, they were scarcely in a position to query. The natural action must have been to retain as much of Stalin's confidence as possible by a display of enthusiastic co-operation in the purge.

But these points were not to be clarified in the course of events. On March 4 it was announced that Stalin had had a stroke two-and-a-half days before, and on the morning of March 6 that he had died the previous night. The same evening far-reaching changes in the leadership were made public. The complicated and obscure plan for a major purge had given way to quite a different, though also obscure, series of manœuvres among the old dictator's diadochi.

This same statement was a theme to Khrushchev, or at least to his superiors.

The final argument is a negative one, though none the less not without point. That is, that there is no sign whatever that Khrushchev has been out of favour with Stalin and nothing that can even be construed that way. In fact, Khrushchev does not even figure in the Secret Speech that he was himself in trouble if it is one that he says that he did follibuto as a whole was menaced by Stalin, but that it is a general enough proposition and it is difficult to take at too seriously. There were several of the pre-1952 Politburo who survived right through the extremely thorough purge of the "thirties," and there is little reason to believe that Stalin could have exceeded the public success that time.

But it is reasonable to think that there are those among the old leadership afraid to try the imminent purge — and perhaps even then compelled to co-operate in it — make have responded it without enthusiasm. As they knew from experience, once these things get started their chances of survival are low. Yet their position must have been difficult. For they could remember that it was precisely those who had attempted to prevent the Yezhovshchina who had been quickest to follow its logic victims. That while they might have taken some hesitant steps unenthusiastically to slow down the course of events, they may well have felt that there was no way of stopping it — apart from the drastic step of assassination. Just as in the 'thirties, Stalin was operating directly and the Security Police, and simply bombing the leadership with the 'protocols' of the convicted, might, when, as Khrushchev complains, they were scarcely in a position to query. The human nation must have been to retain the trust of Stalin's confidence as possible by a display of unhesitating co-operation in the purge.

But these points were not to be clarified in the course of events. On March 3 it was announced that Stalin had had a stroke two-and-a-half days before, and on the morning of March 6 it was said that the previous night, at the some evening the members of the leadership were made public. The announcement told that a plan that a major purge had given way to some more traditional, though also obscure, series of appointments among those who would share the power.

PART III

THE STRUGGLE FOR POWER IN
CONDITIONS OF COLLECTIVE LEADER-
SHIP, 1953–60

CHAPTER NINE

THE DEATH OF STALIN AND THE FALL OF BERIA, 1953

In getting even a hypothetical picture of the events of the days after Stalin's death, it must be remembered that there are factors at whose influence we can hardly even guess. The situation was a completely unique one. We have no way of telling, for instance, how much influence on the survivors real fears of popular trouble, of Army plots, even of the imperialists seizing the opportunity to launch a war, may have exerted. (Their appeal against 'disarray and panic' certainly seems to imply considerable lack of confidence in the stability of the institutions designed to support a one-man dictatorship, now that the man had been removed.)

Yet it depends a good deal on what weight we give this factor how much compulsion we are going to believe was present at the first March meeting for a compromise, makeshift solution. Even the bitterest enemies may postpone a duel and collaborate to prevent the ship that they are in from sinking.

On March 7 the Moscow Press published a decision of a joint meeting of a plenary session of the Central Committee of the Communist Party of the Soviet Union, the U.S.S.R. Council of Ministers and the Praesidium of U.S.S.R. Supreme Soviet. It ran in part as follows:

The Central Committee of the Communist Party of the Soviet Union, the Council of Ministers of the U.S.S.R. and the Praesidium of the Supreme Soviet, in this difficult time of our party and country, deem it the most important task of the party and the government to ensure uninterrupted and correct leadership of the whole life of the country, which in turn demands the greatest unity of leadership and prevention of any kind of disarray and panic, in order by this means to ensure unconditionally the successful implementation of the policy evolved by our party and government both in the domestic affairs of our country and in international affairs.

195

I. *On the Chairman and First Vice-Chairman of the U.S.S.R. Council of Ministers*

(1) To appoint as Chairman of the U.S.S.R. Council of Ministers Comrade Georgi Maximilianovich Malenkov.

(2) To appoint as First Vice-Chairmen of the U.S.S.R. Council of Ministers Comrades Lavrenty Pavlovich Beria, Vyacheslav Mikhailovich Molotov, Nikolai Alexandrovich Bulganin and Lazar Moiseyevich Kaganovich.

II. *On the Praesidium of the U.S.S.R. Council of Ministers*

(1) To recognise the necessity of having in the U.S.S.R. Council of Ministers, instead of two bodies — the Praesidium and the Bureau of the Praesidium — one body, the Praesidium of the U.S.S.R. Council of Ministers.

(2) To establish that the Praesidium of the U.S.S.R. Council of Ministers shall include the Chairman of the U.S.S.R. Council of Ministers and the First Vice-chairmen of the U.S.S.R. Council of Ministers. . . .

On the Secretary of the Praesidium of the U.S.S.R. Supreme Soviet

(1) To appoint as Secretary of the Praesidium of the U.S.S.R. Supreme Soviet Comrade Nikolai Mikhailovich Pegov, relieving him of the duties of Secretary of the Central Committee of the C.P.S.U. . . .

IV. *On the U.S.S.R. Ministry of Internal Affairs*

To merge the U.S.S.R. Ministry of State Security and the U.S.S.R. Ministry of Internal Affairs into one ministry, the U.S.S.R. Ministry of Internal Affairs.

On the U.S.S.R. Minister of Internal Affairs

To appoint Comrade Lavrenty Pavlovich Beria U.S.S.R. Minister of Internal Affairs. . . .

XI. *On the Praesidium of the Central Committee of the C.P.S.U. and the Secretaries of the Central Committee of the C.P.S.U.*

(1) To recognise the need to have in the Central Committee of the C.P.S.U. instead of two agencies of the Central Committee, the Praesidium and the Bureau of the Praesidium, one agency, the Praesidium of the Central Committee of the C.P.S.U., as set forth in the Party Statutes.

(2) In order to ensure more operative leadership, the Praesidium shall consist of ten members and four candidates.

(3) To establish the following composition of the Praesidium of the Central Committee of the C.P.S.U.

Members of the Praesidium of the Central Committee: Comrades G. M. Malenkov, L. P. Beria, V. M. Molotov, K. Ye. Voroshilov, N. S. Khrushchev, N. A. Bulganin, L. M. Kaganovich, A. I. Mikoyan, M. Z. Saburov and M. G. Pervukhin.

As candidate members of the Praesidium of the Central Committee of the C.P.S.U.: Comrades N. M. Shvernik, P. K. Ponomarenko, L. G. Melnikov, M. D. Bagirov.

(4) To elect Comrades S. D. Ignatiev, P. N. Pospelov and N. N. Shatalin Secretaries of the Central Committee of the C.P.S.U.

(5) To consider it necessary for Comrade N. S. Khrushchev to concentrate on work in the Central Committee of the C.P.S.U. and in this connection to relieve him of his duties as First Secretary of the Moscow Committee of the C.P.S.U.

(6) To confirm Comrade N. A. Mikhailov, Secretary of the Central Committee of the C.P.S.U., as First Secretary of the Moscow Committee of the C.P.S.U.

(7) To relieve Comrades P. K. Ponomarenko and N. G. Ignatov of their duties as Secretaries of the Central Committee of the C.P.S.U. in connection with transfer to executive work in the U.S.S.R. Council of Ministers and Comrade L. I. Brezhnev in connection with his transfer to the post of head of the Political Department of the Navy Ministry (*Pravda* and *Izvestia*, March 7, 1953).

The joint meeting of the Central Committee, the Praesidium of the Supreme Soviet and the Council of Ministers has no constitutional validity for making either Party or State appointments. It had been used before, as in the appointment of the State Defence Committee in 1941.

Such a joint meeting can be understood as a demonstration of the unity of State and Party, and as a simultaneous presentation of a common will on the part of all the highest organs in the country, both active and decorative. At the same time it was, in a sense, an illustration of a comparatively reduced role for the Party. What had once been the usual procedure of a Central Committee decision preceding a governmental one was not complied with. Moreover, a meeting of this sort would as far as attendance is concerned add only a handful of Ministers who were not Central Committee members to the hundreds entitled to be present in any case.

What is more to the point is that no provision exists for

registering the vote of a meeting of this sort, so that it is clear that neither debate nor vote was anticipated, but rather unanimity from the start. And this implies that the meeting was held to approve decisions already taken — possibly by a legal majority of the large Praesidium, possibly by the self-constituted small Praesidium.

The changes of March 7, 1953, involved the non-appearance of the following full members of the large Praesidium, on the new small Praesidium, as either members or candidates:

Andrianov; Aristov; Chesnokov; Ignatiev; Korotchenko; Kuusinen; V. V. Kuznetsov; Malyshev; Mikhailov; Shkirya-tov. All these had evidently been junior members, and removal in any given case implies no more than juniority. All the old candidate members were likewise removed.

Except for V. V. Kuznetsov and (though perhaps later) Chesnokov, all kept their extra-praesidial posts, apart from Ignatiev. And he, on the resumption of the M.V.D.–M.G.B. by Beria, was transferred to the powerful compensation of the Secretariat. Mikhailov and Aristov also remained Party secretaries, and Mikhailov gained the additional power of Moscow Party Secretary.

From the Secretariat the removals were Ponomarenko on the one hand, and Pegov, Ignatov and Brezhnev on the other. Ponomarenko clearly lost nothing in status, and the others were the three junior members of the Secretariat, those who had been only candidate members of the Praesidium. Yet in the case of the two last, at least, demotion seems to have been considerable. The associations of the four seem to be: Pegov and Ponomarenko — Malenkov; Ignatov and Brezhnev — non-Malenkov. The most ostentatious demotion (that of Brezh-nev) was of the member of the Secretariat most closely associated with Khrushchev. Yet while Malenkov was thus ridding himself of rivals no signs of disgrace were visited on the ap-paratchiks of Stalin's new promotion, in particular Aristov and Ignatiev. Malenkov's position was further strengthened by the promotion of Shatalin — the only promotion to the upper bodies among this welter of demotion, with the exception of Beria's Bagirov.

It may also be possible to read in Ponomarenko's transfer to be Minister of Culture an intentional strengthening of the State apparatus in the cultural–ideological field as against the Party bureaucrats of the Agitprop and Science and Culture departments of the Central Committee.

The events between Stalin's death and the setting up of a regime with different purposes a few days later are unknown. On March 1 Stalin was alive and well and the country was ruled by the large Praesidium, which Stalin presumably regarded as containing a majority adequate to carry through his grand purge. On March 6 this majority had somehow broken up and a small group, clearly working on a compromise basis, had gained control. It included the prospective purgees and was soon publicly to drop the purge. To reconstruct, hypothetically, the course of events that led to this change is obviously very difficult. But it is an exercise in a method which we have not yet really covered and which we might describe as pure ratiocination.

It will be seen that it involves several steps in argument which it is impossible to refer to evidence. And it need hardly be said that this is a dangerous procedure. The following is therefore simply put forward as an exercise. The writer has, however, considered a variety of alternative hypotheses. In principle, though various adjustments of detail are possible, these range between an immediate amicable compromise and something only just short of a violent open clash. We can certainly take it, from subsequent events, that amicable give-and-take was not a characteristic of relations between those involved. How far friction went in the first days of March, and how far it was inhibited by a common interest in avoiding breakdown, are unknown factors. Meanwhile it will not be out of place to construct a hypothesis on the assumption that the frictions were as intense as usual.

Such an exercise is not, of course, truly necessary to a study of the period. And some new piece of evidence might destroy it lock, stock and barrel. 'Kremlinology' has a characteristic fault, from which other sciences are not indeed exempt. It is, after a theory has been developed, to attempt to fit refractory evidence into it by a series of subsidiary *ad hoc* assumptions. I am sure that this book is not as free in practice as it is in intention of this habit. This is not to say that subsidiary assumptions may not turn out to be perfectly justifiable. But every anomaly that has to be coped with by such an assumption must at least

o

be taken to make the theory less certain, and induce the theoriser to go over the ground again with a reopened mind.

Yet it may be worth essaying one of the possible logical reconstructions, if only because no official information is available about the way in which the actual changes were arrived at so that the reconstruction must proceed from the state of affairs before and after.

The relevant factors seem to be:

(1) The legal power before Stalin's death lay in the twenty-five-man Party Praesidium. On this there was a majority of men recently appointed by Stalin with the express purpose (Khrushchev tells us) of replacing the old leaders. After the reorganisation most of the *novi homines* of the large Praesidium were excluded from the new small Praesidium and some were rusticated to posts of a very minor character. These men eventually returned to the centre during Khrushchev's ascendancy two years later and remained there in 1957 when Malenkov, Molotov and the rest of the Anti-Party Group were being expelled.

(2) Prior to Stalin's death the Ministries of State Security and of the Interior were not under Beria's control. Moreover, the propaganda on the Doctors' Plot had severely criticised previous controllers of the State Security Ministries — i.e. Beria and his subordinates. After the reorganisation Beria was strengthened by gaining control of these organs, now united, and by Bagirov, who can be definitely identified with him, becoming a candidate member of the new Praesidium, though he had not even been a candidate member of the old large one. Beria's increased power can of course be demonstrated in other ways.

(3) The only matter of simple observation involved is that the streets of Moscow were solid with M.V.D. troops when Stalin's death was announced. It is also significant that the Moscow District, Moscow Garrison and Kremlin Garrison Commanders were all removed following Beria's fall.

On this basis it seems reasonable to argue that in theory the beneficiaries and proponents of Stalin's latest intended purge had, at his death, both a majority in the Praesidium and control of the Security Police. There seems no reason to imagine that they would have conceded either position voluntarily. And the conclusion seems to be that Beria regained control of the Police Ministries by what amounted to a coup.

If Beria had thus obtained control of the machine which could give him at least Moscow and the persons of most of his opponents, we next have to seek a reason why he did not carry through his return to power more thoroughly. Again the presumed answer seems to be that his opponents were not without resources. Their constitutional majority on the Praesidium might, indeed, have been destroyed by judicious arrests, as Stalin had destroyed a hostile majority on the Central Committee in the 'thirties. The implication is that other members of the Praesidium held positions of real, and not merely formal, strength. That power can only have resided in two institutions: the Party Secretariat and the Army. With the Army one can only speculate. There were no important bodies of troops in Moscow military district not under M.V.D. control. If there was any hint of a threat to use troops it must have been in terms of other district commands — perhaps Leningrad, where Marshal Govorov was G.O.C. The Party levers, too, were in the hands of capable operators. One is again forced to conclude that there was a political grouping strong enough to present a possible threat in the use of either the Army or the Party machine or both unless it was offered at least some semblance of a compromise. Nobody might be expected to be willing to risk the desperate and uncertain recourse to a direct clash which might involve an open appeal to the country, let alone fighting. Yet on the other hand neither side would be likely to accept less than a strong enough position to guarantee or appear to guarantee at least its safety, even if the alternative was the risk of open conflict.

In Beria's case one of the incentives for avoiding a final showdown would be that he had at this stage no political basis whatever. In the Party and in the country he would be regarded as simply a police terrorist. Over the next few months he started to build himself up a policy basis, as we shall see.

The immediate post-Stalin settlement was thus in the main satisfactory to Malenkov, who took the highest position in State and Party, and to Beria, who regained all the powers that he had lost, and even increased them. It was at least tolerable to other members of the Praesidium, in that Stalin's direct threat to their positions was eliminated and his new men dispersed. The settlement might even be regarded as a legitimate continuation of the Stalin heritage — with the dead man's most recent will having been quietly torn up and reliance placed on an earlier one.

Nevertheless, the most natural solution, and the one most widely expected, was different: this was that Molotov, senior Vice-Premier, should succeed to the Premiership and Malenkov to the leading Party Secretaryship. It seems reasonable to attribute the result to a Malenkov–Beria settlement, based on the Party apparatus and the armed forces of the capital. Molotov's appearance as third in seniority was at least an improvement over his position as suspect of various charges.

The duumvirate's power was not complete, especially in that, for instance, Malenkov's control of the Secretariat was limited by the presence of Khrushchev. Yet so long as Malenkov and Beria remained in alliance it seems that it was well within their power to crush all opposition. And Khrushchev had lost Moscow.

But the mechanics of oligarchy virtually dictate that mistrust and rivalry shall subsist particularly between the two most powerful leaders. If Beria had been unable to strike for absolute power on Stalin's death, both ambition and self-defence might lead him into attempting to weaken Malenkov's position in his own interests. To do this he was bound to seek allies in the Praesidium, and in this balance of forces Khrushchev, Molotov and the others began to carry more weight again. The original solution had probably been accepted by them partly willy-nilly, but partly on a calculation of the potentialities for an increase in their powers. The March 7 solution removed unwanted players from the game, and left the old circle, some with stronger hands, and some with weaker, but all with a stake, and ready for the next round of bidding. The March 14 solution may be thought of as the first hand played under the new rules.

In the meantime Malenkov was to all appearances in possession of both the main levers of political power, the Premiership and the leading Secretaryship of the Party. For a few days a considerable cult of his personality flourished, well exemplified in the famous Faked Photograph published in *Pravda* of March

10, 1953. This purported to show Malenkov with Stalin and Mao-Tse-Tung, but was in fact a manipulation of a photograph originally appearing in *Pravda* of February 14, 1950, which represented a larger scene with many other persons. Three of these separated Malenkov from Mao, and in the 1953 reproduction this section of the picture was simply removed and Malenkov's part blended with Mao's. (This montage was also reproduced as a picture in *Ogonyok* of March 12, 1953.)

Meanwhile nothing had been said in the way of repudiating the Doctors' Plot, though those likely to have fallen in Stalin's purge were already firmly back in power.

Obituaries of Stalin by four doctors appeared in *Meditsinsky Rabotnik* of March 10, 1953. Three were prominent academicians, and one was Dr. Timashuk. Her obituary strongly ran the vigilance line. The significance of this seems to be that neither the editors nor the censors, at this stage, seem to have had any doubts about the Doctors' Plot, and that the vigilance campaign proceeded as before Stalin's death. It seems reasonable to suppose that if there had been any qualms at all, those concerned could and would have played safe by simply printing anodyne obituaries by non-controversial figures.

Some curious listings, at the various ceremonies of mourning, are worth noting (omitting full members of the Praesidium):

March 6: Shvernik, Suslov, Ponomarenko, Mikhailov.
March 8: Suslov, Mikhailov, Ponomarenko, Ignatiev, Aristov, Shatalin.
March 10: Shvernik, Suslov, Ponomarenko, Melnikov, Bagirov, Shkiryatov, Mikhailov, Pospelov.
March 10: Suslov, Mikhailov, Pospelov. (*Pravda* and *Izvestia*.)

The main curiosity here is the anomalous ranking of Suslov, which strongly suggests an attempt to bring him in to a higher position than Malenkov or Beria intended, or (eventually) conceded.

In the week following the provisional settlement of March 7 there must have been lively political activity to secure, while the situation remained fairly fluid, a further major change. We may take the plenum of March 14 as the occasion of the first denunciation of the Doctors' Plot, almost certainly by

Beria. For references to the plot in the central Press now, for the first time, ceased. And the announcement of Ignatiev's removal from the Party Secretariat on April 7, as being partly responsible for the plot, was referred to as a decision of a Central Committee plenum, of which the mid-March one was the latest. It is true that the Secretariat as announced after the plenum still included Ignatiev, but his name now came last (and he was not replaced when his removal was made public). We may therefore perhaps assume that a final settlement of the Secretariat had been made, with a decision to leave the formal removal of Ignatiev until the public announcement of the Doctors' Plot disavowal.

If the new political initiative by which Beria now changed the situation was the attack on the Doctors' Plot, the great political *result* of the second March plenum was the abandonment by Malenkov of the Party Secretaryship. This is not to say that Malenkov himself was attacked in connection with the plot. But at least a majority was found for a programme including both repudiation of the Doctors' Plot and the curtailment of Malenkov's power.

If neither Ignatiev nor Aristov were demoted at the original March 1953 meeting, it must be that there was no animus against them on the part of Malenkov. It was only when Beria took the initiative, at the second plenum, that they fell. So we may conclude that Malenkov had no serious objections to their recent activities, and only threw them to the dogs when forced, in effect, to choose between the new generation of apparatchiks and manœuvres for power based on the state machinery, the economic leaders, and a programme of alliances involving the Stalinists of the older generation. We may regard this as a crucial decision; henceforward the apparatchiks (except for Malenkov's personal *khvost*, like Shatalin) were to turn for protection to Khrushchev, in an alliance that was to remain firm until after the defeat of Malenkov and his colleagues in 1957–58.*

If Beria intended a more thorough counter-purge, and an even greater strengthening of his own position, his allies against

---

* It might be reasonable to date divergence between F. R. Kozlov and Malenkov to this immediate post-Stalin period. Kozlov had served since 1949 in the Malenkov regime in Leningrad, but now he found Malenkov unable, or unwilling, to prevent his demotion.

Malenkov's excessive powers were not prepared to cut these simply in order to strengthen the police chief. We may reasonably regard Khrushchev as an ally of Beria's against Malenkov at this point. If so, he seems nevertheless (to judge by later allegiance) to have done his utmost to save the heads of Stalin's agents in the Doctors' Plot, with a view to using them later. The plenum took Malenkov from his Secretaryship (and thenceforward the brief personality cult of him which the Press had indulged in for a week ceased). It also removed Mikhailov—though leaving him his important Moscow post. On the other hand, the removal and extreme demotion of Aristov now took place.

The plenum taking place on March 14 was announced a week later as follows:

A plenary session of the Central Committee of the Communist Party of the Soviet Union, held March 14, 1953, adopted the following resolution:

(1) To grant the request of Chairman of the U.S.S.R. Council of Ministers Comrade G. M. Malenkov to be released from the duties of Secretary of the Party Central Committee.

(2) To elect the following Secretariat of the Party Central Committee: Comrades N. S. Khrushchev, M. A. Suslov, P. N. Pospelov, N. N. Shatalin and S. D. Ignatiev.

(3) In conformity with Article 32 of the Party Statutes to transfer Comrade N. N. Shatalin from candidate to member of the Party Central Committee (*Pravda*, March 21, 1953).

In this announcement Shatalin is already listed above Ignatiev, and his raising to full membership of the Central Committee also indicates his increased significance. So, of course, does the fact that he was now one of five (and later four) secretaries instead of one of eight. That Ignatiev became junior secretary, after having so recently been a full member of the Praesidium and greatly senior to both Shatalin and Pospelov, seems, as we have said, to confirm that the March 14 plenum was the scene of the main showdown in the Doctors' Plot issue, though the formal investigation by the Ministry of Internal Affairs had to be gone through before the matter could be regularised.

There is some further evidence that the repudiation of the Doctors' Plot had been definitely decided on rather earlier than the April announcement. One of the accused doctors,

Preobrazhensky, had been editor of the bimonthly *Vestnik Oto-Rino-Laringologii*, in which his name had appeared in the issue of November 4, 1952, and been removed in that of January 17, 1953. In the issue of March 31, 1953, his name has already reappeared.

That Ignatov was publicly promised a Government appointment on March 7, but did not appear on the Government list published on March 15 is further evidence of the change which had taken place between the two plenums. It was not until April 1 that Ignatov's appointment to Leningrad (as Second Secretary of the Provincial, and First Secretary of the City, Committees) was announced, Kozlov stepping down to Third Secretary, perhaps as a result of his *Kommunist* article on the Doctors' Plot.

In Aristov's case, at least, revenge for the Doctors' Plot seems the undeniable motive for demotion. Yet the compromise secured by the Praesidium majority saved even him from being publicly blamed. And the postponement until the following month of the official repudiation of the plot and the demotion of Ignatiev adequately dissociated these events from both the fall of Aristov and the coup against Malenkov.

The Doctors' Plot was repudiated on April 4, in a communiqué of Beria's U.S.S.R. Ministry of Internal Affairs, as follows:

The U.S.S.R. Ministry of Internal Affairs has carried out a thorough verification of all the preliminary investigation data and other material in the case of the group of doctors accused of sabotage, espionage and terrorist acts against active leaders of the Soviet State.

The verification has established that the accused in this case, Professors M. S. Vovsi, V. N. Vinogradov, M. B. Kogan, B. B. Kogan, P. I. Yegorov, A. I. Feldman, Ya. G. Etinger, V. K. Vasilenko, A. M. Grinshteyn, V. F. Zelenin, B. S. Preobrazhensky, N. A. Popova, V. V. Zakusov, N. A. Shereshevsky and Dr. G. I. Mayorov, were arrested by the former U.S.S.R. Ministry of State Security incorrectly, without lawful basis.

Verification has shown that the accusations against the above-named persons are false and the documentary sources on which the investigating officials based themselves are without foundation.

It was established that the testimony of the arrested, allegedly confirming the accusations against them, was obtained by the officials of the investigatory department of the former Ministry of

State Security through the use of impermissible means of investigation which are strictly forbidden under Soviet law.

On the basis of the conclusion of an investigatory commission especially appointed by the U.S.S.R. Ministry of Internal Affairs to check this case, the arrested M. S. Vovsi, V. N. Vinogradov, B. B. Kogan, P. I. Yegorov, A. I. Feldman, V. K. Vasilenko, A. M. Grinshteyn, V. F. Zelenin, B. S. Preobrazhensky, N. A. Popova, V. V. Zakusov, N. A. Shereshevsky and G. I. Mayorov and others accused in this case have been completely exonerated of the accusations against them of sabotage, terrorist and espionage activities, and, in accord with Article 4, Paragraph 5, of the Criminal Procedure Code of the Russian Republic, have been freed from imprisonment.

The persons accused of incorrect conduct of the investigation have been arrested and brought to criminal responsibility (*Pravda*, April 4, 1953).

Pravda of the same day announced the revocation of the Order of Lenin awarded to Dr. Timashuk on January 20.

Pravda commented editorially:

This happened primarily because the leaders of the former Ministry of State Security proved unequal to their tasks. They broke away from the people and from the Party. They forgot that they were servants of the people and that their duty was to stand guard over Soviet law. Former Minister of State Security Ignatiev displayed political blindness and heedlessness. It turned out that he was led around by such criminal adventurists as Ryumin, former Deputy Minister and head of the investigation section, who directed the investigation and who has now been arrested.

Having trampled on the lofty duty of officials of government agencies and his own responsibility to the Party and the people, Ryumin and other employees of the Ministry of State Security, guided by criminal aims, embarked on gross violation of Soviet law, including outright falsification of evidence, and dared to mock inviolable rights of Soviet citizens which are inscribed in our Constitution.

Despicable adventurers of the Ryumin type tried, through their fabricated investigation, to inflame in Soviet society, which is imbued with moral and political unity and the ideas of proletarian internationalism, feelings of national antagonism, which are profoundly alien to socialist ideology. For these provocational ends they did not stop at mad slander of Soviet people. Careful investigation has established, for example, that an honest public figure, People's

Artist of the U.S.S.R. Mikhoels, was slandered in this way (*Pravda*, April 6, 1953).

Next day Ignatiev's removal, with its reference to the plenum, was published: 'By decision of a plenary session of the Central Committee of the C.P.S.U. Comrade S. D. Ignatiev has been released from the duties of a Secretary of the Central Committee of the C.P.S.U.' (*Pravda*, April 7, 1953).

Following this, as we have seen, the purge in Georgia was also reversed and those arrested and denounced (in this case Party figures) set free. A link between the central and Georgian purges was established when the local cases were said to have been 'fabricated by the enemies of the people and the state Rukhadze and Ryumin' (*Zarya Vostoka*, April 21, 1953).

Meanwhile another announcement in complete contradiction to the vigilance and embezzlement ones of the Plot period was made in an area of special interest to Beria in a Decree of the U.S.S.R. Supreme Soviet *On the Amnesty*. It said that

observance of the law and socialist order have grown stronger and the incidence of crime has considerably decreased in the country as a result of the consolidation of the Soviet social and state system, the rise in the standard of living and culture of the population, the increase in the civic consciousness of citizens and their honest attitude toward the performance of their social duty . . . (*Pravda*, March 28, 1953).

This second post-Stalin settlement, as is apparent from the later developments, did not consist of a complete victory by any faction over any other.

It seems apparent that the Praesidium was not united even in its opposition to the purge which Stalin had initiated. If it had been, it is difficult to imagine, when other events in Soviet political life are remembered, that the new cadres that Stalin was grooming to replace the old Praesidium would have got off so lightly. As it was, even Ignatiev was only demoted. No one was brought to justice except Ryumin, and that only as a later manœuvre. And the 'new' political figures like Aristov were simply transferred quietly to the provinces. Poskrebyshev, indeed, disappeared. He was simply not mentioned again, apart from a brief sneer in Khrushchev's Secret Speech (or rather the only reference that I have been able to turn up about him is an attack on his speech at the XIXth Congress in *Sovietskoye Gosudarstvo i Pravo*, No. 4, of 1956). And Chesnokov, who had been the ideologist of the purge, was not heard of until 1957. But as the accompaniment of a political victory this amounted to very little. The natural conclusion would be that a powerful section at least of the new Praesidium was determined to protect Stalin's latest protégés and it at least seems possible that this faction in the Praesidium had itself hoped to benefit from the purge. All the evidence points to Khrushchev as the protector of the Aristovs and Ignatievs, as we have already seen (p. 190).

It is curious and noteworthy that the *Large Soviet Encyclopaedia* in its articles on such figures as Ponomarenko and Suslov, appearing before the fall of the Anti-Party Group, while giving their careers in some detail, makes no reference to their having been members of the 'large' Praesidium, and this is one more shred of evidence that we may add. For, on the contrary, the supplementary Volume 51, which appeared in 1958, has the 'large' Praesidium appointments as well as all others. This would, if anything, seem to signify that service in that body was regarded as almost unmentionable *until* Khrushchev reached the height of his power.

All this is to assert the enmities and rivalries which, as the issue showed, certainly existed among the leaders. But it is perhaps a trifle one-sided to insist on nothing else. Even if Khrushchev, say, had been one of those against whom Stalin had no immediate aims, he may well have felt a certain general insecurity, remembering the 'thirties. If Stalin had indeed frequently spoken of the desirability of replacing the Politburo membership in general, as Khrushchev states in his Scret Speech, there was some reason for a certain solidarity among the members of the old Politburo *vis-à-vis* their intended successors. And it may not be too much to read into his motives and those of other members a readiness to rid themselves of the Aristovs, etc., only protecting their lives with a view to future possible use, or in order to avert a counter-purge which would have had the same or greater general disadvantages. The removal of Malenkov from the Party Secretaryship may be read as due less to an increase in Khrushchev's personal power than to a combined desire of the remainder of the leaders to prevent

the double position being in Malenkov's hands. Read in this
way one might imagine something in the nature of a Beria–
Malenkov alliance on March 6 imposing a solution giving
them the maximum power compatible with avoiding an open
breach with the others, followed by an agreement between Beria
and the remainder of the Praesidium to reduce Malenkov's
personal power. It is normal in these matters for the leading
contenders to deal with each other first and to try to make use of
the comparatively minor figures until the major rivals have
been got rid of. And even this is to simplify the possibilities when
a dozen contenders on a basis of comparative equality are
concerned.

It may also be argued that the death of Stalin anyhow prevented any question of a major purge being carried through by
its quondam supporters in the face of the opposition of the now
powerful survivors previously due for purge. In that case it
would be reasonable for Khrushchev or any other tolerably
flexible operator to have genuinely abandoned the purge idea.

Although the result of the March 14 upheaval was the giving
up by Malenkov of a position which was perhaps anyhow un-
tenable, there are countervailing points. His own closest associates did not suffer. The repudiation of the Doctors' Plot, with
its accompaniment of the breaking up of the careers of Stalin's
latest cadre, may have made Malenkov's resignation from the
secretaryship more palatable to him, by removing from the
struggle powerful figures outside his control. Thus the compromise was not entirely unsatisfactory to him either.

The important question remaining is who had charge of the
Party Organs Department after Aristov's and Ignatiev's removal. After April 7 the Secretariat consisted solely of Khrushchev, Suslov, Pospelov and Shatalin. Khrushchev seems, as
has always been the case with the senior secretary, to have had
general responsibility. Pospelov's experience was entirely in
the publicity and cultural world. Suslov had been a Party
Secretary throughout the time when the cadre side was certainly in other hands. His own public activities had been in the
sphere of foreign affairs and ideology, and his service in the
Party Agitprop Department. His attendance at the Cominform
meetings in 1948–49 almost certainly indicates that he was
then in charge of foreign affairs or ideology, or both, and was

present on that account; Malenkov and Zhdanov, as members of the Poliburo, would be representing Soviet policy as a whole.

This leaves only Shatalin. And the assumption is that he now took over the cadres' side. His association with Malenkov is certain, and it is reasonable to think that his retention with increased powers was part of the *quid pro quo* Malenkov extorted for his own abandonment of the Party Secretaryship.

Not only had all the principles, as well as the allegations, of the Doctors' Plot period been repudiated, but during the next months there was greater abstention from over-praise of Stalin than in any period up till February 1956. His methods of rule were indirectly criticised, as in an article in *Pravda* of April 16 'Collectivity is the Highest Principle of Party Leadership', by L. Slepov. And a curious and relevant incident now occurred. G. I. Petrovsky had been a distinguished old Bolshevik. He was a member of the Duma in Tsarist times, and after the revolution was President of the Ukraine and for thirteen years candidate member of the Politburo of the all-Union Communist Party. At the time of the fall of Kossior, during the height of the pre-war terror in the Ukraine, Petrovsky disappeared from public life with the remainder of the Ukrainian Politburo. But, unlike the others, all of whom seem to have been shot, Petrovsky, though removed from all his posts and from membership of the Central Committee, was still employed in a minor job in Moscow. On May 6, 1953, *Pravda* published a decree dated April 28, awarding him the Order of the Red Banner of Labour in connection with his seventy-fifth birthday and 'his services to the Soviet State'. This was the first and for some time unique case of the rehabilitation of an old Bolshevik who had fallen into disfavour under Stalin. Petrovsky had not, indeed, ever been accused of any crime (or, if he was imprisoned at all, it seems to have been for a very short time). But his removal from the Central Committee and compulsory retirement at least indicated that under Stalin he was regarded as *politically* unsound in some respect. But now his period in the shadows was simply ignored.

The matter is even more curious when we find that his real birthday had taken place on February 4, at a time when Stalin was still alive. The timing is peculiar, to say the least. Stalin had been dead, the Doctors' Plot had been reversed and

Beria was at the height of his powers. Clearly the announcement was intended to demonstrate something. It might be argued that a more liberal mood could be easily demonstrated by such an award, and that it had no other significance. But there were many other ways in which this could be done and many other persons to whom it could apply. And in the Soviet context it is at least reasonable to seek a more direct political significance. Petrovsky represented the pre-Khrushchev regime in the Ukraine. The actual First Secretary in the Ukraine, Melnikov, was shortly to be removed, in circumstances which appear to show Beria's influence. The rehabilitation of Petrovsky might most naturally be seen as part of the plan to have ready a leader, or at least a figurehead of great prestige, to assist in breaking up the Khrushchev fief. It is true that Petrovsky was seventy-five. But after all Kuusinen was a year older when, in 1957, Khrushchev called him to the Party Praesidium and Secretariat.

On the other hand, if we seek Beria's obvious allies against exaggerated Russian nationalism and against Melnikov in particular, we are bound to think of Khrushchev. He had not only been at the receiving end of charges of excessive leniency to local nationalism in 1947, but was also the immediate beneficiary of the removal of Melnikov (intruded by Stalin, to the benefit of none but possibly Malenkov in 1950), in favour of his own follower Kirichenko. The Khrushchev–Beria alliance visible in March 1953 was the natural bloc against Malenkov, and he seems to have been the main immediate gainer by Beria's fall. This is not, of course, to say that Beria might not preserve a rod in pickle against Khrushchev, and the powerful presence of his representative, Meshik, in the Ukrainian Bureau cannot have been welcome to the latter.

(After Beria's fall, Petrovsky was not often heard of. He had a few articles in the Press in 1955 and early in 1956, most of which seem to be historical reminiscences designed to cast doubt on the legitimacy of the powers of the Secretariat.)

In any case Beria, even officially the second man in the State and Party, was making the running. His basic asset remained control of the great police machine that he had ruled for so many years and temporarily lost. Basing himself on this power, and on the State and Party positions he held in Georgia and the other Transcaucasian republics, he launched a political initiative.

First he purged the M.V.D., replacing recently appointed figures hostile to him by his own men: in connection with his trial *Pravda* (December 17, 1953) said:

> Having become U.S.S.R. Minister of Internal Affairs in March 1953, Beria began increasingly to promote the participants in the conspiratorial group to a number of leading posts in the Ministry of Internal Affairs. The conspirators victimised and persecuted honest officials of the Ministry of Internal Affairs who refused to carry out the criminal orders of Beria.

In the M.V.D.s of the Union Republics he took similar steps. Meshik was appointed to the Ukrainian M.V.D. on April 11, 1953. On May 29 the Estonian M.V.D. Minister was replaced, on June 3 the Latvian, on June 6 the Lithuanian. These were members of the Bureaux of the republican Central Committees, and thus in a position to raise political issues.

We should now consider the nature of the 'Beria policies'. In dealing with Georgia we have already seen that those accused of nationalism under Stalin were now rehabilitated with honour, and there is good reason to think that one of Beria's lines was to try to obtain the promotion, and support, of local nationals.

The major area of conflict was the Ukraine.

At the Ukrainian Party Congress in September 1952 Melnikov, the Ukrainian First Secretary, had taken a strong Russian line on nationalism:

> The Ukrainian bourgeois nationalists were always the worst enemies of the Russian people; their actions were directed against Russian culture and its highest achievement — Leninism. . . . Their serpent sting was directed against the vital foundation of the Soviet system, the policy of the Communist Party, to which the Ukrainian people owes the prosperity of its economy and culture, the fulfilment of the dream of the union of all the Ukrainian lands in a single Ukrainian Soviet state (*Pravda Ukrainy*, September 25, 1952).

He went on to attack nationalist deviations in Ukrainian literature, by writers including Rylsky, with whose protection Khrushchev was identified (see pp 85-7).

Now, at a plenum of the Central Committee of the Ukrainian Communist Party held in Kiev on June 12, Melnikov was dismissed from the Ukrainian First Secretaryship and from the Party Bureau for 'gross errors in the selection of cadres and the carrying out of the national policy of the Party', and in kolkhoz policy. It was also stated that

'The bureau of the Central Committee and the secretary of the same Committee of the Ukrainian Communist Party, Comrade Melnikov, committed in their practical work distortions of the Leninist–Stalinist national policy of our Party; these distortions took the form of the shameful practice of promoting to leading Party and Soviet posts in the Western regions of the Ukraine mostly people from the other regions of the Ukrainian S.S.R. and of introducing teaching in Russian at the Western Ukrainian universities' (*Pravda*, June 13, 1953).

He was succeeded by the Ukrainian Second Secretary, Kirichenko.

The article on Kirichenko in Volume 51 of the *Large Soviet Encyclopaedia* (2nd edition, 1958) states that he became a candidate member of the Praesidium of the Central Committee of the C.P.S.U. in May 1953, and First Secretary of the Ukrainian Communist Party in June. The fact that only the *Ukrainian* dismissal of Melnikov was publicised at the time may be misleading. A decision to remove him from all his posts had clearly been taken, and taken by the Party Praesidium. That his removal from the centre seems to precede his dismissal from the Ukrainian post is not an essential point, being perhaps only procedural; but at least it demonstrates this yet more clearly.

Another key man in this must have been Serdyuk. He had been Secretary of the Kiev Provincial Committee and candidate member of the Central Committee of the Communist Party, from 1946. On January 31, 1949, he was named as Secretary and candidate member of the Ukrainian Politburo. At the XIXth Congress in 1952 he remained a candidate member of the Central Committee and was First Secretary in Lvov. He would thus be the key man in enforcing Melnikov's policies in the Western Ukraine which were particularly condemned. But, unlike his chief, he was part of Khrushchev's old cadres. And he reappears in a senior position as First Secretary of the Moldavian Central Committee on February 7, 1954, and was to be a most active supporter of the First Secretary.

The substitution of Kirichenko, who was to be a supporter of Khrushchev throughout the ensuing years, for Melnikov gave Beria no obvious advantage except in so far as a strengthening of Khrushchev was a weakening of Malenkov. And it is notable that the published censure referred not only to Melnikov, but to the Ukrainian bureau as a whole. The implication is that some attempt was being made not to let Khrushchev re-establish his old control in Kiev by default (and possibly this is where Petrovsky would have come in). The fact that the Praesidium was willing to let Melnikov go shows that Beria's power was not negligible, and that he had chosen a sound issue. It seems clear that Melnikov was regarded as vulnerable on this, though subsequent events show that the Praesidial majority took the view that Beria's line on the national issue went much too far in the opposite direction.

The Central Committee of the Lithuanian Communist Party performed similar self-criticism on June 17 (*Pravda*, June 18), and the Latvian Central Committee on June 27 (*Pravda*, June 28), in both cases with resolutions about the failure to promote local nationals to high position. (This last was just after the fall of Beria, but no doubt before any policy changes could be transmitted.)

After Beria's fall quite a campaign appeared in the Press on Ukrainian-Russian solidarity, in tones very different from those of the Melnikov censure.

Pravda on July 11, 1953, attacked Beria for trying 'under the false pretext of struggling against distortions of Party nationality policy, to sow discord and enmity among the nations of the U.S.S.R. and to revive the bourgeois-nationalist elements in the Union Republics'. It made a particular point of Ukrainian friendship for Russia:

An all-important date is approaching — the 300th anniversary of the union of the Ukrainian nation with the great Russian nation. Our Ukrainian nation will never forget the fraternal assistance of the great Russian nation and will continue to strengthen our friendship with the Russians and other nations of our country.

Pravda of July 12, 1953, in an article on the national question, again spoke in terms very different from those of the

P

Melnikov censure: 'The working people of the Western regions of the Ukraine know that they owe their happiness and their free and joyful life to the great Russian nation.'

Pravda continued to publish a number of similar pronouncements by local leaders (including Georgians), and on August 8 a Ukrainian deputy, Tychina, was put forward in it to write:

The fraternal friendship of the Ukrainian and Russian peoples, who are so much related to each other, as Vladimir Ilyich Lenin said, 'by their language, their close neighbourhood, their characters and their histories,' has been forged and consolidated during the age-long struggle of the toilers for their social and national emancipation. . . . We will never allow nationalists of any description, any sort of rogues, adventurers and renegades, to bring discord into our friendship with the great Russian and other brotherly nations.

These are some signs that Beria's line may have had some effect on local political leaders in other areas. For example, A. E. Kleshchev, Premier of Byelorussia, was removed from his post soon after Beria's fall (*Sovietskaya Byelorussia,* July 26, 1953), and was not elected even to the Byelorussian Central Committee at the local Congress in February 1954. (He was later to appear in very junior posts in Central Asia.) The same applies to I. L. Cherny, a deputy Premier and Head of the Byelorussian Gosplan. But the study of Byelorussian affairs is full of cross-currents almost as complex as those of Georgia, and there may possibly be some other explanation for these moves.

The Beria line was in any case having political consequences. In both Lithuania and Latvia the post of Second Secretary of the local Central Committee (normally concerned with cadres and under Stalin invariably occupied by Russians) was transferred from a Russian to one of the local nationality at the plenums in June 1953, and given back to Russians at the congresses in January 1956. Plenums held in other border republics, from Moldavia to Karelo-finland, also saw the appointment of local nationals to posts hitherto held by Russians (or at least references to the need to take more trouble about the 'basic nationality') in May–June 1953, and not later.

It is significant that of those executed with Beria all were either from Georgia or the central M.V.D., *except* Meshik, M.V.D. Minister in the Ukraine. Publicity was not thought necessary in the cases of others who seem certainly to have been shot at this time — for instance, Tsanava, who had held the police ministry in Byelorussia, and was mentioned in passing as a member of the 'Beria gang' only in *Sovietskaya Byelorussia* of April 10, 1956. It is at least tempting to see in this a particular intention to repudiate as publicly as possible Beria's action in the Ukraine, and to dissociate its new regime from him.

As part of a campaign to build up support among the national minorities, Beria's move, initially promising, seems a sensible one. If the struggle could have been kept on a political level it certainly seems possible that Beria might have built himself a firm basis in the Party apparatus in the Ukraine and the other Union Republics by securing the promotion of comparatively nationalist-minded cadres. It has always seemed that Beria's failure to seize power at the centre was fatal, and that his operations against Melnikov were sufficiently dangerous to his opponents to provoke them to action without being enough to cause them immediate serious harm. Yet Beria's difficulty was perhaps not so much the seizure of power (which one presumes he could perhaps have done), but of building himself a political as well as a police machine, and at least neutralising those of his enemies. If it is indeed true that the Berlin Rising of June 17 provided a motive for concentration against him in a sense which had not existed before, then it can be said that he had bad luck and that his operational plan was not necessarily defective in itself.

The official indictment against Beria attacks his nationality policy.

It has also been established that Beria and his accomplices undertook criminal measures in order to stir up the remains of bourgeois nationalist elements in the Union Republics, to sow enmity and discord among the peoples of the U.S.S.R., and, in the first place, to undermine the friendship of the peoples of the U.S.S.R. with the great Russian people (Statement of the U.S.S.R. Procurator-General's Office, *Pravda*, December 17, 1953).

There is very little published evidence of a more elaborate sort about what exactly Beria was up to, but the following formulation, made five years later, is significant as well as being interesting in showing the way in which odd leads may be found, years afterwards, embedded in reams of woolly theoretical verbosity:

The party proclaims the principles of promoting national cadres, whereas bourgeois nationalists or people who are influenced by bourgeois-nationalist ideology try to follow a policy of making discriminations between the cadres in accordance with their nationality. That is exactly what was done by enemy of the people Beria, who chose as one of the main forms of his diversionary work in the national Republics the placing of cadres of different nationalities in opposition to one another (*Voprosy Filosofii*, No. 1, 1958).

This can only be interpreted as meaning that Beria was attempting to build support for himself among Communists of the local nationalities, and conducting a definite campaign against Russian officials in possession. Except in Georgia, where there were almost no Russians anyhow, and in the rest of Transcaucasia, Beria had no direct control. His power in the Party organisation could only be exercised through the M.V.D. Minister on the local Party Bureau. Meshik, in the Ukraine, could very well have raised the nationalities issue in the Ukrainian Bureau, and have complained there of discontent among loyal cadres produced by Melnikov's policies.

It may be said that even if Beria had succeeded in removing the whole Ukrainian Bureau, he had no, or almost no, Ukrainian cadres of his own to recommend as their replacements (it seems unlikely that he could have gone to the lengths Khrushchev found possible in the opposite case, when he imposed a Georgian from the Ukraine upon the Georgian Party). But such a demonstration of power would at least begin to attract allegiances. And the more nationally minded cadres might have rallied to the Beria connection on policy grounds. In any case it was a policy of considerable sense as the part of a man needing to build up support rapidly, yet without direct access to the appointments machinery of the secretariat. The question how far Beria sincerely did adopt the policy of relaxation for the minority nations is insoluble. It was, at least, a policy with which he chose to associate himself.

To obtain support in the Party it was necessary for Beria to identify himself with a *political* programme, and one not already adopted by the collective leadership.

Apart from the nationality issue, the main accusations

against him are on agriculture. We can assume that his line differed both from the extreme compulsions of Stalin and the partial concessions being worked out by Khrushchev. From the little that has been said it seems that in this field, too, he was urging relaxations, and probably very considerable ones.

Later Khrushchev was to accuse Beria of blocking the correct solutions in agriculture (in *Kommunist* of August 1957). But even at the time, the Prosecutor's indictment says that Beria set out 'to undermine the collective farm system and create food difficulties in the country' and 'in every possible way sabotaged and interfered with the carrying out of vital Party and Government measures aimed at improving the kolkhozes and sovkhozes and steadily increasing the well-being of the Soviet people' (*Pravda*, December 17, 1953).

It must also be significant that Benediktov was removed from the Ministry of Agriculture and made Ambassador to India in April 1953, only to be recalled from India and made Minister again in August.

What measures Beria advocated is not plain. But his associates had been the spokesmen against the agrogrods in 1951; in 1951–52 the men he later rehabilitated were accused of insufficient disciplinary measures *vis-à-vis* the kolkhozes; criticisms of Melnikov included vague references to faulty kolkhoz policy, which in Western Ukrainian conditions must have been leftist deviations; and the policies associated with Beria in Hungary certainly implied the greatest relaxation of the collectivisation programme (see Appendix IX).

Whether Beria actually 'sabotaged and interfered' is another matter. Except in Transcaucasia the only instrument he had for such direct action was the Police machinery, and the only plausible action within its powers that might have had a direct effect on agriculture would have been a loosening up of the internal passport system, which as it stood (and stands) prevented the peasantry from leaving the soil.

All the attacks on Beria (except those for police and administrative excesses) emphasise a 'Rightist' element in his policies.

In the articles in *Pravda* and *Izvestia* on July 10, 1953, Beria was stated to have planned to 'replace the policy worked out by the Party for many years by a policy of capitulation which would have led ultimately to the restoration of capitalism'.

But, as we have said, where the fine detail of evidence is not available it is only too easy to construct much too crude a version of events. If we consider the policies towards minorities of the Soviet Union and the Communist states of Eastern Europe in the period immediately following Stalin's death, it is only too easy to regard them as 'Beria policies'. That this is in a sense a true description seems undeniable. But it requires a certain amount of reservation.

In the first place, it is inconceivable that policies and acts of policy could have been put through at this point by Beria alone, without the consent of a majority of the Party Praesidium. It may be that the motives for such consent fell short of enthusiastic support: indifference, pressure and even perhaps a desire to see the originator of the policies held to account for their failure might have played a part in securing that consent. But on the whole it seems that the Praesidium felt the force of the arguments which motivated Beria's policy, even when they were not, perhaps, prepared to draw such radical conclusions as he.

The removal of Melnikov for Russifying tendencies in the Ukraine cannot have been carried out without the approval of the Party Praesidium. The fact that, though he received minor posts after Beria's fall, he was never restored even to full membership of the Party Central Committee is an indication that the majority was unprepared to revert to the Russian nationalism which marked Stalin's last years, even though they may not have been prepared to go as far as Beria in the other direction. This conclusion is supported by a number of other facts, such as the attitude of the Party to the history of the minority nations. The treatment of the Imam Shamil, for instance, who led the resistance of the Chechens and Daghestanis to Russia in the middle of the nineteenth century, has always been a touchstone. Under Stalin he was condemned quite simply as 'an Anglo-Turkish agent'. During the period of relaxation in 1956 the editors of *Voprosy Istorii* fell into disfavour very largely because they reverted to the pre-Stalin habit of regarding Shamil, like other nationalist leaders from the past, as entirely progressive. Yet the present view is that though it is wrong to regard the Tsarist annexation of the Caucasus as unbeneficial to the population, yet the resistance to it was up to a point democratic and progressive.

Similarly we may conclude that the new course in Hungary in 1953 was acceptable to the whole Praesidium. Imre Nagy states (see Appendix IX) that Rakosi attempted to bring it to a close on the pretext that it was Beria's policy and was taken to task for this by several members of the Praesidium, who urged a continuance of the new line. (This was presumably at the consultation between Soviet and Hungarian leaders which took place in August 1953.) It may indeed be that the Party Praesidium was not as united on the point as it purported to be, and the effective repudiation of the Hungarian 'new course' which took place at the same time as Malenkov's fall early in 1955 may show that Khrushchev himself was among the doubters. Or he may have changed his mind. Or (for all the alternatives should be kept in mind in matters of this sort) it may have been part of a bargain made between him and more 'Stalinist' members of the Praesidium to secure their support against Malenkov.

In any case, a majority of the Praesidium in July and August 1953 must have taken the position Nagy reports. And yet the fact that Rakosi believed that he could now repudiate the policy on the grounds that it was Beria's presumably indicates that he knew that Beria had in fact been making the running and put-ting the more extreme relaxation view in the matter, which is also in accord with the other evidence. A similar view can be taken of the East German situation. There the policy of relaxa-tion was not abandoned after the rising of June 17. But the rising could be blamed on excesses in implementing it, and when Ulbricht removed the 'Rightist' elements later in the year the Politburo member in charge of the Security Police, Zaisser, was openly referred to as both a Right deviationist and an associate of Beria. This would tend both to confirm our view of Beria's line and to show that he disposed of a powerful apparatus for pressing it.

A similar argument could be advanced in the matter of 'de-Stalinisation'. The absence of reference to Stalin in 1953 is remarkable, and though it seems to have been most complete in the period before the arrest of Beria it did not show much sign of revival for many months thereafter. (And here again it may be argued that the increase in favour-able reference to Stalin which took place later was part of a political move by one faction to secure the support of old Stalinists.)

A Beria programme seems to emerge of a definite congeries of 'liberal' policies. It has often been denied, usually on *a priori* grounds, that this can have been so, but it is difficult to place any other interpretation on the evidence.

The political tensions of this phase of the struggle were resolved by the coup of June 26, 1953, when Beria was arrested. This was not immediately announced. *Pravda* of June 28, 1953, described the attendance on the previous evening of Government and Party leaders at the opera 'The Decembrists'. These were all the members and candidate members of the Party Praesidium elected in March, except Beria, Melnikov and Bagirov, and with the addition of Malyshev.

Pravda, July 10, 1953, gave the first official statement — an account of the decision of a plenum of the Central Committee held 'recently', on a report of Malenkov's about Beria's crimes. *Pravda* of August 9, 1953, announced the appointment of Kruglov as Minister of the Interior, dated June 26, 1953, and *Pravda* of August 10, 1953, printed the official decree dismissing Beria, also dated June 26.

Kruglov was not given Beria's powers. The official announcement of the setting up of a K.G.B. independent of the M.V.D. did not come until April 27, 1954, when Serov was named to the post. But that the K.G.B. was already in existence in 1953 seems to be shown by the statement in an article on V. I. Ustinov, Moscow City Committee Secretary, in 1958 (Vol. 51 of the *Large Soviet Encyclopaedia*), that in 1953 he 'went into directing work in the Committee of State Security attached to the Council of Ministers of the U.S.S.R.'

Other sections of Beria's empire were, in any case, broken up at once. The Ministry of Medium Machine Building was set up on June 26, 1953 (*Pravda*, August 9, 1953). Malyshev was appointed to it on June 29 (*Pravda*, August 9, 1953). This was done quickly and the post was allotted to an important figure. It is widely held that this Ministry is the one responsible for the Soviet atomic programme. And it also seems that no official of this Ministry except the Minister himself and his successors, such as Pervukhin, and his deputies, Zavenyagin and Vannikov, have ever been mentioned in the public Press. On Zavenyagin's death it was said in the funeral speech by Malyshev that he had been the Deputy Minister since 1953 (*Pravda*, January 4, 1957). It is perhaps relevant that Zavenyagin's background was M.V.D., in which he had been Deputy Minister as recently as 1952.

Malyshev's appearance with the Praesidium at the Bolshoi Theatre on June 27 gives the impression that he, if anyone, was to be regarded as the figure promoted in Beria's place. On the other hand, Malyshev could have been in line for promotion to the Praesidium without inheriting the police. And the most natural figure to be put in control, at least for the immediate period, is Shatalin. Ustinov, mentioned above, was at this time not an important political figure, but a secretary in Khrushchev's Moscow apparatus. His appointment shows that the need for political control was appreciated. But he is not said to have *headed* the security organisation, and at this stage a Malenkov associate would be the natural appointment to the top job, quite apart from the Party Organs tradition of transfer to the police. In any case Malenkov appears to have been the main gainer, for the moment at least, from Beria's overthrow. (It is notable that as late as the XXth Congress he spoke at greater length and more violently than anyone else about the dead Police chief.)

The charges against Beria were not only political but of preparing to seize power, and it may be relevant that at this time all the Moscow posts changed hands. General Artemyev, Commander of the Moscow District, was replaced by Moskalenko, and went into obscurity. A member of the 1952 Central Committee, he was not to reappear on it in 1956. Lieut.-General Sinilov had been Commandant of the city of Moscow at least up to about August 23, but was later replaced by General Kolesnikov. At some time in the summer the Commandant of the Kremlin, Lieut.-General Spiridonov, was replaced by Lieut.-General Vedenin.

The documents on the Beria trial are given in Appendix VI.

The selection of Beria supporters for public trial is of interest. From the text issued by the Procurator General's Office (*Pravda*, December 17, 1953) it appears that they were all in positions of power during 1953, and all were, or had been, in the police apparatus. It is interesting that:

(*a*) The most prominent Beria man, Bagirov, was not tried for more than two years, though he was now already disgraced.

(*b*) A number of almost equally prominent Beria police officials — Gvishiani, Tsanava, Mamulov, and so on — who may be presumed shot, were not brought to public trial.

(*c*) Abakumov, who was later to figure as an 'accomplice' of Beria's and who was already in disgrace, was not produced or mentioned.

(*d*) The appearance of Vlodzimirsky may signify something. From his description as 'a former chief of the Investigation Section for Specially Important Cases of the U.S.S.R. Ministry of Internal Affairs' he seems to have been the most recent holder of that office—since the section was not part of the M.V.D., but of the M.G.B. until March 1953. The inclusion of the other names is readily explainable, even if the omissions are less so. But that Vlodzimirsky had attracted special attention may signify that his section was already at work on some 'specially important case', in a way which Beria's rivals disliked. The one really important case we know definitely to have been before the investigation organs is the Ryumin one. If Beria was manœuvring against his rivals in the usual way, it seems very clear that this would have been a powerful weapon.

The extent to which secrecy was maintained in the Beria case may be seen from Khrushchev's Secret Speech. In addressing the delegates to the XXth Congress, a fairly limited and high-ranking audience, one would have thought, on the full record of Beria's crimes, he said: 'It is possible that not all delegates to the Congress have read this document.'

The accusation against Beria of 'sometimes succeeding in protecting from exposure and deserved punishment' some of his contacts 'with foreign intelligence services' raises some problems. None such were ever brought to trial, or at least nothing of the kind was ever announced. These alleged contact men are clearly differentiated from the principals and accomplices actually shot with Beria. Moreover, if Soviet citizens they must be of a particular type, those in fairly easy contact with foreigners. This would virtually limit them to Foreign Ministry officials at home and in posts abroad, M.V.D. agents, and Tass and Press correspondents. The only significant figure who there is at least some reason to think was in trouble at this time was Ivan Maisky, formerly Ambassador to the United Kingdom, a country whose intelligence service Beria was specifically accused of serving. Maisky had disappeared from the public eye early in 1952. More to the point, there was no article on him in the Mai volume of the *Large Soviet Encyclopaedia* (passed for publication April 1954), while this omission was corrected in Volume 51, the supplementary volume with biographies of the wrongly purged, which came out in 1958. This strongly implies not only that he had fallen under Stalin, but that he was still (or again) under a cloud in 1954 and was later rehabilitated. He would fit the bill perfectly, particularly as a Jew, and thus of a category imprisoned by Stalin and favoured by Beria.

This is, of course, very tentative. Only if we knew the date of Maisky's rehabilitation would we be able to use the incident to illuminate other points. He seems to have returned to Moscow academic life in 1954 or 1955. There is in any case a reasonable presumption that his continuance in disfavour after Stalin's death and the (speculative) attempt to link him with Beria, followed by his rehabilitation, represent some dispute in the struggle for power. We may perhaps feel that a struggle to free him was first of all waged by Beria against those unwilling to let the rehabilitation of Stalin's victims go any further; that Beria's fall resulted in an attempt to turn on him; and that one of the surviving factions then took over the rehabilitation line and secured his release. The event most natural to associate this with would be the trial of Ryumin, in which one group belatedly, and with no imputation against Beria and his friends, struck a blow at the 1952–53 purgers. Most of the indications of this period are that Khrushchev was then protecting the Stalinists and making the most of Stalin, and that Malenkov took the opposite line. Later on, Khrushchev became the champion of the anti-Stalinists and pro-rehabilitation policy, so that Maisky's reappearance in the 1958 *Encyclopaedia* would be natural enough.

All the above, I should now say, is an example of the unconfirmed speculation that pervades the field, and at its most typical. It is not that there is anything improbable about it, but it will be seen that quite a large structure has been erected on a small factual basis. There is no harm in this, so long as the tentativeness of the conclusions is made absolutely clear. 'A possible reconstruction of the Maisky case' would not be an unreasonable title. What is plain is that a few more facts are required before it can be regarded as anything more substantial.

Apart from the police officials, and the Georgians covered in Chapter Seven, other major Beria associates fell with him.

Bagirov was dismissed from the Azerbaidzhan Central Committee at a local plenum (*Pravda*, July 19, 1953). The charges made against him at this stage were still political, and not criminal ('dictatorial methods' and so on). He had been Azerbaidzhan First Secretary from 1933 until transferring (on April 20, 1953) to the Chairmanship of the Azerbaidzhani Council of Ministers — perhaps in accordance with the Malenkov precedent of regarding the State machine as a suitable area for the future concentration of power. He was still referred to as 'Comrade' at the February 1954 Azerbaidzhan Party Congress, but a passing reference to his 'anti-State' activity in the oil industry, in a speech by Baibakov in the summer of that year, presumably marks his arrest.

In Armenia Arutinov was dismissed from his post and removed from the Armenian Central Committee at a local plenum later in the year (*Kommunist*, December 4, 1953). He had held the position since 1937, having formerly served under Beria in Georgia since 1931. The Second Secretary, Martirosyan, fell with him, as did several lesser officials.

A lesser figure who had been closely associated with Beria and who lost his post at this time was V. G. Grigoryan, Head of the Press Department of the Ministry of Foreign Affairs and assistant editor of the Cominform Journal. He was a candidate member of the Central Committee (and was not re-elected in 1956). He had started his career as a publicist as a candidate member of Beria's 1938 Bureau of the Georgian Central Committee, editing *Zarya Vostoka* for a number of years. That he owed his career to Beria seems reasonably plain. The question is whether he acted directly for his patron in his later posts, or whether the removal of Beria's associates extended to cases where the link was a weak one. There is some presumption in favour of the former view, as Beria had certainly succeeded in intruding Dekanozov as a Deputy Foreign Minister at one stage. His influence is shown to have been, at lowest, not so restricted as might at first appear.

In conclusion, it throws an interesting light on Soviet political circumstances that the accusers at least, and perhaps the accused too, found no difficulty in envisaging an attempt to seize power — the term *coup d'état* is used, even, as in the account given in *A History of the U.S.S.R. in the Epoch of Socialism* (Moscow 1957).

CHAPTER TEN

MALENKOV'S PREMIERSHIP, 1953–55

THE months following Stalin's death already show some of the differences between the struggle for power as carried on under a supreme arbiter and one in which the contestants are submitted to no such control. But in spite of the differences the similarities are also apparent.

The first solution broke down within a week. The next, reflecting more accurately the balance of forces, collapsed explosively after just over three months. Beria's position was certainly exceptional. He was in complete control of a vast and powerful machine against whose arbitrary use for his own purposes there was no adequate guarantee, now that Stalin had gone (the accusation against him makes this very point).

With the elimination of the Police as an independent political power, the apparatuses still involved were those of the State and the Party, with the Army in the background. None of these was under the monopolistic control of one man. And in the following period the Praesidium majority must be considered as the only decisive force.

That a group so diverse, or indeed any group of (relatively speaking) equals, should manifest a true single will was not to be expected, and in the years that followed a sequence of shifts, balances and manœuvres led first to a partial and then to a total fissure. Meanwhile, for more than eighteen months, we may trace a period in which 'collective leadership' — this sequence of stresses and balances — operated under normal pressure.

To call the leadership 'collective' does not mean that it was unanimous in any sense or on any issue. But the state of affairs, the conditions of equilibrium, were such that committee rule — as against the one-man rule of Stalin's time — was to some extent a reality. For example, the East German Delegation which came to Moscow in August 1953 was met for discussion by the whole Praesidium except Voroshilov and Pervukhin (Malenkov, Molotov, Khrushchev, Bulganin, Kaganovich, Mikoyan and

Saburov, in that order) (*Pravda*, August 21, 1953). And Imre Nagy also mentions that Hungarian delegations the same month were in contact with most members of the Soviet Party Praesidium and that all the Russians took the same line.

This is not to say that a struggle was not on, and that factions had not roughly differentiated themselves, almost immediately. We are no longer so liable to underestimate the speed with which victorious allies fall out, after Khrushchev's removal in October 1957 of Zhukov, promoted in June. And we may take it that the Khruschhev–Malenkov struggle was renewed almost immediately after the fall of Beria.

Malenkov's speech of August 8, 1953, to the Supreme Soviet forecast considerable changes in agricultural policy, which were later taken over by Khrushchev. He stated:

The Government and the Central Committee [Note the order: R.C.] have decided to change seriously our former incorrect attitude towards the personal subsidiary establishments of collective farmers. ... A lowering of income of collective farmers derived from their subsidiary establishments has been taking place during the last few years in consequence of a defective fiscal policy regarding those establishments; a decrease of the quantity of livestock and in particular of cows personally owned by collective farmers has been tolerated ... the Government and the Central Committee of the Party have found it indispensable to accept a notable reduction in the quotas of compulsory contributions from subsidiary establish-ments of the collective farmers and decided ... to change the system of the agricultural tax levied from collective farmers, to reduce by half the cash value of that tax for an average homestead of a collective farmer, and to forego completely the arrears of that tax due to the past few years.

Khrushchev's report on Agriculture to the September 1953 plenum was in accord with what Malenkov had said in this speech of August 8, though that is not to say that differences might not have arisen, with both men speaking to a compromise brief. It is true that Khrushchev later accused the Anti-Party Group of having 'attempted to thwart the implementation of the decisions of the September 1953 plenum of the C.C. and of the XXth C.P.S.U. Congress'. The emphasis on these two par-ticular events is odd, the obvious and natural reference to the Congress going curiously with that of the barely remembered plenum.

This was said in a report on agriculture, and in a general way seems to imply that it was referring to the agricultural decisions of the September plenum, the only ones published. But it may, of course, be a reference to other decisions of the period, such as those concerned with Beria's trial. In any case it implies that a struggle was definitely afoot in 1953, and that a grudge was still borne. That the reference was not accidential is shown by its repetition in the Central Committee Resolution on the December 1958 Report, which says that the Anti-Party Group 'had lost contact with the people, acted against its vital interests, against the decisions of the September [i.e. 1953] and subsequent Plenary sessions of the C.C. of the C.P.S.U., attempted to prevent the implementation of the course worked out at the XXth Party Congress on all the most important questions of home and foreign policy'.

In December 1958 Khrushchev also linked the Anti-Party Group directly with Beria, as opponents of the decisions adopted at the September 1953 plenum.

Thus the three-year plan did not produce the desired results. In 1952 the position of stock-breeding became even worse. The C.C. C.P.S.U. was obliged again to concern itself with the matter of stock-breeding. The commission set up by the C.C. C.P.S.U. for this purpose was instructed to work out measures aimed at increasing the production of animal products. In January 1953 the commission worked out these measures but they remained unratified. One must note here that right up to the September Plenary Session the C.C. could not take the necessary measures for improving stock-breeding.

This was prevented mainly by the rabid enemy of the Party and the people, Beria, and no small role was played in this matter by the members of the Anti-Party Group: Malenkov, Kaganovich and Molotov. In what they said they showed concern for improving stock-breeding, but in fact they did everything they could to prevent the implementation of the urgent measures in this sphere (Khrushchev's Report to the December 1958 plenum of the C.C.).

This seems to mean no more than that the other members of the Praesidium were not prepared to agree with Khrushchev on every detail, or to allow him to execute the agricultural decisions unsupervised. Even so, it shows the frictions in this sphere, and that they existed in others, too, may be not unreasonably assumed.

The first signs of a certain weakness in Malenkov's position may be seen in the recruitment of the Praesidium. Malyshev's presence with the Praesidium at the virtual demonstration at the Bolshoi on June 27, and his new appointment, had been a strong indication that he was to be a replacement for one of the three already eroded from the post-Stalin 'monolith'. (He can be regarded almost without reserve as a supporter of Malenkov.) But his promotion never materialised.

At the July 1953 plenum of the Central Committee, Malenkov delivered the report of the Praesidium on Beria. Thus, at this time there was no question of it being the prerogative of a Secretary (First or not) to be the spokesman of the Praesidium. At the plenum a few months later, in September 1953, Khrushchev delivered the report on agriculture in the name of the Praesidium. This might simply have been taken as a sign that he was the member of the Praesidium responsible for this field. But his nomination in the same plenum to be 'First' Secretary seems to show that it went with a rise in status. And at the February 1954 plenum Khrushchev's report to the Central Committee was to be delivered simply as his own, not in the name of the Praesidium at all.

The September 1953 plenum thus indicated a rise in Khrushchev's status. That this period showed a decline in Malenkov's power leads to the question of on what issue it could have taken place. Khrushchev's agricultural theses were much the same as the views put forward by Malenkov in August. Malenkov's industrial 'consumer-goods' policy was not under attack at this time. The September plenum must have discussed (or rather endorsed the result of a Praesidial discussion on) the full charges to be published against Beria. An 'investigation' of Beria's crimes could scarcely have avoided touching on the Leningrad Case. In later years this was always used as a weapon against Malenkov. If it was raised in the Praesidium in the period June–September, it would have been strongly in Malenkov's interests to prevent any public mention of the case. But though he succeeded in this, the mere discussion must have somewhat weakened his position. In this light we can provide at least a reasonably plausible explanation for the dismissal of Andrianov, Leningrad Province First Secretary from 1949, which now took place. Though he fell at the same time as such Beria supporters

Q

as Arutinov, there is no evidence to link him with Beria. On the contrary, everything points to a Malenkov connection. If he had really been a Beria trusty Stalin might have been expected not to have advanced him to the large Praesidium in October 1952. Even more probably, Beria might have been expected to have the Leningrad secretary, already in the large Praesidium, as his nominee for candidate membership of the small Praesidium in March 1953, rather than the holder of a traditionally lower (and certainly less powerful) post, in the person of Bagirov.

A Malenkov connection is far more probable. Andrianov may simply have been a Stalin nominee, not particularly well regarded by any faction. But he had served in the central apparatus and certainly not as a Zhdanovite, which may indicate the relationship with Malenkov — sometimes deduced simply from his promotion in place of the Zhdanov nominees. In any case, it is tempting to regard the attack on him as constituting the first phase of Khrushchev's assault on Malenkov's position. For, even if he may not have been strictly speaking a Malenkov man, he was at least suitable for an accusation, together with Malenkov, of responsibility for the Leningrad Case. As we shall see, every raising of the issue of this purge was accompanied by a blow at Malenkov, until, in July 1957, he was finally accused in public of responsibility for it. A plausible hypothesis would be that Khrushchev raised the Leningrad Case issue as early as September 1953, in connection with the charges to be laid against Beria.

Andrianov's removal would thus be a stroke at Malenkov's strength in a key area, and at the same time a demonstration of his rival's power. But still, it may be thought of as a compromise, whereby the political blame for the Leningrad Case was put on to a scapegoat, and even then not publicly mentioned as reason for his dismissal.

The circumstances of Andrianov's fall show that it must have been decided about the time of the September plenum. In October 1953 Ignatov reported on agriculture to the Leningrad Provincial Committee instead of Andrianov, though everywhere else the First Secretary made the report.

A plenum of the Leningrad Provincial Committee, attended by Khrushchev, announced in *Pravda* of November 20, 1953, relieved Andrianov of his post, and released Ignatov from the

Second Secretaryship in connection with his transfer to 'work in the apparatus of the Central Committee', F. R. Kozlov being promoted Provincial First Secretary from his then Third Secretaryship. This too seems a partial compromise.

It was not until February 1954 that a fuller report of this XIIth Leningrad Provincial Conference was published, and it was then stated that Andrianov's fault was failure to implement the decisions of the July 1953 plenum of the Central Committee — that is, the actions against Beria.

Meanwhile the Leningrad Case did not figure in the published accusations against Beria. These went back to 1919 (at which times he was alleged to have established his first links with the British Intelligence Service, which he 'maintained and expanded right up to his arrest'). Yet the official indictment mentions only two instances of activity in the 'thirties and 'forties — the 'killing' of a very minor figure, M. S. Kedrov (himself a police official of some notoriety), and 'a criminal struggle of intrigue against' Sergo Ordzhonikidze.

The mere raising of these cases shows that Beria's activity in the relevant period was examined. Crimes far more striking than the vague 'intrigue' were later alleged against him. It seems certain that all his acts were investigated and then examined at a high level, and that a decision was taken to charge him with some, but not others.

The political crimes he was *later* attacked for include the Leningrad Case (in December 1954), and the torture of Politburo members Kossior and Chubar and Komsomol Secretary Kosarev (in February 1956). Both are far more striking accusations than those made public at his trial. (It is true that the full charges have not even now been published, but it is clear that these did not figure among them, if only because no sort of attempt was made to rehabilitate the victims until the later date.) Hence it seems likely that the decision to mention the Ordzhonikidze case, in which others still living were almost certainly more deeply involved than Beria, must imply a manœuvre in the post-Beria struggle. We shall deal with this in connection with the Rapava and Bagirov Cases in 1955 and 1956.

Though most of the actions of the following weeks reflect Khrushchev's increased power, moves attributable to Malenkov continued to take place. For instance, on December 21, 1953, five more Deputy Chairmen of the Council of Ministers were added: Saburov, Pervukhin, Kosygin, Tevosyan, and Malyshev. (In August, Saburov had been reappointed to be head of Gosplan, a post he had held from 1949 to 1953 but handed over to the minor figure Kosyachenko, from the Central Committee apparatus, in the first post-Stalin Government.) This may indicate an increase in the power, or at least the impressiveness, of the State machinery.

But on the whole the general tide will be seen as setting towards the First Secretary. In Moscow, Mikhailov was removed from the Secretaryship on March 31, 1954, and replaced by Kapitonov, and this may certainly be regarded as an advance by Khrushchev. In December 1953 Aristov's fortunes revived. On his fiftieth birthday he was awarded the Order of Lenin 'for services to the State'. In February 1954 he became First Secretary of the Khabarovsk Territorial Committee of the Party, thus re-entering the Party apparatus. S. D. Ignatiev re-emerged as Secretary of the Bashkir Provincial Committee. The past young Stalinists and future Khrushchevists were regaining their footholds at a time of an evident increase in Khrushchev's influence.

In 1953 it is always the Praesidium which is referred to as the highest organ. But early in 1954 we begin to see expressions like 'the Central Committee headed by the Praesidium and the Secretariat' (D. Bakhshiev: *Party Construction in the Conditions of the Victory of Socialism in the U.S.S.R.*, January 1954). This work also claimed that it was false to try to turn the Secretariat into a purely executive organ. Similar claims were made in other publications.

Yet even on February 6, 1954, the Press listing of the Praesidium (renouncing surplus candidatures for the Supreme Soviet election) continues to give Malenkov seniority. It is: Malenkov, Molotov, Khrushchev, Voroshilov, Bulganin, Kaganovich, Mikoyan, Pervukhin, Saburov. Although Khrushchev's appointment as First Secretary and the various personnel changes and so on were advantages to him and disadvantages to Malenkov, the latter was thus still the leading figure in the Praesidium, and the Praesidium still disposed of the essentials of power.

Khrushchev's next move was the first of his spectacular one-man initiatives — the Virgin Lands scheme. The condition of

Soviet agriculture at this time was extremely bad, and Khrushchev frankly drew attention to these defects — in stock-breeding at the September 1953 plenum and in grain production at the February 1954 plenum. The field was open for new policies — and for the allocation of blame. Several of the new reforms of September were of a most useful character and perhaps hardly controversial among the leaders. The Virgin Lands scheme was a different thing again.

The extent to which Khrushchev took up the agricultural problem may be seen from a list of his major speeches in this period:

> On Animal Husbandry, September 3.
> On Machine Tractor Stations, January 28.
> On State Farms, February 5.
> On 'Advanced Workers in Agriculture', February 15.
> On Grain Deficiencies, February 23.
> On the Reclamation of Virgin Soil, February 22 and
> March 8.

Khrushchev used the agricultural issue as an offensive weapon. In his report to the February 1954 plenum of the Central Committee he attacked Skvortsov, First Deputy Minister of State Farms; Demidov, Deputy Chairman of the Planning Commission; Dmitriev, the Head of the Department of Agricultural Planning of the State Planning Commission ('incorrect conduct'); Benediktov, Minister of Agriculture ('engulfed in bureaucracy'), and A. I. Kozlov, Minister of State Farms ('to blame for these mistakes to an even greater extent').

That the Virgin Lands proposal now launched was Khrushchev's personal initative is certain, and henceforward he always treated it as such in speeches and otherwise. But there is no evidence that serious opposition to the scheme was made by other members of the Praesidium, except Molotov. Indeed, the fact that *only* Molotov was criticised on this score at the time of the fall of the 'Anti-Party Group' in June 1957 is strong presumptive negative evidence that the others had not opposed it with any vigour.

On the other hand, their willingness to let Khrushchev make the running seems to indicate that they tended to regard the whole business as less significant than he did. He later quoted

Mikoyan as doubting if the Kazakhstan harvest could be increased as much as he claimed. According to the speech delivered by Khrushchev to the Komsomol on November 8, 1956,

On one occasion I had a conversation from Alma Ata with A. I. Mikoyan. We exchanged opinions on the possibilities of supplying grain to the country. When I said to him that Kazakhstan would produce a milliard poods of grain this year he did not reply. I said to him: 'Why do you say nothing?' He replied: 'I am not arguing, but one milliard, I do not quite believe. Perhaps there may be 750,000,000 poods instead of the 650,000,000 planned, but not a milliard.' This shows that even some of us leaders who raised the question of the reclamation of virgin and waste lands did not expect such splendid results, especially in Kazakhstan, which used to produce only a very little wheat. That is why such surprise on the part of A. I. Mikoyan at that time is understandable.

This (apart from the public implication that Khrushchev was bold and right while Mikoyan was half-hearted and wrong — even though couched in one of those friendly terms of which other examples occur in the Secret Speech) seems to show that even among those leaders who supported the project enthusiasm was variable.

Although Molotov was clearly the main opponent of the scheme (see Appendix VII), there is some evidence that Malenkov was inclined to be at least sceptical of the Virgin Lands. In a speech by Belyaev in August 1957, we read:

The opposition of the Anti-Party Group to such an important measure as the reclamation of virgin and waste land was not accidental. Malenkov and some others had in fact already earlier taken up a wrong position in respect of grain cultivation and were confusing the heads of local workers. Thus, in one of his speeches, Comrade Malenkov stated as follows: 'Now, when the pre-war level of the area under crops has been restored and surpassed, the only correct policy in the matter of increasing agricultural production is the further all-round raising of crop yields.' And further he alleged that the assessing of the successes of agricultural development according to the level of grain production was obsolete (*Pravda*, August 24, 1957).

Malenkov's first point is a plea for intensive rather than extensive farming.

The Group as a whole were belatedly alleged to have opposed

the scheme. But this may have referred to later arguments, or simply be loose talk. Bulganin was significantly accused at the December 1958 plenum of having 'kept silent' about it, merely.

At the December 1958 plenum, too, the Minister of Agriculture, Matskevich, said:

We members of the Central Committee, who took part in preparing materials and various calculations connected with work on cultivating the virgin lands and consequently took part in meetings of the Central Committee Praesidium and of the Council of Ministers which discussed this problem, could see how obstinately and furiously Molotov, Kaganovich and other members of the group obstructed the execution of this scheme which was advanced and demonstrated by Nikita Sergeevich Khrushchev. They were not shy, either in their words or their actions, especially Molotov, in blackening and undermining this measure.

At the December 1958 plenum of the Central Committee, too, T. A. Yurkin, Deputy Minister of Agriculture of the R.S.F.S.R., said that the Anti-Party Group had

fought furiously against the Party policy of cultivating the virgin lands; they threatened that it would lead to a fall in the grain harvest per hectare and that therefore the collection of grain would not increase and that State expenditure on cultivating the virgin lands would not be recovered.

To what tricks did this despicable group not resort! The State Planning Commission of that time declared that there was no money, no material stocks, for cultivating the virgin lands and opposed the allocation of funds for tractors, houses, metal, beams. The supply organisations objected categorically, saying there were no resources. Kaganovich was in charge of this. They tried to call science to their aid. They pulled out ancient Tsarist maps and shouted that we were going into the desert, there would be no corn there.

The charges of Yurkin and Matskevich that Kaganovich and, by implication, Saburov (in 1954 head of the State Planning Commission) organised or permitted obstruction seems no more than the inflation of possibly genuine pleas of shortage of resources into sabotage, in accordance with old Soviet practice, and is not quite the same thing as alleging that they argued or voted against the scheme, as Molotov certainly did.

The reference to Tsarist maps seems to reflect the argument that these lands had been worked before, with the result that they became dust-bowls. The alternative objection must have been that if these dangers were to be overcome, it could only be through the pouring of uneconomic amounts of capital into the rat-hole:

When the idea of reclaiming the virgin lands was born, Molotov and the other members of the anti-Party group, opposing this measure of the Party and State, attempted to prove that allegedly the cost of reclaiming virgin lands would not be repaid and that the matter was allegedly unprofitable from the economic point of view. Subsequent years disposed of these nonsensical assertions and showed the general economic advantage derived by the State from the reclamation of virgin lands (Khrushchev, Report to the December 1958 plenum of the Central Committee).

On August 7, 1954, a conference was held at the experimental station of T. S. Maltsev, the soil expert. It was attended by Matskevich, Deputy Minister of Agriculture, A. I. Kozlov, Minister of State Farms, Ponomarenko, First Secretary of Kazakhstan, and others. Maltsev claimed to have developed a system which rendered crop rotation unnecessary and made the growth of grain possible on poor land without the loss of soil fertility, so that ley farming could be rejected. By this method, he hoped, it would be possible 'not to repeat the mistakes of our fathers when they ploughed the virgin lands . . . and very quickly destroyed their fertility'.

Maltsev's system (and other variants) became one of the foundations of Khrushchev's Virgin-Lands development, and also of his view that ley farming was not the best basis for livestock development — contrary to Stalin's line. The new method seems to have been only doubtfully successful, and (admittedly on the eve of the Anti-Party Group's bid for power) the *Journal of the Academy of Sciences* said that crops raised in the Maltsev fashion were actually less drought-resistant than under ordinary methods, and that it gave 'no advantage over the usual system and was even inferior to it'.

Stalin's last project for the countryside was the 'Plan for the Transformation of Nature'. the essence of which was soil conservation, moisture-catching by tree-belts, irrigation and grass-farming for cattle on marginal lands. This was dropped in 1953, and Khrushchev went on to a different scheme. His view was that livestock could be better fed on grain, and that this could be grown successfully even on marginal land. His advocacy of maize was vociferous. All his adversaries are said to have opposed this, as well as other measures. For example:

When Comrade Khrushchev put forward new urgent matters these fractionists divorced from life failed to understand them and looked at them like sheep at a new gate. Reclaim virgin land? What for? Reorganise the management of industry and construction? What if anything happens? *Grow maize? More news!* [my italics]. Use personal contacts in foreign policy? That's the limit! And so on and so forth (Kuusinen's Speech to the XXIst Party Congress, February 3, 1959).

The most obvious of all the ideological stigmata of the Stalin period had been the imposition of Lysenkoism on Soviet biology. However, Lysenko had already been attacked in the *Botanical Journal* No. 6 of November/December 1952, though he replied in the same journal's issue No. 1 of 1953. *Pravda* of May 21, 1953, carried a long article of his, and a number of others appeared through the summer. By July, however, some criticism of him, at least by implication, was appearing and the views of his opponents such as Tsitsin were getting quoted. *Kommunist* No. 9 of 1953 attacked dictatorial methods in the biological sciences. Yet criticisms were indirect and recommendations of his methods continued to appear.

But at the beginning of 1954 an open attack was made on him. Khrushchev, in his speech of February 23 to the Central Committee (*Pravda*, March 21, 1954), criticised V. S. Dmitriev, formerly Chief of the Agricultural Planning Department of Gosplan, who had advocated ley crop rotation and after being relieved of his post tried to get a doctor's degree 'enjoying the protection of Academician T. G. Lysenko, although he did not deserve one'. *Pravda* of March 26, 1954, printed a letter from the scientist Prof. Stankov which revealed that Lysenko had bullied the Academy of Agricultural Sciences into giving Dmitriev a degree, but that this had since been cancelled. Various other criticisms appeared, such as the leading article in *Kommunist* No. 5 of 1954 (published early in April) — condemning, not Lysenko's theories, but his methods of controversy.

On the other hand, the attack was a limited one. Lysenko was awarded the Order of Lenin on February 12 and elected a Deputy to the Supreme Soviet on February 14. This is the only recorded instance of Khrushchev criticising him, and in 1957 he was to support him strongly and in 1958 gave him back his monopolistic position. The censure seems to have been based on two motives. Firstly Lysenko's conduct was clearly incompatible with the general cultural relaxation, so long as scientists were allowed to draw attention to such malpractices. Secondly, ley farming, Stalin's method, was a technique Khrushchev personally opposed. The theoretical basis of Lysenko's biology continued to be accepted, if not by the scientists, at least by the Party Secretariat.

Various other themes centred on the Virgin Lands: for instance, the issue of State versus Collective Farms, in its ideological context as well as its practical one. A good deal of prominence was given in the May Day slogans for 1954 to the task of 'building Communism'. The April 1954 issue of the Party theoretical journal *Kommunist* contained an article by Stepanyan (who in a similar article in 1950 had given the outlines of the themes later put forward by Stalin in *Economic Problems of Socialism*, and had spoken approvingly of the fusion of kolkhozes into 'kolkhoz towns').

Stepanyan's new article revives the theme of the undesirability of the insufficiently 'all-national' kolkhoz form of property and repeats arguments used by Stalin (omitting only Stalin's line that commodity barter should take the place of the present method of exchange). He says, for example:

The further development of Socialist production relations at the present stage of the construction of Communism demands, in the first place, a strengthening and development of the two forms of communal property, that of national property playing a leading part. This is the requisite for the creation in the future of that higher synthesis between industry and agriculture about which Marx and Engels wrote. The quantitative and qualitative growth of machine tractor stations, the transfer of collective farmers working in the M.T.S. to the permanent staff of workers employed by Government undertakings, the gradual transition of all agricultural processes in the kolkhozes on to basis of modern technical methods, reflect the process of the all-round development of the two forms of communal property and of their increasingly close fusion.

Voprosy Ekonomiki (No. 7 of 1957) states that the 'Anti-Party

Group of Malenkov, Kaganovich and Molotov' resisted the development of State farms, especially in the Virgin Lands.

At the December 1958 plenum of the Central Committee a speaker asserted:

Molotov and other members of the Anti-Party Group affirmed that the expenditure on the organisation of State Farms would apparently not be repaid for decades (V. A. Telyakovski: *Pravda*, December 17, 1958).

Another said:

Malenkov and other members of the Anti-Party Group failed completely when they objected against the development of the new lands in Altai. You remember, Nikita Sergeyevich, you came to us in the summer of 1954 and saw that corn was growing in the new State Farms which we organised. But Malenkov, who was at that time Chairman of the Council of Ministers, signed a decree condemning us for organising State Farms on the new lands; we were forbidden to organise new State Farms. I say this because Malenkov not only did not agree with the development of the virgin lands: he hindered this national cause. But the Anti-Party Group did not succeed in carrying out its plans (K. G. Pysin: *Pravda*, December 19, 1958).

This seems to indicate — not of course that Malenkov was initiating an independent sabotage movement, as implied — but that a majority against the development had arisen in the Party Praesidium. It seems that this was in the summer of 1954, a period already believed on other grounds to be one of a Khrushchev decline. It also seems that the 'decree' may have been as much directed against Khrushchev for encouraging the move without the permission of the Council of Ministers, as against the particular farms.

Yet Khrushchev seems soon to have reversed this during the period when he was regaining his strength in the autumn. Originally the share to be contributed by the collective farms had been the major one, since they were to bring into cultivation some two-thirds of the thirteen million acres originally planned. But later, as a *Pravda* article (October 5, 1954) by Puzanov, Chairman of the R.S.F.S.R. Council of Ministers, said, 'In future the reclamation of virgin and waste lands in territories, provinces and autonomous republics of the U.S.S.R.

is to be organised mainly through the development of new State Farms'.

Subsidiary agricultural quarrels with Molotov, some of them of very minor importance, arose. In one of these at least Molotov won the vote (though it is not certain from the context that this took place in 1953–55):

> How in fact can one reconcile with the aim of raising agriculture a proposal by Molotov that every province must provide its own supplies of potatoes? Despite objections, Molotov succeeded in having this proposal accepted. Could this problem have been solved in this way, in those conditions? To supply Moscow and Leningrad with potatoes from Moscow and Leningrad provinces for instance, it was essential substantially to increase the area under potatoes * (Khrushchev's Report to the December 1958 plenum of the Central Committee).

The evidence we have examined, such as it is, implies that agriculture was the key issue of the early part of 1954 and that Khrushchev's Virgin Lands project, which was the main centre of dispute, was regarded as follows by the main contenders:

(1) Molotov strongly opposed it.
(2) Kaganovich and Saburov found its demands a nuisance.
(3) Malenkov favoured more attention to intensive farming.
(4) Mikoyan supported it with reservations.
(5) Bulganin was more or less neutral.

The key indication that Khrushchev was not at this stage enforcing policies on a totally hostile group was seen when in February 1954 Ponomarenko, Malenkov's ally, was relieved at the Ministry of Culture and sent as First Secretary to Kazakhstan, the Virgin Lands area, with Khrushchev's nominee, Brezhnev, as his second-in-command. That this was a move from strength was shown when Ponomarenko's old post was simply handed over to another, and even closer, Malenkov associate, G. F. Aleksandrov.

In any case the Virgin Lands issue does not seem to be one in which Khrushchev obtained much *active* Praesidial support. A vote to let him go ahead was no doubt taken, but it seems to

---

* It was in fact Stalin who at the XVIIth Congress had urged that every province should grow its own potatoes — a dictum quoted with approval by Aristov at the XIXth Congress (*Pravda*, October 11, 1952).

have been permissive rather than encouraging, and Praesidium members made few and perfunctory statements in favour of it: on the contrary, it was allowed to stand very obviously as Khrushchev's own scheme.

It was thus clearly enough an issue arousing strong opposition from at least Molotov, and was quite unusable against Malenkov. The immediate result, if anything, was probably to weaken Khrushchev's position in the Praesidium.

In the spring and summer of 1954 there were a number of indications of a strengthening of Malenkov's position. He was still listed first in Praesidium orders of appearance. And he continued to emphasise State authority.

The Government approved by the Supreme Soviet on April 28, 1954, had as leaders:

Premier: Malenkov
First Deputy Premiers: Molotov, Bulganin, Kaganovich
Deputy Premiers: Mikoyan,   Saburov,   Pervukhin,
                             Tevosyan, Malyshev, Kosygin.

On May Day 1954 the leadership appearing on Lenin's Tomb for the parade showed one quite new feature. In addition to the Praesidium and Secretariat, the three other Vice-Premiers were on the stand and listed in the papers (Malyshev, Tevosyan and Kosygin in that order). This was repeated at the parade for the 300th Anniversary of Russo-Ukrainian unification (*Pravda*, May 31).

This demonstration of the significance of the Governmental machine had not been seen before: for instance, the November 7 parade in 1953 had shown only the Praesidium and Secretariat, plus Shkiryatov of the Party Control Committee. Nor were purely governmental representatives to appear again until 1959. November 7, 1954, was back to normal practice. There seems little reason to doubt that this upgrading of the Government was a move of Malenkov's.

On June 13, 1954, *Pravda* published a speech made in Prague by Khrushchev on the previous day, in a version which omitted a number of the more aggressive points made in the foreign-policy sphere.

Some further slight pointer to a loss of power by Khrushchev in the summer of 1954 may be seen in his report to the

December 1958 plenum of the Central Committee, where he says:

> In this respect the February–March plenum of 1954, and the January 1955 plenum of the Central Committee, were of special importance. They discussed the matter of the taming of virgin and abandoned lands and the increase in output of animal produce.

The June 1954 plenum is omitted, and it may be deduced that it failed to discuss the First Secretary's favourite scheme, or discussed it wrong. The rapporteurs on agriculture to this plenum were, significantly, not Khrushchev, but the Ministers concerned.

The *Tass* announcement on the Ryumin trial, published on July 23, 1954 (see Appendix VI), says that it had been conducted by the Military Collegium of the Supreme Court 'from July 2 to July 7'. We can certainly take it that the belated decision to try and execute Ryumin was a political one. The delay itself is significant and clearly associated with the fall of Beria. It was possible to bring Beria's group to trial seven months after his arrest, although even the published material on the case shows that allegations dating back to the 1930s, and even to the Civil War period, were presented. Ryumin, whose criminal career concerned only a few years prior to 1953, had to wait fifteen months. Judicially this would be an unaccountable anomaly. We must seek the reasons elsewhere.

Although Ryumin alone was brought to trial, the original statements had referred to other guilty parties. The M.V.D. communiqué had condemned, in the plural, 'officials of the investigating department of the former Ministry of State Security' (*Pravda*, April 4, 1953); and the keynote editorial had spoken of 'Ryumin and other employees of the Ministry of State Security' as criminal. That the trial was limited to one man may show that opponents of it had contrived to water it down. Even so, it demonstrated strongly against the Doctors' Plot and its accomplices.

Khrushchev states in the Secret Speech, referring to the Leningrad Affair, 'Had a normal situation existed in the Party's Central Committee and in the Central Committee Political Bureau, affairs of this nature would have been examined there in accordance with Party practice, and all pertinent facts assessed. . . .' This indicates that major trials of political significance are examined by or at least reported on to the Central Committee. And hence the Ryumin case must presumably be taken as having been discussed at the June 1954 plenum. This strengthens the view that it was an important political move. It lasted six days. This is a very long time for a trial with one accused: for instance, the Pyatakov–Radek trial in 1937, with its fifteen defendants, lasted only eight days. One can conclude that a great deal of dirty linen was washed.

At the time of Ryumin's arrest, *Pravda* had commented on his activities as an attempt 'to inflame in Soviet society . . . feelings of national enmity which are profoundly alien to socialist ideology'. But curiously enough Ryumin was sentenced under Article 58, Section 7, of the Penal Code (see Appendix VI), which seems quite inapplicable to what had previously been said of his aim, its emphasis being rather on 'the undermining of State industry, transport, trade, the financial and credit system'.

If the original accusations had been proceeded with he could have been charged, straining the wording at least no more, under Section 10 of the same Article, for 'propaganda or agitation containing an appeal to overthrow, undermine or weaken the Soviet regime or to commit individual counter-revolutionary crimes . . . under conditions . . . involving the exploitation of the religious or national prejudices of the masses', which also involves the death sentence. The announcement of the execution mentioned 'provocational cases' against 'Soviet citizens, *including* [my italics] prominent medical figures'.

It has been very plausibly argued by Mr. Boris Nicolaevsky that all this is a sign that Malenkov wanted to present Ryumin's crimes as having been the preparation of a purge against the khozaistveniks — the great industrial bureaucrats. He points, quite truly, to the fact that the Press campaign for 'vigilance' which preceded the announcement of the arrest of the doctors was directed almost entirely against cases in the Ministry of Supply, Ministry of Non-ferrous Metals, and so on — ministries controlled by such men as Malyshev (an alumnus of the Baumann Technical College, like other leading figures, including Malenkov and Saburov).

Thus Ryumin's case seems to imply that whatever the situation

in 1953, Malenkov was now in a position to use the Doctors'
Plot against his opponents. And as against Beria's line of attacking it for its anti-Semitism Malenkov was employing it as an
object lesson, to convince a section of the Party that they must
rely on him for protection against opponents who were still
dangerous; and that he retained sufficient control to do this.

Meanwhile there had been activity on the 'cultural front'.

In 1953 the anniversaries of Zhdanov's death, and of his cultural decrees, in August and September, were ignored by
Pravda for the first time.

On October 21–24, 1953, there was a meeting of the Board
of the Union of Soviet Writers, attended by Ponomarenko,
Minister of Culture. The intention was to prepare the ground
for the forthcoming Second Writers' Congress. A number of
speeches of 'liberal' tendency were made. Books such as those
of Vasily Grossmann, which had been condemned in the first
months of the year, were rehabilitated, as were the works of Ilf
and Petrov, censured in Zhdanov's time. And, while the
Zhdanov decrees were scarcely mentioned, Malenkov's speech
to the XIXth Congress was quoted by almost every speaker.
The speech had sounded entirely orthodox at the time, and its
use to justify the new line can be taken to indicate mainly that
Malenkov's interest had been sought and probably (in view of
the unanimity and of Ponomarenko's presence) obtained for the
relaxation.

In the ensuing months the first 'Thaw' took place. Novels
like Vera Panova's *Seasons of the Year* and F. Panferov's *Mother
Volga* were both printed and praised, in spite of their large
quota of unpleasant, and even criminal, Soviet characters.
L. Zorin's play *The Guests*, which closely resembled in tone and
action Dudintsev's later *Not by Bread Alone*, was brought out
and given favourable criticism. There also appeared Ehren-
burg's overt attack on the pressures put on writers under Stalin
(*The Thaw* Part I). And in the December 1953 issue of *Novy
Mir* the critic Pomerantsev wrote a powerful and satirical
attack on stereotyped literature. He even went to the length of
demanding 'sincerity' as the quality which 'distinguishes the
author of a book or play from the compiler of a book or play'.

Literaturnaya Gazeta of January 30, 1954, counter-attacked
with the orthodox reply that sincerity is not the important

thing, 'the first test for a Marxist' being 'evaluation of the ideological-artistic quality of the work'. But publication of 'thaw' literature continued. Even Pasternak, who had published virtually nothing except translations since 1946, had some highly subjective poems (later to form part of the epilogue of *Dr. Zhivago*) in *Znamya*.

It was not until May 1954 that a concerted barrage against the new freedom came, from *Pravda*, *Party Life* and *Kommunist*, as well as the literary papers. Zorin and Pomerantsev were the main targets, but a whole list of writers (and periodicals) came in for censure. Pomerantsev's 'subjectivist criteria of sincerity' were condemned by *Party Life* in favour of 'a Party attitude to literature'. The playwrights Surov and Virta were expelled from the Writers' Union for immorality, but that there were other motives was made clear by *Pravda*, which said: 'It is no accident that precisely these writers have recently brought out ideologically corrupt, vulgarly naturalistic and dull literary works.' Writers' meetings called in Moscow and Leningrad in June vilified the offenders (though some leading writers were accused of failing to speak, and Zoshchenko went to the length of defending himself). In the debates, though the Zhdanov decrees were frequently appealed to, I have only come across one reference to Malenkov's October 1952 speech. Yet the victory of the ideologists was not complete, and though the Pomerantsev's thesis and much of the thaw literature were sacrificed, the Writers' Congress in the autumn of 1954 did not revert completely to Zhdanovist rigour.

To interpret these trends it seems rational to treat the apparent association of Malenkov and the thaw as real. (Not that there is any need to believe that Malenkov would have defended Pomerantsev and the 'extreme' liberalisers, and he may well have agreed to some counter-action.)

It seems certain that the departure of Ponomarenko from the Ministry of Culture in February 1954 strengthened the hand of the cultural sections of the Party apparatus. So long as the Minister of Culture was himself a candidate member of the Party Praesidium it would be difficult for the secretariat to over-ride him, or do much more than carry on a guerilla warfare on the cultural issues. His replacement, G. F. Aleksandrov, was inevitably a lower-ranking figure.

R

Aleksandrov had been head of the Agitprop Department after the war, and had been removed mainly as a result of Zhdanov's attack on his philosophical work in the decree of August 25, 1947, to be succeeded by Suslov. Like other Malenkov cadres, he was never then demoted very far, in spite of further censure. But it is significant that when Malenkov fell from the Premiership in February 1955, the associates quickest to follow him down were Shatalin, his representative in the Party Secretariat, and Aleksandrov in the Ministry of Culture.

The literary struggle was a complex one with many cross-currents, tactical retreats and partial victories. Nor is there any reason to look on it as an *immediate* reflection of political events, or of its fortunes developing *pari passu* with changes in the fortunes of the political struggle. Nevertheless, after making all the necessary reservations, we can with great probability link Malenkov with a tentative patronage of the thaw tendency, and Khrushchev, and doubtless even more Molotov, with the trend to greater ideological control.

But though the cultural front played its part, it did not now have the major significance it had had in 1946–48.

Khrushchev's problem in building up a decisive majority against Malenkov was to find an issue on which he could unite with Molotov and the more conservative elements. Even then the presumable line-up in mid-1954 would only have been Khrushchev, Bulganin, Molotov, Kaganovich, Voroshilov versus Malenkov, Saburov, Pervukhin, Mikoyan — a mere 5 to 4.

The first signs of an adequate anti-Malenkov majority may perhaps be seen in the delegation to China in September 1954, consisting of Khrushchev, Bulganin, Mikoyan and Shepilov. The delegates returned by stages, rather demonstratively, through the Asian parts of the U.S.S.R. Whether with Chinese encouragement or otherwise, Mikoyan's attachment to Khrushchev seems to date from about this time. If Mikoyan really now determined to go along with the coalition against Malenkov it would presumably provide a potential 6–3 majority on the Praesidium. Though it is probably wrong to assume that solidarities of this sort were other than very tentative and shaky, a potential 6–3 provides a reasonable certainty of a majority at some suitable crisis in a way that 5–4 does not.

On November 7, 1954, Khrushchev had moved, for the first time, to the right-hand position of the non-uniformed Praesidial members, with Malenkov second.

The political issue found was Malenkov's public sponsoring of a policy of more consumer goods for the population.

In his speech to the Supreme Soviet in August 1953 Malenkov had launched the new line:

The Government and the Central Committee of the Party consider it necessary to increase significantly the investments in the development of the light, food, and fishing industries, and in agriculture, and to improve greatly the production of articles of popular consumption. . . .
Our immediate task is within the course of two or three years to raise sharply the supply to the population of foodstuffs and manufactured goods — meat and meat products, fish and fish products, butter, sugar, confectionery, fabrics, clothing, footwear, utensils, furniture and other articles of cultural and household goods, considerably to raise the supply to the population of all consumer goods. . . .
Our task is to make a sharp improvement in the production of consumer goods and ensure a more rapid development of the light and food industry.
But in order to ensure a sharp development in production of consumer goods, we must, first and foremost, be concerned for the further development and growth of agriculture which provides the population with foodstuffs and light industry with raw materials (Malenkov, Speech to the Supreme Soviet, August 8, 1953).

Although this promise seems to have been highly popular in the Soviet Union, and was at least a departure from the extreme rigour of the policy of heavy industry at all costs, it was by no means the Rightist deviation that it was later made out to be by Khrushchev, and might better be read as an application of a reasonable incentive system to Soviet society as a whole, just as Khrushchev had to make incentive concessions to the peasantry. For Malenkov was at pains to emphasise the basic importance of heavy industry and added:

We shall continue to develop by all means the heavy industries — metallurgical, fuel, power-producing, chemical, timber, machine-construction, factory-building, and to develop and perfect our transportation. We must always remember that heavy industries are the main foundation of our socialist economy, because it is impossible without them to secure the further development of light industries, increase of the productivity of agriculture, and improvement in the defence capacity of our country.

Mikoyan in a speech on October 17, 1953, supported Malenkov's line saying:

Despite an enormous increase in production and consumption we have not yet overcome the well known disproportion between the production of goods and popular consumption and the saturation of the increasing needs of the popular masses of the Soviet Union (*Izvestia*, October 25–27, 1953).

Khrushchev, however, had to some extent reserved his position:

The Communist Party has steadily maintained a course of overall development in heavy industry as essential to the successful development of all branches of the national economy, and it has achieved great success on this road. Chief attention was turned to solving this immediate national economic problem, and basic forces and means were diverted to it. Our best cadres were occupied with the work of industrialising the country. We did not have the means for high-speed, simultaneous development of heavy industry, agriculture, and light industry [note the order: R.C.]. For this it was necessary to provide needed prerequisites. Now these prerequisites exist. We have a mighty industrial base, strengthened collective farms and cadres trained in all branches of economic construction (Khrushchev's Report on Agriculture to the September 1953 plenum of the Central Committee).

In his speech to the Supreme Soviet on April 26, 1954, he again spoke in terms of concentrating on heavy industry ('the very basis of Soviet economy'), agriculture and consumer goods, in that order. Yet this hardly amounts to a divergence from Malenkov's view as expressed in 1953. During 1954, however, the Malenkov line began to be expressed more emphatically; as by Mikoyan, in his speech of March 11, 1954, who said: 'The giant successes in the growth of our heavy industry have created the necessary preconditions for posing the question of sharply increasing the production of consumer goods.'

Economists were found to support Malenkov's theme. An article by A. N. Maslin in *Voprosy Filosofii* No. 4 of 1954, 'The

Principle of Material Interest under Socialism', explicitly called for a change in the relationship between producer-goods and consumer-goods production, in favour of the latter.

It should be pointed out that Malenkov's plans involved very little actual reduction in capital-goods production. In the Budget of 1954 the increased allotment to consumer goods is marginal. The only cut of some significance is in the defence industries, and this is a doubtful case because much defence expenditure is anyhow hidden under other items, and this sort of manipulation may be increased in a given year simply to support Soviet propaganda claims about peaceful behaviour.

The 'heavy industry' issue thus seems to have been more a dispute on a point of doctrine, convenient for allegations of deviation, than a major matter of policy. It was an issue on which Molotov's rigorous conservatism could be rallied against Malenkov, and which could be used in the higher levels of the Party apparatus.

The opening of the full-blown campaign on priority for producer goods was an article by Prof. S. Strumilin in *Voprosy Ekonomiki* No. 11 (November 1, 1954). For the following seven or eight weeks *Pravda* put the view that producer goods were basic, while *Izvestia* continued with the old Malenkov line that consumer goods needed attention. There was no formal contradiction between the two papers, but the difference in approach was very obvious, as was the amount of space now being devoted to the issue.

Izvestia's last firm defence of the Malenkov line was on December 21, and in the next few days it began to temporise. Khrushchev had spoken to a conference on building on December 7, and this speech, not published until December 28, put the implied attack on consumer-goods priority very clearly. The Abakumov trial was announced on December 26, with its Leningrad Case implications against Malenkov. And we may presumably date the beginning of the final attack on Malenkov's position in this week.

For the published material on the trial was specific (see Appendix VI) solely on the issue of the Leningrad Affair. That it was directed against Malenkov was absolutely clear. Although Abakumov's links with Beria alone were mentioned even at the time the public rehabilitation of Malenkov's defeated rivals obviously struck at him, and since then we have several times been informed that Malenkov was personally responsible for the case. It is an interesting example of the use of a police trial as an implied threat, not yet made explicit. The fact that it was held before a plenum rather than after one may show that it was discussed in the Praesidium only, and was intended to bring pressure on a plenum.

The trial, with its further attack on police excesses, was clearly also helpful in giving the regime the credit for curbing these. But, as if to show that the right sort of security police apparatus was still in good odour, the Order of the Red Banner was almost simultaneously awarded to Serov, on December 25, 1954.

The heavy industry campaign was now stepped up further. Voroshilov spoke on January 1, 1955, of 'heavy industry, which was and remains the main basis of the socialist economy, of the increased well being of the people and of the strengthening of the defence capacity of our country'. This may be taken as the voice of the adherents of orthodox Stalinism in the Praesidium. The reference to defence seems one of the many almost overt appeals for the support of the military.

Early in 1955 articles in the theoretical Press, too, began to take a particularly sharp tone. M. T. Iovchuk, in *Voprosy Filosofii* No. 1 of 1955, called 'Some economists', who rejected production goods priority, 'vulgarisers and falsifiers of Marxism'. In *Kommunist* No. 2 (January) 1955, I. Doroshev and A. Rumyantsev again referred to 'some economists' who took this line as 'distorting the substance of the action carried out by the Party and the Soviet Government steeply to raise agriculture and increase production of products of popular consumption'. (Stalin's authority was later brought in. F. Konstantinov in an article 'J. V. Stalin and Questions of Communist Construction' (*Pravda*, March 7, 1955), cites Stalin against the consumer-goods line, which he calls 'a revision of Marxist–Leninist economic theory and the Party's general line'.)

An article by Shepilov (in *Pravda* of January 24, 1955) is usually taken as the moment of decisive assault on the Malenkovist position. For hitherto the putting of the heavy industry line in the central press, as apart from the economic journals, had been mainly unaccompanied by direct attack on the alternative, implication being allowed to do the work. Shepilov's article, 'The General Line of the Party and Vulgarisers of Marxism', attacked a number of economists by name for complaining that heavy industrialisation distracted attention from consumer-goods needs. They were charged with 'grossly distorting the substance of the decisions of the Party and Government', by claiming that 'since 1953 the Soviet land has entered a new stage of economic development . . . the centre of gravity has been shifted to . . . the production of consumer goods'. It will be seen that while what is being attacked is not far from what Malenkov had said in August 1953 (and even less far from what his organs had more recently been advocating), Shepilov adheres to the common Soviet practice of implying that the actual decisions taken in 1953 had been correct in themselves, and simply distorted.

Shepilov referred to the economists as 'bourgeois types', accused them of 'a gross distortion of Marxist-Leninist economic theory', quoted Stalin against them, and added that 'it is difficult to think of a theory more anti-scientific, rotten and demoralising for our people'. He also said, with rather sinister significance, that 'right-wing elements once pushed our Party on to this path' — an obvious reference to Bukharin.

One of his other major arguments, which is repeated throughout this controversy, is that the danger from outside the U.S.S.R. means that heavy industrialisation is a military necessity.

In spite of all this, on January 25, 1955, the day the plenum opened, the papers published the usual list of top names — those selected for many constituencies, but renouncing all but one (in the elections for the R.S.F.S.R. Supreme Soviet). The multiple selection arrangements had been made rather earlier, when Malenkov was stronger, and the official crisis before the Central Committee was yet to come. But this publication may yet be regarded as a demonstration for Malenkov on the eve of the plenum. The list is particularly interesting in, presumably, presenting the Malenkovite candidates for higher office. In addition to all those Praesidium and Secretariat members not holding posts outside the R.S.F.S.R. there are four names: Andreyev, Kosygin, Malyshev and Tevosyan. None of these was promoted in the ensuing Khrushchev ascendancy, except that Kosygin became a candidate member of the Praesidium in June 1957 and a full member in May 1960. Before that he and the others had been passed over by half a dozen juniors of Khrushchev's selection. Andreyev was Khrushchev's rival in agriculture in 1950–51, and Malyshev and Tevosyan can be definitely associated with Malenkov. Tevosyan was demoted from Vice-Premier to Ambassador to Japan in 1956. He and Malyshev both died within the following year.

That Malenkov was able to carry on the struggle so long is rather remarkable. The concessions made in August 1953, under the stress of the various recent crises, were unlikely to prove attractive to orthodox elements after stability had returned. Malenkov could, in theory at least, have moved back to orthodoxy with the other members of the Praesidium. That he did not do so seems to indicate first of all that he, and others, actually believed that a policy of economic concession, or at least apparent economic concession, was required by the Soviet economy and polity, and secondly that he thought the power situation such that it was a policy that he might put through while maintaining, or strengthening, his power.

The first asset he could count on was an intangible: the policy was popular (as was, to a lesser degree, his foreign policy). This no doubt cut little ice in the Kremlin, but it cannot have been without effect at various lower levels of the Party. Yet we must also conclude that his following in the higher levels of the Party, at Central Committee level, remained strong. Certain positions had been lost — Leningrad, for example — but the turnover in 1955, *after* his fall, shows that up to then he had retained a lot of support. It seems that the calculation that Shatalin could prevent mass removals of Malenkov followers, even if he could not stop occasional specially mounted operations like the Leningrad one, was sound. By January 1955 it was evident that his policy was opposed by Khrushchev, Bulganin, Mikoyan, Voroshilov, Molotov and Kaganovich — a great majority in the Praesdium. At the same time such evidence as there is implies that Army thought was against him, too. Yet to break him a considerable campaign, and weapons such as the Abakumov trial, had to be brought into play.

The plenum was announced as having taken place from

January 25 to 31, in *Pravda* of February 2, 1955, which carried also the Central Committee decision on an agricultural report to it by Khrushchev on the production of animal products. His report itself appeared the following day, with its highly aggressive beginning denouncing Right deviationism:

In connection with the measures taken recently for the increase in the production of consumers' goods, some comrades have introduced confusion into the question of the respective tempos of the development of heavy and light industry in our country. 'Basing themselves on the fundamental economic law of socialism', which they have misunderstood and vulgarised, these 'theoreticians' — if you will allow me to call them such — are trying to prove that at a certain stage of the construction of socialism, the development of heavy industry ceases to be the main task and that light industry then can and should outstrip all other branches of industry.

These are totally wrong views, contradicting the law of Marxism–Leninism. They are nothing but a slandering of the party. They are a belching forth of the right deviation, a belching forth of the views hostile to Leninism, which in their time were preached by Rykov, Bukharin and their ilk (Khrushchev's Report 'On the Production of Animal Products', *Pravda*, February 3, 1955).

This direct and threatening attack on Malenkov was given special point by the unusual naming in the first place as a Rightist of Rykov — who, like Malenkov, had been Prime Minister of the U.S.S.R.*

At the January 1955 plenum Malenkov was 'sharply criticised for a bad style of leadership' (F. R. Kozlov, *Pravda*, July 3, 1957). And his removal from the Premiership was doubtless voted at this point. The fact that the plenum did not remove him from the Party Praesidium as well is striking, and indicates either that he had considerable support, or that some of those supporting Khrushchev up to a point were yet not prepared to let him go further at the moment.

On February 8 the newly elected Supreme Soviet heard a statement by Malenkov read to them by Deputy Volkov. In it he resigned the Premiership, claiming that the post needed

---

* According to the Italian Communist paper *Unita* of July 7, 1957, Malenkov had been reproached for the Leningrad Case in the January 1955 plenum: 'During the session of the Central Committee in which he was criticised, and for which he then had to abandon his post of Prime Minister . . . Malenkov revealed on that occasion that a "moral responsibility" for it also fell upon him.'

'some comrade who possesses greater experience of government activity' and an administrative background in local work and particular ministries. Malenkov then said: 'I see particularly my fault and responsibility for the unsatisfactory state of affairs in agriculture because, over a number of years, I was entrusted with the duty of control and leadership.' He added that the present increases were to be credited to the Central Committee, and that further development of the economy must be firmly based on heavy industry. The statement, with its various nuances, speaks for itself.

Bulganin formed a government the same day.

On February 28, 1955, the new Government announced changes in its structure. The position was:

COUNCIL OF MINISTERS OF THE U.S.S.R.

	February 8 to 28	From February 28
Chairman:	*Bulganin	*Bulganin
First Deputy Chairmen:	*Kaganovich	*Kaganovich
	*Molotov	*Mikoyan
		*Molotov
		*Pervukhin
		*Saburov
Deputy Chairmen:	Kosygin	Zavenyagin
	*Malenkov	Kosygin
	Malyshev	Kucherenko
	*Mikoyan	Lobanov
	*Pervukhin	*Malenkov
	*Saburov	Malyshev
	Tevosyan	Tevosyan
		Khrunichev

Thus Malenkov became the only Praesidium member to rank as a simple deputy Premier, sharing the level with seven others. The position was anomalous and can hardly be interpreted as other than part of a move to remove him from the Praesidium. But this removal did not take place.

Malenkov's fall involved a number of his supporters.

Shatalin, as we have seen, almost certainly represented Malenkov in the Secretariat, and the latter may have found it reasonable to assume that the Secretariat would at least be unable to act independently of orders from the Praesidium. In this

* Members of the Party Praesidium.

he seems to have been justified, and the struggle for power was largely fought out in the Praesidium itself. Nevertheless, once a majority had been found against Malenkov in the Praesidium, leading to his removal from the premiership in February 1955, even though Khrushchev's presumed allies were not prepared to go the whole hog and dispose of his rival entirely, the First Secretary was able to eliminate Shatalin from the Secretariat and thereafter to make a start in appointing his own nominees in the provincial apparatus of the Party, and hence in the long run to provide himself with extra strength in the Central Committee itself. Even though the Central Committee can scarcely be regarded as playing an important role in the ensuing events, these implied changes in its composition might perhaps be presumed to have had some effect on the minds of wavering members of the Praesidium.

Pravda much later (July 3, 1957) stated that at plenums held in connection with the XXth Congress sharp criticism was made of certain members of the Central Committee, and some were excluded from it. It seems likely that this refers to the July 1955 plenum in particular, by which time Khrushchev had removed a number of Malenkov supporters from their local Party posts, as he had not been able to do in the days of Shatalin's presence at the key point.

Pravda of March 22, 1955, listed the presence of Praesidium and Secretariat (without Shatalin) at the lying-in-state of Marshal Gororov. *Pravda* of March 24 showed him as absent from the opening sessions of the Supreme Soviet. It seems certain that he must have been removed at the January plenum (the plenum alone having the power to do this). He was transferred about this time to be Secretary of the Maritime Territory Party Committee, on the Pacific coast.

On March 3, 1955, *Pravda* announced the dismissal of Zasyadko as Minister of the Coal Industry, for 'unsatisfactory work'. At the time this was regarded as probably a blow to Malenkov, since Zasyadko was replaced by Zademidko, a Ukrainian more closely associated with Khrushchev. Later on, it is true, Zasyadko's position became rather equivocal. He was removed from membership of the Central Committee at the XXth Congress. But after working in the Ukraine for a period he was again promoted, becoming vice-premier of the U.S.S.R. in 1957. (Later still a peculiar incident occurred, when two separate editions of the *Political Dictionary* appeared in February and April 1958 respectively, the only significant difference in them being the omission in the latter of Zasyadko and the insertion there of Ustinov — the only vice-premier left out of the earlier edition. The precise significance of this is not yet apparent. But Zasyadko's speech at the XXIst Congress was notably mild towards the Anti-Party Group.)

Pravda of March 3, 1955, also announced the removal of A. I. Kozlov, Minister of State Farms, and formerly Stalin's Head of the Agricultural Department of the Central Committee, for not coping with his work. His fall must almost certainly be seen in connection with the recent plenum's decree on agriculture, and hence as an attack on Malenkov.

Pravda of March 22, 1955, carried the removal of G. F. Aleksandrov as Minister of Culture, for 'failing to carry out his work'. Ostrovityanov, Zhdanov's economist, who now became a great Khrushchev publicist, indirectly involved Aleksandrov in the economic accusations against Malenkov by an article in *Pravda* of March 27, 1955, criticising consumer-goods advocacy in the book *Dialectical Materialism* which Aleksandrov had edited. The removal of Aleksandrov was accompanied by charges of scandalous immorality. It seems hard to imagine that such conduct can have gone unnoticed for years, and suddenly come to the horrified attention of the authorities just at the moment when the sinner's faction suffers political defeat. It will be remembered that the inquiry into Beria's crimes revealed 'profound moral degeneration'. We may take it that the situation is much as described by Evelyn Waugh's fictional Archimandrite of Sofia, explaining his removal (in *Put Out More Flags*): 'They are not expulsing . . . for fornications unless there is politics too.'

In May 1955 a further blow to the economic managers came with the division of the State Planning Committee (Gosplan) into two: Gosplan, with long-term responsibilities, under the untrained and therefore more pliable Baibakov, and Gosekonomkommisiya, with short-term powers, under Saburov, who was thus shorn of much of his power.

In May 1955 Ponomarenko was removed from the First Secretaryship in Kazakhstan and sent to be Ambassador in

Warsaw. His case is illustrative of several points. He had been a candidate member of the Praesidium since March 1953. His appointment as Ambassador to Poland was universally regarded as a downgrading from the First Secretaryship in Kazakhstan which he had hitherto held and where he was now replaced by Khrushchev's protégé, Brezhnev, who had been serving under him as Second Secretary. Ponomarenko had been regarded as an associate of Malenkov's. And it was generally felt that the ambassadorial post was far too low to be compatible with candidate membership of the Praesidium. However, in the article on Ponomarenko in the *Large Soviet Encyclopaedia*, Vol. 34, passed for publication in June 1955, he is described as a candidate member of the Party Praesidium, and at the same time his appointment to the Embassy in Poland is mentioned. It might have been thought that this was a temporary anomaly due to the fact that no Central Committee plenum had met since the fall of Malenkov which could regularise Ponomarenko's dismissal from the Praesidium. But in fact, when a plenum was called in July 1955 Ponomarenko was not removed. Kirichenko and Suslov were promoted over his head to be full members of the Praesidium, and this was at least confirmation that his star was not in the ascendant. It is true that the fact that he was not mentioned might not necessarily have meant that he had not been quietly removed. However, at the XXth Party Congress he is mentioned as appearing in the Praesidial lodge in his correct position as a candidate member, the only one apart from Shvernik. He lost this position only when the new Praesidium was elected at the plenum immediately following the Congress.

This shows in the first place how gradual a downgrading may be. But it is also some indication of an equally significant point. For Ponomarenko's new post in Warsaw was not an unimportant one, and all indications are that he carried it out strictly in accordance with the wishes of the new majority on the Praesidium (if a trifle clumsily).

There are a number of other cases in which something similar could be shown, but this is a good opportunity to make the substantive point. The fact that the struggle of policies and personalities within the ruling body in the U.S.S.R. is an extremely bitter one does not mean for a moment that factional considerations are the only ones. A man like Ponomarenko could be entrusted with an important job and would carry out orders. As against the outsider, even the outside Communist Party or state, a certain solidarity seems to prevail. (And see Appendix IX, where some remarks by Nagy, which he presumably regarded as incontrovertible facts in putting them forward in arguments with the Hungarian Central Committee, show that he was given identical advice by all parties in the Kremlin.) This solidarity has several aspects. The most obvious is that any plain and overt breach of it renders the offender extremely and immediately vulnerable to censure. This is not, of course, to say that concealed action may not often be taken — for instance, there is some reason to believe in collusion between Nagy and Malenkov in the 1953–55 period, even more between Zhdanov and Tito up to 1948, and between Beria and a number of political figures in Eastern Europe who had worked in the M.V.D. But still, the rules were enforceable to the extent that Zhdanov could be sent as the Party's representative to destroy his own policy at the Cominform meeting of June 1948 and Beria to remove his own appointees in Georgia in 1952, with at least the certainty that they would carry out the letter of their instructions.

As Malenkov's associates fell completely or declined in power, his policies continued to be attacked. Not only his agricultural and industrial ideas, but his foreign policy, too, came under direct censure.

Molotov concluded his speech to the Supreme Soviet on Foreign Policy (February 7, 1955) with a passage emphasising the end of Malenkovism. Malenkov, addressing the Supreme Soviet on March 13, 1954, had said that 'a fresh world carnage, given modern methods of warfare, means the ruin of world civilization'. Now Molotov declared:

What will perish will not be world civilisation. . . . It will be rather that social system with its imperialist basis soaked in blood, which is moribund and is being denounced for its aggressiveness and rejected because of the exploitation of the working people and the oppressed peoples, that will perish (*Pravda*, February 8, 1955).

Kommunist, No. 4 (March) 1955, carried an assault on those who identify 'the consequences of atomic war' with 'the destruction of world civilisation' — another clear reference to Malenkov's speech mentioned above. 'Such identification', *Kommunist* added sinisterly, 'serves the cause of the American imperialists, whether willingly or not.' It also alleged the imperialists were seeking 'weak-nerved and unstable people' to whom they could 'speak the language of dictation and ultimata'.

A conference held under Communist auspices in Warsaw in February 1955 had proposed simultaneous withdrawal of occupation armies from Germany and of Soviet troops from Poland, the unification of Germany and free elections under the plan put forward by Eden at the Berlin Conference in January 1954 (and then rejected by Molotov), and urged that Germany should not enter any military coalition and her frontiers be guaranteed by the European states and the United States (*Trybuna Luder*, February 9, 1955). Malenkov fell at this time, and no further mention of this conference's decisions was ever made.

The charges against Miss Anna Louise Strong (see Chapter Five) were withdrawn in a *Tass* announcement of March 4, 1955, which blamed them on the former leadership of the Ministry of State Security. This rehabilitation at this particular time seems a trifle curious. The Minister of State Security at the time of her expulsion had, of course, been Abakumov. And, as we have seen, there is reason to associate the business with the attack on Yugoslavia, though the reference to incompetence in the Ministry of Foreign Affairs may conceivably have involved Molotov. In any case, the original expulsion seems to have had something to do with Malenkov's successful attack on his opponents, and the almost simultaneous fall of Voznesensky and the other Zhdanovites. Her rehabilitation, coming shortly after the reversal of the 'Leningrad Affair' and at the time of the fall of Malenkov from the Premiership, seems to link it with a counter-attack on the latter. Malenkov's fall seems almost certainly to have been brought about by an alliance of Khrushchev and Molotov, which may well mean that the Titoite issue as such was not the point. (For this had not yet been raised, publicly at least, and, when it was, was a question dividing Khrushchev and Molotov and not uniting them.) If the original attack on Miss Strong and 'officials of the Foreign Ministry' had been even apparently a blow at Molotov, the rehabilitation might be seen as, at least partly, a strengthening of the latter's position. Even if the original trouble in 1949 had, at the time, seemed a minor criticism of the Foreign Ministry, yet it is just the sort of thing that later on might have provided Stalin with a weapon against Molotov. In 1952, when, as Khrushchev tells us, in the Secret Speech, Molotov was facing grave charges, and not only his wife but also several officials of the Foreign Ministry seem to have been under arrest, Miss Strong might well have appeared to be the imperialist spy most readily available as a link to prove Molotov's treachery. It may be some confirmation of this that *Pravda* of March 5, 1955, carrying the announcement, also had a long article condemning the idea that world civilisation might be destroyed in an atomic war — i.e. an attack on Malenkov's foreign policy views.

CHAPTER ELEVEN

TO THE XXth CONGRESS, 1955–56

ONCE again the victors fell out among themselves almost at once. Apart from the failure of Khrushchev to use the defeat of Malenkov to upset the balance of power within the Praesidium, as rather plainly intended, there were other signs that the struggle had merely entered a new phase.

For a brief period after Malenkov's fall from the premiership, Molotov and Kaganovich appeared to be in strong positions, and on May 24, 1955, Kaganovich was appointed Chairman of the important State Committee for Labour and Wage Questions under the U.S.S.R. Council of Ministers.

Malenkov might well have been considered, from July 1953 to February 1955, the man most likely to concentrate all power in his hands. And so Molotov and his colleagues may have supported Khrushchev simply as the lesser danger (though he certainly made it easier for them by concentrating on an issue — industry — on which they were in sympathy with his views).

This is to some extent confirmed by a curious change which took place after the fall of Malenkov from the Premiership. In the first place Khrushchev was not able to secure his ouster from the Praesidium, and though he eliminated Malenkov's supporter Shatalin from the Secretariat, he was not at this stage allowed to replace him by one of his own nominees.

In the early part of the period between February 1955 and the plenum of July 1955 we can, in addition, trace a definite campaign to limit the power of the Secretariat.

G. I. Petrovsky, the only old leader of the Ukraine who had survived the Yezhov purge with the loss of his offices, and who had been resuscitated at the height of Beria's power after Stalin's death, again appeared. *Pravda* of April 20, 1955, printed an article by him as an old Bolshevik, for Lenin's birthday. Among general reminiscences the extremely actual point suddenly emerges: 'Lenin taught us collectivity of work, often reminding

us that all members of the Politburo are equal and that the
secretary is chosen for the carrying out of the decisions of the
Central Committee of the Party.'

Kommunist in its April 1955 issue made the same point, that
Lenin required that 'only collective decisions of the Central
Committee adopted in the Orgburo or Politburo or in a plenum
of the Central Committee, exclusively such matters are carried
out by the Secretariat of the Central Committee of the Party'.

A further curious detail, which has been interpreted in the
light of a sniping at Khrushchev, was the appearance at the end
of the *Encyclopaedic Dictionary* (March 1955) article on Stalin of
the expression 'J. V. Stalin worked at this post [General Secre-
tary] until October 1952, and subsequently until the end of his
life was secretary of the Central Committee'. As Mr. Myron
Rush has pointed out in his *The Rise of Khrushchev*, Stalin was
never formally elected to be 'General' Secretary at any Congress after 1930; and, on the other hand, he was on occasion
referred to as General Secretary as much after October 1952
as before it. Historically the sentence is meaningless: read as an
implied attack on the pretensions of the First Secretary it gains
some significance. This last is a minute particular of information
and interpretation, and is only mentioned as such. It is not that
these subtleties may not be useful in supporting other evidence,
but the dangers of reading too much into them, and especially
the danger of treating them in isolation, is an obvious one.

We may interpret the statements on the limited power of the
Secretariat as a definite attempt, presumably by Molotov and
those who thought like him, to use a Praesidium majority
against the further strengthening of Khrushchev, who had become, with Malenkov's downgrading, the main threat to the
power of the other members of the collective.

During the first part of 1955 Khrushchev had not gained
definite control, in the Stalinist sense, of a majority of the
Praesidium; nor even of the Central Committee, an estimate of
the proportion of whose members actually owing their appointments to him comes out at about one-fifth, though with fairly
thoroughly committed allies this should be higher. He had to
rely, therefore, on manœuvre. And it is reasonable to read the
Tito reconciliation which now took place as at least in one
aspect an attempt to isolate Molotov.

The overt attack on Molotov started as early as March. *Pravda* (March 10, 1955) did an unprecedented thing: it carried extracts from a speech by Tito, two half-columns in all, including a direct criticism of Molotov by the Yugoslav President: 'Undoubtedly the formulations of Mr. [sic] Molotov about Yugoslavia in his declaration to the Supreme Soviet do not correspond with reality. . . . We consider that this is an attempt to hide the facts from his people.'

This must be the only time the Soviet Press has ever published a foreign criticism of a member of the Praesidium in good standing. Its significance is obvious enough.

The issues on which Molotov was being attacked at the time are summarised in a commentary from Radio Moscow's English service on July 3, 1957:

His erroneous stand on the Yugoslav issue was unanimously condemned by the plenary meeting of the C.C. in July 1955 as not being in line with the interests of the Soviet State and the socialist camp and not conforming to the principles of Leninist policy.

Molotov hindered the conclusion of the State Treaty with Austria and the improvement of relations with that State which lies in the centre of Europe. The conclusion of the Austrian Treaty was largely instrumental in lessening international tension. He was also against normalisation of relations with Japan, while that normalisation has played an important part in relaxing international tension in the Far East. He opposed the fundamental proposition worked out by the Party on the possibility of preventing wars in the present conditions, on the possibility of different ways of transition to socialism in different countries, on the necessity of strengthening contacts between the C.P.S.U. and progressive parties abroad.

Molotov repeatedly opposed the Soviet Government's indispensable new steps in defence of peace and the security of nations. In particular he denied the advisability of establishing personal contacts between Soviet leaders and the statesmen of other countries, which is essential for the achievement of mutual understanding and better international relations. Later he was removed from the post of Foreign Minister. But after this Molotov still held to his conservative, dogmatic views, and with his associates in the group opposed measures for easing international tension.

The negotiations for the Austrian Treaty, which Molotov was later accused of opposing, started on February 8, with Soviet proposals. Agreement in principle was reached in April, when Molotov and Mikoyan conferred with the Austrian Government delegation. The treaty was signed on May 15.

The attack on Molotov involved squeezing him out from foreign policy. The career Ambassadors in Eastern Europe had already largely been replaced by Party officials. On May 14, 1955, the State visit to Yugoslavia was announced, and it took place at the end of the month. Molotov was not on the delegation, whose leading figures were Khrushchev, Bulganin, Mikoyan and Shepilov (who, as it later appeared, was being groomed to take charge of foreign affairs in Molotov's place). In Belgrade, Khrushchev blamed the 1948 accusations against Yugoslavia on Beria and Abakumov.*

Earlier in May, the Conference setting up the Warsaw Pact had been managed by Bulganin as Prime Minister, without any assistance from the Foreign Minister.

The next plenum met on July 4–12, 1955. That it involved an attack on Molotov is clear. In the Secret Speech Khrushchev says: 'The July plenum of the Central Committee studied in detail the reasons for the development of the conflict with Yugoslavia.' 'Study of the reasons for' indicates that this was no mere reversal of policies with no questions asked, as sometimes occurs, but a post mortem with blame allotted. The Central Committee resolution against the Anti-Party Group in June 1957 accuses Molotov (but not the others) of opposing the *rapprochement* with Yugoslavia.†

By this plenum Khrushchev had thus weakened the positions of both Malenkov and Molotov, and had in effect removed foreign policy from the hands of the latter. And he was now able to strengthen his position on both Praesidium and Secre-

---

* According to Lecoeur, at the time Secretary of the Central Committee of the French Communist Party, when Beria fell a confidential letter, circulated by the C.P.S.U. to the other Party leaderships, charged him with being in touch with Tito for subversive purposes. Possibly he really had intended to anticipate Khrushchev's 1955 move.

† It so happens that the July plenum is one on which what appears to be a reliable account of the minutes, as circulated, has been given in the West, by the Polish defector Mr. Seweryn Bialer. He states that Molotov kept up his opposition to the point of taking it to the floor of the Central Committee, but was then opposed by *all* the other members of the Praesidium, and voted down. This is, in any case, only a slight extension of what can be deduced from the official sources. In his speech to the XXIst Congress Pervukhin said that he 'and others' had criticised Molotov's errors on Yugoslavia at this plenum.

tariat — Shepilov, Aristov and Belyaev joining the latter body (see Appendix I). The disposal of cadres was now clearly in his hands as far as the Secretariat was concerned, at least as against the other members of the Praesidium. (Aristov was head of the Credentials Commission at the XXth Congress, which confirms his role as, once again, Secretary in charge of Party organs.)

The promotion of Kirichenko and Suslov to full membership of the Praesidium does not appear as a clear-cut victory for Khrushchev. It seems highly unlikely that he had, at this stage, much more power to impose a change in the leadership than he turned out to have later on, at the XXth Congress. In that case the move must be seen as, at least to some extent, a compromise. Kirichenko is plainly a Khrushchev nominee pure and simple. Suslov is therefore the question mark. There is nothing in his previous career to associate him with Khrushchev. It seems likely that he was acceptable, as a makeweight, to some other members of the Praesidium.

It is notable that not only Ponomarenko, but also Shvernik were passed over. Although the latter was later to be an outspoken ally of Khrushchev, he had associated himself in 1953–54 with Malenkov's consumer-goods campaign. On the other hand, he seems to have been ill from about February 1955 for the greater part of the year.

The plenum of July 1955 called a XXth Congress, with the following agenda, for February 14, 1956:

(1) Report of the Central Committee, delivered by Khrushchev;

(2) Report of the Central Revision Commission, delivered by its Chairman, P. G. Moskatov.

(3) Election of central Party organs.

It seems clear that the intermediate period saw a number of steps calculated to lead up to a final victory at the Congress.

In the first place, the new Secretariat stepped up its replacement of non-Khrushchevite by Khrushchevite nominees as the provincial First Secretaries (see p. 285). By the Congress they had increased the numbers owing their positions directly to Khrushchev to about two-fifths of the senior provincial secretaries.

On July 29, 1955, Patolichev was removed from the First

Secretaryship of Byelorussia and made a Deputy Foreign Minister. Heirarchically speaking this is a very definite reduction in rank. On the other hand, it was also the intrusion of a skilled apparat figure into Molotov's apparatus.

In *Kommunist* of October a public humiliation was inflicted on Molotov. The journal carried an article signed by him in which he apologised for having said in his speech to the Supreme Soviet on February 8, 1955: 'The Soviet Union, where the foundations of a socialist society have already been built'. This is, of course, erroneous: the foundations of socialism had been laid by 1932, and socialism completed by 1939, according to all orthodox formulae. It is sometimes held that Molotov's formulation was intentional — perhaps implying a state of affairs in which stern class-struggle and 'Stalinist' methods were still appropriate. This must seem doubtful. Still, *Kommunist*, in its covering editorial, spoke of 'attempts' to carry over obsolete formulae, and Molotov did not claim that it was a mere slip. It seems true that, slip or not, the incident was slightly more than an attack on Molotov's prestige, though the whole affair certainly represents a debunking of Molotov's presumptions as a theoretician (which, however, he was to resume in 1956). His retraction admitted that the Socialist forces had irrevocably triumphed in the U.S.S.R. And it is tempting to link this with the argument about rehabilitating purgees and denouncing Stalin which must have been going on in the Praesidium at this time. For the *theoretical* basis of the denunciation of Stalin was his view that the class struggle would become more intense. *Kommunist* spoke of 'the theoretical bankruptcy of using the formula of a state passed through long ago'.

In his speech at the XXIst Party Congress on February 3, 1959, Kuusinen said: 'Such a pseudo-theorist as Molotov proved to be organically incapable of understanding this Leninist proposition. I remember how at one of the plenary sessions of the Central Committee Molotov, who did not hatch a single theoretical chick himself, hurled reproaches at other Comrades for theoretical heedlessness.'

Thus, Molotov had been inclined to theoretical denunciation of his opponents not merely in the Praesidium but actually before the Central Committee. It seems possible that the plenum referred to was that of July 1955, where Molotov was certainly arguing against a Praesidial proposal (that on Yugoslavia). And the *Kommunist* episode may be seen as a revenge, and at the same time a theoretical manifesto in favour of the rehabilitation now beginning.

In September 1955 came the Rapava–Rukhadze trial (see Appendix VI). Rapava and his co-defendants were tried in Georgia, mainly on local charges. At first sight the trial might appear to be simply a winding up of some loose ends of the Beria conspiracy. But in the first place numbers of Beria's supporters were shot without publicity. Secondly, we have seen that trials of this sort do not take place in the Soviet Union without both their timing and their content, as well as any publicity given them, being decided on political grounds. There is only one element in the Rapava trial that has any probable significance from the point of view of the struggle for power in Moscow. That is, the reference to their having persecuted Ordzhonikidze.

Beria was vaguely accused at his trial of having persecuted Ordzhonikidze. The issue was now raised again and Khrushchev, in his Secret Speech of February 1956, revealed for the first time officially that, far from having died naturally, Ordzhonikidze had been forced to kill himself. It is most unlikely that Stalin could have done this without accomplices. And it is at least possible that Malenkov or Kaganovich, or both (and possibly Molotov, too), were also involved. In that case the obscure references to the matter, without any direct blame being laid on them, would parallel the way in which the Leningrad Case was referred to in the Abakumov trial and later in the Secret Speech — as a weapon against Malenkov, but without the charge being pressed home until June 1957.

For a time there appears to have been no direct affront to Kaganovich (unless the award of the Order of Lenin on March 19, 1955, his sixtieth birthday, to the Ukrainian poet Maxim Rylski, whom Kaganovich was later alleged to have viciously persecuted in 1947, may be so considered). Nor was he excluded from Eastern European affairs: he led the Soviet delegation to Prague in May 1955, and his speeches were prominently reported. In the autumn he was usually reported high in the Praesidial listings, and was seen near the centre of photographs in which Molotov and Malenkov were on the periphery. During Khrushchev's and Bulganin's visit to India and Burma, Kaganovich and Mikoyan figured as the ranking stay-at-homes.

In November, however, there were signs of a drop in his power.

In the Revolution speech made by Kaganovich on November 6, 1955, he voiced some criticism, saying that there had been talk about the difficulty of work in the Virgin Lands. This was deleted by *Tass* and every Soviet newspaper. Then a decree of the Supreme Soviet of November 25, 1955, renamed the 'Kaganovich' Moscow Metro after Lenin, while, 'noting the services of Comrade L. M. Kaganovich in building and organising the work of the Moscow Metropolitan', one of the stations on it (the Okhotny Ryad [Lenin] Station) was named for him.

Thus the Praesidium approached the XXth Congress with Malenkov and Molotov certainly, and Kaganovich most likely, under attack. They were, however, being dealt with on different issues: on the heavy industry question Molotov and Kaganovich had sided with Khrushchev; on the Tito issue Molotov seems to have been isolated; and even on the discussions evidently going on about de-Stalinisation there is no reason to assume any great identity of opinion. In fact the forces Khrushchev was attacking at this stage seem to have had little solidarity.

Yet if the opposition was divided on positive policies, it seems as if Khrushchev's majority must have been anything but solid on the issue of *finally* destroying the anti-Khrushchev forces. It is easy to imagine that some of those who wavered in the crisis of June 1957 were already at least unwilling to alter the balance.

On the organisational side, the turnover of new appointments became even more rapid in December and January. The removal of Kruglov from the M.V.D. and his replacement by Dudorov from Khrushchev's Party apparatus was a particularly significant step.

It was not an isolated incident. A number of other senior M.V.D. officers of the old service had been quietly dropped over the past two years — for example, the M.V.D.'s other representatives on the Central Committee, Maslennikov and Ryasnoi, who had both been Deputy Ministers of Internal

Affairs under Kruglov in 1952. In the new Central Committee neither they nor their chief were to figure.

Provincial secretaries were being replaced at an increasing tempo. Their allegiances were mostly those of one of their number, Shatalin, who was again demoted at this time, being referred to on Radio Moscow of January 23, 1956, as having been replaced as Secretary of the Maritime Territorial Committee, and who was not re-elected to the new Central Committee.

Several organisations under Khrushchev's control now began to speak of 'the Praesidium of the Central Committee headed by the First Secretary of the C.C. C.P.S.U., Comrade Khrushchev' (Resolution of the Kazakh Party Congress January 24, 1955) and 'the Praesidium headed by Comrade Khrushchev' (Nazarenko at the Ukrainian Party Congress January 24, 1956). There is no constitutional basis for speaking of the First Secretary as 'heading' the Praesidium, and it had not previously been done. There were, in addition, many other expressions of adulation, and almost none for anyone else. The commonest was 'the Central Committee and Comrade Khrushchev personally'.

At these preliminary meetings almost nothing was said about Stalin — at least, in the published records. The man closest to Khrushchev, however, Kirichenko, gave him one favourable reference.

On the ideological side, too, pressure was kept up. *Kommunist* (No. 12 of 1955, which appeared early in the following year) spoke in favour of a more flexible application of *partiinost* in literature. Attacking the 'philosophising mannequins' which many characters in fiction had become and the 'naked abstractions' which prevailed, it criticised the conception of typicality which had been the essential point on art in Malenkov's speech at the XIXth Party Congress. And, in general, the views it attacked were put in the terms of that speech. Though not overt (since, after all, the speech had been the official report of the Central Committee), it seems as if the article was designed to give the impression that Malenkov had been personally responsible for the line now repudiated. This is natural enough in the political circumstances.

The major issue, ideological and political, was a different one. The Abakumov trial had been a great demonstration of the utility of blaming rivals for the crimes of the past. At the same time, the rehabilitations which had ensued had been popular, and had led to further requests for reconsideration of cases. When this became the main point in dispute is uncertain, but as Kaganovich was one of those most clearly threatened by any exposure of the facts of the 'thirties, we may assume that it was in the autumn of 1955, at the time when hostility between him and the majority begins to show itself.

We may consider how the question of rehabilitations got started and attained such scope that it would have been virtually impossible to write it off, leaving the leaders with the alternative of making use of it.

The investigation of the Beria Case already implied a look at the relevant material. In the Beria indictment (in *Pravda* of December 17, 1953) reference is already made to the Kedrov Case. Kedrov, it was made clear in Khrushchev's Secret Speech, was executed about 1940 (since a letter of his from prison is quoted, which mentions his being sixty-two years old). Thus at least one rehabilitation from the pre-war period was already made. Also 'it has been established by the inquiry' that Beria had intrigued against Ordzhonikidze and his relatives, so that the scope of the inquiry must have gone into sensitive matters directly involving Stalin as early as 1937.

As Khrushchev said in the Secret Speech:

Lately, especially after the unmasking of the Beria gang, the Central Committee looked into a series of matters fabricated by this gang. This revealed a very ugly picture of brutal wilfulness connected with the incorrect behaviour of Stalin.

That the Supreme Court was examining the material as early as 1954 is made clear in the Secret Speech:

A large part of these cases is being reviewed now and a great number of them are being voided because they are baseless and falsified. Suffice it to say that from 1954 to the present time the Military Collegium of the Supreme Court has rehabilitated 7,679 persons, many of them posthumously.

There is some implication that the cases directly involving Beria came first, as when Khrushchev quotes the declaration of a witness against him. In this declaration Snegov writes:

In connection with the proposed rehabilitation of the former Central Committee member Kartvelishvili-Lavryentiev, I have entrusted to the hands of the representative of the Committee of State Security a detailed deposition concerning Beria's role in the disposition of the Kartvelishvili case and concerning the criminal motives by which Beria was guided.

In my opinion it is indispensable to recall an important fact pertaining to this case and to communicate it to the Central Committee, because I did not consider it as proper to include in the investigation documents.

That such cases led only gradually to the key crimes of the Stalin era with which Beria had *not* been associated seems to be shown by the fact that Khrushchev states that the Rudzutak and Komarov cases were examined 'in 1955'.

This widening of the scope of the inquiry led to the setting up of a special commission, which Khrushchev describes as follows:

Having at its disposal numerous data showing brutal wilfulness towards Party cadres, the Central Committee has created a Party commission under the control of the Central Committee Praesidium: it was charged with investigating what made possible the mass repressions against the majority of the Central Committee members and candidates elected at the XVIIth Congress of the All-Union Communist Party (Bolsheviks).

The commission has become acquainted with a large quantity of material in the N.K.V.D. archives and with other documents and has established many facts pertaining to the fabrication of cases against Communists, to false accusations, to glaring abuses of Socialist legality — which resulted in the death of innocent people. ... The commission has presented to the Central Committee Praesidium lengthy and documented materials pertaining to mass repressions against the delegates to the XVIIth party Congress and against members of the Central Committee elected at that congress. These materials have been studied by the Praesidium of the Central Committee.

It was determined that of the 139 members and candidates of the party's Central Committee who were elected at the XVIIth Congress, 98 persons, i.e. 70 per cent, were arrested and shot (mostly in 1937–38) ...

The same fate met not only the Central Committee members but also the majority of the delegates to the XVIIth Party Congress. Of 1,966 delegates with either voting or advisory rights. 1,108 persons were arrested on charges of anti-revolutionary crimes, i.e. decidedly more than a majority. This very fact shows how absurd, wild, and contrary to common sense were the charges of counter-revolutionary crimes made out, as we now see, against a majority of participants at the XVIIth Party Congress.

This extends the matter far beyond Beria's responsibility, directly involving the whole Yezhov period.

It will be seen that three separate organisations are concerned: the Military Collegium of the Supreme Court (whose 7,000-odd rehabilitations certainly covered a wider field than that of the Commission); the Committee of State Security, for which the only quoted case is one of a victim of Beria's; and this Commission of the Central Committee.

Meanwhile the public trials had covered a certain amount of ground. The Abakumov trial (December 1954) confined itself to rehabilitating Voznesensky and the Leningraders. This was certainly a more recent case, but it, too, was one in which Stalin was directly involved, and covered a wide field in the State and Party apparatus. The Rapava–Rukhadze trial in September 1955 again mentioned Ordzhonikidze, and also rehabilitated a number of Georgians headed by Orakhelashvili, who had been shot in the Yenukidze-Karakhan case of December 16, 1937, one of the key publicised (though not public) trials in the great purge.

Some pressure for rehabilitation was also now being brought by the Polish Communist Party, most of whose leaders were shot in Moscow in 1937–38. Certain of these had been rehabilitated as early as April 1955. On February 9, 1956, a communiqué announced the official repudiation of the charges against the Polish Communist Party. (Nevertheless, even as late as this, the Poles found it necesssary to put the blame on the 'criminal work of Beria'.)

And now we come to a peculiar and significant episode. In the Secret Speech, Khrushchev says that the investigative judge who had handled the 'cases' (or possibly case, for they are now all stated to have been executed in 1939) of Kossior, Chubar and Kosarev was questioned by the Party Praesidium 'only several days before the present Congress'. That such an individual witness should be interrogated by the Praesidium at all is a trifle odd, for it is difficult to imagine what information they supposed they could obtain from him that had not already been extorted by the other inquiries, or could be extracted by them on instructions from above. The fact that this interview was taking place on the very eve of the Congress seems to show that general decisions had not been made, that points of detail were still being looked into and, from its very oddity, that manœuvres were afoot and pressures being put.

Though Khrushchev in his speech dissociates himself strongly from the matter and expresses disgust at the Kossior purge, it is difficult to escape the presumption that the reason it had become so much of an issue before the Praesidium was that the member who could be most plausibly blamed for the Kossior–Chubar case was Khrushchev himself.

The extent, and the details, of the rehabilitations decided on were of obvious importance to most members of the Praesidium. But there was a further issue. To what extent should the implied disavowal of the past go?

There were obviously good political motives of a general nature for dissociating the rulers from the heavy debit balance in people's minds arising from their continuity with Stalin's rule. And it is clear that some attempt to dissociate the actual regime from its origins had been decided upon. The key question was how far, in order to dramatise and emphasise the point, Stalin himself should be disavowed and attacked, and in what way.

The history of the attitude to Stalin since his death is interesting. After the transports at his funeral (of which Khrushchev was later to say, 'We were sincere when we wept'), the repudiation of the Doctors' Plot brought a period of cold silence.

Bulganin's speech of May 1, 1953, made no mention of Stalin. Nor did his order for V.E. Day anniversary on May 9. *Pravda* of June 28 — that is, immediately after the fall of Beria — carried an article 'The People — Creator of History', by F. Konstantinov, which was an attack on the idea of the role of 'eminent personalities' in social history. The Communist Party was referred to as 'the leader'. An editorial in *Pravda* of July 13, 1953, strongly in favour of collective leadership, said: 'Decisions taken by individuals are always or almost always one-sided.'

The cult of personality and collective leadership issues were raised at the July 1953 plenum, as we know from Aristov's report to the XXth Congress:

As is known, the July 1953 plenary session of the Central Committee revealed very blatant violations of this most important principle of Party leadership engendered by the cult of the individual, and demanded the constant implementation of Lenin's instructions regarding collectivity in Party leadership. . . .

At a joint session of certain sections of the Academy of Sciences on October 19, 1953, several speakers, including Pospelov and F. Konstantinov, attacked the cult of personality. (Pospelov advanced the argument that Stalin himself was opposed to such a thing.) *Voprosy Filosofii* (No. 4 of 1953, which went to press in August) had an article on the fiftieth anniversary of the Party, in which Stalin is downgraded not to the 1956 level, but to very much the position he was to occupy in 1957–59. Lenin is frequently referred to, the Party and the Central Committee are given boundless praise, but Stalin appears only twice — once in a quotation from Malenkov's XIXth Congress Speech, and once as leader of the Central Committee in the struggle with the Trotskyites and other deviationists. The 1936 Constitution, hitherto almost always called the Stalin Constitution, is now referred to simply as the New Constitution. Victory in World War II is attributed no longer to Stalin, but to the Party.

The edition of the *Philosophical Dictionary* published in November 1953 had a number of changes, entirely omissions, from that published in 1952, on the role of Stalin. Although it was a longer edition, its biography of Stalin was considerably shorter and it omitted a number of the strongest adulations and the most absurd of the falsifications — e.g. the claim made in the earlier edition that Stalin created the Constitution and wrote the *Short Course History of the Communist Party*.

Stalin's birthday on December 21, 1953, was passed over in silence. But in December 1954 *Pravda* published a long article with a photograph of Stalin, writing, among other things, 'It was he who mercilessly exposed the enemies of the people. Under the leadership of its Central Committee and of Stalin the Communist Party destroyed the traitors and defeatists.' *Izvestia*, still under Malenkov's influence, devoted no more than a short note to the birthday.

Stalin's birthday anniversary in 1955 was again celebrated with some enthusiasm by the Press. *Izvestia* (December 21, 1955) spoke of 'a great revolutionary and profound thinker . . . the name of Stalin is close and dear to millions of toilers in all corners of the earth. Stalin — great fighter for the peace and security of the peoples. In millions of hearts burns the inextinguishable flame of his word.' *Kommunist*'s 1955 anniversary article linked Lenin, Stalin and Khrushchev, naming no others. The decision to go ahead with a downgrading of Stalin seems to have been taken about mid-January. On January 12, *Tass* was announcing the publication of Vol. 14 of his collected works, covering the purge period, which never in fact emerged. (*Literaturaya Gazeta* of January 12, 1956, even said that it would appear in connection with the XXth Congress.)

On January 21, 1956, addressing a Komsomol meeting, Khrushchev made no mention of Stalin. The previous year on the same occasion he had spoke of him several times. The last time Stalin's name appeared in a leading article in *Pravda* was January 16, 1956. The Soviet Press at large, on the other hand, continued to praise Stalin right up to the Congress. (Shepilov was then editor of *Pravda*.)

On Voroshilov's seventy-fifth birthday (February 4, 1956) for the first time on such formal occasions the conventional description of a leader as a 'companion of Stalin' is omitted. This seems the first absolutely hard piece of evidence.

The latest figures to be reported as speaking favourably of Stalin were Furtseva, Kapitonov and Kirichenko, all close associates of Khrushchev. (Bierut, the Polish leader, is indeed reported in *Pravda* of February 13 with the old conventional remarks about Stalin. But it is conceivable that he had not been briefed, and there is in any case no reason to believe that a final and formal decision had been taken, such as would enable the editor of *Pravda* to censor the Polish leader.)

The conclusion would be that rehabilitation was taking place, and that it was intended to play Stalin down. But there is no reason to suppose that even the mass rehabilitations would necessarily affect Stalin's public status in a *direct* fashion, any more than the reversal of the Leningrad Case and the Doctors' Plot had done. Confusion about the status of the late dictator seems to have prevailed: some local party organs praised him and others ignored him, which could scarcely have been the case if proper directives had gone out. Thus, although we may assume that a general decision had been taken to do something about the past, it seems unlikely that the precise line to be taken at the Congress had been decided. Moreover, there was not only this 'negative' controversy: at a January Conference of the Readers of *Voprosy Istorii*, Burdzhalov (later to be the stormy petrel of anti-Stalinist historiography and to be purged from his assistant editorship early in 1957) attacked Stalin's *Short Course* Party history. He was counter-attacked by historians from the Party apparatus, and it was officially stated that no historical re-estimate was intended.

The theme of collective leadership was not new, as we have seen. And nor was that of attack on the cult of personality. *Voprosy Filosofii*, No. 2 of 1955, had strongly attacked the 'cult of personality' as 'alien to the spirit of Marxism–Leninism', contrary to the collective principle, and tending to hamper the initiative of the Central Committee and 'leading cadres'.

This was one of a number of similar articles. The point is that the theme was thoroughly established long before the XXth Congress. Although the phrase naturally derogates a certain amount from Stalin's reputation, it does not in itself imply any violent denunciation of him. On the contrary, the formula as it stands limits criticism to little more than a charge of insufficient attention to collegiality of leadership. If I accuse a man of vanity it rather implies that I am restricting myself to that and associated errors, and am not going to mention the fact that he is a murderer. Yet the formula, unaltered, was used to cover Khrushchev's uninhibited assault in the Secret Speech, and is still the basic phrase in discussion of the whole of Stalin's errors. One might conclude that Khrushchev was stretching things further than the collective had agreed on when he went so far.

There is little doubt that some sort of attack on the cult of personality had been agreed on. But that it took the form it did seems to have been something of a last-minute improvisation. The Speech itself is far more incoherent in construction than is usual in Soviet addresses — and is even improperly briefed on details, as when Khrushchev wrongly states that no Lenin prizes had ever been awarded.

As a general conclusion from the Congress, the impression may be formed that Khrushchev's timing was wrong. The essentials of the attack on the personality cult, which might otherwise have been used as a powerful weapon against Malenkov at least, were still in dispute when the Congress was already upon the leadership and it was no longer possible to force a conclusive assault through.

Khrushchev's position as he approached the XXth Congress was thus not entirely satisfactory. He had been able to secure the public branding of Malenkov as an incompetent, had removed him from the Premiership and had dismissed a number of his followers, from Shatalin and Aleksandrov down to provincial Party secretaries. But he had not secured his removal from the Praesidium. He had then contrived to isolate Molotov, and to humiliate him as an ideological incompetent. But here again no further progress had been made. And although the initiative was in his hands and he had strengthened himself in Praesidium, Secretariat and Central Committee alike, he had not been able to secure a majority on the Praesidium decisive enough to let him destroy his rivals. It seems likely on these grounds alone that there was always a Praesidium majority which included both his enemies and some of those prepared to give his policies a trial and which was strong enough to prevent a decision being reached. That this was so even after the promotion of Kirichenko and Suslov is evident from the events of 1956–57. Even if we assume that both the new men were prepared to back Khrushchev to the hilt, it is at least possible to imagine that most, if not all, the other eight might have opposed such a move. Khrushchev's presumed intention at the XXth Congress was to secure a Praesidium more favourable to the development of his plans, to put it mildly.

In this he was, without any doubt, quite right. The lesson of our whole period is that the leading figure in a 'collective leadership' is in constant danger unless he crushes his enemies in the Praesidium completely and assures himself of a solid and devoted majority. We can assume that anyone in Khrushchev's place is compelled by the logic of his position to strive for such a result.

The opposite is also true: 'collective leadership' is the resultant of a number of conflicting forces. A balance can only be

T

kept by constant manœuvre and adjustment by all concerned.
Those not themselves in the running for supreme power must
work tirelessly to provide counterweights. The calculations
involve so many unknowns that even the most skilled operators
must be expected to make wrong guesses, and chance must play
a big part. It is not a system that is self-regulating, even on these
terms, and crises come almost yearly. It seems likely that on a
chance basis alone sooner or later one of these would lead to
the establishment of a single man's supremacy. If the Anti-
Party Group had triumphed in 1957 the struggle would have
gone on longer, and between different protagonists, but it
appears at least probable that sooner or later oligopoly would
have given way to monopoly.

The XXth Congress opened on February 14, 1956. On the
first day Khrushchev delivered his official report, in which he
said that 'shortly after the XIXth Congress death took Josef
Vissarionovich Stalin from our ranks', adding that in spite of
enemy hopes of confusion the Party had 'rallied still more
strongly around its Central Committee'. On the Leningrad
Affair he said:

> The Central Committee verified the so-called Leningrad case and
> established that it had been fabricated by Beria and his henchmen in
> order to weaken the Leningrad Party Organisation, to discredit its
> cadres. Having established the inconsistency of the Leningrad case,
> the Central Party Committee also verified a number of other
> doubtful cases. The Central Committee took steps to restore justice.
> On the recommendation of the C.C. the falsely condemned people
> were rehabilitated.

This way of putting the matter on the Leningrad Case and
other purges is very different from the way Khrushchev put it
in his Secret Report a few days later.

In this open Report Khrushchev made a number of attacks
on his opponents. After significantly remarking that collective
leadership did not imply any 'mutual amnesty', he went on to
bring up (though without naming names), first Molotov's error:

> The Central Committee has had to correct persons who introduced
> disorder and confusion into certain clear issues which had been
> settled by the Party a long time ago. . . . The speeches of some
> people contained erroneous formulations, such as the one that so far

only a basis for socialism, only the foundation of socialism, had been erected in our country.

and then Malenkov's:

Some wiseacres began to counterpose light industry and heavy industry, assuring us that the preponderant development of heavy industry had been essential only at the early stages of Soviet economic development. . . .

(F. R. Kozlov also attacked 'the right-wing opportunist theory of benighted Communists who proposed to reduce the pace of development of heavy industry'.)

Khrushchev's open reference to Stalin was fairly friendly. But on February 16 Mikoyan, in his speech, made several remarks which constituted an attack on Stalin and a hint that more was required. He called for a revision of *Economic Problems of Socialism*, and described 'a well-known dictum of Stalin's' as 'hardly helpful, hardly correct'. He referred not very indirectly to Lenin's Testament and dropped other anti-Stalinist hints, such as one to the effect that histories of the Transcaucasian Party organisation falsified the facts. Above all, he spoke of 'Comrade Kossior' and 'Comrade Antonov-Ovseenko', 'wrongly declared enemies of the people'.

A link of sorts may be established between Mikoyan and the 'liberal' historian Burdzhalov. The same book which Mikoyan had used from which to demonstrate the wrong treatment of Kossior and Antonov-Ovseenko had been attacked by Burdzhalov at the historians' meeting, and Burdzhalov's chief on *Voprosy Istorii*, Pankratova, also attacked it at the Congress in her speech on February 20. Mikoyan's speech was not automatically given at once in full in all the organs of international Communism, as was the case with all the other senior speeches. The Cominform journal *For a Lasting Peace, For a People's Democracy* did not print it until a later issue, when the matter had, as we shall see, been settled. Between Mikoyan's speech and the Secret Speech of Khrushchev nine days passed.

In his speech to the Congress on February 18, 1956, Kaganovich seems to be directly condemning any 'unprincipled' personal attack on Stalin:

After the XIXth Congress of the Party the Central Committee boldly (I have in mind boldness which has to do with ideas, which is principled, theoretical) raised the question of the struggle against the cult of the individual. This is not an easy question. But the Central Committee gave a correct, Marxist–Leninist Party answer to it.

On February 24, 1956, a substantive resolution was adopted on Khrushchev's open Report of February 14. It instructed the Central Committee 'not to weaken the struggle against vestiges of the cult of the individual'. This is so different from the line taken in the resolution on the cult a few days later, that it is reasonable to conclude that a final decision on the Secret Speech had not *yet* been taken. It may also be noted that the Secret Session was postponed from 6 p.m. on Friday, February 24, until early in the morning of Saturday, February 25.

At the beginning of the Secret Speech Khrushchev emphasised previous attacks on the cult of Stalin:

In the report of the Central Committee of the Party at the XXth Congress, in a number of speeches by delegates to the Congress, as also formerly during the plenary C.C. C.P.S.U. sessions, quite a lot has been said about the cult of the individual and about its harmful consequences. After Stalin's death the Central Committee of the Party began to implement a policy of explaining . . . that it is contrary to the spirit of Marxism–Leninism to elevate one person, to transform him into a superman . . .

The reason he put for giving the secret report, which in the circumstances might sound unnecessary, was:

Because of the fact that not all as yet realise fully the practical consequences resulting from the cult of the individual the Central Committee considered it absolutely necessary to make the material available to the Congress.

(It may be noted that, according to Khrushchev, Lenin's Testament had already been distributed to and read by delegates.)

The impression remains strong that, although some sort of intention to disavow the purges had developed some weeks before the Congress, the precise tactics had not been decided on up to the last moment. That such should be the position right in the middle of a Congress was unprecedented and, inevitably, confusing in the extreme. It seemed at first as if the Congress would go on in accordance with old routine, leaving the question unresolved for the time being. Yet the opportunities must have seemed as attractive to some as the dangers seemed appalling to others. We may perhaps read Mikoyan's speech as a definite attempt to force the issue. He appears as the most consistent anti-Stalin man throughout. And there can be little doubt which way his influence was cast. But to read his intervention as a threat to Khrushchev may not be exactly the right way of looking at it. Khrushchev may well, by this time, have been undecided about rather than opposed to the intransigent anti-Stalin line, and a little goading, a sharp reminder that the awkwardness of the Kossior business would now have to be faced anyway, might well have turned the scale.

Another point that seems evident is that all this confusion and hesitation followed by decision must have taken place within the Praesidium. No larger body, such as the moribund Central Committee, could have handled it (and the re-election of the old Praesidium en bloc could only have been a Praesidial decision). On the other hand, a group determined to press the issue regardless could possibly have threatened to appeal to the Central Committee, or even the Congress, with facts which the others were in no position to deny, and the Secret Speech, unopposed, may represent a very reluctant compromise. The situation was extremely fluid, the dangers pressing and the possible consequences very various. The final result may be interpreted, in so far as the field of power alone is concerned, as the development by Khrushchev of a 'platform for further struggle' against Malenkov, Kaganovich and to some extent Molotov, while not for the moment throwing the position of the whole ruling group into jeopardy by entering into an uncontrolled and inadequately prepared battle in the presence of the shaken delegates.

It is hardly necessary to elaborate on the extreme and dramatic nature of the Secret Speech's attack on Stalin; the fact that many reservations and praises of the old dictator, scarcely compatible with the attacks, were also included suggests an ambivalence in the matter — perhaps on the part of Khrushchev himself, as seems possible from his later development on the Stalin issue, but if not, representing an inadequately melded draft in which several hands had put in amendments.

The Secret Speech contained references to all the senior members of the Praesidium: Malenkov, Molotov, Voroshilov, Kaganovich, Mikoyan and Bulganin:

Mikoyan appeared three times, once criticising Stalin to his face, once as his prospective victim and once as an unprotesting witness of a minor injustice. In the first two cases he was given his forenames.

Malenkov appeared twice, as the immediate intermediary to Stalin, when the latter was refusing the correct requests of Khrushchev and the generals during the war. No forenames were given.

Voroshilov appeared twice, once as a prospective victim of Stalin, and once as a man rather patronisingly urged to tell the truth; in both cases with his forenames.

Molotov appeared twice, once as a prospective victim of Stalin, and once as the recipient of orders to increase the terror. In the first case he was given his forenames.

Kaganovich appeared twice, once as the recipient of orders to increase the terror, and once as the uncomplaining witness of a minor injustice. No forenames were given.

Bulganin appeared once, complaining of Stalin in private. His forenames were given.

A pattern of sorts seems to emerge. And though amenities are, in general, preserved, it appears from this that the Speech as delivered was a personal draft, even if finally and perhaps reluctantly approved or even amended by the Praesidium before delivery.

The election of the new Central Committee must be presumed to have been on the old principle of the Congress assenting to a list presented to it by its managers. And just as the Praesidial election represents an obvious compromise, the Central Committee's composition shows no sign of a walk-over for Khrushchev or anyone else.

Khrushchev had nevertheless made a number of gains. And it is instructive to look at the position of the Provincial Secretaries who also became full members of the C.C. (We may leave out Moscow and Leningrad for this purpose, as really ranking with the republican secretaryships, among which relevant changes also took place, as can be seen in Appendix I.) And the result will show both the power and the limitation on the power of the Secretariat as a machine for packing the Party organisation in the then circumstances. Seventeen of the provincial First

Secretaries who were C.C. full members and had been removed from their provincial posts in 1954–55 were dropped from the new Central Committee. Thirteen of their replacements were elected to the new one: but of these, five had figured in the old Central Committee, though holding other posts. The net gain to Khrushchev through these replacements was thus only eleven, even assuming that all the removals had been for straight faction motives. On the other hand, ten Provincial Secretaries serving in provinces not previously represented on the Central Committee were brought in, mainly from the Ukraine and Siberia. Most of these were evidently Khrushchev nominees. Thus the gain made by direct negotiation in the Praesidium was about as great as that secured, or staked, through the Party Organs Department.

The method by which Stalin had gained control of the Party was thus shown to be indecisive in present conditions, though still useful. The reason why it was more effective in Stalin's time is plain. Then the Secretariat, through its appointees in the provinces, could strongly affect the composition of the delegations to Congress, *and the Congresses actually voted*. No (non-unanimous) voting took place in February 1956. The Congress was faced with the decisions of the Praesidium and accepted them.

The formulation of the attack on Stalin in the Secret Speech (and afterwards) can be simply summarised. Stalin 'played a positive role' in defeating 'the Trotskyite–Zinovievite bloc' and the 'Bukharinites', and in the industrialisation and collectivisation policies. Later, while still in general on the right line in 'socialist construction', he introduced the 'cult of personality', ruled despotically, and abandoned 'Leninist norms' — practices which led to terrorism against loyal cadres.

The theoretical basis of Stalin's errors (or what we could probably call their rationalisation) was his thesis that the class struggle becomes stronger as socialism is approached. This theory of Stalin's was now formally abandoned.

A suitable reconstruction of the Stalin and rehabilitation themes which dominated the Congress might be something on these lines: a further move had been agreed on, and the report of the investigating commission set up to go into the purges must have made it difficult for members of the Praesidium to resist the rehabilitation of at least some of the victims of the 'thirties, even though such rehabilitations tended to implicate them. But rehabilitation itself could have been carried out in such a way that the blame was put on the police chiefs alone. This had already been done in the rehabilitation of Voznesensky at the Abakumov trial in December 1954. What is more, in the partial rehabilitation of Stalin which took place in 1957–58 there was a reversion, as far as possible, to this method, and all the emphasis began to be that Stalin, with all his merits, had been led astray by Yagoda, Yezhov and Beria in turn. It would have been perfectly possible to attack the cult of personality in a general way, and to emphasise collectivity and quietly drop Stalin — as had indeed been done in the period April–September 1953. One interpretation is that the leadership approached the XXth Congress without final agreement having been reached, that Mikoyan forced Khrushchev's hand with his remarks both on Stalin's economic errors and on Kossior and Antonov-Ovseenko. That no very simple explanation is likely to fit the facts will be apparent even *a priori* if we look at the considerations affecting various members of the Praesidium. The attack on Stalin was an attack on one-man rule, and hence a blow at Khrushchev if he was hoping to secure complete victory at the Congress. At the same time it was a blow at other members of the Praesidium who were particularly identified with Stalin's more reprehensible (from a Party point of view) acts. Mikoyan, who was comparatively unaffected on either count, may have been whole-heartedly in favour of de-Stalinisation. Khrushchev, with the two considerations pulling him different ways, may have been in two minds. But as soon as it became apparent that the matter had anyhow got partly into the open, and that it would certainly be adequate to prevent his own immediate assumption of supreme power, there was an excellent motive for him to take over the project, assume control of it and credit for it and direct it as far as possible against his opponents. The text certainly looks like a draft angled against Molotov and Kaganovich, for the 'thirties purges, and Malenkov, for the Leningrad Case. But this itself, in an oblique way, shows that open attack was not yet possible. At the same time it is full of reservations often quite contrary to the trend of the rest of the text, and presumably inserted as the result of insistence on the part of elements wishing to defend Stalin, at least in part. To obtain a majority in the Praesidium for some such procedure would be explicable on the equivalent and opposite argument: that the same two major considerations operated on Khrushchev's opponents. Though the speech involved their own political pasts, at the same time it was a blow at one-man rule. That a compromise was reached in the matter may further be deduced from the obvious fact that a compromise was reached on the composition of the ruling bodies. That Khrushchev would have wished to intrude his own supporters into the Praesidium is shown by the fact that he did so intrude them among the candidate members and the Secretariat. That the Praesidium proper remained unchanged shows that a majority were unwilling to let Khrushchev increase his representation in the decisive organ. (That he was unable to do so proves that it *was* the decisive organ.) The balance of forces must have been both complex and delicate for such a quasi-deadlock, reminiscent to some extent of the situation in March 1953, to have been the accepted solution for a moment.

We may certainly take the composition of the new Praesidium, after the XXth Congress, as at least a partial defeat for Khrushchev. He had not contrived to increase his power among the full membership at all, nor to eliminate any of his rivals, not even Malenkov, whose continued low status in the State apparatus pointed so clearly to the anomalous nature of the freezing of the *status quo*. Among the candidates he had managed to remove the adherent of the opposition, Ponomarenko, to intrude his own men, and to bring in to play the rather perilous card of the Armed Forces, personified in Zhukov. It was an advance, but a minor one.

Shvernik's demotion to junior candidate, to some extent resembling Pervukhin's in 1957, may perhaps be read as confirmation that he had inclined to support Malenkov's economic policies in 1954–55. In the ensuing period he became a strong supporter of Khrushchev.

Following the XXth Congress a new Party organ was announced on February 28, 1956 — the 'Bureau for the R.S.F.S.R.', consisting of Khrushchev (Chairman), Belyaev (Vice-Chairman), Yasnov (Chairman of the Council of Ministers of the R.S.F.S.R.), Kapitonov (Moscow Provincial Secretary), Kozlov (Leningrad Provincial Secretary), Churaev

(Head of the Central Committee Department for Party Organs for the R.S.F.S.R.), Mylarshchikov (Head of the Central Committee Department for Agriculture for the R.S.F.S.R.), Puzanov (First Deputy Chairman of the Council of Ministers of the R.S.F.S.R.). N. G. Ignatov (Provincial Secretary, Gorki) and Kirilenko (Provincial Secretary, Sverdlovsk). A Central Committee announcement of March 14, 1956, added Aristov and Pospelov. This body was composed entirely of associates of Khrushchev's. Its powers were not defined. The anomaly whereby all the republics except the R.S.F.S.R. have their Central Committees and Bureaux was thus partly changed. A certain differentiation of Russian from non-Russian Party affairs had already taken place with the creation of separate R.S.F.S.R. Central Committee departments for Party Organs (first mentioned by Khrushchev in his speech of January 25, 1954) and for Agriculture. It was later stated (see Appendix VIII) that the R.S.F.S.R. Bureau worked in close contact with the Central Committee Departments for the Union Republics, a curious point being the evident primacy of the Department of Party Organs (Union Republics). One function of the Bureau may have been to interpose another Khrushchevite organ between the Party Secretariat and a large part of the Central Committee apparatus. The composition of the Bureau, with its fairly junior apparat officials, resembles that of the old Orgburo.

The new Bureau was thus a preserve of Khrushchev and his allies in the Party apparatus and the publicity given it was at least a prestige victory for him, perhaps particularly necessary after his failure in the Praesidium. The extent of the increase in his actual powers is more doubtful. The Bureau in effect co-ordinated work already being performed in the Secretariat and the Central Committee apparatus, and while perhaps making it easier to put through minor changes more or less repugnant to the other factions of the Praesidium, could not detract substantially from the power of the senior body. The formation of the new organ is perhaps best regarded as a sign of a determination on Khrushchev's part to keep the pot boiling, to grasp the initiative and to warn the Party public against drawing conclusions about his comparative impotence from the stalemate suffered at the Congress.

Another significant action taken within weeks of the Congress was the bringing to trial of Bagirov, Beria's supporter and accomplice. Publicity was only given to this trial (stated to have taken place April 12–26, 1956), in the local *Bakinski Rabochy* of May 27, 1956, but we may be sure that its circumstances were circulated to the Party aktiv, and may presume that the trial went forward on a decision of the Central Committee (i.e. presumably in February 1956), or at least the Praesidium. Bagirov and his five accomplices are announced as having confessed to a series of local Transcaucasian crimes and, in addition, of plotting against Ordzhonikidze. This had been an allegation against Beria, and had been the only non-local accusation against Rapava and Rukhadze at the Tiflis trial in September 1955. These had only spoken in a general way about intrigues against and persecution of Ordzhonikidze. But Bagirov was charged with 'compelling arrested people to give false testimony against Ordzhonikidze'. This strongly implies that Ordzhonikidze was out of favour some time before his death, and perhaps that Stalin collected the 'testimony' and used it to compel Ordzhonikidze to commit suicide, as alleged in Khrushchev's Secret Speech. If true, this proves that Ordzhonikidze must have been under powerful and organised pressure involving numbers of people, and not just suddenly threatened in some abrupt ultimatum. Moreover, if this charge could have been made against Bagirov, who was in Baku at the time, it could equally well have been made against Beria, then in Tbilisi. In any case, to raise the issue so strongly, and on the *corpus vile* of a former candidate member of the Praesidium, must almost certainly be regarded as a blow by Khrushchev against those of his enemies who may have been involved.

I may now develop the speculation about the whole Ordzhonikidze business. The persistence with which it was raised — at Beria's trial, at the Rapava–Rukhadze trial, in the Secret Speech and now again at Bagirov's trial — may well not be accidental. It resembles in many respects the persistent and gradually developing use of the Leningrad Case — for which Abakumov and Beria were blamed in December 1954, Stalin as well in February 1956 and finally Malenkov in July 1957. The point is that the raising of the Leningrad Case at Abakumov's trial in 1954 was already a blow against Malenkov, and was widely understood to be such, although his name was never mentioned. I incline to the view that the Ordzhonikidze case may be treated similarly. It is, of course, a far more sinister matter. The Leningrad Case, though a frame-up, was presumably conducted with the formalities of a trial, and not merely a vulgar murder, illegal by even Stalinist standards. I take it that Stalin could not have organised Ordzhonikidze's death without the assistance of at least a few individuals, no doubt Yezhov on the one hand, and his private secretariat — that is, Poskrebyshev — on the other (with both of whom Malenkov was closely associated), and that rumours of this, which were widespread among the defectors of the period, were also known at all high levels in the Party.

On this view, every reference to the matter was a threat to Malenkov, just as mention of the Leningrad Case was. It may also have been an attack on the others later accused of responsibility for the period of 'mass-repression' — Molotov and Kaganovich. It is difficult to believe that Kaganovich, at least, was not privy to all that went on in 1937. (And the Rapava–Rukhadze Case may have been decided on at the July 1955 plenum, which saw Molotov's defeat on the foreign policy issue.)

A future decision to proceed yet further with the Ordzhonikidze Case would depend on the relative status of Stalin. During the period in which Khrushchev was rebuilding the old dictator's reputation it would be scarcely usable. But if there is a further de-Stalinisation, as seems possible, I would expect allegations about Ordzhonikidze to begin to be made against Malenkov. And if he comes to trial in the circumstances, I would expect the trial to be made the occasion of an official disavowal of the terrorist past, with the Ordzhonikidze murder and the Leningrad Case as major charges against Malenkov, Poskrebyshev, Andrianov and their co-accused. But we should recall that the precise circumstances of Ordzhonikidze's death are unknown, and it is possible that Kaganovich, say, was the more deeply implicated. In any event it remains a powerful potential weapon against someone.

From the time of the XXth Congress rehabilitations began to take place in great numbers. It was only exceptionally that a direct announcement on their fate was made. More usually their names began to reappear in favourable contexts, after years of complete silence. This was a departure from the procedure with Voznesensky and the Leningraders, and may show that restrictions were being enforced.

Meanwhile, the attack on the cult of personality had two main areas of result: in Eastern Europe and in the cultural field at home. In the latter, which we shall deal with later, Shepilov seems to have made the running with the new liberal line. In Eastern Europe the Secret Speech, which had been distributed to the local leaderships, had a strong effect. At first, in spite of 'negative' phenomena, it was not obvious that this was likely to lead to serious crisis. And the position of Khrushchev and his allies grew if anything stronger.

On March 20, Khrushchev attended a Polish Central Committee meeting. The other Praesidium members to take part in various visits and negotiations with the foreign Communist parties were Bulganin and Zhukov (to Poland in July), Mikoyan (to Hungary in July, and in negotiations with the Hungarians in Moscow in early October) and Suslov (to the French Communist Party in July, and with Mikoyan in the October negotiations).

The central event of the period, apart from a rather formal resolution of the Central Committee on the cult of personality (dated June 30 and published in *Pravda*, July 2, 1958), was Tito's triumphant visit to the U.S.S.R. from June 1 to 23. As a result a declaration of the Soviet and Yugoslav Parties was issued (unlike the previous year's negotiations, which had only produced a declaration by the two Governments). This was to the theme developed rather vaguely at the XXth Congress of 'different roads to socialism'. This phrase, now interpreted amicably, though hardly more than formal agreement, was later to prove capable of considerable contraction.

For the moment things appeared to be going Khrushchev's way. In the humiliating circumstance that it was the day of Tito's arrival. Molotov gave up the Ministry of Foreign Affairs to Shepilov on June 1, 1956. On June 6, 1956, Kaganovich gave up the Chairmanship of the State Committee on Labour and Wage Questions.

But critical events which would change the whole outlook were just round the corner.

CHAPTER TWELVE

THE ANTI-PARTY GROUP, 1956–57

As the attack on Stalin and the *rapprochement* with Tito started to produce difficulties in Eastern Europe, those who had opposed Khrushchev began to recover their influence. Poznan, and the beginnings of Hungarian unrest, came in July 1956 and aroused immediate qualms. Kaganovich was appointed U.S.S.R. Minister of the Construction Materials Industry (a post he had held in 1946) on September 4, 1956, and on October 19 the most definite sign of a return of the old guard's influence was seen: up till now Khrushchev, Bulganin and Mikoyan had handled Eastern Europe. Now a delegation consisting of Khrushchev, Kaganovich, Molotov and Mikoyan, flew to Warsaw in an attempt to prevent Gomulka's election as First Secretary of the Polish Workers' Party. This must be read as a sign of revulsion on the part of a Praesidial majority from Khrushchev's Eastern European policies, due certainly to the evident signs of its collapse.

On November 20, 1957, Molotov was appointed Minister of State Control. The then State Control Ministry supervised the work of other Ministries and saw that Government decrees and instructions were implemented, and that budgetary allocations were properly spent. To carry out its work the Ministry had a large staff of so-called State Controllers in offices and State enterprises. It had the right to demand documents, accounts and explanations from every Ministry, State Administration and State Committee. For breaches of the law it could impose both fines and disciplinary punishments, reprimands, severe reprimands and dismissals from posts — though to inflict the more drastic penalties the Minister needed the permission of the whole Cabinet.

Under a minor figure (like Zhavoronkov, the previous incumbent, only a candidate member of the Central Committee) the Minister would have little real power to intervene in the affairs of bodies run by his seniors. With Molotov in charge, the

State Control machinery could easily become a powerful instrument. And in the following year Khrushchev was to complain
strongly and frequently of its capacity to interfere with his
plans.

The same month Molotov also made a return to ideological
power, representing the Praesidium at a Conference held by
the Ministry of Culture to lay down the correct attitude on
Socialist realism in art, where he sponsored a strong line against
those objecting to 'Party leadership in art'. The cultural field
was one in which Khrushchev's policies could be said to have
done obvious damage from the Party point of view, and
Molotov's appearance on this and other occasions must represent a decision by the Praesidium to entrust him with intervening to restore order in an area controlled by Shepilov.

The line on Stalin put forward earlier in the year now began
to be modified. On December 23, 1956, *Pravda* published an
article by the ideologist Azizyan pointing out that: 'such a
teaching — Stalinism — is unknown to us. It must be clear to
those who are versed in Marxism–Leninism that Stalin has not
left any separate teaching of his own. He was a major Marxist
and was guided by the teaching of Marxism and Leninism in his
activity.' Khrushchev's own rehabilitation of Stalin at the
Chinese reception in Moscow on January 18, 1957, is equally
striking. In the officially edited Soviet version of his remarks
(*Pravda*, January 19, 1957), he declares his belief that 'the term
"Stalinist", like Stalin himself, is inseparable from the high title
of Communist'. Though later events seem to show that this was
a reasonable statement of Khrushchev's own opinions, it remains
true that the opposition could legitimately blame him for
having caused the troubles of 1956 by sponsoring the earlier
line, now being amended.

Besides foreign affairs and culture, there was a third field
in which Khrushchev's policies had produced bad results. The
Sixth Five-Year Plan, launched in February 1956, had proved
grossly over-ambitious. On December 16, 1956, a plenum
of the Central Committee was called — ten months after the
last, instead of the prescribed maximum of six. The published
data on it were entirely economic, and as such we may cover
them here, though it is reasonable to imagine that other matters
were discussed.

The published resolution of the Central Committee on the plan stated that the Five-Year Plan and the Plan for 1957 must be amended to 'eliminate excessive strain in the plans of certain industries and bring the production and investment programmes into accord with material resources'. This task the 'numerous cadres of skilled personnel' were to fulfil, their 'profound competence' being praised. Revision of the plans was entrusted, not to the State Planning Committee (Gosplan), under Baibakov, but to the State Economic Commission (Gosekonomkomissiya) now made a high-powered cabinet of technocrats under Pervukhin, with Kosygin and Malyshev as his First Deputies, and Khrunichev, Kucherenko, Matskevich and Benediktov as Deputies. At the same time Kosygin, Malyshev, Khrunichev, Kucherenko and Matskevich ceased to be Deputy Chairmen of the Council of Ministers, leaving Malenkov alone in that position, and thus no longer ranked for State purposes as equal to men below him in Party position.

On the other hand, the resolution sponsored by Bulganin on the improvement of management criticised the managerial class and vaguely proclaimed 'democratic centralism' in economic administration.

Soon after the December plenum, Tevosyan was demoted to the Ambassadorship to Japan. It is difficult to estimate what this may signify, though it seems that Tevosyan's affiliations were with his State-economic colleagues (and remained so, if we are to judge by the failure to recall him for the June 1957 plenum). But in dealing with the December plenum we are certainly faced with a complicated semi-deadlock, with many cross-currents. The economic troubles were undoubtedly regarded as stemming, at least in part, from faulty execution, and if a scapegoat were wanted, it is possible that Tevosyan had made specially notable miscalculations. (Even the removal of Saburov from planning duties may be regarded at least partially in this light, for his replacement, Pervukhin, though in general a supporter of 'managerial' policies, was later shown at least to be less unacceptable to Khrushchev than his predecessor was.)

But in general the December 1956 plenum may be seen as a partial defeat for Khrushchev. Economic power was transferred to the Gosekonomkomissiya, and that body was made so powerful that it could scarcely be overruled except by direct decision of the Party Praesidium. Centralisation of this power, as against Khrushchev's decentralisation schemes, was also a repudiation of his policies. Yet there was no full recapture of their old positions by his opponents: Malenkov was not, for instance, made a First Vice-Premier. The indications are of a majority of anti-Khrushchev votes for certain purposes, but neither a large nor a reliable one. Yet, even as to Malenkov, he now re-emerged to accompany Khrushchev in the Soviet Party delegation to Budapest in January 1957, thus appearing in more influential circumstances than he had done for two years. The voting of Malenkov on to this delegation must at least mean that he was now in the confidence of Molotov and Kaganovich. He had already been given favourable reference, with Molotov, in *Voprosy Istorii* of November 1956, as a wartime defender of Leningrad.

The Supreme Soviet met in early February. On February 6 Pervukhin delivered to it the report on the revised 1957 Plan. He stated that plans for some branches of heavy industry, including iron, coal, steel and cement, had 'not been fully fulfilled' in 1956, and that the 'expansion of consumer goods production' was a main object of the revision. But he acclaimed as a 'striking success' Khrushchev's Virgin Lands scheme, largely ignored at the December plenum, and added that in capital investment the Government 'has proceeded, as in the past, from the need to ensure priority in developing heavy industry'. In fact, the main change was a slowing down of the rate of expansion from 11 per cent. in 1956 to 7·1 per cent. in 1957, with the relative rates of growth of heavy and light industry left as before. Though the report was rather less critical of the economic arrangements of the XXth Congress than the resolution had been in December, it was still substantially in accord with the decisions of the December plenum. The next Central Committee plenum, meeting on February 13–14, made nonsense of it.

This February plenum passed a decree on 'further perfecting' the administration of industry and building. This decree reiterated the slogan which had been made the keynote of the XXth Congress — 'in an historically brief period to overtake and outstrip the most developed capitalist countries in output

U

per capita'. It ignored the failures that had agitated the previous plenum, and described the 1956 results as showing that the Soviet Union 'is advancing confidently, selecting the rates of its development'. On the other hand, it questioned the adequacy of the industrial administrative system.

The Ministerial system was condemned for 'departmentalism', waste and inefficiency; for its remoteness from the 200,000 industrial enterprises and 100,000 building projects involved; for the immobilisation of ' talented organisers of production, engineers and technicians'; and for limiting the 'opportunities of local Party, Soviet and trade-union organs in direct economic construction'.

Specialised Ministries should be replaced by 'such forms of economic administration as will most fully combine concrete and operative direction by economic regions with strict observance of the principle of centralised planning on the scale of the whole country'. Whereas the role of Gosplan, 'guided by the general Party line on preferential development of heavy industry', must now be 'enhanced', Gosekonomkommisiya must be 'simplified', made 'less cumbersome', refrain from 'duplicating the work of the State Planning Committee' and from 'interfering in the functions of administration', and 'reconstruct its work' to cover only current planning and the co-ordination of regional organs in fulfilling annual plans. At the same time the 'content and methods of work' of Molotov's State Control organs must be improved and 'radically reconstructed'. The Party Praesidium and the U.S.S.R. Council of Ministers were to submit to the Supreme Soviet concrete proposals which should, first and foremost, 'further strengthen the Leninist principle of democratic centralism in economic construction'.

The reversal of the economic reorganisation made in December, combined with the attack on Molotov's Ministry of State Control, drew the lines clearly enough.

The plenum also appointed F. R. Kozlov a candidate member of the Praesidium: Kozlov certainly figures as an ally of Khrushchev's throughout the ensuing period. Even so, he was not one of those who had depended for his career entirely on the First Secretary's protection, like Brezhnev, Furtseva and, to a lesser extent, Mukhitdinov, of the February 1956 promotion. In fact, in 1957–59 it seems that Ignatov, whose rival for the Leningrad secretaryship Kozlov had been in 1953, was by now the more thorough Khrushchevite or at least anti-Malenkovite. This may show, first, that Kozlov's 1953 promotion in Leningrad was a compromise, as seems likely enough; second, that his election as a Praesidium candidate in 1957 was of a man held reliable by Khrushchev, yet felt by his more critical allies not to be too inclined to support him in any extremes of one-man rule. On the other hand, the appointment was certainly rather distasteful than not to the opponents of Khrushchev.

At the same time Shepilov returned to the Secretariat, giving the Foreign Ministry up, not to Molotov but to the professional diplomat Gromyko, who lacked the status to promote policies unapproved by the Central Committee. Shepilov, as was soon seen (for instance, from his appearance at the Congress of Soviet Composers on March 28, 1957, and at the Congress of Soviet Painters the same month), took over the supervision of culture, and thus intruded on Molotov's sphere once more. It seems as if the deadlock of December–February had warned Khrushchev that he must move soon and effectively against his opponents or expect trouble, and that this was a first step. It was followed by the great campaign against bureaucracy in which Khrushchev consciously put forward the destruction of the power-basis of the economic managers.*

It is quite unknown (though several interesting guesses exist) what led to the virtual reversal in February 1957 of the December 1956 decisions. The implication is strong that in December Khrushchev had no majority on the Praesidium, and perhaps none, or an unreliable one, on the Central Committee itself; and that by February this had been changed. But the industrial proposals of the February plenum were later debated without any speeches of support from Praesidium members, which seems to imply that any Praesidial approval at the time was permissive, or abstentionist (as in the Virgin Lands project in 1954), rather than based on a solid majority. The fact, too, that the February Supreme Soviet meeting,

---

* Quite a considerable reduction of administrative staffs had already been achieved without these drastic measures: Khrushchev at the XXth Congress had given a figure, over the past two years, of 750,000.

preceding the plenum, took a different line, rather seems to show that the proposals had not obtained the support of the Praesidium, which was — until a plenum should meet — the deciding body on policy issues. We may certainly deduce opposition to the proposals from a strong Praesidial minority — Malenkov, Molotov, Kaganovich, Pervukhin and Saburov, and later developments indicate that Voroshilov and Bulganin at least might have wavered or been neutral. It may be that Khrushchev had a potential majority to allow him to put forward the plan as a personal one, for 'discussion', as was done. And this may mean some slight shift of opinion in one or more members of the Praesidium — Voroshilov, say: but it is impossible to deduce the details. That members of the Praesidium 'work on' other members was stated in June 1957 in connection with the 'Anti-Party Group'. What may also have happened is the 'working on' the rank-and-file members of the Central Committee, a task which the Secretariat was equipped to perform.

It seems certain that it was, in any case, *after* the February plenum, and therefore as a result of Khrushchev's conduct in the ensuing months, that a potentially decisive majority against him in the Praesidium came into being.

That Khrushchev's proposals on the reorganisation of industry and the economic administration were made on his own initiative was evident from their reference back to the Praesidium and their reappearance on March 30, 1957, as 'Theses on Comrade Khrushchev's report' to be made to the Supreme Soviet on May 7.

At the outset Khrushchev put his case bluntly, as on February 19 to the American journalist Joseph Alsop:

We mean to do away with the industrial Ministries altogether, both at the centre and in the Republics. Instead, all industrial enterprises . . . will be directed by territorial departments (*New York Herald Tribune*, February 21).

But the theses themselves, after dilating on 'democratic centralism' and 'departmentalism', were less forthright:

There should evidently be a transition from the previous forms of administration through branch Ministries and departments to new forms of administration according to the territorial principle. The forms of such administration could be, for instance, National Economic Councils.

The theses admitted opposition to the whole idea:

Some Comrades express a fear that reorganisation . . . on the territorial principle . . . may result in weakening the centralised planning element in developing our Soviet economy.

But Khrushchev was not in any way opposed to centralisation as such, and added 'But this is, of course, incorrect.'

He warned against 'localist' tendencies:

The detection of, and the struggle against, these harmful localist tendencies . . . must be kept constantly in view by Party, Soviet, economic and trade union organs.

Khrushchev insisted on the State aspect of centralisation being through Gosplan. He again admitted the existence of alternative proposals:

In this connection there is no need to create new central organs of economic direction in place of the liquidated branch Ministries. . . . Various Comrades propose to create special economic organs under the Council of Ministers, as, for example, committees . . . which they propose to charge with direction of the chief branches of heavy industry. This means that some industries will have to be centrally administered as formerly. . . . These Comrades are apparently concerned that in fulfilling annual and Five-Year Plans operative questions will arise which some organ must decide,

and he spoke of attempts to 'circumvent' the Gosplan–N.E.C. set-up.

For Gosekonomkomissiya, he now proposed not 'reconstruction' but liquidation, and he envisaged a similar fate for another technocratic institution:

The question should be considered of creating under the U.S.S.R. Council of Ministers an Engineering-Technical Committee in place of the present Gostekhnika.

Malyshev had long been chairman of this State Committee on New Techniques, whose organ, *Promyshlenno-Ekonomicheskaya Gazeta*, alone of all the major Moscow organs, had not responded editorially to Khrushchev's February decree but had merely reprinted its text. By contrast, it 'would clearly be expedient to retain' the State Committee for Building Affairs (Gosstroi), under the chairmanship of Khrushchev's nominee, Kucherenko.

The essential point in the new controls, however, was that over all there would be the Party apparatus:

Under existing forms of direction whereby plans have been worked out and executed through branch ministries and departments, local Party organisations have in a number of cases been deprived of the opportunity to influence more actively the work of enterprises. . . . The new administrative forms . . . give republican, territorial and personal Party organisations greater rights and opportunities to influence the course of fulfilment of State plans and the production activity of enterprises and projects, to organise implementation of Party and Government decisions. . . .

Supervision by local officials would complement control of the whole economy by the First Secretary through Gosplan and the central Party apparatus.

The theses also stipulated that the Soviets, i.e. the local governmental machinery, should have no effective control:

Autonomous Republican Councils of Ministers and also Provincial and Regional Soviets have the right to hear reports of chairmen of the Sovnarkhozy of corresponding economic regions and in this way to participate in managing the development of industry and building in their Republic, Region or Province, to influence actively the course of fulfilment of the national plan. It would not be expedient at present wholly to subordinate the direction of industry and building to local Soviets, in view of the considerable increase in the scope of production in industry of local subordination and also the great and responsible tasks in directing the further development of agriculture.

But though the attack on the State-economic structure had been launched, its success was by no means clinched. The communiqué accompanying the theses said:

The Central Committee of the C.P.S.U. and the U.S.S.R. Council of Ministers have decided to publish the theses and hold nation-wide consideration so as to work out, on the basis of a broad exchange of opinions and the all-round assessment of our experience, the most expedient forms for administering the country's national

economy. . . . It is not their purpose to give in final form recommendations on all concrete questions connected with the new
central and local administrative structure.

During the ensuing weeks a curious phenomenon was seen:
Khrushchev and his supporters made a wide publicity campaign for the theses, but he was not backed by any other full
members of the Praesidium, except Kirichenko. Indeed, apart
from these two, no member of the Praesidium spoke about the
theses at all, either during the publicity campaign which ensued, or at the Supreme Soviet session in May. At the same time
open controversy sprang up in the Press.

Khrushchev himself visited Voronezh, Gorki and elsewhere
making speeches reported almost daily in *Pravda* (April 2-19).
Meanwhile, in spite of some talk in the communiqué about the
Soviets being concerned in making proposals for the layout of
the N.E.C.s, Furtseva in Moscow addressed the City Party Committee plenum on April 3, in a speech in which she 'characterised in detail the Moscow economic region and the intended
structure for administering industry and building'. The City
Party Committee Bureau would 'work out . . . proposals on
administrative reorganisation and the structure of the city's
National Economic Council'. The Moscow Provincial Party
Committee plenum considered proposals elaborated by a 'Party
commission with the participation of managers, Ministerial
and scientific workers, production innovators, Party and Soviet
leaders'; and the Leningrad Provincial Party Committee
plenum left its bureau to 'work out final proposals on administrative organisation and the structure of the Leningrad
National Economic Council and submit them for consideration
by the Central Committee of the C.P.S.U.' This procedure was
general.

On April 12 the most open and violent attack on the State-
economic apparatus was made in *Literaturnaya Gazeta* by Academician Strumilin, who had made the running for Khrushchev
in 1954-55. For almost the first time he used the deadly phrase
'technocracy':

The bureaucracy, and its latest offspring the technocracy, are
alien in principle to the creative endeavour springing from the thick
of the people. Grandly scornful of everything not yet taught from

above . . . demanding unconditional trust from the popular masses, the bureaucracy is not at all inclined to show them the same trust. . . . For decades the workers' democracy, headed by the Communist Party, has struggled most energetically against all manifestations of bureaucratism. But this struggle is not at all easy. The bloated administrative apparatus was relentlessly cut well-nigh every year but would not yield and again increased . . .

On the State–Party issue it was later, at the November 1958 plenum, to be said that:

The June plenum unmasked and defeated the Anti-Party Group of Malenkov, Kaganovich, Molotov, Bulganin and Shepilov who ioined them, which waged a struggle against the Leninist general line of the Party, against the political course adopted at the XXth Congress of the C.P.S.U., against the directing role of the Party, entering on the road of fractional splitting activity (*Pravda*, November 12, 1958).

Accusations follow of errors in industry, foreign policy and agriculture (the Virgin Lands being mentioned). But the most significant point seems to be the reference to 'struggle . . . against the directing role of the Party', which appears definite confirmation of the Group's tendency to concentrate on the State machinery.

On April 14, 1957, *Pravda* printed a letter from a Moscow engineer criticising the abolition of the Ministries. Counterattacks followed, but the Press continued to contain letters and speeches by minor officials critical, by implication or directly, of the essence of the new scheme. Factory directors complained of the prospect of Party interference. For example, in *Izvestia* of April 12 the director of the Stalino metallurgical plant wrote:

The question of the structure and apparatus of the N.E.C.s is inseparably linked with extending the rights of leaders of enterprises. The Party has made no small effort to train hundreds of thousands of leaders able to run the economy in the general State interest. They need no petty tutelage and could often direct their enterprises much better if they had greater powers.

On April 30, 1957, Pervukhin was again given an important, though less important, post: the atomic 'Ministry of Medium Machine Building'. On May 3, Baibakov became Chairman of the R.S.F.S.R. Gosplan, now a significant body, and the hitherto unknown I. I. Kuzmin was appointed Chairman of the U.S.S.R. Gosplan and First Deputy Chairman of the Council of Ministers.

The raising to these major posts of an obscure member of the Revision Commission looked surprising. But it later became known that Kuzmin's past was not insignificant. From 1952 he had been Deputy Head, then Head, of the Industrial and Transport Section of the Central Committee, and then Head of the Machine-Construction Section. He thus worked closely in the apparatus with the Party Secretariat. Before 1947 he had been Deputy Chairman of the Party Control Commission. More interesting, perhaps, is the fact that from 1947 to 1952 he had had 'leading work in the Council of Ministers of the U.S.S.R.', and been 'Member and Deputy Chairman of the Bureau for Rural Economy and Procurements, assistant to a Deputy Chairman of the Council of Ministers of the U.S.S.R.' (Vol. 51, *Large Soviet Encyclopaedia*). This seems to point to his having been assistant to Andreyev, but not to have shared in the latter's disgrace. From which might be deduced that he had inclined to Khrushchev, as Andreyev's rival in the struggle about agriculture.

In the Supreme Soviet session of May 7, 1957, Khrushchev proposed that every 'basic question . . . should be settled at this session' and organisational matters left to the Government. In the ensuing two-day debate on the Draft Law no member of the Party Praesidium spoke, and Khrushchev was supported from the floor only by his picked officials like Kalchenko, Kapitonov and Kuzmin. The law was a basic summary, and laid down that the main lines of the reorganisation should be completed by July 1, 1957.

Khrushchev therefore had formal sanction for his scheme; and meanwhile he had 'cultivated' his own personality. On May 14, 1957, *Pravda* publicised his interview with the Chief Editor of the *New York Times*; on May 15 and 17 it reported his reception of Polish and Yugoslav journalists. In Leningrad on May 20 he harangued workers of the Kirov Plant. On May 21 he was warmly greeted at the Skorokhod Works and on May 22 'enormous attention' and 'stormy applause' awaited him at a Leningrad mass meeting and an agricultural conference, to which he put a new slogan: 'to overtake the U.S.A. in the next

few years in per capita production of meat, milk and butter.'
On May 27 *Pravda* said: 'Already from all corners of the
country . . . come reports that collective and state farms are
raising their undertakings.' Thereafter *Pravda* carried such
reports almost daily. Though opposition was still conceded,
it was no longer voiced.

By this time the descriptions of economic failure which had
characterised the December plenum had disappeared and been
replaced by confident boasts. In fact 'opposition' attitudes had
been replaced by 'government' ones.

The precipitate nature of the actions of Khrushchev and his
associates may be seen in the fact that Kozlov and Ignatov,
Party secretaries at Leningrad and Gorki respectively, usurped
the prerogative of the R.S.F.S.R. Council of Ministers and
appointed their own local Economic Councils even before the
law on the reorganisation had been passed.

Khrushchev's dissolution of a large part of the governmental
machinery in 1957 can certainly be read as a blow at the
apparatus which had sustained his rivals. It was, as we have
seen, stated openly that the local Party apparatus, itself
centralised as ever on Moscow, would play a dominating part
in the decentralised economic machinery. The economic
arguments for decentralisation have substance. But even a
decentralised economy, particularly of the Soviet type, requires
a considerable amount of economic expertise. If the whole
government and economic apparatus were abolished to-morrow
and replaced by organs of the Party, the problems would
remain much the same. No one had suggested quite so radical a
change. Yet as long as two apparatuses exist there are bound to
be areas of conflict. Moreover, in the extreme hypothetical
case I have imagined, the obvious result would be the rise of an
economic apparatus, formally part of the Party machinery,
but in practice consisting of economic managers, which would
soon develop into the same sort of group as the previous
governmental economic managers. The name would be
changed and the conflict of influence would be within the forms
of Party nomenclature rather than between Party and Government. But that would be all. Even if the whole managerial
class were transferred to 'useful work' and replaced by ideologists, the new men, or at least those of them who did not prove

useless, would soon develop the habits and interests of their predecessors, just as happened before. This is not, of course, only an economic question: when the cadres of Yagoda's professional N.K.V.D. were shot and imprisoned they were replaced by men from the Party apparatus. Within a few years they, too, had become professionalised and had developed their own organisational loyalties.

We may, indeed, see something of the smallness of the change from certain points of view in the number of deputy chairmen and departmental heads of Gosplan who figured as members of the Council of Ministers — to the number of eight in the Government announced under Khrushchev's premiership in February 1958.

That Khrushchev was in practice attacking the whole managerial set-up does not of course mean that he would pursue tactics of crude frontal assault on the whole group of leaders identified with the managers. Simply as tactics, it is in accord with Communist practice everywhere to attempt to isolate the main enemy and to detach or confuse his allies (just as the Group itself detached the apparatchik and ideologist Shepilov from Khrushchev). Though Malenkov had become politically representative of the managerial class, he was far less intimately identified with it than Saburov, Pervukhin and the others. And it is noticeable, at the June 1957 plenum, how much more mildly Pervukhin, and even Saburov, were treated than the 'Group' proper. It seems almost certain that Pervukhin compromised under pressure: yet even this implies either (a) that an opportunity or incentive for him to change sides was provided; or (b) that he was not nearly so deeply committed to the anti-Khrushchev line as the Group; or both.

Khrushchev's efforts to win over, or neutralise, the economic leaders should not, however, be viewed solely as a manœuvre to split the opposition. For he had great need of experienced economic cadres, and the fact that he had had to go right outside the Central Committee to the lowly Kuzmin, for chief planner and First Vice-Premier, is indicative of a shortage of economic cadres wholly devoted to his line. In the circumstances the support, however undependable, of men like Kosygin and Zasyadko was of obvious value.

At every stage in the campaign attacks had been made not

only on the old economic organisation but even more strongly on Molotov's Ministry of State Control, already scheduled for reorganisation in the resolution of the February plenum. In Khrushchev's Theses this Ministry is accused of massive interference:

The contents and methods of work of the U.S.S.R. Ministry of State Control and the Ministries of State Control of the Union Republics should evidently be radically reorganised. The Ministry of State Control has now a cumbersome apparatus which is based on the departmental principle and tries to embrace literally all matters, including the control of the technical level of that or this industry, and the level of development of science and technology. This is of no benefit at all. Controllers try to give instructions on problems of production, thus usurping the functions of economic organs. A big shortcoming in the work of State Control organs is that they try to use their staff in order to collect voluminous data on diverse questions, concentrating them in the apparatus of the Ministry, instead of seeking to remove on the spot, with the help of the public at large, the shortcomings brought to light.

Proceeding from the new tasks arising from the reorganisation of the management of industry and construction on the territorial principle, it is obviously necessary to draw up a new Statute on control organs both in the centre and in the localities, having in view the implementation of the Leninist directives on the organisation of control and on the improvement of the work of the State apparatus (*Pravda*, March 3, 1957).

Khrushchev made the same point at the Supreme Soviet Meeting:

Comrades Deputies, the measures to improve the organisational forms of industrial and building management require a change in the content and methods of work of bodies engaged in state control.

It must be said that there are grave defects in the work of the Ministry of State Control and its local agencies. In its investigations the ministry tries to embrace literally everything bound up with economic and cultural development, even including such matters as the development of science and technology, and of the various industries, and has accumulated in its apparatus voluminous data on various subjects. Furthermore, the ministry has an extremely cumbersome apparatus built on the departmental principle (Report to the Supreme Soviet, May 1957).

After the decisive clash in June, Molotov was accused of failing as Minister of State Control, to carry out the decisions

of the February plenum, instead 'writing letters against them'
(Petukhov in *Pravda*, July 4, 1957).

At the XXIst Congress Kuzmin was to attack Pervukhin in
curious terms: 'It was you who with Molotov and Shepilov
formed that same triumvirate in the Anti-Party Group which
waged an active struggle against the reconstruction of the direction of industry and building. It was you who talked of an
"organising itch", who talked of some sort of "tendency" in
the idea of reconstruction' (*Pravda*, February 5, 1959).

This 'triumvirate' — a peculiar alliance of an old-fashioned
Stalinist, a spokesman of the new managerial class and a
'liberalising' ideologist — casts a considerable amount of light
on the struggles of the period. It seems to indicate that Shepilov
was opposing Khrushchev some time before the June crisis.
The absence of Saburov is peculiar, and may mean that he was
in the background, having perhaps taken some of the blame
for the collapse of the sixth Five-Year Plan which culmin-
ated in his replacement in the State Economic Commission
by Pervukhin in December 1956.

Bulganin claimed in his speech to the December 1958 plenum
that he did not oppose the reconstruction at all. But Malenkov's
and Kaganovich's absence from the triumvirate is odd, and may
imply that it represented some sort of division of labour among
the group.

The whole group's general opposition to the reorganisation
was afterwards asserted on many occasions, as in the following:

Everything the party did to fight against bureaucracy, to reduce
the swollen government apparatus, also encounted either the open
or the hidden resistance of the Anti-Party Group. This Group is
organically opposed to methods of work which develop the independence of party organisations (*Party Life*, July 1957).

At the same time they were offering opposition to Khrushchev's agricultural proposals. They 'tried to prove' that the
slogan of catching up with America in livestock products was
'the wrong line' (Kuusinen in *Pravda*, July 7, 1957). They
'collected data' to show the impossibility of a increase in livestock (Kosygin in *Pravda* July 4, 1957). A reference to the
struggle during this period also occurs in the speech of V. V.
Matskevich to the December 1958 plenum:

I must say that when the question of preparing materials for re-organising the M.T.S. actually arose, Molotov and Kaganovitch literally tried to terrorise the machinery of the Ministry of Agriculture in order to dig up, or rather cook up, materials which would damn this measure.

On the opposition's line of argument on the reorganisation, Bulganin later said:

Molotov, Malenkov, Kaganovitch and Shepilov said at that time that we would have anarchy in the management of industry and construction and that extension of the rights of the Union Republics and local Party and government bodies, and specifically, vesting the Union Republics with the rights of planning and transferring to them some of the duties of the State Planning Committee — would even be contrary to Lenin (Bulganin's speech to the December 1958 plenum of the Central Committee, *Stenographic Report*).

On the other point mainly at issue in this period, he put their line as follows:

I well remember the situation in the Praesidium of the Central Committee when Comrade Khrushchev raised the question about the virgin lands and their reclamation, and when he almost simultaneously submitted the proposal for the new agricultural planning procedure. 'This is an adventure,' Molotov said. 'We will be left without bread,' Molotov, Malenkov and Kaganovich said. 'It is necessary to squash the movement for the slogan to overtake the United States in per-capita output of animal products, we will not have enough fodder,' they said. (Ibid.)

This seems to imply that the slogan on overtaking the United States was originally proposed by Khrushchev in 1954, or earlier, at the time when the Virgin Lands Scheme was afoot, but that it, at least, was then voted down. The opposition's objection about fodder appears to mean not merely that the plan was impracticable, but also that it would lead to a shortage of grain products.

The opposition to the agricultural plans was given a definite ideological basis:

Malenkov, Molotov and other participants in the Anti-Party Group, every time the matter concerned the production of meat and milk, accused our cadres of opportunist expediency and narrow-minded utilitarianism, of endeavouring to oppose economics to politics (Speech of Ignatov at the XXIst Party Congress, February 2, 1959).

It is extraordinary to realise that during this period, in which the signs of a clash were so numerous and so plain, commentators were to be found who continued to assert that all was harmony. So misleading is an outlook rooted in a basic fallacy about Soviet political life.

Things were, in fact, tending towards crisis. Around the end of May the Press (e.g. *Pravda* of May 24) urged the end of further dallying in completing those parts of the crash reorganisation still meeting with 'delay'. On May 30 Voroshilov, who had been in India and the Far East for over a month, returned. On June 5, Khrushchev and Bulganin left on a visit to Finland, returning on June 15. During this trip *Pravda* only referred once to the reorganisation, reporting on June 6 that the Moscow City N.E.C. would 'be ready to start work in the next few days'.

On June 17 it reported Khrushchev as saying 'the reconstruction . . . will have an enormous political and economic effect, but this effect will be considerably greater if we all set to work in a friendly manner'. On June 18, and on various days thereafter, it spoke of failures and difficulties in the plan. On July 1, the target date, it said that 'some N.E.C.s' had not yet settled their organisation. Meanwhile the promised Government statutes had not appeared.

But by this time the leadership was locked in decisive struggle. For a Praesidial majority against Khrushchev had been found.

Many detailed differences on policy can be deduced, but the essential charge against Khrushchev from his enemies on either flank seems to have been one of unprincipled adventurism. It was later said:

The Anti-Party Group — Malenkov, Kaganovich, Molotov, Bulganin and Shepilov — accused our Party's Central Committee and also Comrade N. S. Khrushchev of practicism and of being too engulfed in the practical tasks of economic construction. As is known, such accusations were also raised by the Yugoslav revisionists . . . (I. I. Kuzmin: Speech to the XXIst Party Congress, *Pravda*, February 5, 1959).

If the 'Yugoslav revisionists' could agree with Molotov on this issue, it to some extent accounts for the reconciling of Shepilov and Molotov, and of Malenkov and Kaganovich, who had hitherto held opposite views on most major issues.

Celebrations of the two hundred and fiftieth anniversary of Leningrad were to be held on June 23. Khrushchev later said (*Pravda*, July 7, 1957) that 'consideration of the visit of the Praesidium and Secretariat to the Leningrad celebrations was the occasion for direct action'. He interpreted this as due to Malenkov's fear of meeting the Leningraders, owing to his guilt for the Leningrad Case.

The whole business of holding the two hundred and fiftieth anniversary of the foundation of Leningrad in 1957 is peculiar, to start with. The city's first building took place in 1703–4. It became the capital of Russia in 1712, and the original building was completed in about 1721. In the article on 'Leningrad' in the *Large Soviet Encyclopaedia* (2nd Edition), which goes into considerable detail about the city's origins and gives several other intermediate dates, 1707 is not mentioned in any connection.* At least some suspicion remains that a political motive lay behind the selection of this curious year for the celebration. It is hard to believe that Malenkov was reluctant to face the celebrations, owing to his guilt for the Leningrad Case. Taken at its face value, such an attitude is unlikely in a Soviet leader: otherwise how could most of them even remain in Moscow itself? If interpreted to mean that Malenkov feared that the celebrations might be made the occasion for an overt attack on him, it becomes intelligible.

In that case we would have to assume that the Anti-Party Group's blow for power was more or less forced on them, if they were to anticipate a projected coup of Khrushchev's. In any case this coincided with an access of strength to them. For now the power at the disposal of the anti-Khrushchev elements seemed adequate. It was later said:

The participants of the Anti-Party Group, immediately after the death of Stalin, had almost at every meeting of the Praesidium of the C.C. attacked everything new which followed from the teaching of

* The *Leningrad Encyclopaedia* (1958) (giving 1703 as the date of the city's foundation) mentions almost every year from 1700 to 1724 in one connection or another. 1707 is one of the few not referred to.

Lenin and from life, and which concerned the questions of exercising leadership over the country, the building of armed forces and foreign policy. But it was particularly after the XXth Congress that they took up arms and began their fierce attack on the general line of the Party. The Anti-Party Group cast off its mask, and on June 18, 1957, it took organised action against the course planned by the XXth Party Congress, that is, at the time when its participants had counted their forces in the Praesidium of the C.C., and when they came to the conclusion that they had, as they imagined, forces at their disposal strong enough to change the policy of the Party and the Government (Speech of Kirichenko to the XXIst Party Congress, January 31, 1959).

The Group is also accused of having 'tried for demagogic purposes to shelter behind the collective principle' (*Kommunist*, No. 10, 1957), which can best be translated as having a majority on the Praesidium.

'It recruited supporters, held secret meetings behind the Praesidium's back, placed its cadres with the intention of seizing power' (Shvernik in *Pravda* July 7, 1957). They had 'striven to "work on" Praesidium members, individually so as to knock together a temporary formal majority' (Kozlov in *Leningradskaya Pravda*, July 5, 1957). They 'tried to effect a change in the composition of the Praesidium and Secretariat of the Central Committee of the C.P.S.U. elected by the plenum of the Central Committee', and they 'counted on presenting the Central Committee with the changed leadership and policy of the Party as a *fait accompli*' (*Party Life*, No. 13, July 1957). As I. V. Spiridonov, First Secretary of the Leningrad City Party Committee, said on July 2: 'they reckoned ... that a plenum would vote for a resolution proposed by them in the Praesidium's name' (*Leningradskaya Pravda*, July 5, 1957).

The Praesidium met on June 18, remaining in session until June 22, on which date a Central Committee plenum started, lasting until June 29.

Not all the Praesidium membership was in Moscow. The absentees were Saburov, Kirichenko and Suslov. Saburov was in Poland, and is reported in *Glos Pracy* of June 22–23, 1957, as being in Poznan on June 21, so that he can hardly have played any part in the praesidial phase of the crisis. Kirichenko was attending a Ukrainian Central Committe plenum which closed on June 20, but might have arrived earlier, while Suslov was on a provincial tour and easily recallable.

On June 18 a delegation of Hungarian journalists was received 'in the Praesidium' by Bulganin, Voroshilov, Kaganovich, Malenkov, Mikoyan, Molotov, Pervukhin and Khrushchev (*Pravda*, June 19). The candidate members present were Zhukov, Brezhnev, Shepilov and Furtseva. Shvernik returned from the Urals on June 19 (*Pravda*, June 20), and the other candidates could probably have arrived within the same period. Even though they had no votes, their voices would have an effect — especially Zhukov's on the one hand and Shepilov's, as that of an adherent on Khrushchev who had changed his views, on the other.

We know that the anti-Khrushchev element was, initially, a majority in the Praesidium: of the eight present on June 18, clearly Molotov, Malenkov, Kaganovich, Bulganin and Pervukhin at least were now to be relied on to vote against Khrushchev 5–3, or, on the return of those absent, the above plus Saburov 6–5.

But it seems unlikely that a bare majority in the Praesidium could possibly have been considered adequate to force through the intended changes, and it is difficult to avoid the conclusion that men not particularly committed to Khrushchev would have gone along with the tide. If Khrushchev was left in a minority of two or three, it seems on the face of it that the 'Group' could have presented its recommendation to the plenum in the name of the Praesidium. And it is scarcely likely that the hostile majority would have wavered simply at the idea of meeting the Central Committee, which it knew it would have to do sooner or later. Until the C.C. actually assembled, the Praesidium was the legal authority. It must therefore have been prevented, by force or the threat of it, from making its recommendations public, as it had every right to do. The obvious wielders of the threat of force were Zhukov (and that he was considered too free with his power was certainly the conclusion reached by Khrushchev, after his work had been done); and Serov, plainly in Khrushchev's confidence.

The threat need not even have been a positive one. The mere refusal of *Pravda* to print, or Moscow Radio to announce a decision would have been an insurmountable blockage, in the absence of any possibility of relying on the enforcement authorities to compel them to do their duty.

Under these various pressures it is reasonable to suppose that weaker members of the majority started proposing compromises, and that finally all but Molotov, Kaganovich, Malenkov and Shepilov had slid over into accepting the final terms.

Not only does it seem unlikely that a bare majority in the Praesidium would have been felt anything like sufficient to effect a complete coup, but it should also be pointed out that only five of the members *present* (Bulganin, Molotov, Malenkov, Kaganovich and Pervukhin) have been identified with the Anti-Party Group, and that this would not constitute a majority of the whole membership of the Praesidium. It is true that Saburov would vote with them when he returned, but there is no reason to believe that proxies are allowed, let alone that they would be available in such a hurried crisis (and even on Saburov's return the majority, allowing only for members of the Anti-Party Group already named, would be a mere 6–5). There is a strong presumption, from both lines of argument, that the anti-Khrushchev forces disposed of at least six votes, on the spot, out of nine. Of those available, Voroshilov and Mikoyan, we can almost certainly conclude that Voroshilov sided, at least temporarily, with the anti-Khrushchev coalition.*

As to how the majority was originally assembled, the position is clearly that Malenkov, Kaganovich and Molotov had been opposing the First Secretary for some time. On the industrial issue at least there seems little doubt that they could rely on the votes of Saburov and Pervukhin. Bulganin's adherence must have come later.

At the December 1958 plenum T. A. Yurkin said:

Yesterday Comrade Bulganin gave an explanation of his anti-Party activity to the plenum and presented the case as if he had all the time supported the general Party line and as if it was only in

* This has since been confirmed, in the *History of the Communist Party of the Soviet Union* (1959), which lists all the current full members of the Praesidium as having contributed to the defeat of the Anti-Party Group, with the single exception of Voroshilov; (i.e. of the June 1957 full members it gives Khrushchev, Mikoyan, Kirichenko and Suslov).

June 1957, that the devil confused him and that he jumped into the Anti-Party Group.

Such a naive explanation will not convince anybody, of course. I, for example, and other Central Committee members, were present several times at meetings of the Central Committee Praesidium, during discussions on ploughing up virgin and waste lands, on agricultural planning and on organising sovkhozes in the virgin lands. We saw Nikita Sergeyevich struggling desperately against Molotov, Malenkov, Kaganovich, Shepilov. Bulganin, however, was silent as a rule. He can say that silence is a sign of agreement. But with whom he was agreeing was shown last June when the office of the Prime Minister became a place of conspiracy. It wasn't the devil confusing people then, but a previously prepared attack on the general line of the Central Committee of the Party. That is why all members of the Central Committee plenum consider Comrade Bulganin's explanation completely unsatisfactory (*Stenographic Record* of the December 1958 plenum).

If anything, this seems to mean that Bulganin had only become *actively* involved in the scheme to oust Khrushchev in June 1957.

In this speech Yurkin was objecting to the remarks of Bulganin, who had said:

Objectively, I must honestly declare that until the events of June 1957 I was not with Malenkov, Kaganovich and Molotov, on the questions concerning the reorganisation of the management of industry and construction, on the question concerning the virgin lands and their reclamation, and on other questions. I was with the majority of the Praesidium of the Central Committee, I was with the Central Committee. I spoke and fought for the Party line and carried it into life in my practical work. But no matter how sad this is for me, the fact remains that when in 1957 the anti-Party work of Malenkov, Kaganovich, Molotov and Shepilov developed actively, I joined them, supported them, and became their adherent and accomplice. Being then Chairman of the Council of Ministers I turned out to be not only their accomplice, but even nominally their leader. In my office the Anti-Party Group gathered and intrigued about its anti-Party factional work. Thus, if at a definite stage I behaved correctly and adhered to Party principles, later I in fact shared with them the entire anti-Party dirt (*Pravda*, December 19, 1958).

This was held to be an inadequate evasion, as far as his own role is concerned, but no assertion that he had opposed the

industrial reorganisation was made; and Bulganin's flat assertion that he did not join the Group until June must at least be
considered plausible. At the same time he says he joined them
when their anti-Party work 'developed actively', which seems
to mean that the actual attempt to seize power was only
planned in June. He also implies that Shepilov was working
with the others before his own accession to the Group, which
would mean that the ideologist was not a last minute adherent.

On the other hand, at the December 1958 plenum, too,
L. R. Korniets stated:

> Bulganin said in his speech that before June 1957, he was not with
> the Group and later on he says himself, and it was said at earlier
> plenums too, that long before June members of the Anti-Party
> Group gathered in Bulganin's office, that is, at the time when this
> fractionist group was being knocked together.

As Molotov, Malenkov and Kaganovich were Vice-Premiers,
it might seem natural for them to meet in the Premier's office,
even in the occasional absence of other Vice-Premiers. But the
implication is perhaps that Khrushchev's opponents tried to
obtain Bulganin's support, but did not do so effectively until
June 1957, after argument. The decision to strike in June may
then be read simply as going ahead as soon as their majority
was secure. The Agricultural Exhibition (see pp. 67-8) was on
June 2nd.

On the role of Shepilov, 'who joined them', and is described
as a 'most shameless double-dealer' (Khrushchev, quoted in
Pravda, July 16, 1957), we may conclude that his change of
sides was fairly recent; yet, as we have seen, it was also stated
that he had been involved against Khrushchev in the policy
disputes on the industrial reorganisation.

He is also later referred to as having got involved at this
time in opposition to Khrushchev's agricultural plans:

> And Shepilov and his henchmen, like Academician Laptev, tried
> 'theoretically' to demonstrate the 'mistakenness' of the proposals
> which were being worked out. As you know, Shepilov tried to
> separate himself from the Group and to reckon that he had adhered
> to it at the last moment; but this is not true. In practice he has done
> a great deal to slow down the development of the science of economics
> and at the same time the solution of urgent tasks in developing the
> kolkhoz system (V. V. Matskevich at the December 1958 plenum).

So far this is rather vague, but may indicate that Shepilov's 'joining them' was genuinely based on policy qualms, or partly so.

At the XXIst Congress, I. I. Kuzmin developed the point about Laptev. 'Academician Comrade I. D. Laptev' had continued research on 'the mutual economic relations of the M.T.S. and the collective farms' when the Central Committee had already decided the issue and was 'working on the question of reorganising the M.T.S.' This implies that Shepilov, like Molotov and Kaganovich, was opposing the new M.T.S. proposals and that these had been decided on already — although not announced until the February 1958 plenum, which gives some idea of the time-lag preceding the presentation of this sort of proposal to a plenum. All the same, the Laptev accusation is a remarkably weak one, and if it is all that can be said may mean that Shepilov's agricultural heresies were negligible.

Bulganin was not removed from the premiership until February 1958, nor from the Praesidium until September 1958, and was not publicly denounced as a member of the Group until November of that year. Pervukhin and Saburov were not named as such until the XXIst Party Congress in January 1959. We can deduce that the Praesidium majority crumbled, with these three finally leaving it (if indeed Saburov was present until the plenum) under a compromise which saved something from the wreck.

An attack on Pervukhin at the XXIst Party Congress was to describe his and Saburov's role at the time as follows:

Comrade Pervukhin claims that he helped the Central Committee to unmask the Anti-Party Group: he presents himself to the Congress as a hero. Is that so, Comrade Pervukhin? We, the members of the Central Committee, all remember what the facts were. Did you not come out against the reconstruction of the direction of industry and building? Were you not in disagreement with proposals of Nikita Sergeyevich Khrushchev on important questions of international policy? Did you not move over to the camp of the conspirators? . . . You, Comrades Pervukhin and Saburov, were compelled to talk to the June plenum of the Central Committee of the Party about the activities of the Anti-Party Group only after the members and candidate members of the Central Committee of the Party had unanimously condemned the Anti-Party Group (Denisov, in *Pravda*, February 5, 1959).

This perhaps means that they accepted a set-piece *fait accompli*. In general, the unanimity of the very Central Committee which the Group had expected to accept an opposition- ist Praesidial diktat can only be a sign of agreement reached outside its competence — that is, in the Praesidium itself.

Some further hints on the development of the struggle were given in Saburov's statement to the XXIst Congress on February 4, 1959 (*Stenographic Record*, Vol. II). He claimed that he had supported the Party line on all major themes as against the Anti-Party Group, but that he had criticised faults in the work of the Praesidium

not from the position of the healthy part of the Praesidium of the C.C. C.P.S.U., but from the position of the Anti-Party Group which, using as a screen small and easily corrected faults, attacked Comrade Khrushchev, sought changes in the leadership of the Central Committee, and consequently in the policies of the Central Com- mittee.

He added that

already at meetings of the Praesidium of the C.C. C.P.S.U., before the June plenum, I took a quite different position; I protested against the dirty attempts of Kaganovich and other participants in the Anti-Party Group to smear the name of N. S. Khrushchev, and stated that collective leadership existed in the Praesidium of the C.C.

This makes it clear that one of the 'smears' was an accusa- tion that Khrushchev was aiming at dictatorship.

Saburov continued, 'maintaining correct positions on the basic questions of the policy of the party, I saw the actual aims of the Anti-Party Group, leading to a change in the leadership of the Central Committee' and then 'with the aid of some comrades from the healthy section of members of the Prae- sidium — Comrades Mikoyan and Kirichenko — I broke strongly with the Anti-Party Group'. This last sentence shows that the practice of 'working on individual members of the Praesidium' was not confined to the Anti-Party Group. It also may seem to imply that these two were Khrushchev's only reliable allies at the time, casting a slight shadow on Suslov as well as Voroshilov.

We now have to consider the fact that Bulganin, later to be named as a full member of the Group, and Pervukhin, who was attacked as a leading opponent of the industrial reform, should have been left in the Praesidium, or demoted only to candidate member, respectively, while Saburov, who on the face of it simply acted as an irritant, went so much lower. It may be that the issue was, in general, fixed before Saburov's return, so that only a minimum incentive needed to be offered for his defection. And we may perhaps think of him as both more closely linked with Malenkov in the past and more identified with the managerial class.

The defeat of the Anti-Party Group is perhaps best regarded as a coup (or counter-coup) by the Party Apparatus, the Army and the Security Police against a majority in the Praesidium which might otherwise have obtained a majority — or unanimity! — in the Central Committee.

If the Praesidium majority against Khrushchev had been broken on the substantive issue even before going to the Central Committee, that in itself would not prove that everything was settled. Yet the fact that *all* speeches at the C.C. are said to have condemned the Group seems to show that the debate was prejudiced in advance.

There is no reason to believe that the calculation that the Central Committee would vote a resolution presented by the Praesidium was a mistaken one. The Committee was by no means a Khrushchev preserve, as had been shown before and was to be shown later. And the most natural conclusion is that the majority had crumbled under threats and inducements before the Committee met. The official description of its session is as follows:

The plenum of the C.C. C.P.S.U. lasted for a week. It was attended by members and candidates of the C.C. and by members of the Central Revision Commission — 309 persons in all. The plenum proceeded under the conditions of the very widest, entirely unrestricted democracy. Speakers were not regulated by rule. Malenkov, Kaganovich and Molotov spoke twice, and their written declarations were read out at the final session of the plenum. 215 Comrades put down their names to take part in the debate. 60 of them expressed their views. All the remainder who were unable to speak submitted their views in written form. And not a single member of the plenum of the C.C. supported the Anti-Party Group (*Party Life*, July 1957, No. 13).

Kozlov was to say that the Anti-Party Group's speeches to the plenum 'developed a platform for further struggle' (*Leningradskaya Pravda*, July 5, 1957).

Finally a resolution was passed (see Appendix VII) and a new Praesidium and Secretariat were elected (see Appendix I). The new Praesidium included a majority of the old — Bulganin, Voroshilov, Kirichenko, Mikoyan, Suslov, Khrushchev — to justify the assertion that the opposition's 'incorrect utterances and acts were constantly rebuffed in the Central Committee Praesidium which consistently implemented the XXth Congress line'.

The accusations against the Anti-Party Group in the Central Committee Resolution are revealing, though not amounting to total clarification by any means:

They had 'in the last three to four years' shown opposition 'direct or indirect' to the struggle to rectify the errors produced by the cult of personality, and also to the struggle against revisionism.

They had attempted 'in effect' to oppose peaceful coexistence.

In foreign policy Molotov had opposed the *détente* with Yugoslavia; the signing of the Austrian Treaty; better relations with Japan; the idea that war might not be inevitable; the idea of possible 'peaceful roads to Socialism'; contacts with foreign 'progressive' parties; and personal contacts among statesmen. He had been backed on 'many points' by Kaganovich, and on 'a number' by Malenkov.

So far there is nothing to indicate anything remotely like a bloc; on the contrary, it is virtually admitted that the three men frequently did not see eye to eye. Molotov's personal programme, which might be defined in both foreign affairs and ideology as one of no adventures and no concessions, is interesting. The ideological points give some idea of the discussions before the XXth Congress.

Some light on the foreign policy 'platform' of the Group was thrown at the XXIst Party Congress (on January 29,

1959), when Gromyko accused them of urging a passive foreign policy (presumably disapproving of various adventures and pressures):

> But the objective favourable conditions, created for the foreign policy of the U.S.S.R. by the very nature of its social order, must, of course, be used skilfully and one must not allow them to remain unused. However, there are people who draw conclusions harming the Party and the people. The Anti-Party Group of Malenkov, Kaganovich, Molotov, Bulganin and Shepilov tried to push our foreign policy into such a road and seriously prejudiced not only internal developments of our country but also the foreign policy of the Soviet State. Our Party and its Leninist Central Committee removed these fractionists, paved the way for a more creative, flexible and active policy of the Soviet State, fully in keeping with the interests of our people (*Stenographic Record*, Vol. I).

In Kirichenko's speech to the XXIst Congress on January 31, 1959 (*Stenographic Record*, Vol. I), there is also an allegation that the Group disputed the Party line on 'the structure of the Armed Forces'. Malinovsky's speech at that Congress (February 3, 1959) also spoke of the Group, but for its defeat, causing 'great damage' to the Armed Forces. What this refers to is not clear.

It is only on matters of recent policy that the Group is alleged to have offered joint and unqualified opposition — to decentralisation, debureaucratisation, the National Economic Councils and the new proposals for material incentives to the kolkhozes and the catching up of the U.S. in milk, meat, etc. The inference is that the Group, as a group, only started operating within the past six or seven months — not earlier, perhaps than the December 1956 plenum, and not later than the aftermath of that of February 1957. That a struggle had certainly been taking place on these recent issues was, anyhow, confirmed, as was the fact that there had been sporadic disputes on various issues as far back as 1953–54.

Kosygin, who was now made a candidate member of the Praesidium and Deputy Chairman of the Council of Ministers, said that the Group's 'basic motive' was 'personal resentment and ambition'; they 'considered that they had little power'. 'Opportunists', they had 'gathered facts about shortcomings . . . to discredit the Party line' (*Pravda*, July 4, 1957).

A few of the substantive points in the Resolution were elaborated shortly afterwards. For instance it was said that:

As Chairman of the U.S.S.R. Council of Ministers Comrade Malenkov . . . made crude political mistakes, distorting the Leninist line on the preferential development of heavy industry, and giving confused and harmful directives on questions of foreign policy and the international situation. . . . As Secretary of the Central Committee for a number of years in charge of agricultural questions, he did not take steps to correct the clearly unsatisfactory state of agriculture, but practised deception. At the plenum in January 1955 he was sharply criticised for a bad style of leadership (Kozlov, *Leningradskaya Pravda*, July 5, 1957).

Meanwhile the public announcement was being prepared.

On June 30 *Pravda* carried a long interview given by Khrushchev to the Japanese newspaper *Asahi Shimbun* on June 18.

On July 2 *Pravda* reported only Bulganin, Voroshilov, Mikoyan, Suslov and Khrushchev as present at a Kabardine Balkar Art Concert. That is, members of the old Praesidium were listed, with neither the fallen, nor their replacements. On July 3 *Pravda* carried a leader on 'Unbroken Unity' — a sure sign of trouble.

Then the matter became public. Denunciatory meetings were held throughout the country. Bulganin and Pervukhin are among those listed as addressing a meeting of the Moscow Party aktiv on the theme of Anti-Party Group (*Tass*, July 3, 1957).

The fall of Malenkov, Kaganovich and Molotov was followed by a lively propaganda campaign against them. In so far as this did not consist of general abuse it may be differentiated into three main types of allegation:

(*a*) that they had opposed certain policy decisions;
(*b*) that they had acted in a 'fractional', intriguer's manner;
(*c*) that they had committed criminal offences.

Examples of (*a*) and (*b*) have been given in other connections. The criminal charges can now be considered.

In Leningrad, Khrushchev took a decisive step. After appropriating the policy with which Malenkov had been popularly identified:

'We wish that Soviet people should have enough meat and

butter and milk and fruit, that in the shops there should be plenty of cheap and pretty textiles, dresses, everything that beautifies the life of man,' he added: 'Malenkov . . . was one of the chief organisers of the so-called Leningrad Case' (*Pravda* July 7, 1957).

Shvernik repeated the accusation:

'The Leningrad Case, in organising which Malenkov took an active part, was fabricated.' He also associated the opposition with the Great Purge of the 'thirties:

> Correcting the violations of revolutionary legality committed by Malenkov, Kaganovich and Molotov in the period of mass repressions, the Party Control Committee has examined in 1957 many personal dossiers of former Party members rehabilitated by the judicial organs (*Pravda*, July 7, 1957).

Marshal Zhukov in Leningrad on July 15 made the point even more strongly:

> Malenkov, Kaganovich and Molotov . . . stubbornly opposed steps taken by the Party to liquidate the consequences of the personality cult, especially in the sphere of unmasking and calling to account the chief culprits who in their time committed violations of legality. Now that their utterly un-Party deeds have been revealed it has become clear why they were against unmasking the illegal acts committed. They feared responsibility before the Party and people for exceeding their rights and for illegal actions.

He went on, according to *Pravda*, to 'adduce facts of violations of legality by participants in the Anti-Party Group'. These were not published (*Pravda*, July 16, 1957).

Certain criminal accusations of a general nature were made against Kaganovich alone. Kozlov said:

> The inactivity and crude violations of revolutionary legality committed by Kaganovich as First Deputy Chairman of the Council of Ministers, as Chairman of the State Committee for Labour and Wages and as Minister of the Building Materials Industry, have also been revealed (*Leningradskaya Pravda*, July 5, 1957).

In Kiev Kalchenko said:

> For a short time Secretary of the Ukrainian Central Committee, Kaganovich . . . defamed and insulted Party workers, discredited many honest people devoted to the Party, degraded them. Without

proof he made grave accusations against many leading workers and representatives of the progressive Ukrainian intelligentsia. If he had not been recalled from the Ukraine in time he would have done immense harm to the Ukrainian Party and people (*Pravda*, July 3, 1957).

This plainly refers to 1947.

General Gorbatov in Riga (*Sovietskaya Latvia*, July 5) said that the Anti-Party Group attacked Khrushchev because he had been the first to fight against the illegalities they had committed in 1937-38 and subsequently.

The Group were also branded as responsible for opposition to reform of the Stalinist system, because they expected that any inquiry would implicate them. This is no doubt true, as far as it goes:

> The Anti-Party Group put up a constant resistance to the measures which were introduced by the party for the liquidation of the consequences of the personality cult, for the removal of the infringement of socialist legality which had occurred in the past and for the creation of conditions which make it impossible for them to be repeated. No small part was played in this by the fact that Malenkov, Kaganovich and Molotov were particularly deeply implicated in the grossest errors and shortcomings which had happened in the past (*Party Life*, July 1957).

Khrushchev repeated his allegations against Malenkov the following month:

> Great blame in this matter attaches to Comrade Malenkov who fell completely under the influence of Beria, was his shadow, and was a tool in his hands. Occupying a high position in Party and State Comrade Malenkov not only failed to restrain J. V. Stalin, but very adroitly exploited Stalin's weaknesses and habits in the last years of his life. In many cases he egged him on to actions which merit severe condemnation (*Pravda*, August 28, 1957).

Such were the voices calling, in effect, for the trial of the Group. The speeches of Khrushchev and others directly accuse Malenkov and almost directly the others, too, of definite criminal acts. Yet they were not brought to trial, nor even expelled from the Party. The natural conclusion is that those who made the charges were representatives of a view which they had urged, but been unable to find a majority for, in the

June plenum. (The accusation against Bulganin at the December 1958 plenum that he had 'defended Malenkov' may be a pointer to the struggle in the Central Committee on the issue of bringing Malenkov to trial.)

The June 1957 plenum's decision was evidently a compromise — as indeed is shown by the resolution's references to the machinery of expulsion from the Party not being followed by such expulsion. The speeches of criminal accusation following it may be regarded as the first agitation by those favouring a trial, in a campaign to have the June decisions amended. This campaign was evidently pursued in the Central Committee throughout the following eighteen months. And the issue may be regarded as the basic one in the power struggle up to the XXIst Congress. (A cross-current was, of course, provided by the fall of Zhukov, who, for different reasons, had spoken strongly in favour of the criminal accusation line.)

It may be relevant that (leaving aside Zhukov) the public accusations made by major figures can be divided as follows:

Direct accusations of crime:
  by Khrushchev (against Malenkov),
  by Shvernik (against all three),
  by Kozlov (against Kaganovich).

General accusations of evil motives and 'conspiracy':
  by Kosygin (and in general in the Party Press).

Most of the other attacks, however violent, are usually on points in *political* dispute, or accusations of vanity, incompetence, etc. (In the Ukraine, Kalchenko, presumably under Kirichenko's aegis, accused Kaganovich of criminal, though unconsummated, plans.)

The fact that so few praesidial figures (and not very many minor ones either) supported the criminal charges may show a general reluctance to follow Khrushchev any further in the matter at that time. The silence of his new colleagues resembled the silence of the old ones in the reorganisation of industry.

And thus, the decision of the June plenum which at first sight seems such a total defeat of Khrushchev's opponents, appears as a compromise after all. The opponents of one-man rule had suffered losses and had retreated, but they were still to be reckoned with.

It is beyond the scope of this book to deal with the great literary and intellectual Thaw of 1956–57; with the purge of *Voprosy Istorii* for bourgeois objectivism; with the controversy about *Not by Bread Alone* by Dudintsev; with the 'liberal' editors of and contributors to *Novy Mir* and *Literaturnaya Moskva*, and their tribulations; with the 'unsatisfactory' meetings of the Moscow and Leningrad Writers' Associations. But we should note in the first place that the machinery for giving leave to print, and especially for books, is extremely complicated and thorough under Soviet law, and that definite permission is required from the Publications Sector of the Agitation and Propaganda Department of the Central Committee (*Soviet Union Laws*, No. 57/589). It is not only unlikely, it is practically inconceivable that a junior official in this apparatus would start allowing heterodox literature without a definite directive from higher up. We may conclude that in the early days after the XXth Congress, Khrushchev ruled for a relaxation, hoping (as with his Eastern European policy) that this would lead, in spite of odd abuses, to the manifestation of voluntary attachment to his rule, which would be a welcome change from the insecure and unfruitful forced attachment which had hitherto done duty.

This was not due to any acceptance of liberal principles, and when it was apparent that the writers, like the Hungarians and Poles, had used their freedom of choice to choose wrong, Khrushchev rapidly went back to a modified Stalin position in this field, too. At the same time the old guard, and especially Molotov, were able to blame him for this error as well.

During most of 1956, and again after February 1957, Shepilov was in charge of culture. He seems to have taken the 'liberal' line a little more seriously. And when the Anti-Party Group, which he 'joined', fell from office, accusations began to be made against him, and in general against them, too, on this point.

When Shepilov was still in favour, *Kommunist* could assert:

Our enemies slander us, asserting that in the Soviet Union the 'supervision' of the party over art and literature has been established. But that is what enemies are for, to use every type of weapon against us. As we see, they do not hesitate to use dirty slander. The actual fact, however, is that Lenin's principles for direction in the sphere of literature and art are definitely directed against any kind of 'supervision', against interference in the process of artistic creation (*Kommunist*, February 1957).

This was soon to be put very differently. The denunciation of the Anti-Party Group, in so far as questions of policy and ideology were involved, centred on accusations of dogmatism and bureaucratic methods. Yet apart from the Tito issue (which was mainly blamed on Molotov) there were few specific cases given. And it is noticeable that in *Voprosy Filosofii* No. 4 of 1957 (passed for publication September 9, 1957), although the general charges of dogmatism are again made, the only *specific* point is:

It should be noted that D. Shepilov who occupied himself with problems of ideological work and who joined the Anti-Party Group, avoided the Leninist principle of party spirit in socialist ideology in a number of his speeches to the intelligentsia. He did not give the due party rebuff to the attacks of various demagogues on this Leninist principle in Soviet science, art, literature. He ignored it, and displayed rotten liberalism towards the anti-socialist ideological propositions of a certain section of our literary and artistic intelligentsia, among whom there had spread a bourgeois-anarchist, individualistic conception of the creative liberty of the artist, directed against the party supervision of art.

This is, of course, if anything, a charge of *insufficient* bureaucracy and of rightist deviation. (Perhaps it is significant that this is a case in which the orders are given, the bureaucracy exercised, by the *Party* Organisation, not by the State. And this may go some way to justify the view that Khrushchev was not opposing bureaucracy as such but bureaucracy exercised otherwise than through the Party machine.)

Shepilov is also accused of having failed to 'submit to criticism' certain literary and cultural figures (*Sovietskaya Kultura*, July 18, 1957.) He was alleged, too, to have played down, and criticised, the meeting between Party leaders and writers — a reference to the meeting of May 9 at which Khrushchev attacked recalcitrant intellectuals (*Literaturnaya Gazeta*, July 9, 1957). At a meeting of the Armenian republican aktiv of literary and artistic workers on November 18, 1957, Tovmasyan, First Secretary of the Armenian Central Committee, went so far as to say: 'People have been found who, leaning upon the mistaken theses of D. Shepilov, have stated that the Party leadership, as it were, does not help but hinders the development of literature and art.'

On July 31, 1957, *Kommunist*, the Party's theoretical magazine, attacked Shepilov. It said that he had departed from the XXth Congress line and adopted a liberal position, that he was intent not so much on genuine freedom of artistic creation as on making concessions to anarchistic elements, that his references to the Zhdanov decrees were totally inadequate, and that he failed to underline the Leninist principle of Party-mindedness. In the case of Hungary great harm had been done by liberalism; Shepilov had not learned the lesson of Hungary: as a result 'certain demagogic elements among the artistic intelligentsia had the chance of indulging themselves to the limit'. At the XXIst Party Congress in January 1959 he was curiously accused of defending the intellectual's right to political instability (see p. 380).

These accusations were occasionally directed against the Anti-Party Group as a whole, as when they were accused of having 'supported the decadent mood of certain writers, precisely those who were parading their imaginary "objectivity", attempted to distort splendid Soviet reality and tried to inflate particular shortcomings' (*Pravda Ukrainy*, July 12, 1957). The Secretary of the Board of the Uzbek Union of Writers, S. Azimov, even went so far as to omit Shepilov when saying: 'The Anti-Party Group of Malenkov, Kaganovich and Molotov to a certain extent inspired those literateurs who try to deny the Party spirit in literature' (*Pravda Vostoka*, July 1957). It seems certain, however, that the views of Molotov as least are quite the opposite of what is here implied — and it is interesting that such diverse elements could sink their differences to form a single group. No direct and clear attempts to blame as individuals his three seniors, rather than Shepilov, for the relaxation were made. Malenkov's pronouncements at the XIXth Congress on the 'typical' were attacked (e.g. in *Sovietskaya Kultura*, July 18, 1957) — a very different point. Molotov was accused much more vaguely of never having 'raised any serious questions on improving work in the field of culture' (*Sovietskaya Kultura*, July 6, 1957). But, much in

Y

line with the accusations of dogmatism, both Molotov and Malenkov are accused of having, with Beria, adversely influenced Stalin into making the Zhdanov music decree far more rigorous than it should have been (Central Committee Decree of May 28, 1958: see p. 356).

The episode is, in any case, instructive.

CHAPTER THIRTEEN

ZHUKOV AND THE ARMY, 1953-57

AT the end of October 1957 Marshal Zhukov was suddenly expelled from the Praesidium and the Central Committee, and removed from his post as Minister of War under grave political charges.

Zhukov served on the highest body from February 1956 to October 1957. His original promotion may be read in terms of a situation at once so tense and so well balanced that resort was made to the expedient of dealing in the Army, in the hope of manipulating it to the disadvantage of rivals in some crisis. It was, in principle, an expedient full of danger to the whole political system, but it seems to have served its purpose in June 1957. After that the victorious faction was left with the risks but no longer with the reasons that had caused it to accept them. And it took the first opportunity of normalising the position, with the removal of the Marshal.

Thus, following the fall of the Anti-Party Group, the Army briefly beomes the centre of political attention. We have said little of its role in previous cases, and it will be convenient to go back a little in time.

Soviet Army politics is almost as vast and complex a subject in itself as Soviet political life proper. Here we can only sketch the main lines, give a sample of the often inadequate and sometimes confusing data and deal with the major crisis of October 1957.

In the Army we see in a particularly pure form some of the phenomena which are fairly general in Soviet ruling groups. Military professionalism is far more of a specialisation than the economic professionalism of the khozaistvenniks or the police professionalism of the security forces, let alone the political–ideological specialisation of the Party apparatchiks. Yet it has something in common with them.

And just as the Army is an area of skill where it is difficult to replace the specialist, and an area in which professional resentment at interference by the uninformed is likely to produce solidarities, so it is also a source of power which may, if improperly handled, be capable of intervention in affairs of State. We can certainly trace, in Soviet military politics, attempts to control the Army through political nominees, the rise of a professional solidarity and, partly counterbalancing it, the emergence of factions within the Army leadership. During periods of crisis we can see the attempts of rival political groups to secure the general support of the Army. At the same time we see the politician's distrust of the Army, and readiness to crush it as an independent force whenever such action seems possible.

We have so far dealt with Army issues only in Chapter Eight in connection with Stalin's last months. From that period we may perhaps distinguish roughly three main trends:

(a) Zhukov, Sokolovsky and their associates, ready to extend the power of the Army and not strongly engaged by Party considerations.

(b) Konev, Govorov and so on — professional soldiers more involved in Party manœuvre;

(c) F. F. Kuznetsov, Zheltov, etc., the political apparatus of the forces — not really soldiers at all and in constant conflict with (a).

(d) Shtemenko, etc. — an intermediate case, professional soldiers given rapid promotion for political reasons and becoming identified with political manœuvres almost to the exclusion of their military links.

Of the normal military view of Stalin it is possible to be absolutely clear. The first flat criticism of the old dictator of any sort was made in a book by a general, published by the Military Editions, in November 1953 — *On Soviet Military Science* by Major-General N. V. Pukhorsky, who attacked the 'cult of the individual' and the habit of quoting authority, as having 'voluntarily or involuntarily' hindered Soviet military thought. Stalin was not named. But in the semi-secret organ *Military Thought* (No. 3, March 1955) the habit of 'quoting J. V. Stalin' is frankly stated to have caused harm. Again 'the cult of the individual' is mentioned.*

The direct military interest was particularly great because

---

* The quotations from *Military Thought* have been obtained from Dr. Raymond L. Garthoff's invaluable *Soviet Strategy in the Nuclear Age* (New York, 1958).

these scholastic habits had practically prevented any thought whatever being given to real problems, since military science was considered to have been settled once and for all by 'Stalinist genius'. In 1953 the military papers already started to cope. And, naturally, the whole bias of the soldiers, as 'military scientists', was the same as that of scientists in other fields — to exclude 'Marxist–Leninist' considerations and Party interference altogether. *Military Thought* carried a long discussion (1953–55) on whether military science should include Marxism–Leninism in its scope, and finally concluded that, correct though Marxism–Leninism undoubtedly was, too wide an interpretation of the subject-matter of military science distracted it from its tasks, and this would mean 'to ruin military science as a specific branch of knowledge'.

We may also consider that disputes may arise on simple questions of purely military significance, which may then play a part in other quarrels. For instance, *Military Thought* mentioned in its editorial of March 1955 that it had 'baselessly' held up an article by Marshal of Tank Troops Rotmistrov, 'On the Role of Surprise in Contemporary War'. It is part of the Party's view of war that surprise cannot be decisive, and that the essential of victory is the industrial potential and political maturity of the winner — a Marxist view, and one which suited the *results* of World War II and played down the effect of the original German surprise. This is not a point, in the long view, on which the Marshals usually differ from the Party. The conservative professional's interest in lengthy strategies leads to a bias against surprise which even leads in cases like this to a sort of faction fight against a leading soldier who does little more than examine its practical advantages, not as a war winner, but simply as a help.

At the time of Stalin's death, when Beria resumed control of the M.V.D. in unknown circumstances and the capital was filled with Security Troops, one line of speculation as to why Beria's victory was not more complete lies, as we have seen, in searching for an actual centre of armed force capable of balancing the Moscow M.V.D. garrisons. This could have been nothing but some Army centre — with some preference for the nearest and most powerful military district, that of Leningrad under Marshal Govorov.

Whatever the possibilities of Army intervention in March, there seems to be a strong case for the Army having played a role in the fall of Beria. The same *a priori* argument remains, in that the Army was the only armed group to whom appeal could anyhow be made against the power of the armed police, if it came to the point. Moreover, the removal of the Police Generals commanding Moscow District, Moscow City and the Kremlin and their replacement by military men following the fall of Beria, suggests that they and their units constituted one of the Georgian's power bases, and that if, as the indictment against him says, he was really preparing to seize power, they would have supplied part of the means. Artemyev's disappearance, in particular, can clearly be interpreted as disgrace, as it involved also his removal from the Central Committee.

Following Beria's fall, meetings and declarations of Army figures were given publicity. The promotion of Marshal Zhukov in July to the vacant place as full member of the Central Committee (*Encyclopaedic Dictionary*, September 1953) was a significant move, particularly as it would have been possible to co-opt him earlier — on his promotion to Vice-Minister in March 1953, say.

Pravda of July 16, 1953, prominently reports a meeting, undated but having taken place 'recently', of high military officials expressing their support for the Party against Beria. Those listed as present included Zheltov, Bulganin, Zhukov, Sokolovsky, Govorov and others. The — quite unprecedented — presence of Konev and of Moskalenko on the court which tried Beria can hardly be read as otherwise than a demonstration of Army solidarity with the regime against the Police Chief. In particular, Moskalenko, as the replacement of Beria's nominee in the Moscow command, plays an obvious part.

In any event the Army now carried more and increasing weight.

On February 6, 1954, the conventional letter in which prominent candidates for the elections to the Supreme Soviet announced their renunciation of all but one of the many candidatures thrust upon them was signed, by a great departure from the norm, not only by the Praesidium, the Secretariat and the Secretary of the Young Communist League, but also by three marshals. One of these was indeed Budyonny, who had been singled out for this exceptional favour in Stalin's time and who must be regarded as more a decorative pensioner of the regime than a genuine soldier. But the others, by a genuine novelty, were Vasilevsky and Zhukov.

In the campaign against Malenkov's consumer-goods heresy in 1954-55 the evidence is that the Army supported Khrushchev. *Krasnaya Zvezda*'s editorials of December 30 and 31, 1954, and a series of articles afterwards, take his line. Malenkov's opponents made continued appeals for Army support with the argument that heavy industrialisation priority was required in the interest of national defence. *Krasnaya Zvezda* itself, on January 27, 1955, attacked a military economist who held Malenkovite views, on the grounds that such policies would 'weaken our defence'. Zhukov (in *Pravda* of February 23, 1955) Sokolovsky (in *Izvestia* of February 23, 1955) and other leaders rubbed it in with notable enthusiasm when Malenkov was removed.

Another point on which Zhukov and the Army leaders evidently differed from Malenkov was the latter's view of nuclear warfare. In his speech of March 1954 Malenkov had said that an atomic war 'would mean the end of world civilisation'. After Malenkov's fall in 1955 Molotov and other leaders replaced this by the formula that a new war would only mean the end of capitalism, a doctrine that remains in force to this day. But it is notable that the military spokesmen, too, have never treated atomic war as being as destructive as it is usually held in the west. A whole series of articles in the military Press take the line that atomic weapons cannot be decisive. Zhukov himself stated: 'One must bear in mind that one cannot win a war by atomic bombs alone' (*Pravda*, February 13, 1955) precisely at the time of Malenkov's fall, and repeated the point later (e.g. *Pravda*, August 7, 1956). The line is consistently taken that victory can be achieved even after 'tens of thousands' of atomic bombs have been used, since 'operational balance or equality achieved by reciprocal atomic blows will be broken to the advantage of one side or the other' (*Militarism* by V. Skopin, 1956). Dr. Raymond Garthoff, in his *Soviet Strategy in the Nuclear Age*, gives numerous similar quotations, and says that he found fifty-five in support of Zhukov's words in the three years 1954-57.

On the other hand, if they regarded the Malenkov formula as unrealistically pessimistic, Zhukov and his associates were equally disinclined to underestimate entirely the dangers of atomic warfare. In his V.E. day speech in May, Zhukov spoke at some length on this theme, and failed to repeat Molotov's sanguine thesis that atomic war would destroy not civilisation but only capitalism. If we can deduce a military view, different from either Molotov's or Malenkov's, on this key question of foreign policy, it seems to be that while an atomic war would not (as Malenkov had said) destroy civilisation and it might be possible to be victorious in one, yet the Molotov formula was unduly optimistic and played down both the extent of the probable destruction and the risks not only to capitalism, but to the U.S.S.R. as well. In this issue we see a vital political point on which the professional interests of the Marshals were bound to be strongly engaged.

When Bulganin became Premier, Zhukov moved up to be Minister of War. A series of promotions followed, including the creation of six new Marshals of the Soviet Union: Bagramyan, Biryuzov, Grechko, Eremenko, Moskalenko and Chuikov, on March 12, 1955.

It would perhaps not be far-fetched to regard Khrushchev's 'association' with certain Marshals in the Ukraine as significant — notably Konev, Chuikov and Moskalenko. Moskalenko's position seems specially relevant. He was on Khrushchev's First Ukrainian Front during the war, and in the Ukraine thereafter until 1949. He then came to Moscow with Khrushchev and was a member of his Moscow Party Committee. As we saw, in 1953, when only a Colonel General, he replaced Artemyev as G.O.C. Moscow District, and served (with Konev) on the tribunal which sentenced Beria.

Among the changes following the removal of Malenkov from the Premiership came a new method of treating the activity of Party leaders during the war. Where previously the State Committee of Defence, of which Khrushchev was not a member, used to be named, now there was regular reference to the Party having sent to the front Zhdanov, Scherbakov, Khrushchev and Bulganin.

Marshal Konev was one of the few soldiers who used this formula. In *Pravda* of February 23, 1955 — Soviet Army Day —

his article, but not those by other Marshals, took it up. Again, in the V.E. day celebrations of May 1955, Konev and Zheltov ran this line, naming Khrushchev first. Zhukov, Vasilevsky and Sokolovksy did not mention the politicians at all. An article in *Pravda* of February 3 on Stalingrad gave Stalin and Khrushchev much of the credit. An article in the Army's *Krasnaya Zvezda* of the same date did not mention them. Moreover, when the *Pravda* article was repeated in the Soviet Army-in-Germany's organ *Tägliche Rundschau*, the reference to the politicians was omitted. Meanwhile, Zhukov had given an interview to the Hearst Press, in which he claimed credit for the planning of the Stalingrad, Kursk and other operations.

In June 1955 an article (in *News*, No. 11) gave Konev credit for the Berlin operations usually given to Zhukov — of interest in view of Konev's violent attack on Zhukov on this very point after his fall (*Pravda* of November 3, 1957).

In the Secret Speech Khrushchev's bid for personal support from Zhukov was strong:

> Stalin was very much interested in the assessment of Comrade Zhukov as a military leader. He asked me often for my opinion of Zhukov. I told him then, 'I have known Zhukov for a long time; he is a good general and a good military leader.'
>
> After the war Stalin began to tell all kinds of nonsense about Zhukov, among others the following, 'You praised Zhukov, but he does not deserve it. It is said that before each operation at the front Zhukov used to behave as follows: He used to take a handful of earth, smell it and say "We can begin the attack," or the opposite, "The planned operation cannot be carried out." ' I stated at that time, 'Comrade Stalin, I do not know who invented this, but it is not true.' It is possible that Stalin himself invented these things for the purpose of minimising the role and military talents of Marshal Zhukov.

A different estimate of these talents was to be made after October 1957.

In the Secret Speech Khrushchev spoke in a general way about Stalin's purge of the Army. He condemned the 'repression against the military cadres', and mentioned those who had 'perished in camps and jails'. But he did not rehabilitate any of the victims by name, as he had done in the case of certain political leaders.

During the ensuing year the executed generals of 1937–40 were gradually rehabilitated, though in a quiet and undemonstrative manner. They simply reappeared, one by one, in historical and military journals and reference books, as former good comrades now dead. (This evident reluctance to give much attention to them, in spite of what was plainly heavy pressure from the Army, has been attributed to Voroshilov's direct implication, as Defence Commissar, in the military purge.)

The Secret Speech well illustrated, through the Marshals, a point of Soviet political psychology. Rokossovsky was, Khrushchev tells us, one of those arrested in the purges of the 'thirties, surviving 'despite the severe tortures to which they were subjected in the prison'. Yet Stalin had found it possible to release him and raise him to important military posts. And it is clear from his conduct when transferred to be C.-in-C. of the Polish Army, that his views remained 'Stalinist'. One is reminded of the high court official at Byzantium, mentioned by Gibbon, who was publicly beaten unconscious on the Emperor's orders, but soon afterwards readmitted to favour. In most cultures such a thing would be hardly conceivable.

At the XXth Congress Admiral N. G. Kuznetsov was dropped from full membership and a number of military figures who had been candidate members of the 1952 Central Committee were not re-elected.

One of these was Shtemenko. Others came from all arms: Marshal of Tank Troops Bogdanov, Stalin's C.-in-C. Armoured Formations, who had already been given a lower post; Admiral Basisty, Deputy Minister of the Navy under Stalin and Deputy Minister of Defence in the March 1953 Government, who had lost this post in 1954; Marshal of Aviation Vershinin; and Admiral Yumashev. It seems clear that, like Shtemenko himself, these men were not the forces' choice. Their replacements were, on the whole, men with higher military reputations.

At the same time General F. F. Kuznetsov, Head of the Political Administration of the Army, was reduced from candidate member of the Central Committee to membership of the Revision Commission — a step in line with the policy Zhukov was later to become publicly identified with, of downgrading the political machine in the Army. The other political officer to have been a candidate member of the Central Committee, Admiral Zakharov, Head of the Navy Political Directorate, was not even elected to the Revision Commission.

Of the fighting Marshals of the late war, only one lost status — Meretskov, who (in spite of a favourable reference to him in the Secret Speech) fell to the Revision Commission. The reason is not clear. General Malinin, first Deputy Chief of General Staff, had a similar demotion.

In the Central Committee, the military full members (omitting Artemyev) had been Konev, Sokolovsky, Vasilevsky, Admiral N. G. Kuznetsov and (promoted from candidate in 1953) Zhukov. The candidates, apart from those mentioned above (and omitting Budyonny) were Chuikov, Grechko, Gorbatov, Govorov, Luchinsky, Malinovsky, Nedelin, Timoshenko and Zhigarev.

Malinovsky was now promoted to full membership, which was also significantly given to Moskalenko who had hitherto not served in the leading Party bodies at all. The new candidate members were Marshals Biryuzov and Eremenko and Admiral Gorshkov.

The new appointments do not on the face of it strengthen Zhukov's position notably, but the total removal of representatives of the Army Political Department does. And at the plenum following the Congress Zhukov became the senior candidate member of the Praesidium, an unprecedented position for a soldier.

As against the oblique hints of dispute on history which had been seen in 1955, Zhukov's ascendancy now appeared unchallenged. And *Kommunist* No. 10 of 1956 for almost the first time mentions the Army commanders, headed by Zhukov, as the leading war-winners.

Zhukov continued to develop the independence of the armed forces from any Party control otherwise than through himself, in a way paralleling the manner in which Beria had extricated the M.V.D. from any effective control by the Administrative Organs Department, and turned it into a power controlled solely by its chief. The key to Zhukov's progress was to break the already weakened power of the Political Department under Zheltov, which sits for practical purposes precisely as a Department of the Central Committee.

In the winter of 1956 at the Party conferences of the Military Districts there were strong criticisms of the political departments — except at that of Chuikov's Kiev District. *Krasnaya Zvezda* of December 16 published an editorial referring sympathetically to delegates who had 'sharply criticised defects in party political work'.

In May 1957 there was formally issued a full-blown Central Committee 'Instructions to C.P.S.U. organisations in the Soviet Army and Navy', accompanied by an Order of Zhukov's. The key sentence of the decree was, 'criticism of the orders and decisions of commanders will not be permitted at Party meetings' (*Krasnaya Zvezda* and *Sovietski Flot*, May 12, 1957). After Zhukov's fall a different view of Party criticism of commanders was to be taken: 'Regardless of the rank or position of a Communist he not only can, but must, be subjected at Party meetings or conferences, to criticism for shortcomings in his service' (*Sovietski Flot*, November 1, 1957). Zhukov was criticised in the same article for 'trying to diminish the importance of Party-political work in the army and navy'.

During Khrushchev's economic reforms in the spring of 1957 it was originally proposed to decentralise even the ministries dealing with defence production — or at least they were not among those specifically exempted. When the project went through, however, the Ministry of the Defence Industry and the Ministry of the Aviation Industry remained. That this was a concession to the Army seems to be confirmed by the abolition of these ministries in December 1957, after Zhukov's fall, in favour of State Committees.

In the Anti-Party Group crisis Zhukov was plainly one of the most extreme opponents of the Group, and his support may have been decisive.

After the June plenum and the petering out of public references to the criminal nature of the Anti-Party Group's acts, the political struggle appeared to die down. On October 4, 1957, Zhukov left on a visit to Yugoslavia. His send-off was prominently reported. On October 26 his replacement as Minister of War by Marshal Malinovsky was announced by *Tass*. He returned the same day, an event given briefly, in small type, on the back page of *Pravda* (October 27).

On October 19 and 22 *Krasnaya Zvezda* had published long

articles on the Party as the 'guiding and directing force of the Army' — which may indicate that the operation to remove Zhukov had been definitely launched. It is not known when the plenum which expelled him from the Praesidium and the Central Committee took place (the *Tass* announcement, on November 2, says only 'late October'); but it must have been after Zhukov's return, since he is quoted as speaking at it. He was therefore removed from his Ministry before being disposed of at a Party level — a reversal of the procedure in the case of Malenkov and the 'Group'. This is most easily explicable by the idea that Khrushchev did not wish to risk allowing him access to control of the Armed Forces while his political liquidation was being put through. That the plenum was hastily assembled appears from the absence of most of those Central Committee members who were ambassadors abroad.

The substantive portion of the plenum's resolution (adopted unanimously) ran as follows:

The Plenary Session of the C.P.S.U. Central Committee notes that of late the former Defence Minister Comrade Zhukov has violated the Leninist Party principles for the guidance of the armed forces, pursued a policy of curtailing the work of Party organisations, political organs and military councils, of abolishing the leadership and control of the Party, its Central Committee and Government over the Army and Navy.

The Plenary Session of the Central Committee has established that the cult of Comrade Zhukov's personality was cultivated in the Soviet Army with his personal participation. With the help of sycophants and flatterers he was praised to the sky in lectures and reports, in articles, films and pamphlets, and his person and role in the great Fatherland War were over-glorified. Thereby, to please Comrade Zhukov, the true history of the war was distorted, the actual state of affairs was presented in a wrong light.

Comrade Zhukov did not justify the confidence reposed in him by the Party. He proved to be a politically unstable leader disposed to adventurism, both in his understanding of the main tasks of the Soviet Union's policy and in heading the Defence Ministry.

In connection with the aforesaid, the C.P.S.U. Central Committee Plenary Session has resolved to remove Comrade Zhukov from the Central Committee Praesidium and the C.P.S.U. Central Committee, and has instructed the C.P.S.U. Central Committee Secretariat to provide Zhukov with another job.

Zhukov is quoted as saying at the plenum:

In the course of the investigation some Comrades said that I had been once before excluded from the C.C. during Stalin's lifetime, in 1946, and that I had failed to understand the necessity of correcting those mistakes for which I was excluded. Then, Comrades, I could not recognise and did not recognise, that my exclusion from the C.C. was correct; I did not recognise that the accusations which had been made against me were correct. Now, it is a different matter. I recognise my mistakes; I have become profoundly aware of them in the course of the Plenary Session, and I give my word to the C.C. of the Party that I will eliminate completely those shortcomings which I possess (*Pravda*, November 3, 1957).

This is interesting on two counts: first as official confirmation that Zhukov had been disciplined in this way in Stalin's time; and, more curious still, that some Central Committee members were prepared to take up the Stalin line again — even though the printing of this point at all is evidently a rebuke to them. Zhukov's way of putting it, in fact, seems to be quite a well-considered attempt to divide his opponents, perhaps with a view to future possibilities.

The Marshals were assembled to condemn their late chief:

Among speakers at the Plenary Session of the C.C. of the C.P.S.U. were outstanding military leaders: Marshals of the U.S.S.R. Comrades Malinovsky, Konev, Rokossovsky, Sokolovsky, Eremenko, Timoshenko and Biryuzov; Admiral Gorshkov; Generals of the Army Gorbatov, Zakharov, Kazakov and others. Many of them had known Comrade Zhukov for decades in their joint work. They pointed out the serious shortcomings of Zhukov, sharply criticised the mistakes and distortions allowed by him and unanimously condemned his wrong, un-Party-like behaviour in the post of U.S.S.R. Minister of Defence (*Pravda*, November 3, 1957).

An article by Marshal Konev in the same issue of *Pravda* spoke of 'a separation between the Army and the Navy on the one hand and the Party on the other', and of 'a definite tendency to regard the Soviet armed forces as his own domain' on Zhukov's part.

Konev went on to attack Zhukov for failing to prepare for the German invasion of 1941, when Chief of Staff; of falsely claiming credit for Stalingrad; of responsibility for the failure of the Demyansk operation in 1943 and the Kamenets-Podolsk operation in 1944; and of blunders in the Berlin campaign — all these in some detail.

The accusation of a Zhukov 'cult of personality' was also rubbed in by his rival:

Lickspittles and toadies began to praise and extol Comrade Zhukov in lectures and reports, pamphlets and films. The artist Vasili Yakovlev particularly excelled himself in this respect. He painted a picture in which, against the background of the Brandenburg Gate and the burning Reichstag, he pictured Zhukov on a prancing white horse which had under its feet the banners of the defeated fascist Germany, exactly like St. George Nikephoros on an old ikon. From the artistic point of view this picture is of no value, but from the ideological point of view it is harmful. However, Comrade Zhukov gave an order for this picture to be displayed in the Museum of the Soviet Army.

Comrade Zhukov also had a hand in the script of the film 'The Battle of Stalingrad' which is being refilmed by a film studio. In the new version of this film, which is called 'The Great Battle', everything that related to the cult of Stalin has been removed, but Zhukov has taken a completely undeserved place. In the text of the film, read by the announcer, have appeared the words, personally introduced by Zhukov, that the evolving of the plan and practical preparation of the Stalingrad offensive operation was headed by Deputy Supreme Commander, Army General Zhukov and also the representative of H.Q., Col. Gen. Vasilevsky. As has been mentioned above, this assertion does not correspond with historical reality. Scenes picturing Zhukov in battles near Moscow and Berlin were included in this film artificially and without any connection with events.

It is characteristic that Comrade Zhukov himself spoke more than once against the cult of Stalin's personality, severely criticising him for his errors. However, this criticism was calculated not to assist the Party to eliminate the negative after-effects of the cult of personality, but to extol himself.

The account of the film is very reminiscent of Khrushchev's account, in the Secret Speech, of Stalin's 'Fall of Berlin' film.

It will be noted that Vasilevsky is not quoted against Zhukov and the above contains at least a hint that he too was under criticism. The *Small Soviet Encyclopaedia* (Vol. II, October 1958) has an article on Vasilevsky which concludes with his 'retirement through illness in December 1957' — that is, not until after the plenum. He had not been among the Marshals who attacked the Anti-Party Group, and it at least seems possible that he had shown himself favourable to them in some way. In the Secret Speech he is named, almost in the same breath as Malenkov, as one of those at the Centre under Stalin's thumb and not daring to put to Stalin the correct demands of Khrushchev from 'the front'. The treatment of him in 1957–58 was not too degrading, however. He is given a biography in the *Political Dictionary* (February and April 1958) as none of the Anti-Party Group are — (though Zhukov is). So his fault may have been merely one of omission, of unappreciated neutrality: his association with Bulganin may conceivably be relevant too.

A brief summary of Zhukov's offence, which seems sound, was:

The October plenum of the C.C. of the C.P.S.U. of 1957 severely condemned the harmful line of the former U.S.S.R. Minister of Defence, Zhukov, tending towards the curtailing of the work of Party organisations in political organs and military councils, towards the liquidation of Party, C.C. and Government leadership and control over the Army and Navy (Radio Moscow, February 6, 1958).

With Zhukov's fall the Army no longer had a spokesman at the highest policy level. The old line of giving Party figures credit for military achievement soon returned.

The *Large Soviet Encyclopaedia* says:

Great work for the strengthening of the fighting capacity of the forces and the mobilisation of the effort of the local population for the defence of Stalingrad was carried out by the member of the Politbureau of the Central Committee of the All-Union Communist Party, N. S. Khrushchev, a member of the Military Council of the Stalingrad Front.

Harassing and weakening the enemy, the Soviet forces prepared the Stalingrad counter-offensive. In working out the plan for a counter-offensive, the following took an active part: the Commander of the Stalingrad Front, General A. I. Eremenko, and the member of the Military Council, General N. S. Khrushchev; the Commander of the South-Western Front, General N. F. Vatutin, and the member of the Military Council, General A. S. Zheltov; the Commander of the Don Front, General K. K. Rokossovsky, and the member of the Military Council, A. I. Kirichenko. In working out the plan General

G. K. Zhukov also took a certain part as Deputy C. in C., and also the leading workers of the General Staff, headed by General A. M. Vasilevsky (*Large Soviet Encyclopaedia*, Vol. 50).

Vol. 50 was passed for publication on August 15, 1957. But later some last-minute alterations were made. Zhukov's removal is already reported, and his name is left out of a list of the Party Praesidium. The *Encyclopaedia*'s description is of interest not only because of the condescending tone concerning Zhukov, and the importance given to Khrushchev, but also because of the special mention made of Kirichenko. It is not that such praise was unprecedented so much as that it was now formally incorporated into history, to the exclusion of others.

Tribute to Khrushchev as an important figure in the Battle of Stalingrad was reiterated in, e.g., *Kommunist*, No. 1, 1958, in an article written by General Eremenko.

After Zhukov's fall, Zheltov was transferred from the Army Political Department to the Central Committee apparatus. We may perhaps regard this in the following light. As the Party enforcement officer he had attracted to himself over a period of years the main resentment of the professional generals, whether Zhukov supporters or not. To sacrifice him at this stage was to make it easier to rally anti-Zhukov sentiment behind the new arrangements. At the same time his long preservation of his post may have been due to Bulganin, whose views no longer counted. He was replaced by Lieut.-General Golikov, a career officer, though one much associated with the political apparatus (*Pravda*, January 10, 1958).

That some voices were raised in the Army against the new arrangements, and that some sort of purge of Zhukov supporters took place, is shown by a Party conference of the Soviet Armed Forces in Germany which heard a report on the October plenum. At this

The delegates did not agree with opinions voiced by Comrade Shaposhnikov. Comrade Shaposhnikov was right in stating that the demagogic statements of those who tried to use criticism as a means to settle personal accounts, and not for the further strengthening of the combat readiness and a higher level of Party-political work, should be condemned as contrary to Party principles. However, the conclusion of Comrade Shaposhnikov's statement was in effect a call for restraint of criticism (*Sovietskaya Armiya*, February 13, 1959).

z

The rapporteur, Lieut.-General Efimov, had already spoken:

Comrade Efimov gave convincing examples of *many* commanders and political workers who, during the discussions of the decisions of the October Plenary Session of the C.P.S.U. Central Committee, had been criticised but are now striving to eliminate their shortcomings. [My italics: C. R.]

The removal of Army General Luchinsky at about this time from G.O.C. Turkestan Military District may also be relevant.

A rather comic episode, which yet has something of the spirit of the times, was when, the following year, Major-General I. Petrov, chief of the Soviet Army's Military Band Service, was accused of the 'cult of personality' and dismissed. *Krasnaya Zvezda* of October 14, 1958, said that Petrov had failed to draw any of the necessary conclusions from Zhukov's dismissal, accused him of 'organising commercial performances' from which he 'produced an income', and declared that his music was 'at times artistically feeble'. In reply to the charges levelled against him the paper said, Petrov 'accused the Party officials of deliberate exaggeration of the facts'.

Attacks on Zhukov remained scarce, however, unlike those against the Anti-Party Group. The essence of the accusations against the Marshal may be seen in two speeches early in 1959. One was when, in the only reference to Zhukov at the XXIst Party Congress, Malinovsky said on February 3, 1959,

The C.C. of the C.P.S.U. discerned in an extremely timely manner the aspiration of the former Minister of Defence, Marshal Zhukov, to sever the Army from the Party, and gave this new Bonaparte a sharp rap over the knuckles.

The 'Bonaparte' is only a vague accusation of seeking power. But the 'extremely' timely action of the Central Committee gives a curious impression that some dangerous move was just thwarted.

At the Ukrainian Congress just before the XXIst Congress, Marshal Chuikov had said:

The October plenum of the C.C. of the C.P.S.U. cut short the revisionist line of the former Minister of Defence Zhukov, which was directed towards the liquidation of the direction and control over the army and navy by the Party, its Central Committee and Soviet

Government, and restored the Leninist principles of the control of troops (Speech of Marshal Chuikov at the XXth Congress of the C.P. of the Ukraine) (*Pravda Ukrainy*, January 18, 1959).

'Revisionism' in this context may signify no more than a denial of the Party's claim to competence and control in every sphere. Yet Zhukov appears to have been a more consistent opponent of 'Stalinism' than Khrushchev was, and it may to some extent have a general political significance. A revisionist Bonaparte is, in any case, a phenomenon the regime was glad to be rid of.

The career of Zhukov makes it clear that all factions united in regarding him as the one leading figure who could, in any real sense, 'speak for the Army'. He seems to have been the one man who could be thought of as being capable of wielding the Army's influence as an independent political force with a reasonable certainty of being backed up.

When the situation was fluid in 1953, his support seemed necessary. But once he was in a position of strength it became even more necessary, and he rose with each crisis, until he was, to all appearances, so strong as to represent a real danger to Party rule in its present form. This happened at the same time that his support was no longer needed, all other factions and power centres having been crushed. The motives compelling Khrushchev to turn on him were thus very strong ones.

CHAPTER FOURTEEN

KHRUSHCHEV'S ASCENDANCY AND THE XXIst CONGRESS, 1957–59

BETWEEN the fall of Zhukov and the XXIst Congress a period ensued which was marked, as became clear at the Central Committee plenum of December 1958, by a long-drawn-out struggle on Khrushchev's part to break the compromise by which the Anti-Party Group had been expelled only from the Central Committee, and at the same time to destroy the influences still prepared both to defend them and to oppose certain of his policies. This campaign originally centred on Bulganin.

On July 3, 1957, in addition to the expulsion from the Central Committee of Malenkov, Kaganovich, Molotov and Shepilov — always given in this order, which is hard to interpret unless it be one of criminal responsibility — Pervukhin was demoted to junior member of the Praesidium and Saburov was removed from it entirely. The four main culprits were removed from all their Government posts on July 3, 1957, but at that time, while Saburov also lost his posts, Pervukhin, though demoted from his First Deputy Chairmanship of the Council of Ministers, retained his Ministry of Medium Machine Building. He was transferred from this to the less important State Committee for Foreign Economic Relations on July 24, 1957.

No public accusations were made at this time against Saburov or Pervukhin, any more than against Bulganin. The demotion was demonstration enough that the first two had erred. And it is curious that their emergence as full members of the Anti-Party Group came only in January 1959, two months after Bulganin's. The inference seems to be that during the intervening period Bulganin had continued to make himself obnoxious to Khrushchev.

Khrushchev's new Praesidium was still hardly monolithic. A superficial breakdown of its full members might be:

346

(a) Khrushchev himself, Kirichenko, Furtseva, Brezhnev and probably Belyaev, whose careers had depended very largely on his patronage.

(b) Aristov, Ignatov, Kozlov, Kuusinen, who had reached high posts without a Khrushchev connection, but who now attained or returned to the highest under his auspices.

(c) Mikoyan, Shvernik, Suslov, Voroshilov, Bulganin, whose rise had been quite independent of Khrushchev, and some of whom had opposed him even in the recent crisis.

(d) Zhukov.

This Praesidium thus showed signs of the compromise — further indicated by the retention of Pervukhin as a candidate member. In spite of the apparent scope of Khrushchev's victory, there were still forces in being capable of organising resistance to him in controversial matters, and of hindering any attempt to take absolute power. In particular, it is important to stress again that however appropriate it may have been to speak of such men as Aristov, Suslov and Kozlov as Khrushchev supporters when dealing with the struggles of 1953–57, it is necessary to remember that this was an alliance due to circumstances, some of them fortuitous, and not a master–client relationship. Organisationally speaking, the apparatchiks naturally supported the proponent of apparat rule against the representatives of the State; but this did not signify that Khrushchev had yet turned the apparat itself into a personal appanage, as Stalin had done.

The Government as constituted on July 5, 1957, with Bulganin still as Premier, had two First Deputy Chairmen — Mikoyan and Kuzmin, and one Deputy Chairman, Kosygin. From the end of July all three began to be referred to as Deputy Chairmen simply. On December 14 D. F. Ustinov was added to their number.

The plenum held on December 16 and 17, 1957, promoted Mukhitdinov to be a full member of the Praesidium and at the same time made Kirichenko, Ignatov and Mukhitdinov members of the Secretariat. This increased the Secretariat to ten members, all of them full members of the Praesidium, except for Pospelov the senior candidate member. The Secretariat in itself thus comprised a majority of the members of the Praesidium, an extraordinary and unprecedented hypertrophy of the Party machine. Moreover, it now included, as its second senior member, Kirichenko — that is to say a figure who, unlike Suslov and others, was from Khrushchev's personal following.

Meanwhile agricultural issues were again rearing their heads. The 1957 harvest ran into difficulties, especially in the Virgin Lands. On January 20, 1958, a joint statement by the Central Committee and the Council of Ministers announced that

For agriculture the year 1957 was a difficult one. A prolonged drought caused a serious situation in a vast territory, particularly in the areas of the Volga region, the South Urals and Kazakhstan. In the areas of the Lower and the Middle Volga region the drought was more severe than in the memorable year 1921. . . .

Dr. T. Yakubov of the Soil Research Institute of the Academy of Sciences of the U.S.S.R. had already written:

The area of the virgin and fallow lands of Kazakhstan is placed almost entirely within the boundaries of the steppe zone, the climatic conditions of which are characterised by several un-favourable peculiarities. . . .

Data obtained from observation show that in the area of the virgin and fallow lands of Northern Kazakhstan, dust storms pro-ducing wind erosion occur every year, and that the number of such storms rises from North to South, i.e. from the forest-steppe towards desert-steppe zones.

Due to unfavourable weather conditions, wind erosion of soil was widespread in the areas of virgin and fallow lands of Northern Kazakhstan in 1955. . . . The wind erosion has occurred again (*Kazakhstanskaya Pravda*, November 20, 1957).

Thus among the troubles in agriculture was precisely the erosion in the Virgin Lands against which the Anti-Party Group seem to have warned. Academician Tyurin, Director of the Soil Research Institute, went further, writing that new dust-bowls had been created in the last few years by wholesale ploughing of waste and virgin lands. This might lead to 'rapid and catastrophic improverishment of the soil' and even 'com-plete destruction of its fertility'. He adds that he is not referring to older trouble regions, but to the new areas in the east (*Izvestia*, May 7, 1958).

Tyurin urged a number of elementary precautions which

were apparently being neglected, but also called for crop rotation and more fallow. There had been various articles and speeches against erosion before, but none had put the dangers quite so flatly. In the circumstances it might seem either that this represented a view hostile to Khrushchev's agricultural schemes which was now evidently being put to the Central Committee, or, alternatively, a method for Khrushchev to transfer the blame for the troubles besetting his arrangements.* Even if the second view is the true one, there is still an implication of Khrushchev being on the defensive.

In any case it seems that agricultural questions became the main area of policy dispute in the early part of 1958. They were the main (published) theme at the plenum held on February 25–26, when Khrushchev put forward his thesis for merging the Machine Tractor Stations into the collective farms, a measure which Stalin had opposed (and 'preparations' for which the Anti-Party Group were later alleged to have hampered). Stalin's view was that to transfer the centralised and State-controlled stations to the 'lower form' of Socialist property not under State control, the kolkhozes, would *ipso facto* be a retrograde step. Khrushchev took the opposite view — that the introduction of the M.T.S. personnel and organisation into the farms would bring these closer to being State property and thus make their final absorption into it easier. Although this was argued ideologically, the matter of principle is a minor one. Both sides were thinking in terms of how to complete the evolution of the countryside into State property. The real question resolves itself into the practical one: would it be possible to exert more State control under the new system or the old? This remains to be seen.

But though the ideological issue was not truly important the whole business was the sort of thing which most easily creates controversy in Soviet conditions. And it seems likely that the opposition within the Praesidium argued against it. In any case, Bulganin was now under direct, though as yet unpublished, attack.

---

* It should be noted, however, that Khrushchev had hedged on the Virgin Lands at the XXth Congress, as follows: 'If, out of five years we have two good harvest years, one average, and two poor ones, it is still possible to farm to considerable advantage. . . .'

The election campaign for the new Supreme Soviet earlier in the month had given definite evidence of Bulganin's decline. In a leading article in *Pravda* of February 2, 1958, at the start of the campaign, other key figures were enumerated, but the Chairman of the Council of Ministers was not mentioned. The seven Praesidium members listed by name as candidates were Voroshilov, Kirichenko, Mikoyan, Mukhitdinov, Suslov, Shvernik and Khrushchev.

A surer sign of Bulganin's decline was now given.

An analysis of nineteen central newspapers and sixteen Republican newspapers for the period February 1–10, 1958, made by Radio Liberation's research team collates all the instances of members and candidate members of the Party Praesidium being put forward (vystavlenie) as candidates for election to the Supreme Soviet — i.e. as distinct from the final nominations. The result, in terms of the times each individual was put forward, is:

Full Members		Candidate Members	
Khrushchev	664	Pospelov	19
Voroshilov	309	Mzhavanadze	18
Kirichenko	223	Kosygin	16
Mikoyan	215	Kalnberzins	14
Suslov	141	Mazurov	13
Shvernik	117	Korotchenko	12
Aristov	109	Kirilenko	7
Brezhnev	107		
Ignatov	95		
Furtseva	94		
Mukhitdinov	71		
Kuusinen	61		
Kozlov	61		
Belyaev	54		
Bulganin	52		

This indication of Bulganin's decline was at once accepted as such by most experts.

The list may also be taken, up to a point, as symbolising a general order of seniority among the full members — though Kozlov and Belyaev, identified at this point with particular republics (the R.S.F.S.R. and Kazakhstan, respectively), seem to have received little nomination outside their own areas, and

there are other considerations affecting it slightly. But the first
five, for example, were to figure as the leading group throughout the year following.

If we divide the scores into three groups, with natural breaks,
we find that these come between Shvernik and Suslov and between Mukhitdinov and Furtseva. There is very little differences,
certainly not enough to be significant, in the scoring among the
second five, or among the third five. And though Shvernik later
is given in appearances lower than he stands here, Aristov,
Brezhnev, Ignatov and Furtseva come together in various
orders, which seems to show a comparative equality.

Some relevant public appearances early in 1958 are:

(1) Komsomol Celebrations (*Pravda*, April 16, 1958):

> Voroshilov, Khrushchev, Mikoyan, Kirichenko, Sus-
> lov, Aristov, Ignatov, Bulganin, Brezhnev, Furtseva,
> Mukhitdinov, Shvernik.

(2) Lenin's Birthday (*Pravda*, April 23, 1958).

> Khrushchev, Mikoyan, Kirichenko, Suslov, Aristov,
> Shvernik, Ignatov, Kuusinen, Mukhitdinov.

(3) May Day (*Pravda*, May 2, 1958)

> Voroshilov, Khrushchev, Mikoyan, Kirichenko, Suslov,
> Furtseva, Kozlov, Bulganin, Aristov, Ignatov, Brezhnev,
> Shvernik, Kuusinen, Mukhitdinov.

Bulganin had by this time been removed from the Premiership. His formal listing is here higher than his practical position,
just as in the case of Molotov at the XIXth Congress. Shvernik's position also seems low. But the first five, apart from the
purely ceremonial status of Voroshilov, is solid, and henceforward became constant. Towards the end of the year it was
often given even in print (with Khrushchev before Voroshilov)
and not merely in appearance — though the alphabetical
method continued also to be used. After the XXIst Congress in
January 1959 several foreign Communist delegations were received by Khrushchev, Mikoyan, Kirichenko and Suslov, as if
by a committee of senior members of the Praesidium, and in
that order.

Saburov was not elected to the new Supreme Soviet. Peruvkhin was appointed, on February 20, 1958, to the junior post of Ambassador to East Germany.

When the Supreme Soviet met, Bulganin was removed from the Chairmanship of the Council of Ministers and on March 31, 1958, Khrushchev became Prime Minister as well as First Secretary of the Central Committee. D. F. Ustinov and Zasyadko became Deputy Chairmen of the Council of Ministers, and F. R. Kozlov, who had previously briefly served as Chairman of the Council of Ministers of the R.S.F.S.R. (having been replaced in his Leningrad First Secretaryship by the unknown Spiridonov), was made a First Deputy Chairman.

Bulganin figured in the Government as its forty-fourth ranking figure, Head of the State Bank. This was final confirmation that he had been under fire at the February plenum. The demotion was a much greater one than Malenkov had suffered in February 1955, and may indicate a far heavier defeat. Yet Bulganin anomalously remained a member of the Praesidium, even when further demoted to be head of the Stavropol C.N.E., through two more plenums, only being removed in September. This most probably represents a struggle on the part of still powerful interests to save him, just as he himself was later accused of trying to save Malenkov.

Khrushchev's new team of vice-premiers deserves looking at. Mikoyan's and Kozlov's positions speak for themselves. The other four were Kuzmin, Kosygin, Zasyadko and D. F. Ustinov.

Ustinov had been Minister in Charge of the Armaments Industry since the war. The position of Zasyadko is odder, in certain respects. He had become Minister of the Coal Industry in January 1949, when Zademidko's Ministry of Fuel Construction undertakings was merged with it. On March 2, 1955 he was heavily criticised and dismissed (to reappear later as Ukrainian Coal Minister). Meanwhile Zademidko got his post. In 1956 Zasyadko was not elected a member of the new Central Committee or even of the Revision Commission. So far, one would have said, the tie-up with Malenkov seems extremely probable. If so, he must have worked his passage in the Ukraine. On April 27, 1957, he was made a Hero of Socialist Labour for his Ukrainian coal work. In May he very strongly urged the Khrushchev plan to abolish the central ministries — to the extent, in fact, that in his speech of May 11, 1957, Khrushchev took him to task for suggesting the abolition of the Defence Industry Ministries. In this he was perhaps only a stalking-horse, for he was almost at once appointed a Vice-Chairman of the new central Gosplan and now in April 1958 became Deputy Chairman of the Council of Ministers.

The new Council of Ministers numbered forty-five (not counting the Chairmen of the Councils of Ministers of the Union Republics, who are ex-officio members of the U.S.S.R. Government under Article 70 of the Constitution), as against thirty-five in the post-purge Government of July 1957. The changes, apart from the transformation of the Ministries of State Control, the Defence Industry, the Aviation Industry, the Radio-technical Industry and the Ship-building Industry into State Committees, were, first, the entry of no fewer than seven Deputy Chairmen and departmental heads of Gosplan into the Government as well as its chairman — a probable indication of the virtual growth of its sections into something resembling the Ministries dissolved early the previous year, and secondly the increase in the number of Deputy Chairmen of the Council — Khrushchev having Kozlov, Mikoyan, Kosygin, Zasyadko, Kuzmin and Ustinov, as against Bulganin's July 1957 Deputies, Mikoyan, Kuzmin and Kosygin.

Khruschchev's double appointment was a major assertion of one-man leadership, of a sort that had not been seen in the U.S.S.R. since Malenkov's abandonment of the Secretaryship in March 1953.* The concentration can hardly be seen as necessary, or even useful, from any other point of view.

The appointment was accompanied by comments very much in the 'cult of personality' line, as in *Party Life* (No. 7, 1958), which said:

In appointing Comrade N.S. Khrushchev Chairman of the Council of Ministers of the U.S.S.R., the Supreme Soviet gave expression to the will of the entire Soviet people. Comrade Khrushchev has already been serving the interests of the working people and of the great cause of Communism for over forty years. It is generally recognised that the last few years in the life of our country have been

---

* Indeed, Khrushchev is said by Imre Nagy to have condemned one man holding the two posts in Hungary as contrary to collective leadership. (See Appendix IX.)

heralded by substantial new successes in all fields of Communist construction. Soviet people know that a great share in this belongs to Comrade N. S. Khrushchev, to his outstanding creative talents and truly inexhaustible energy and initiative.

Another ideological event of key interest was the appearance of the *Sta* volume of the *Large Soviet Encyclopaedia* (Vol. 40) in 1958. There had been a delay of over eighteen months, during which all the subsequent alphabetical volumes had appeared. The trouble was plainly the Stalin biography. Its final form may be taken as representing the considered position of the Khrushchev regime on the subject.

The article is one of only six pages, as against forty-four in the previous edition. Stalin's role in the revolution is toned down, though not to the extent of giving credit to the 'opposi-timists'. He is praised for exposing Trotskyite and Rightist deviations and carrying out collectivisation and industralisa-tion. The biography, unlike Khrushchev's Secret Speech, has little to say on the purges in the 'thirties, and what it says is far more moderate in tone. Stalin is said to have applied unneces-sary mass repression against ideological opponents. This he did, it is stated, on the basis of the mistaken thesis he advanced in 1937 that the class struggle would become increasingly intense during the construction of Socialism. Besides neglecting the pre-1937 purges, the *Encyclopaedia* places most of the responsi-bility for the liquidation of the innocent on other shoulders:

In this situation the accursed enemies of the people, Yagoda, Yezhov and Beria, who had wormed their way into J. V. Stalin's confidence, slandered and destroyed many honourable and devoted Party people.

As far as his war policies are concerned, Stalin is credited with making 'a serious contribution to the defence of the coun-try and the struggle against Fascism' and with taking all pos-sible measures for strengthening the anti-fascist coalition. On the other hand, he is said to have attached excessive significance to the Nazi–Soviet Pact and, as a result, to have disbelieved reports of German military preparations and rejected proposals for strengthening Soviet forces on the frontier. This was partly responsible for the early defeat of the Soviet Army. Further, in his conduct of certain important military operations he disregarded the opinions of members of the Central Committee engaged on military duties on the spot, with disastrous consequences. This recalls the passage in Khrushchev's Secret Speech, where he attacked Stalin for refusing his advice on the Kharkhov operation. There is no mention in the biography of Stalin's part in the wartime mass deportations of several Caucasian nationalities.

Very little is said of Stalin's post-war activities. The publication of his works, *Marxism and Questions of Linguistics* and *Economic Problems of Socialism* is noted, the latter with the warning that certain of its propositions, including that on the inevitability of a decrease in capitalist production after the war, were fallacious. It is also stated that Stalin often made mistaken decisions on economic questions; rejected measures proposed by members of the Central Committee; and made serious mistakes in foreign policy — e.g. the break with Yugoslavia.

Considerable space is given to the personality cult theme. Seeking to prove that the personality cult is not endemic in the Soviet system, the biography attributes its emergence both to negative features in Stalin's character and to specific conditions which prevailed during the period of the construction of Socialism. As a result, although the lower Party organisations continued to function normally, Central Committee plenums and Party Congresses were not held for a number of years, and Stalin became impervious to all criticism.

In conclusion it is emphasised that while the personality cult inflicted considerable damage on Soviet life, it had no great influence on the development of the Soviet State. This provides the key to the whole biography. The final passages include,

His name is inseparable from Marxism–Leninism and it would be a most flagrant distortion of historical truth to spread the mistakes made by Stalin in the last years of his life to all his Party and State activity extending over many years. The campaign undertaken by reactionary imperialist circles against the 'Stalinism' they themselves have contrived in fact constitutes a campaign against the revolutionary workers' movement. The attacks by revisionists against so-called 'Stalinism' are also essentially a form of struggle against the fundamental positions of Marxism–Leninism.

A further ideological announcement gave a clear idea of both the differentiation and the similarities of the Khrushchev and

Stalin lines, and asserted a 'Molotov–Malenkov–Beria' link, of a sort which was to appear again. This was the resolution of the C.P.S.U. Central Committee of May 28, 1958, referred to earlier, on the rectification of mistakes made in the assessment of the operas 'Great Friendship', 'Bogdan Khmelnitsky' and 'From the Bottom of the Heart':

The C.P.S.U. Central Committee notes that the Central Committee's Resolution of February 10, 1948, on V. Muradeli's opera 'Great Friendship' on the whole played a positive role in the development of Soviet musical art. This Resolution set out the tasks of developing musical art on the basis of the principles of socialist realism, stressed the importance of the bonds of art with the life of the Soviet people, with the finest democratic traditions of classical music and the creative work of the people. It justly condemned formalistic tendencies in music, fanciful 'innovation' which divorced art from the people and made it a possession of a narrow circle of epicure aesthetics. The subsequent development of Soviet music confirmed the correctness and timeliness of these Party recommendations.

At the same time, the assessment of the work of some composers given in the Resolution was in a number of cases groundless and unjust. V. Muradeli's opera 'Great Friendship' had shortcomings which merited businesslike criticism, but there was no ground for declaring the opera to be an example of formalism in music. Such gifted composers as D. Shostakovich, S. Prokofyev, A. Khachaturyan V. Shebalin, G. Popov, N. Myaskovsky and others, some of whose works revealed incorrect tendencies, were described in a sweeping manner as exponents of an anti-popular formalistic trend in art.

Contrary to historical facts, an artificial contrasting of some North Caucasian peoples to others had been permitted in the Resolution in connection with criticism of Muradeli's opera. Some of the incorrect assessments made in the aforesaid Resolution reflected J. V. Stalin's subjective attitude to individual works of art and creative endeavour. J. V. Stalin's subjective attitude to the evaluation of individual works of art was also manifested in the one-sided and tendencious criticism of K. Dankevich's opera 'Bogdan Khmelnitsky' and G. Zhukovsky's opera 'From the Bottom of the Heart' contained in the editorial articles published in *Pravda* on his orders in 1951. In deciding these questions Stalin is known to have been very negatively influenced by Molotov, Malenkov and Beria.

The next plenum, held on May 6–8, 1958, discussed the chemical industry. Its main unpublished theme was certainly Yugoslavia. This was the period following the publication of the Yugoslav Party programme, which had led to the refusal of the Soviet delegation to attend the Yugoslav Party Congress in spite of previous arrangements to do so. Relations with Yugoslavia had been cool since the refusal of the Yugoslav delegation to the Moscow Conference of Communist Parties the previous November to sign the substantive manifesto, but it was only now that a definite break was decided on. There is no particular reason to see any direct implications for the Soviet struggle for power as it then was in this episode. On the other hand, the immediate blow against revisionism — the execution of Imre Nagy (whose trial had significantly been held in two parts, one in February and one in June) — must certainly have been regarded even by those wholly out of sympathy with the Hungarian ex-Premier as a precedent with unfortunate implications for the Soviet Union's own leaders of inadequately Khrushchevite leanings.

In June a further agricultural plenum was held, and Podgorny and Polyansky were made candidate members of the Praesidium, Podgorny, First Secretary in the Ukraine, was a veteran of Khrushchev's Ukrainian machine. Polyansky's affiliations with the First Secretary were less complete, but his rise had been entirely under his auspices. These additions to the candidate members gave Khrushchev remarkably little advantage, and the removal of Bulganin was even now not consummated.

It finally took place in September, at a one-day plenum which called the XXIst Congress, with a single item on the agenda — the 'control figures' of the Seven-Year Plan, on which Khrushchev was to be rapporteur.

This XXIst Congress was to be 'Special'. The Party statutes provide for normal congresses and for 'Extraordinary' ones. The latter has or can have all the powers of an ordinary one. An ordinary congress was due by February 1960, and there seems no reason why — even with the launching of the Seven-Year Plan being an important event — a regular congress should not have been convened. The XXIst Congress agenda was simply this item, the Plan. But there could have been no difficulty in preparing the other usual items of a congress agenda. An important difference between the XXIst and other congresses was that no new Central Committee was elected. Even a conference (though these are no longer permitted) used to be able to make considerable changes in the Central Committee, in spite of not being allowed formally to elect a new one. At the Party Conference of February 1941 four members and fifteen candidate members were removed, and two members were reduced to candidate: four candidates were promoted to full membership, together with two hitherto not in the Committee at all, and seventeen new candidates were brought in (the whole procedure leaving the numbers in each case exactly as before). But the 'Special' XXIst Congress did not even do this. It is natural to conclude that this was the true distinctive feature of the Congress, perhaps forced upon the First Secretary by a majority not wishing a change.

During the earlier part of the year the organisation, or at least the practical results, of the economic decentralisation schemes had been under attack.

A decree of April 28, 1958, reveals serious defects:

The non-implementation by leading and other official persons in enterprises, economic organisations, C.N.E.s, Ministries and departments of plans and tasks for the delivery of products to other Economic Areas or Union Republics, as well as for all-Union requirements, is a gross violation of State discipline and involves disciplinary, material or criminal responsibility. Leading and other official persons of enterprises, economic organisations, C.N.E.s, Ministries and authorities found guilty of not implementing, without valid reasons, plans and tasks for such deliveries are liable to strict disciplinary penalties or to a monetary fine amounting to the equivalent of up to three months' salary, according to the legislations to be enacted by Union Republics. In the case of repeated failures without valid reason to implement plans and tasks for the delivery of products to other Economic Areas and Union Republics, as well as for all-Union requirements, the above mentioned persons will be prosecuted as for a criminal breach of trust (*Pravda*, May 19, 1958).

The following day *Pravda* (May 20, 1958) commented upon the decree in these terms:

Facts . . . show that in a number of places violations of State discipline are permitted. This finds its expression in the fact that individual economic, Government and Party workers are acting against the interests of the State to please local interests. They permit the non-implementation of plans for co-operation deliveries, sometimes they arbitrarily alter confirmed plans and switch funds intended for capital construction work to other secondary purposes, to so-called 'local requirements'.

This 'localism' — 'myestnichestvo' — was complained of in numbers of localities. *Pravda* spoke of Alma Ata's 'priority delivery of material to enterprises under its own jurisdiction to the detriment of other economic areas'. *Pravda Vostoka* (the Uzbek organ) of May 22 criticised the Uzbek C.N.E.s in general, in almost the same words, speaking also of 'gross violation' at Tashkent and elsewhere and 'extremely unsatisfactory' cotton supply work.

The violations that had led to the decree had been mentioned since the previous year. *Pravda* (December 2, 1957) speaks of Bashkiria paralysing the building industry of Tataria by withdrawing its labour, as soon as the new system came into force. In the Ukraine the Stalino-Donbas C.N.E. had failed to comply with Gosplan instructions to send steel elsewhere, and had kept it; Dnepropetrovsk C.N.E. had, 'without any justification', appropriated thousands of tons of its steel and iron allocated to others; 'such cases are not exceptional'.

The reasons for this sort of thing were clearly understood — the absence of any medium of exchange to replace the old system of orders from above. But the remedy does not seem to have suggested itself:

The most difficult problem of all in the new conditions appears to be that of supplies. . . . Let us be frank: The search for new ways of supply and circulation of goods has taken longer [than expected]. . . . Moreover, a patently unhealthy state of affairs has developed. A large number of 'go-betweens' have appeared, who travel all over the country looking out for some additional raw materials and equipment and disorganise the normal supply (*Pravda*, January 19, 1958).

The Sixth Five-Year Plan directives, in line with Khrushchev pronouncements, had been approved by the XXth Congress in February 1956; nevertheless the detailed plan failed to materialise, and by the end of 1956 long-term planning had

A A

broken down. In December the Central Committee had adopted Saburov's proposal that the annual plan for 1957 should be scaled down and a revised, detailed, Sixth Five-Year Plan prepared by mid-1957. There had been, however, no sign of its appearance when, at the end of June, Khrushchev's enemies made their abortive stand.

In September 1957 the Sixth Five-Year Plan had been abandoned without the Central Committee being consulted, and the planning and economic organs had been instructed to prepare, by July 1, 1958, a draft plan for a seven-year period, 1959–65. In his speech on the Fortieth Anniversary, on November 11, 1957, of the Revolution, Khrushchev proclaimed grandiose targets for the next twenty-five years.

With such targets in view the 1959–65 Plan would have had to return to something like the tempo of the Sixth Five-Year Plan; it seemed that, politically, Khrushchev was now in a position to effect this. Yet July 1, 1958, passed without the draft appearing; and when the Central Committee met on September 5 it was only to authorise its publication in due course as 'Theses' for a report by Khrushchev to the XXIst Congress.

After two months' further delay the 'Theses' (together with proposals for reorganising education) were presented on November 12 to a one-day plenum of the Committee, approved and published. Evidently this plenum was purely formal; it served to furnish Khrushchev's 'Theses' with a further stamp of approval, not apparently contemplated in September and best explicable on the assumption that opposition to his policies had not been eradicated. The delay in producing the outline of the plan had suggested as much; Khrushchev provided confirmation at the plenum by naming Bulganin as a member of the Anti-Party Group.

At this stage Bulganin was simply intruded into the old list of the Anti-Party Group as if he had figured there all along, and nothing further was said:

Creatively developing Marxism–Leninism, the Party is waging a determined struggle against all who cling to old and outlived forms and methods of work, and who, infected with conservatism, resist the implementation of the Lenin general line of the Party. The June Plenary Session of the C.C. of the C.P.S.U. unmasked and routed the Anti-Party Group of Malenkov, Kaganovich, Molotov, Bulganin, and Shepilov who joined them, which waged a struggle against the Lenin general line of the Party, against the political course adopted by the XXth C.P.S.U. Congress, against the leading role of the Party, and slid along the path of fractional, dissident activity (Theses on Khrushchev's Report on the Seven-Year Plan to the November 1958 plenum of the C.C., *Pravda*, November 14, 1958).

In the theses a leading ideological point was made:

As a result of the victory of socialism, the U.S.S.R. has entered a new historical period of gradual passage from socialism to communism. The long-term plan for the development of the Soviet Union in the next 15 years provides for the creation of the indispensable conditions for the completion of the transition to communism. The putting into practice of the seven-year plan for the development of the national economy of the U.S.S.R. for 1959–65 will represent a decisive stage in the creation of the material and technical basis of communism (ibid.).

This was developed in its main area of practical application, agriculture, as follows:

The programme outlined for the further development of agriculture will be accompanied by a perfecting of socialist production relations, the bringing closer together of the two forms of socialist property, the collective farm type and the all-national. This will be manifested in the further development of the collective farm system, the growth of production funds, the increase of the non-distributed funds of collective farms and their correct use, the expansion of inter-collective farm production relations through the joint organisation of industry, building and other economic enterprises, the joint construction of electric power stations, roads, irrigation and drainage systems, enterprises for the processing and storage of agricultural produce, schools, and especially boarding schools, homes for those of advanced years, hospitals and clubs.

As collective farm production develops, in conditions in which the collective farms become major enterprises equipped with leading machinery and with qualified cadres at its disposal, the material and social requirements of the collective farmers will come to be met more and more at the expense of communal husbandry. And, therefore, the private, supplementary husbandries of collective farmers will gradually lose their significance.

The State farms, whose role in socialist agriculture has in the recent period increased considerably, will develop as model socialist enterprises, setting an example to the collective farms in the best way of exploiting land and machinery to obtain a maximum yield of agricultural produce with the least expenditure of funds and labour. The development of the State farms will be directed towards a more active involvement of male and female workers in direct control of production.

The new stage in the development of the collective farm system, the enhancement of the role played by the State farms in raising agricultural production, will enable an abundance of agricultural produce to be created more swiftly, and this is a most important condition in the transition to communism (ibid.).

As *Oktyabr*, No. 12 of 1958, stated, it was planned to set up 'large-scale monolithic farms of the industrial type, that is farms which would realise the maximum specialisation and division of labour'. As a practical means 'we shall introduce an exclusively cash payment for labour, as in any State enterprise . . . within from six to eight years'. Hence the amalgamated collective farm-M.T.S. would in practice become no longer even formally co-operative, but something resembling in most ways a State farm.

There is also a reversion to something closely approaching the Stalinist attitude proper in a number of formulations. We may appropriately quote a typical one by D. Chesnokov, the ideologist of the Doctors' Plot Praesidium (who had long been in obscure posts) in *Questions of History of the C.P.S.U.* (No. 5 of 1958): 'the withering away of the state in communist society will come about by an increase in its role. This will all take place in the very distant future. . . .'

With the attack at the November plenum the public campaign against the Anti-Party Group, which had notably slackened, began to pick up again. In *Pravda* of November at least seven issues carry attacks on them. Kuusinen wrote a typical article there giving the new line associating the Seven-Year Plan with the defeat of the Group:

This is a majestic programme for bold development of communist society. Now it seems that even the blind must see what great harm the group of Malenkov, Molotov, Kaganovich, Bulganin and Shepilov would have done the cause of the Party, had this Anti-Party Group not been exposed in good time and routed. These bankrupt conservatives, who had separated themselves from the life of the people, were struggling against Lenin's general Party line, against the political line accepted by the XXth C.P.S.U. Congress, against the vital indispensable measures undertaken by the Party in the fields of home and foreign policy, and drifted on to the road of splitting activities. By removing the Anti-Party Group from the road, our Party has still further strengthened the Leninist unity of its ranks, and gathered them closer under the great banner of Marxism–Leninism. By doing so, the Party has opened the road to living Marxism–Leninism and mobilised the energy and initiative of the millions strong popular masses for the speediest construction of communism (*Pravda*, November 22, 1958).

This is typical of the more moderate of two lines to be taken about the group in the coming months. Its characteristics are:

(*a*) It is mainly an attack on the policy views of the Group.
(*b*) It refers briefly, and not in abusive terms, to their 'splitting' activities.
(*c*) It speaks of them as having been 'routed' and 'removed' as a matter that is over and done with.

In December, Serov was removed from the K.G.B. in circumstances roughly paralleling the removal of Kruglov from the M.V.D. just before the XXth Congress. This meant the departure of the last of the 'professionals' from the top leadership of the Police apparatus. It can be read, in part at least, as a popular gesture in favour of that 'Socialist legality' which the Anti-Party Group were being accused of ignoring

On December 29 Shelepin was appointed to the vacant post. The transfer of a leader from the Central Committee apparatus to head the Police is no guarantee of relaxation: the previous such moves were of Yezhov and Ignatiev respectively. Shelepin's background becomes relevant. He had been a Secretary of the Komsomol Central Committee since 1943, but was only made its First Secretary in November 1952, at the time of Stalin's preparation of cadres for the Doctors' Plot. He kept this post until April 1958, when he became head of a Central Committee department — evidently Party Organs (Union Republics).

In December 1958, too, a new Decree on State Crimes replaced the articles of the Criminal Codex of the R.S.F.S.R. hitherto dealing with the theme. The new Decree has Sections I to X under the heading 'Particularly Dangerous State

Crimes'. Article I covers 'plotting with the aim of seizing power', prescribing ten to fifteen years' imprisonment or death. This offence was not dealt with as such under earlier codes, and it has been plausibly interpreted as aiming at the June 1957 events.

There had also been some signs of a 'Vigilance Campaign'. An article in *Party Life* (No. 21 of November 1958) by Moskovsky, Head of the Central Committee Department of Agitation and Propaganda (R.S.F.S.R.), said that 'Carelessness and complacency have gained strength in recent times'. It argued that Soviet successes had given 'some short-sighted people' the wrong impression. But ordinary citizens must back the State Security Organs and be 'its billions of eyes and billions of ears'. In quite the style of 1952, the writer criticises some institutions, organisations and individual enterprises for 'slipshod carelessness in keeping secret documents'. 'Chatterboxes are a real find for the enemy's agents', and they exist even among those who are entrusted with State secrets — these being 'direct accomplices of imperialist intelligence'. Moskovsky comments: 'Some people imagine that since we have now lived for forty-one years under the Soviet Government and our cadres have grown up under socialism there is no reason to doubt anyone's political reliability' and refers to the Stalinist decree of June 1947 on 'Those Guilty of the Violation of State Secrets' as still in force.

Thus, as the Congress approached there were at least some signs of the preparation of a purge atmosphere. And throughout the year there had been indications of struggle taking place on the issues of agriculture, industrial organisation and the new Plan, and the Anti-Party Group. Opposition in all these fields seems to have been rather of a harassing or delaying nature than anything in the form of a challenge. Nevertheless, the amount of manœuvring and the time involved in forcing Bulganin gradually downwards in plenum after plenum, show that the struggle was a hard fought one.

On December 15 yet another plenum was assembled — the sixth of the year. The mere holding of these November and December plenums, between that which called the Congress and the Congress itself, is peculiar. The themes — approval of the Theses, and Agriculture, were hardly ones requiring sessions at this time. That there were at least some other motives is shown by the Bulganin developments — removed from the Praesidium in the September plenum, mentioned as a member of the Anti-Party Group in the November one, and now publicly attacked in the December one. The constant appeal to the Central Committee also seems to show that the Praesidium was not giving the answer Khrushchev wanted. But the Central Committee, too, was proving slow and reluctant.

The fierceness of the attacks made on the opposition at the December 1958 plenum certainly led a number of speakers to blur the truth about the Anti-Party Group. Whereas the June 1957 plenum had only spoken of the Group, as such, coalescing quite recently, now *all* previous opposition to proposals by Khrushchev was treated as *group* activity, which it had not really been. However, in the report Khrushchev gave certain fresh information. He said:

In this report, I shall not dwell in detail on all the shameful activities of this group. But speaking of the Party's and people's struggle to achieve a sharp upsurge in agriculture, it is impossible not to mention how this group in recent years stubbornly resisted the implementation of the most important measures in agriculture, thereby delaying the development of the country's economy. As known, the Anti-Party Group fought against the Party's policy of cultivating the virgin lands.

In June 1957 Molotov alone had been blamed for this particular sin. And in certain agricultural matters the emphasis is still put on him. He is named first or alone in the following passages:

The Anti-Party Group's opposition to the Party's most important measures to strengthen collective farms and to improve the collective farmers' prosperity bears witness to the fact that Molotov, Kaganovich, Malenkov and others did not understand agriculture, that they had a wrong attitude to the peasantry, regarding it as a force resisting socialist construction. This false line which is contrary to Lenin's views with regard to men and women collective farmers led in practice to the difficult agriculture situation which existed until 1953.

How in fact can one reconcile with the aim of raising agriculture a proposal by Molotov that every province must provide its own supplies of potatoes? Despite objections, Molotov succeeded in having this proposal accepted. . . .

Or let us take for example another proposal by Molotov — to increase the amount subscribed to loans in the countryside. He motivated this proposal by stating that collective farmers were playing only a small part in subscribing to loans — signed for small sums and less than people in towns. Molotov succeeded in having this proposal adopted. . . .

When the idea of reclaiming the virgin lands was born, Molotov and the other members of the Anti-Party Group, opposing this measure of the Party and State, attempted to prove that allegedly the cost of reclaiming virgin lands would not be repaid and that the matter was allegedly unprofitable from the economic point of view. Subsequent years disposed of these nonsensical assertions.

At the December 1958 plenum the number of Central Committee members was stated to be 124, plus 115 candidates. This shows that the places of those who had died or been expelled since the XXth Congress had not been filled. This can only have been as the result of some sort of standstill agreement. It is inconceivable that the First Secretary would not have wished to intrude Spiridonov and Kuzmin, for example, into the Committee,

Eighty-five members and candidates entered their names to speak. The theme, agriculture, may have been one on which a number of members felt incompetent to intervene, but a rough estimate would be that about half of those who might have spoken did not do so. Those who did were all, of course, enthusiastic for the Khrushchev proposals.

In his report Khrushchev hinted strongly at the expulsion of the Group from the Party. He said of Malenkov, Kaganovich, Molotov, Bulganin and Shepilov, that 'one cannot bring oneself to refer to such people as "comrades", even though they remained members of the Party'.

Khrushchev also brought up the Beria link, saying of the impossibility of getting a correct agricultural policy before September 1953, 'Beria, the inveterate enemy of the Party and the people, hindered this most of all. No minor role was played in this affair by the members of the Anti-Party Group — Malenkov, Kaganovich, Molotov.'

The circumstances of Bulganin's 'confession' at the December 1958 plenum illustrate many of the processes of the power-struggle. He made his confession, in terms which at first might appear to be adequately abject. But it then appeared that he was failing to do all that was required of him. The episode resembled in many respects what occurred in the early 'thirties in the cases of the opportunists of that period, and seemed to indicate that Party conventions which had been in disuse had not become obsolete. He was attacked for insincerity, for concealing the extent of his activities. And (so many speakers said) he had tried to maintain that his adherence to the Anti-Party Group had been a last-minute aberration. Then, he had failed to 'disarm himself completely' (an expression also used of Zinoviev and others in their time) 'and tell honestly about his subversive work and about the roots which have still remained' (speech of V. V. Matskevich). This last phrase foreshadowed the implication of yet other anti-Party cadres.

Several speakers mentioned Bulganin's 'earlier speeches' (Ignatiev) and his 'speech at a previous plenum' (Snechkus) as being equally unsatisfactory, and it is thus clear that the matter had been discussed before, and that Bulganin had continued to take an unsatisfactory line.

Bulganin's confession made points which were not of a desirable sort from Khrushchev's point of view. For instance, he said that the Anti-Party Group had held that the economic decentralisation was liable to lead to 'anarchy in the direction of industry and construction' and that it was 'even in contradiction of Lenin'. This was, in a sense, to develop the Group's arguments once more, as a 'platform for further struggle'. Bulganin also made it clear that Khrushchev's victory had not been foredoomed, when he spoke of the danger to the Party and State 'if Molotov, Malenkov and Kaganovich had come to power'. Bulganin's defence, to the effect that he had supported the industrial and other measures suggested by Khrushchev, and had *yet* come out against him in June 1957, is particularly striking. For he is saying, in effect, 'even people who agree with Khrushchev's views find him intolerable as a ruler'.

The violence of the attacks on the ex-Premier was pointed up by the fact that the first blow at his speech was struck by none other than S. D. Ignatiev, who had been Stalin's Minister of State Security at the time of the Doctors' Plot. He said:

Bulganin's speech to-day sounded just as feeble and unconvincing as his earlier speeches. . . .

He presents the case as if it is only just now that he has seen the true face of the Anti-Party Group of Malenkov, Kaganovich, Molotov, Shepilov, and that, allegedly, it was not visible to him during those days of ruthless malicious assaults on the Leninist section of the Central Committee Praesidium and Party policy, during those days when they even raised the question of the leadership of the Central Committee and of the Party. Bulganin is not a schoolboy that he could not see through the aims of the Anti-Party Group. Anyway, even our schoolboys now can find their way about in politics. No, Nikita Sergeyevich was right when he said: Bulganin ran after a piece of gingerbread which the Anti-Party Group offered him. Although the gingerbread was poisonous, Bulganin, being dissatisfied with his position in the Party, nevertheless ran after it when it was promised to him (*Stenographic Record*).

Two comments emerge. First, that Ignatiev was the one member of the Central Committee who had himself been branded for 'political blindness' when the Doctors' Plot was repudiated. Second, that it is highly unlikely, to say the least, that the Anti-Party Group was in a position to bribe Bulganin with a higher post than that of Prime Minister unless he was their candidate for First Secretary.

Ignatiev's attack on Bulganin and the Anti-Party Group was repeated in general terms by a number of speakers. Most of these used the agricultural sabotage theme. But there was an interesting organisational revelation from A. Yu. Snechkus, Secretary of the Lithuanian C.C.:

Comrade Ignatiev has expressed his attitude to Comrade Bulganin's speech. I agree completely with Comrade Ignatiev's speech, and would add only that, as Bulganin's speech at a previous plenum showed, he himself has not revealed all his connections with the anti-Party grouping, and particularly with Malenkov. If you remember, at that time a number of members of the Party Control Committee spoke, Comrade Shvernik spoke, and it was clear to everyone how close Bulganin's relations were with Malenkov and that Bulganin himself tried in every way to protect Malenkov. Bulganin did not admit this at that plenum, and now again in to-day's speech he has also said nothing about it, has given no explanation of what he was accused of by the Party Control Committee. It seems to me that Bulganin's speech to-day cannot satisfy us (*Stenographic Record*).

The occasion of the intervention of the Control Committee against Bulganin must presumably have been either the September 1958 plenum, when he was removed from the Praesidium, or the November 1958 one, when he was first publicly referred to as a member of the Group. When he is supposed to have defended Malenkov is not so clear; it seems either to refer to the circumstances of June 1957 — when the speeches of the Khrushchev faction after the plenum seem to have indicated a desire to bring Malenkov to trial, rather than the milder decision actually arrived at at the time; or to the plenum of January 1955, when the removal of Malenkov from the Praesidium as well as the Premiership was blocked by a majority which may have included Bulganin. (Another Malenkov supporter, not yet mentioned by name seems to have been attacked at the December 1958 plenum, when T. A. Yurkin spoke of the 'tricks' of 'this despicable group' against the Virgin Lands scheme as including obstruction and opposition from 'the State Planning Committee of that time' — i.e. Saburov.)

Nor was Bulganin's characterisation of the three senior members of the Anti-Party Group held adequate. Although Bulganin said:

Molotov is divorced from life and the Soviet people, completely ignorant of industry and agriculture. Kaganovich is a phrasemonger, who hindered work with his long, confused speeches. Malenkov is an intriguer, capable of any vileness,

this was vigorously attacked in a very interesting drawing of distinctions between the right and wrong ways of condemning the Anti-Party Group by Kolushchinsky, who said:

Bulganin here, in the plenum of the C.C., again spoke of that conspiratorial group and made the following estimate of it: Molotov — frightened of life, knowing absolutely nothing of industry or rural economy; Kaganovich — a phrasemonger, muddling work up with his empty talk; Malenkov — an intriguer, capable of any vileness; but about himself he was silent and said nothing. But Molotov, Kaganovich and Malenkov — were not merely windbags and intriguers knowing nothing of industry and rural economy. The Party has given a true characterisation and estimate of the base, treacherous, conspiratorial group of fractionists and splitters.

Kolushchinsky also said that the 1952 faking of agricultural statistics alleged against Malenkov by Khrushchev was a 'monstrous provocation', a 'foul provocation' and must be investigated afresh.

At precisely the same time as the December 1958 plenum, at which Khrushchev was able to press ahead with this renewed attack on the Anti-Party Group, and extracted the inadequate mea culpa from Bulganin, there was another highly significant article. *Pravda* published (December 14, 1958) a full-scale attack on a number of opponents of Lysenko, and in particular biologists, including a 'shameless reactionary', on the board of the *Botanical Journal*. It claimed that 'the so-called discussion which has been conducted for a number of years' in that periodical was 'of no help in the development of materialist biology'. It asked if the editorial board was 'capable' of working correctly.

A few days later the board was purged. Meanwhile Lysenko had been granted an even more extraordinary sign of distinction. He had addressed the plenum itself, although not even a member of the Party, let alone of its Central Committee. This can hardly be interpreted otherwise than as due to support from Khrushchev, and a sign that the sciences were, as in earlier times, closely involved in the struggle.

In April 1956 Lysenko had resigned as President of the Agricultural Academy, probably as part of the post XXth Congress liberalisation. The great biologist, Nikolai Vavilov, his predecessor in the post, who had died in an Arctic camp in 1943 as a result of opposing the new biology, was rehabilitated at that time. Much of the new thaw literature had attacked the Lysenko type in Soviet science (for example Prof. Avdiev in Dudintsev's *Not by Bread Alone*). But in March 1957 Khrushchev had said that he 'gave his vote to Lysenko'. This seemed another sign of the return to quasi-Stalinist orthodoxy.

Now he spoke up more strongly — not a vote in a controversy, but a suppression of one side of it. When, at the plenum itself, I. D. Mustafaev attacked the *Botanical Journal* Khrushchev commented:

'The cadres must be looked at. Evidently people were selected for the editorship who are opposed to Michurinist science. While they remain nothing will change. They must be changed and others put in — real Michurinists. Here lies the basic solution to the question.'

Mustafaev: 'Nikita Sergeyevich, not only this journal has such a tone. Sometimes scientist-Communists cannot think of how to behave. Not long ago ill rumours reached me that our delegation in China, among whom there were some biologists, declared that Comrade Lysenko was finished now, not only in theory but also in fact.'

Khrushchev: 'It was Tsitsin who said that' (*Stenographic Record*).

(N. V. Tsitsin is a prominent expert on plant reproduction and an old opponent of Lysenko's.)

It is also notable that the other favourite, Maltsev, was one of those specially added, on Khrushchev's proposal, to the Commission for drafting the Central Committee's resolution on agriculture.

The new campaign about the criminal nature of the Anti-Party Group, which had been dropped between August 1957 and December 1958, was kept up after the plenum. Rudenko, the Procurator-General, told the Supreme Soviet on December 25 that:

These dissidents, especially Malenkov, Kaganovich, Molotov, Bulganin, having themselves committed crude arbitrariness and criminal violations of Socialist legality, hindered urgent and vitally necessary measures of the Party Central Committee for strengthening Socialist legality (*Pravda*, December 26, 1958).

There are two views of the XXIst Congress. One sees it as simply a vast demonstration in favour of Khrushchev's Seven-Year Plan, with odd blows at the Anti-Party Group considered as just tying up a few loose ends in the campaign against a defeated and forgotten faction.

The other sees it as a clash between a moderate element on the one hand and on the other Khrushchev, wishing to crush his opponents and put an end to influences lukewarm about giving him full powers. On this view Khrushchev was blocked by the moderates.

The Congress was marked by a number of attacks on the Anti-Party Group. For the first time not only the original members and Bulganin, but also Pervukhin and Saburov, were named as figuring in it. Both of them, and Bulganin too, were still members of the Central Committee, and Pervukhin was still a candidate member of the Praesidium.

The Praesidium was listed complete (except for Polyansky), as to both members and candidates, when attending the opening of a Dzerzhinsky memorial meeting in Moscow on December 20, 1958, following the December plenum. Pervukhin was given in his correct seniority, before Podgorny. Pervukhin was again listed in his correct position on the Party Praesidium at the opening of the Congress on January 27, 1959 (i.e. before Podgorny and Polyansky). He was not elected to the Praesidium of the Congress, which of course included all the rest of the Party Praesidium members. And he was the only Praesidial figure omitted from the list of important persons choosing one among several constituencies offered them in the Union Republic elections (*Tass*, January 31, 1959). Thus all the signs of demotion were visited on him, but the formal removal had not taken place — rather as in the case of Ponomarenko in 1955 or Bulganin in February–September 1958.

On the eve of the Congress, *Party Life* (No. 2, January 1959) published an article by Spiridonov, the Leningrad First Secretary, whose rise had taken place entirely under Khrushchev's auspices. He raised once more the issue of the Leningrad Affair. Little had been said of this since Khrushchev's abortive campaign in July–August 1957, and the timing cannot be coincidental. Spiridonov wrote:

The Communists of Leningrad are especially sharply aware of the anti-Party essence of this despicable group. To them it is well known that through the guilt of some of these leaders the Leningrad Party organisation in the past was subjected to impermissible discrimination, its militant traditions were flouted and humiliated and a great loss was inflicted on its cadres.

At the Congress itself it was Spiridonov (on January 29, 1959) who launched the direct challenge:

'They must be asked to account for their actions before the Supreme Organ of the Party — the Congress — especially those who have remained members of the Central Committee'. Bulganin had at least spoken at the December plenum, 'but Candidate Member of the Praesidium of the C.C. Pervukhin and C.C. Member Saburov have not come out once in one and a half years to denounce the Anti-Party Group and their own role in it'.

On February 3 Pervukhin made a speech. He said that he had been unable to discern the anti-Party plans of the Group. 'I have condemned and am condemning the dissident activity of the Anti-Party Group. I have already spoken about it at the June plenary session.' He went on to say that he had supported the Central Committee line on the Virgin Lands and on Yugoslavia and had only opposed the industrial reorganisation. (He says that he opposed it 'in the Central Committee', which may indicate a debate at the February 1957 plenum.) It was as a result of his policy disagreement that he had 'committed a great political blunder by supporting the Anti-Party Group'. He had supported attacks on Khrushchev. Even so, he had not agreed with the changes of leadership put forward by the Group.

Uldzhabaev said later in the morning session of February 3, 1959, that it had been right to raise the issue of 'long-silent members of the Anti-Party Group. They must give explanations to the delegates of the Congress about their fractional activity, though their explanations will scarcely make amends. It will hardly be suitable to retain them in the make-up of the Leninist Central Committee of our Party.'

This definite proposal to remove them is as striking as Khrushchev's remarks at the December plenum about their unworthiness to retain the Party members' title of comrade. It also seems significant that Uldzhabaev spoke without reference, oblique or otherwise, to Pervukhin, who had spoken earlier in the day. For this appears to show that Uldzhabaev's speech (and hence others, too) had been carefully drafted and approved by some caucus and that he did not feel authorised to alter it. (There is some parallel here with Ignatiev's attack on Bulganin at the December plenum, where the first seven or eight speeches after Bulganin's did not refer to his confession at all, again implying the careful preparation of a set-piece counterblast.)

However, by the afternoon session there had been time for preparation, and I. I. Kuzmin made a particularly long and sustained attack on Pervukhin, accusing him of failing to mention his 'activity in the Anti-Party Group and inactivity in high state posts'. In strong language he accused Pervukhin of having, with Molotov and Shepilov, formed the 'triumvirate' within the group for carrying out the attack on the industrial reorganisation; of urging the use of hydro-electric generating stations rather than thermo-electric ones, as suggested by Khrushchev (the point here is that hydro-electric plants require a bigger capital outlay, but much smaller running expenses); and of failing to expand the production of mineral fertilisers when Minister of the Chemical Industry. He also attacked Saburov for errors over power-generation and of responsibility for faults in the oil industry.

On February 4 Saburov admitted to 'political instability', but said that he 'did not share the views of the Anti-Party Group', though he had criticised faults in the work of the Praesidium

not from the position of the healthy part of the Praesidium of the C.C. C.P.S.U., but from the position of the Anti-Party Group which, using as a screen small and easily corrected faults, attacked Comrade Khrushchev, sought changes in the leadership of the Central Committee, and consequently in the policies of the Central Committee.

He added, as we have seen (in Chapter Twelve), that

already at meetings of the Praesidium of the C.C. C.P.S.U., before the June plenum, I took on a quite different position; I protested against the dirty attempts of Kaganovich and other participants in the Anti-Party Group to smear the name of N. S. Khrushchev, and stated that collective leadership existed in the Praesidium of the C.C.

As we have said, the implication is that one of the smears was that Khrushchev was aiming at dictatorship. Significant in 1957, its public repetition in 1959 was no less so. For the treatment of Saburov's remarks was peculiar. Alone of the speeches it was not given or even summarised in *Pravda*. A very short version was broadcast in the Soviet Radio's Foreign Services. But when the *Stenographic Record* of the Congress was published (passed for publication, April 29, 1959) it was printed at length; though it was indeed still distinguished from all the others by being referred to in the index as a 'statement' while the rest were described as 'speeches'.

Next day Kolushchinsky, who had already spoken strongly at the December plenum, said 'the C.C. was very merciful in retaining them then in the ranks of the Party. The C.C. showed particular humanity in connection with Bulganin, Pervukhin, Saburov, but they did not draw any conclusions from this.' He went on to condemn Pervukhin (who, he said, had spoken 'only when compelled to do so by the intervention of Comrade Spiridonov') for an unsatisfactory speech full of cunning and evasion.

Instead of speaking to the Congress of his base role . . . with the dirty conspiratorial group and honestly repenting before the Congress . . . he then, on the tribune of the Congress, maintained that he had helped the C.C. plenum to settle with the disgusting conspirators. That is a lie! (*Pravda*, February 6, 1959).

Pravda of February 10, 1959, said that 'literally not one statement at the Congress did not contain angry condemnation for the base fractional activity of the Anti-Party Group'. In fact about a quarter of them avoided the subject — even including important officials like the Ministers Elyutin and Novikov, and, as we shall see, many of the condemnations sound far from angry.

The XXIst Congress was not the scene of any major explosion. This had led certain commentators to maintain that there was never any question of an extension of the purge, and that the efforts of Kremlinologists to imagine such a thing are extravagant. It seems to the author that it is quite clear that a conflict on this major issue did take place: there is enough direct evidence in the Congress speeches themselves (far more than at the XXth Congress), and a good deal more which can most suitably be interpreted in these terms.

At a very superficial level there was a certain unanimity about the Anti-Party Group at the Congress. Everyone was against it — including its own members. But there is more to it than that.

In his speech attacking Bulganin at the December plenum Khrushchev's supporter Kolushchinsky had put the issue clearly. A division was announced as a crucial one between those referring to the Anti-Party Group as political windbags and even intriguers and those prepared to go the whole way in accusations of treachery and conspiracy. So there is a good publicly formulated reason, even apart from commonsense, distinguishing between the ways various leaders expressed themselves on the matter and for regarding the results as significant of a clash on something openly defined as a major issue. For we

B B

may reasonably apply to the speeches at the XXIst Congress what might be called the Kolushchinsky Criterion. If we take it precisely as Kolushchinsky lays it down, the extreme Anti-Party Group speakers of praesidial rank are even fewer than in our more general analysis (that Khrushchev himself does not figure as a pace-maker scarcely counts: it would only be suitable for him to do so if the matter was definitely being forced to an issue).

The statements can be divided quite clearly into three main groups on this issue.

One (which included Pervukhin and Saburov themselves!) condemned the Anti-Party Group in moderate terms and on the grounds that their political line had been incorrect. This view was put by Mikoyan, Suslov, Mukhitdinov, Kosygin, Zasyadko and others.

Mikoyan's formulation was as follows:

Among the many questions I was asked at meetings and receptions in the U.S.A. was this question: How was it to be explained that recently (they had in mind the December plenum of the C.C. on rural economy and the period after it) we had again come out against the Anti-Party Group? Did that mean that the opposition had become stronger and represented some threat? I answered: In no case: with us there was full unity in the Party and there were no struggles. This group had not increased by a single member in that time.

This can hardly be taken as other than a hint that further attempts to link people with the Group were to be deplored. He added that the December plenum's attacks on the Group had been simply designed to show how wrong had been 'the political position of this fraction'.

At the opposite pole were those most closely identified with Khrushchev who himself spoke of the 'basest methods of factional struggle' — a phrase echoed in the Resolution: Ignatov ('criminal', 'loathsome', 'perfidious'); Kirichenko ('intriguer', 'baseness', 'despicable'); Furtseva ('intriguer', 'despicable', 'dirtiest means'); Belyaev ('criminal'); Podgorny ('treacherous'). The junior Khrushchevites Spiridonov, Denisov, Kolushchinsky, Uldzhabaev and Kuzmin launched even more direct attacks.

Between the two main ways of putting it, lie another category of speakers which confined its criticism to the fact that the Group had been in error politically and did not refer to the 'conspiratorial' tactics pursued in stronger language than 'splitters'. These included Aristov, Brezhnev, Pospelov, Polyansky, Mazurov, Mzhavanadze and Shvernik ('fractionists'), the latter speaking as Head of the Party Control Committee emphasised his disinterest by attacking by name for violations of discipline only — certain members of the new Councils of National Economy. Kozlov and Kuusinen ('despicable fractionists' and 'shameful intrigues' respectively), yet took a more or less intermediate position, arguing mainly on the political issues. Kuusinen said: 'I am convinced that there is not a single delegate to our Congress who does not condemn the members of the Anti-Party Group' — very different from the views of the critics of Pervukhin — and 'I am convinced that there is not a single conscious Soviet person who considers that the Central Committee has treated these people too severely' — rather different from threatening further measures.

If these speeches represent definite positions in the Praesidium it appears that the extreme policy of further action against the group was supported in the Praesidium only by Ignatov, Kirichenko, Furtseva and Belyaev, while the remainder were prepared, to one degree or another, to consider the affair closed. The speeches of Spiridonov and others suggest that some attempt was made to rush the Congress into further measures, but that this was resisted.

We now give here the *most extreme* phrases used by given speakers about the Anti-Party Group. It is also the case that some — in particular Suslov and Mukhitdinov — referred to them very briefly indeed in passing. Some of those who treated them at greater length, such as Shvernik and Kozlov, confined themselves almost entirely to analyses of the political mistakes of the Group rather than their factiousness.

Aristov	'Petty and wretched.'
Belyaev	'The criminal activity of the fractionists.'
Brezhnev	'Anti-Leninist positions . . . political bankrupts.'
Furtseva	'Filthy methods . . . despicable intriguers and splitters.'

Ignatov	'Filthy lot of bankrupts. Criminal lot of fractionists.'
Kirichenko	'The abominableness of the splitting activities of these political intriguers and double-dealers.'
Kozlov	'Wretched fractionists.'
Kuusinen	'Shameful intrigues.'
Mikoyan	'Anti-Party Group.'
Mukhitdinov	'Showed elements of chauvinism.'
Shvernik	'Fractionists.'
Suslov	'Anti-Party Group.'
Voroshilov	'Fractional activity . . . Splitters group . . . Shame.'
Pospelov	'Wretched group of bankrupts, splitters and fractionists.'
Kirilenko	'Wretched and shameful . . . splitters group of fractionists and bankrupts.'
Kalnberzins	'Hostile acts of this lot of political bankrupts.'
Kosygin	'Fractionists and splitters.'
Mazurov	'Wretched group of fractionists and splitters.'
Mzhavanadze	'Anti-Party, anti-national little group.'
Podgorny	'Disgusting, treacherous attempts.'
Polyanksy	'Wretched fractionists.'

It almost looks as if an agreed line of defence was being taken by those most determined to prevent further action. This was to condemn the Anti-Party Group, dissociate those present from it and speak of the matter as closed. At the same time it had been secured that no new Central Committee more loyal to the Secretariat would be elected at least until 1961. The fact that the Congress was only a 'Special' one was insisted on by Suslov and Mikoyan in almost identical terms, while other speakers (including Khrushchev) only used the adjective in passing, if at all.

Suslov started his speech:

Comrades, the XXIst Congress is not a regular Congress of our Party and therefore no report of the Central Committee has been heard at the Congress. In fact, however, the brilliant, comprehensive and profound report of Comrade Khrushchev illumines all the results of the activity of the Party and the whole Soviet people during the period between the XXth and XXIst C.P.S.U. Congresses.

Mikoyan started:

Chosen delegates of the Communist Party of the U.S.S.R. have gathered here to-day to discuss the only question on the agenda of this special Congress, the control figures for the U.S.S.R. national economy plan for 1959–65,

and went on similarly to praise the report.

It must be remembered that the Central Committee, as it stood in 1959, was a body elected at the XXth Congress, at a time when Khrushchev was not in a position to dictate its composition. A rough analysis of its 124 surviving full members in January 1959 gives results of the following type:

(a) 62 likely to support Khrushchev.
(b) 7 likely to support Khrushchev on most issues, while not bound to him closely.
(c) 47 Independents.
(d) 8 Opponents.

This is a very schematic division, in any case, and with many of the minor personalities is based mainly on the machinery through which they come and the circumstances of their rise. These may not be reliable. For instance, I have included both Kapitonov and N. F. Ignatov under (a), but their removal from their Moscow posts in March 1959 may indicate that they failed to run true to form at the XXIst Congress. In any case a *potential* majority against Khrushchev seems to exist, even without allowing for any disintegration of (a).

On the eve of the Congress, Khrushchev announced that the Congress had received 'appeals against decisions of expulsion from the Party, Party censure, and other personal Party questions. The Congress instructed the Central Committee to look into these appeals.'

That the original members of the Anti-Party Group were still submitting pleas to the authorities, and that these pleas were still not of an acceptable type, seems to be shown by an attack made on Shepilov (whose line appears to be that the intelligentsia must be allowed a certain amount of latitude to think):

But it is impossible to concede that the schismatics and fraction-
alists of the Anti-Party Group have drawn correct conclusions from
the decisions of the Central Committee of the Party. For example,
Shepilov continues to slander Soviet actuality and the Soviet intelligentsia: he asserts that irresolution is of the essence of the
intelligentsia and that he, to be sure, 'as a Russian intellectual' also
does not escape this irresolution. Such assertions are alien to our
party, such accusations are alien to our Soviet intelligentsia (Denisov
at the XXIst Congress: *Pravda*, February 6, 1959).

And in the meantime the differentiation between attitudes
to the Anti-Party Group had been formalised in *Voprosy Filosofii*
No. 2 of 1959 (passed for press March 5, 1959). It printed a
letter from an M. I. Sosnin attacking an article by Shershunov
and Shiglov in the periodical's issue No. 11 of 1958 (passed for
press December 1, 1958). This article had referred, very much
in passing, to the Anti-Party Group: 'A typical example of
dogmatism showed itself in the well-known platform of the
Anti-Party Group of Malenkov, Kaganovich and Molotov,
which dragged the Party backwards towards already outmoded
methods of leadership.'

The letter criticising this formulation ran in part:

Thus the authors characterise the fractional anti-Party activity of
the group of Malenkov, Kaganovich, Molotov, Bulganin and
Shepilov only as a manifestation of dogmatism. How could the
authors limit themselves to such a toothless, passive-contemplative,
liberal-complacent characterisation of the Anti-Party Group? The
authors may say that it was not their job in their article to give
characterisations of all the activity and essence of the Anti-Party
Group. But a Marxist–Leninist cannot approach abstractly, passive-
contemplatively, such a manifestation as the fractional anti-Party
conspiratorial activity of the group of Malenkov, Kaganovich,
Molotov, Bulganin and Shepilov.

The editors of *Voprosy Filosofii* add a note that they agree with
this criticism and regret not having demanded the necessary
corrections from the authors.

The Congress had closed without the 'accounting for themselves' or removal from the 'Leninist Central Committee'
which had been demanded for the new anti-Party trio Bulganin,
Saburov and Pervukhin. But though the demand was evidently

blocked, it was at least publicly established as a political platform.

And now within weeks major changes were put through in
a number of important areas. In the year that followed tensions
expressed themselves in various ways. Moreover, controversy,
which had briefly concentrated on the issue of the Anti-Party
Group's future, again arose over a wide field of policy.

POSTSCRIPT

1959–60

IT had been my intention to end this book with the aftermath of the XXIst Congress. I would have touched on the wave of changes which followed that ambiguous crisis, and gone on to envisage the general, though not of course the particular, ways in which the struggle might be expected to develop as the XXIInd Congress, promised for 1961, approached.

A book of this type, however, takes a good time to pass through all its publishing stages, and as it goes from galley into page proof in the late summer of 1960, actual changes have taken place in Russia so important that they can hardly be left untouched. In particular the changes of May 4, 1960, are on a greater scale than any since the fall of the Anti-Party Group. I am therefore adding to my concluding remarks a brief account and analysis of what passed between February 1959 and July 1960.

One good reason for brevity is the comparative obscurity which has again fallen upon the scene. Not only are the 1960 shifts of a complexity rivalling those of March 1953 but, for the first time since Voznesensky, a leading figure (Kirichenko) has been catastrophically degraded without any reason whatever being publicly advanced. The investigator, spoiled by the overt accusations at the debate at the December 1958 plenum and the XXIst Congress, has since had to face silence.

We may conclude that the XXIst Congress was the scene of a phase in Soviet political life in which any intended climax was aborted, leaving the proponents of different views on policy still in the positions which various initiatives had vainly attempted to alter. An impression was given that, as throughout the previous period, a majority of members of the Praesidium, and of the Central Committee (for of course no votes were taken in the Congress itself, notoriously a body to be manipulated, not to decide), were concerned to hinder any change in the political line or in the balance of power, even to the extent of defending against further attack the members of the faction defeated in 1957. It was reasonable to suppose that further attempts would be made to break this impasse.

It is sometimes held that Khrushchev has in a sense repeated Stalin's attainment of supreme power, by using the Party machine to overcome his opponents. It is certainly the case that he has in turn defeated the police (in the person of Beria), the State and economic apparatus (in the persons of Malenkov and the Anti-Party Group), and the Army (in the person of Zhukov). And it is perfectly true that Stalin similarly overcame his enemies by reliance on the Secretariat. What is sometimes forgotten is that having overcome all rival sources of power, Stalin then turned on the Party apparatus itself and in effect replaced it, just as much as the Government, by his personal machine.

And so the fact that Khrushchev had been supported during the struggles of recent years by the representatives of the apparat — men like Suslov and Aristov — does not necessarily mean more than that they were naturally on the side of the First Secretary in his struggle against other apparatuses.

For Khrushchev truly to consolidate his power, and to ensure the adoption of his policies on the Anti-Party Group and other matters, the logic of the situation seems to dictate the replacement of allies by dependants in the Praesidial majority and in the key posts of the secretariat. This is not to say that if such a manœuvre proved impossible, a watchful compromise might not be acceptable to all parties, *faute de mieux*.

Though it is not easy to interpret the detail, it may be remarked that the XXIst Congress was followed by a wave of demotions, some accompanied by grave accusations, such as had not been seen over the previous year. (The only major purge in that period — and that not long before the Congress — had been in Turkmenistan. There the First Secretary S. Babaev and others were purged (*Turkmenskaya Iskra*, December 16, 1958) under charges developed into cliquery, ignoring Leninist 'norms of leadership' and some suggestion of nationalism. What link, if any, this had with the main campaign is unknown. He was later expelled from the C.C. (*Turkmenskaya Iskra*, January 23, 1959).)

The most important of the post-Congress changes seemed to have been those imposed on the Moscow Provincial Party

Committee. A meeting of this committee was attended by Kirichenko and Aristov (*Pravda*, March 3, 1959). Kapitonov was removed from his position as First Secretary and from membership of the Bureau, another of whose members, N. F. Ignatov, was also removed. While Kapitonov had hitherto been considered a Khrushchev appointment, he and the other spokesmen of the Moscow Committee had been particularly mild in their remarks about the Anti-Party Group.

The same month saw purges in Uzbekistan, where the First Secretary, Kamalov, was removed with a number of his colleagues; and in Byelorussia, where the Prime Minister, Avkhimovich, was dismissed, with others, and the entire Bureau criticised.

On March 20, 1959, a different type of change took place, with the replacement of Kuzmin by Kosygin as head of Gosplan. Kuzmin also lost his deputy premiership and was given the lesser post of Chairman of the State Committee for Science and Technique.

Further important changes among key personnel followed. In March Semichastny, till then First Secretary of the Komsomol, was identified as Head of the Central Committee Department of Party Organs (*Pravda*, March 26, 1959). A Ukrainian, he was another close associate of Khrushchev, who had also taken the extreme line. In April it was announced that N. G. Ignatov had become Chairman of the Praesidium of the Supreme Soviet of the R.S.F.S.R. (*Tass*, April 16, 1959). Although it was explained that this post needed strengthening, it seems fairly plain that it remained, as it had been, a decorative position of little real significance, and it does not seem unreasonable to read the move as a diminution of Ignatov's power. At the lowest, the post's official duties, even though mainly honorary, were likely to make it difficult for him to keep up with his work on the Secretariat, and seem to imply an intention to remove him from that body.

The next plenum of the Central Committee, held in June 1959, did not register any further advance for any faction. In fact, perhaps because it was obvious that nothing could be done with the recalcitrant majority, the occasion was organised so as to be not a plenum at all in any ordinary sense, being diluted by the attendance of a large number of minor officials.

Through this period the issue of the Anti-Party Group was kept before the Party membership, if not to the extent seen round the time of the Congress. (For example, Kaganovich was accused of deviation in the early twenties (*Sotsialisticheski Zakonnost*, April 1959); of using threats of arrest for political purposes (*Pravda*, June 4, 1959); and of sanctioning arrests for careerist motives in 1937 (*Partiinoye Poruchenie*, No. 7 of 1959).).

The second half of the year saw a notable reversal of what had hitherto taken place. Semichastny was sent to Baku as Second Secretary of the Azerbaidzhan Central Committee, to cope with the situation produced by the purge there. This departure from the Party Organs Department, in view of later developments, seems to reflect a weakening of a 'Khrushchevite' attempt to gain full control of the Party machinery.

During the autumn and winter Kapitonov and N. F. Ignatov reappeared in fairly important positions — Kapitonov as First Secretary of the Ivanovo Province (*Pravda*, September 23, 1959) and N. F. Ignatov as First Secretary of the Tula Province (*Sovietskaya Rossiya*, January 14, 1960). In November N. G. Ignatov gave up the Chairmanship of the R.S.F.S.R. Supreme Soviet Praesidium to 'devote his chief efforts to his work as Secretary of the Central Committee' (*Pravda*, November 27, 1959), a confirmation of the speculations which had arisen on his appointment.

In the second half of 1959 a whole cycle of purges took place in the peripheral republics. Some of these, particularly in Latvia, struck at a large section of the local leaderships; and in all the theme was one of accusations that insufficient resistance was being made to nationalist tendencies in politics and culture. Such manœuvres began in Latvia in June and continued there with increasing scope throughout the year. (In November 1959 Kalnberzins was demoted from Latvian First Secretary to Chairman of the Praesidium of the republic's Supreme Soviet. This was plainly not because he was in any way compromised as a 'nationalist', unlike a number of the other Latvian leaders who fell at this time; but presumably his activity against them had been inadequate, or possibly too crudely Stalinist. It is remarkable that he retained, in May 1960, his candidate membership of the Praesidium of the All-Union Central Committee.)

Similar campaigns began in August in Lithuania and Azerbaidzhan (where the First Secretary, Mustafaev, fell); in September in Moldavia; and in October in Kazakhstan.

In the last named of these republics a variety of other troubles had produced something like a crisis. The Virgin Lands harvest was a failure. Working conditions produced strikes and riots. The gravity of the position was emphasised by the despatch of Lunev, Deputy Chairman of the U.S.S.R. K.G.B. to be Chairman of the K.G.B. in that republic (*Kazakh-stanskaya Pravda*, October 11, 1959).

At the December 1959 plenum Khrushchev attacked Belyaev for the failure of the Kazakh grain harvest. At the same time A. I. Kozlov (who had fallen with Malenkov) was salvaged from headship of a State farm and made Minister of State Farms in Kazakhstan (with powers which made him virtual dictator of the Virgin Lands project), to the accompaniment of praise from Khrushchev. Belyaev's dismissal from his Kazakh post (*Pravda*, January 21, 1960) and his appointment as Party Secretary at Stavropol (*Pravda*, January 29, 1960) followed.

The December 1959 plenum also went a step further in pro-letarianising the collective farms. It was announced that instead of receiving a proportion of the farm's profits, a new system would be introduced whereby the peasant would be paid by the hour or the day, as in factories. Among other moves fore-shadowed on the same lines was the building of communal houses — again an urbanising move.

With Belyaev fell a far more important figure. *Pravda* of January 13 announced Kirichenko's downgrading to be Party Secretary at Rostov. An almost simultaneous Central Committee announcement on propaganda (January 10, 1960) made a par-ticular point of the fact that many party organisations 'do not give a due rebuff to manifestations of nationalism, cosmopoli-tanism and apolitical attitudes' and that they were defensive towards 'an idealistic and revisionist ideology hostile to Marxism–Leninism'. There are other references to the national problem.

It seems clear that Kirichenko was in general charge of cadres. In the republics he had evidently been practising a policy which made him vulnerable to charges of insufficient strictness towards the allegedly nationalist elements. It will be remembered that Khrushchev had himself suffered under similar imputations in 1947; that Kirichenko — clearly with Khrushchev's support — had become First Secretary in the Ukraine in 1953 on a platform of opposition to Melnikov's denationalising policies; and that one of the charges against the Anti-Party Group (made by Mukhitdinov at the XXIst Congress) was of 'chauvinism' towards the minorities. There seems to be an implication that the 1959-60 campaign in this sphere was, if not overtly, directly against Khrushchev himself. In that case we may feel that he maintained himself by hedging on the policy and sacrificing a scapegoat, just as with Belyaev in agriculture, and Kuzmin in industry.

The extent of Kirichenko's downgrading (for he was removed in June 1960 even from his Rostov post) indicates an animus against him far greater than could be accounted for simply by the failure of one or other of his moves in the policy field. Yet we may find the pretext, if not the reason, for his disgrace in the purges in the national republics.

The fall of Kirichenko and Belyaev was formalised at a plenum which met on May 4, 1960. This brief meeting made a number of changes, of which the loose ends were tidied up at another plenum in July.

The net result of the changes announced at these May and July 1960 plenums was as follows:

(a) The dismissal of Kirichenko and Belyaev from the Praesidium and Secretariat.

(b) The retirement of Voroshilov from both membership of the Praesidium and Chairmanship of the Praesidium of the Supreme Soviet.

(c) The promotion to full membership of the Praesidium of Kosygin, Podgorny and Polyansky.

(d) The transfer from the Secretariat of Brezhnev (to be Chairman of the Praesidium of the Supreme Soviet), Furtseva (to be Minister of Culture) and Ignatov (to be Deputy Chairman of the Council of Ministers).

(e) The transfer to the Secretariat of F. Kozlov (from being First Deputy Chairman of the Council of Ministers).

(f) The promotion of Kosygin to be First Deputy Chairman of the Council of Ministers.

(g) The giving up of their posts on the Secretariat by Aristov
and Pospelov, to concentrate on their work in the
Bureau for the R.S.F.S.R.

This last change does not seem to have affected the actual
powers or duties of Aristov, at least. *Pravda* reports him on
June 15 as attending a meeting of the Rostov Committee to
supervise the removal of Kirichenko from his Provincial secretaryship there, just as he had seen to his installation in January.

On the other hand, it is certainly true that the balance between
State and Party appointments among the Praesidium members
is drastically altered. The proportions now became: State, 6;
Party, 6; both, 1 (omitting Shvernik). This may perhaps indicate the beginnings of a revival of the old method of rule.
Possibly it originates with a Khrushchev unable, for the moment
at least, to gain control of the apparat, and turning to the
setting up of an alternative power-source; but it is equally
likely that the true motives are as yet not deducible.

Khrushchev's reply, when asked about the significance of the
December 1957 increase in the number of Secretaries, was
straightforward:

Question: Does the appointment of a greater number of
secretaries of the party indicate the increasing role of the
Central Committee of the Communist Party?

Khrushchev: You understand this question correctly. Yes, the
changes you have mentioned indicate the continually
strengthening role of the Communist Party in the life of
our country, and evidently this role will continue to
increase.

(Interview with *The Times*, January 31, 1958: *Tass*, February
15, 1958.)

Yet there is nothing to indicate that the actual power of the
apparat has ever depended on the number of Secretaries, and
in fact the main element of the 1957 increase was the intrusion
of Kirichenko rather than the increase in numbers.

The more essential change seems to be the removal of
Khrushchev's closest associates from key positions. Kirichenko
and Belyaev have gone; Brezhnev has a post of considerable
decorative value — yet one which in Stalin's last years was not

even held by a full member of the Politburo; Furtseva's new post may be the State equivalent of her old cultural secretaryship, and this could be interpreted in the context of a strengthening of the State machine — yet she is the first Praesidium member in a government post not to rank as Deputy Chairman of the Council of Ministers (except for the special case of Zhukov). Nor does it seem that the new Council of Ministers is any more of a Khrushchev preserve than the new Secretariat.

Nevertheless, and in spite of the effective opposition certain of his policies seem to have run into, his position remains a very strong one. In theory a perpetuation of the *status quo*, even after the XXIInd Congress, appears to be quite possible. Yet all experience leads us to expect the contrary: the nature of the Communist method of rule, and the personal and political attitudes of those whose activities have been our study, all imply that a struggle will continue, not improbably accompanied by extraordinary crises.

That the Praesidium's membership and candidate membership was unaltered apart from the removals and promotions listed above was indicated by a listing in *Pravda* of May 6, 1960, which continued to show Kalnberzins and even Pervukhin in the same positions as before the XXIst Congress. But meanwhile another factor had come into play which, if not producing immediate organisational results, at least seems to have weakened the position of some members of the Praesidium.

The fall of Kirichenko had taken place in a period when foreign affairs were producing little of significance. But in April came the U2 incident, and the curious sequence of events following it. It was at this period too that the latent tensions between the Soviet and Chinese Communists became translated into virtually undisguised polemics.

To take the second point first: although the Chinese may well prefer a more intransigent foreign policy from Moscow, and favour any Soviet group that advocates it, there is no reason to suppose that Chinese support as such is of any particular benefit to any Kremlin figure who may be receiving it. It is important to remember that from the point of view of even the most leftist or Stalinist elements in Russia, the Chinese interpretation of Marxism–Leninism, both internally in the Communes and externally in the attitude to war, is the crudest and most unacceptable of leftist, adventurist deviations. In addition to which, every Soviet leader wishing the support of his fellows must avoid anything that could possibly be interpreted as abandoning the absolute primacy and independence of the Soviet apparatus. In a very real sense, therefore, Chinese support may be a liability to any Soviet grouping. And in fact, in its power-struggle aspect, we may perhaps see the attacks on Chinese views made at this time as an attempt, by Khrushchev or others, to smear those of their colleagues who urged a harder foreign policy with the stigma of being little better than Maoists.

The U2 incident seems to have produced a definite, though not perhaps a major, crisis in the Praesidium. It would be hazardous at this stage to do more than sketch a few possibilities. Given the original incident, it would have been contrary to all Soviet notions not to exploit it. Yet it seems that it was intended to combine this with Khrushchev's co-existence theme, on the basis of blaming it on warmongering generals in the Pentagon. When President Eisenhower admitted having personally approved the flight, this manœuvre became impossible and, even if only to contain and satisfy more extreme elements, Khrushchev had little choice but to increase the violence of his language. At the same time he did not cancel the Paris Summit meeting. His immediate break-up of that meeting when it did start seems to indicate a later, last minute decision.

It had been one of the accusations against the Anti-Party Group that they had opposed the meetings of heads of state, as well as the general Khrushchev theory on the reduction of international tensions. His prestige seems therefore to have been heavily involved. And, following the breakdown, having demonstrated an attitude tough enough to avoid any accusation of weakness, he launched a campaign against Chinese and other opponents of 'peaceful co-existence', and at the same time reserved his position with regard to a summit with a future American president.

Such seems a plausible general interpretation of an obscure subject. The key to the situation within the Kremlin on the issue is the position of Mikoyan (the leading proponent of a peaceful, or peaceful-sounding, foreign policy). Here we are on firmer ground.

The May Day photographs show the following order: Voroshilov, Khrushchev, Kozlov, Brezhnev, Furtseva, Mikoyan, Shvernik, Kuusinen, Aristov, Ignatov, Mukhitdinov.

In fact, Mikoyan's position is unprecedentedly low. His name was also omitted from an account of the establishment of Soviet power in Azerbaidzhan, which appeared in *Party Life* of May 1960 — an event with which he had always been associated in previous references to it. And after the beginning of May the Soviet Press no longer described Mikoyan as *First* Deputy Premier, but as deputy Premier simply: i.e. the equal of Ustinov, Zasyadko and Novikov. Kosygin, at the same time was described carefully, and frequently, as *First* Deputy Premier (e.g. *Pravda*, June 15).

Thus the signs of discomfiture were visited on Mikoyan before the May 4 plenum, let alone the presumed belated decision to wreck the summit. There seems no reason to doubt that this signifies that a majority in the Praesidium had emerged against the methods of foreign policy hitherto associated with Khrushchev and Mikoyan. (It is notable that it was Kozlov, and not Khrushchev, who reported on the Bucharest meeting of Communist Parties to the July plenum — (*Pravda*, July 17, 1960).)

But Mikoyan was not actually degraded at the May, or the July, plenums. And this may confirm the idea that Khrushchev, unable to beat his critics, had joined them, offered Mikoyan as a prospective scapegoat, and gradually led them back to the starting-point again, with his attacks on the Chinese, saving Mikoyan on arrival. We can only say that this sounds not unreasonable, not that it is the only conceivable way of looking at the matter. Manœuvres of great complexity were evidently afoot, and little evidence was forthcoming. But in any case the whole episode can be seen as one deeply affecting the position of the First Secretary.

From the policy point of view, 1959-60 had seen a series of failures. The trouble in the Virgin Lands had led to the fall of Belyaev. It was perhaps the difficulties with bourgeois nationalism which provided the pretext for Kirichenko's downfall. Foreign policy issues seem to have at least shaken the position of Mikoyan. And in addition to these, the other main group of policies associated with Khrushchev seem to have come under attack. The July 1960 plenum dealt with industrial as

c c

well as diplomatic problems. This followed a decree of June 18, 1960, setting up a new centralised All-Russian Council of National Economy, to co-ordinate the work of the local C.N.E.'s, and thus to a considerable extent reversing the original de-centralisation of Khrushchev's 1957 reorganisation.

It is natural to associate this abandonment of the idea that the Party machinery would be able to provide adequate co-ordination, with the decrease in the size of the Secretariat. And, in particular, we may link it with the rise of Kosygin.

This senior figure, associated if anything with an earlier anti-Malenkov 'left', had supported Khrushchev in June 1957, but had only received promotion to a low position on the list of candidate members of the Praesidium. Though by far the most experienced economic administrator of the non-Malenkovists, he served as simple Deputy Chairman of the Council of Ministers, with the unknown Kuzmin above him as First Deputy Chairman in charge of economic planning. In March 1959 he had taken over Kuzmin's post as head of Gosplan. The summer of 1960, with Kosygin's promotion to full membership of the Praesidium and First Deputy Chairmanship of the Council of Ministers, also saw the despatch of Kuzmin, who had already lost his governmental post, to be Minister to Switzerland.

As in earlier periods, we seem to detect various majorities within the Praesidium on particular matters of policy. For example, Mikoyan might be seen as supporting Khrushchev on foreign policy, and opposing him on the issue of trying the Anti-Party Group. On the central issue of extending or contain-ing the First Secretary's power, it appears that a sharp, though not explicit, struggle has continued through 1959–60, with no advantage to Khrushchev.

It is quite conceivable, indeed, that Khrushchev, faced with the evident failure of the current attempt to place his own *khvost* in power, willingly sacrificed Kirichenko, and accepted, or even suggested, the compromise whereby other close ad-herents were removed from sensitive power positions, while retaining their seats on the Praesidium — ready, perhaps, for next time. We now await the XXIInd Congress.

If Khrushchev succeeds in destroying all his enemies, and his less enthusiastic friends too, we may still be sure that new factions would arise, and that we should soon see developments similar to those of 1946–53. And, since Khrushchev cannot normally be expected to live more than another decade, we would then find ourselves again among events similar to those of 1953–57, with the whole cycle beginning once more, as in Byzantium or Bagdad.

But this would be to assume that no democratisation of the Soviet regime takes place. It seems to the author that we cannot make that assumption. On the contrary, the relevant forces within and without the Soviet Union are anything but static, and he would expect, barring a war, that another decade or two may see enormous changes. The cycle cannot go on indefinitely amid circumstances which ensure that the regime must evolve or perish.

Meanwhile the struggle for power at the top is the only area of serious political action in the U.S.S.R., and its developments are likely to be important in that evolution, or at least in its early stages. Nor is it likely that the 'new ideas', clearly exerting great attraction to the students and the intelligentsia, are having any effect at all on the minds of the party officials.

We do not end this study at any decisive stage in the permanent struggle. Recent events only gave a few indications of how things were going.

In a way, this is an advantage. For a certain obscurity hangs over them which is far more typical of the circumstances normally requiring interpretation than are the occasional bursts of clarity. And since the precise significance of the present changes cannot now be proved, they constitute a useful test-case for checking, at some future date, the general accuracy of the conceptions presented here as well as, and far more importantly than, the more hypothetical particular conclusions which have been drawn.

A colleague once asked me, 'What is the use of this study?' He was not so obtuse as to imagine that a study may not be worthwhile even if it is not of immediate utility. And I do not really feel that his question required any more answer than that it is justified whether or not it has any more practical value than the history of Cromwell's political life, so long as the subject interests. But he felt, I think, that a work on present-day Russia should contribute to our ability to predict Soviet development, and to cope with Soviet action. The short answer is, I suppose, that for such purposes *any* relevant knowledge is valuable. But I would also take the view that within its limits the study gives us priceless insights into not only the nature of the Soviet political world but also the special characteristics of the members of the Soviet ruling group. Moreover, the basic habits of thought and modes of action which can be followed in these pages are likely to manifest themselves in international affairs as well. The standards of truth and humanity thought suitable in dealings with colleagues may be felt relevant to those likely to be adhered to in relations with foreigners and enemies.

THE RULING GROUP OF THE U.S.S.R.

(i) *The Politburo 1939–49*

The Politburo as elected at the XVIIth Congress in 1934 and recruited at a Central Committee plenum in 1935 consisted entirely of Stalin's supporters against the oppositionist groups. It almost immediately lost nine of the seventeen persons involved — one murdered, one allegedly murdered, one forced suicide, five executed and one dismissed. The XVIIIth Congress in 1939 elected the eight survivors, plus Khrushchev, to be full members of the Politburo, and named two new candidate members. Its composition was as follows (names in alphabetical order):

1939. Andreyev, Voroshilov, Zhdanov, Kaganovich, Kalinin, Mikoyan, Molotov, Stalin, Khrushchev.
Candidates: Beria, Shvernik.

1941. Three new candidates co-opted: Voznesensky, Malenkov, Shcherbakov.
(Shcherbakov died in 1945 and Kalinin in 1946.)

1946. Raised to Members: Beria, Malenkov.
Co-opted as candidates: Bulganin, Kosygin.

1947. Raised to Member: Voznesensky.

1948. Raised to Members: Bulganin, Kosygin.
(Zhdanov died in 1948 and Voznesensky was expelled in 1949 and shot in 1950.)

(ii) *The Secretariat 1939–49*

The *Secretariat* elected after the XVIIIth Congress in 1939 consisted of Stalin, Andreyev, Zhdanov and Malenkov, the only change from its previous composition being the substitution of Malenkov (who was Head of the Cadres Administration of the Central Committee) for Kaganovich. At the Party Conference in 1941 Shcherbakov, a close associate of Zhdanov's and Secretary of the Moscow Provincial and City Party Committees, was added. Shcherbakov died in 1945 and was replaced in his Moscow posts, and then in the Central Committee Secretariat, by G. M. Popov; Andreyev was dropped at this point in favour of A. A. Kuznetsov, transferred from Leningrad, where he had been Zhdanov's successor. In 1946 Patolichev became a Secretary. Later that year Malenkov seems to have been taken off the Secretariat for a time during this period of Zhdanov's ascendancy. Patolichev ceased to be a Secretary on being sent with Kaganovich to the Ukraine during the attack on Khrushchev's position there in 1947. Suslov was appointed a Secretary in 1947. In 1948 Zhdanov died and Ponomarenko was appointed. Kuznetsov lost his post and was shot in 1949, and G. M. Popov was dropped shortly afterwards, being replaced both in his Moscow posts and in the Secretariat by Khrushchev. This left the position as it is, in the following tables, listed vertically:

(iii) *Politburo, Praesidium and Secretariat, 1949–60*

THE LAST POLITBURO

1949–52

(in order of January 1952)

Stalin	Voroshilov	Khrushchev
Molotov	Kaganovich	Bulganin
Malenkov	Mikoyan	Kosygin
Beria	Andreyev	

Candidate:

Shvernik

Secretariat:

Stalin	Khrushchev	Ponomarenko
Malenkov	Suslov	

THE (LARGE) PRAESIDIUM

OCT. 1952–MARCH 1953

(English alphabetical)

Andrianov	Kuusinen	Ponomarenko
Aristov	V. V. Kuznetsov	Saburov
Beria	Malenkov	Shkiryatov
Bulganin	Malyshev	Shvernik
Chesnokov	Melnikov	Stalin
Ignatiev	Mikhailov	Suslov
Kaganovich	Mikoyan	Voroshilov
Korotchenko	Molotov	
Khrushchev	Pervukhin	

Candidates:

Brezhnev	Patolichev	Vyshinsky
Ignatov	Pegov	Yudin
Kabanov	Puzanov	Zverev
Kosygin	Tevosyan	

Secretariat:

Stalin	Suslov	Brezhnev
Malenkov	Mikhailov	Ignatov
Khrushchev	Aristov	
Ponomarenko	Pegov	

'BUREAU OF THE PRAESIDIUM'
OCT. 1952–MARCH 1953
(hypothetical — see pp. 159–163)

Stalin	Kaganovich	Pervukhin
Malenkov	Molotov	Saburov
Bulganin	Beria	Shvernik
Khrushchev	Voroshilov?	Mikoyan?

Candidates (?):

Ponomarenko	Suslov?
Melnikov?	Shkiryatov?

PRAESIDIUM
MARCH 1953

Malenkov	Khrushchev	Saburov
Beria	Bulganin	Pervukhin
Molotov	Kaganovich	
Voroshilov	Mikoyan	

Candidates:

Shvernik	Melnikov
Ponomarenko	Bagirov

Secretariat:
(March 7)

Malenkov	Mikhailov	Pospelov
Khrushchev	Aristov	Shatalin
Suslov	Ignatiev	

(March 14)

Khrushchev	Pospelov	Ignatiev *
Suslov	Shatalin	

JULY 1953

Malenkov	Khrushchev	Mikoyan
Molotov	Bulganin	Saburov
Voroshilov	Kaganovich	Pervukhin

* Out April 1953.

Candidates:

| Shvernik | Ponomarenko | Kirichenko |

Secretariat:
(April 1953)

| Khrushchev | Pospelov |
| Suslov | Shatalin |

JULY 1955
(alphabetical)

Bulganin	Malenkov	Saburov
Voroshilov	Mikoyan	Suslov
Kaganovich	Molotov	Khrushchev
Kirichenko	Pervukhin	

Candidates:

| Shvernik | Ponomarenko |

Secretariat:

| Khrushchev | Shepilov | Belyaev |
| Suslov | Aristov | Pospelov |

FEB. 1956
(alphabetical)

Bulganin	Malenkov	Saburov
Voroshilov	Mikoyan	Suslov
Kaganovich	Molotov	Khrushchev
Kirichenko	Pervukhin	

Candidates:

| Zhukov | Mukhitdinov | Furtseva |
| Brezhnev | Shepilov | Shvernik |

Secretariat:

Khrushchev	Shepilov *	Belyaev
Suslov	Furtseva	Pospelov
Brezhnev	Aristov	

FEB. 1957
The same as Feb. 1956

Candidates:
The same as Feb. 1956 *plus* Kozlov

Secretariat:
The same as Feb. 1956
* Out Dec. 1956–Feb. 1957.

JULY 1957
(English alphabetical)

Aristov	Ignatov	Mikoyan
Belyaev	Khrushchev	Shvernik
Brezhnev	Kirichenko	Suslov
Bulganin	Kozlov	Voroshilov
Furtseva	Kuusinen	Zhukov

Candidates:

Mukhitdinov	Kalnberzins	Mazurov
Pospelov	Kirilenko	Mzhavanadze
Korotchenko	Kosygin	Pervukhin

Secretariat:

The same as Feb. 1957 *less* Shepilov, *plus* Kuusinen

NOV.–DEC. 1957

The same as July 1957 *less* Zhukov, *plus* Mukhitdinov

Candidates:

The same as July 1957 *less* Mukhitdinov (promoted)

Secretariat:

Khrushchev	Furtseva	Mukhitdinov
Kirichenko	Aristov	Pospelov
Suslov	Kuusinen	
Brezhnev	Ignatov	

SEPT. 1958

The same as Nov.–Dec. 1957 *less* Bulganin

Candidates:

The same as Nov.–Dec. 1957 *plus* Podgorny and Polyansky
(May 1958)

Secretariat:

The same as Nov.–Dec. 1957

MAY–JULY 1960
(English alphabetical)

Aristov	Kosygin	Podgorny
Brezhnev	Kozlov	Polyansky
Furtseva	Kuusinen	Shvernik
Ignatov	Mikoyan	Suslov
Khrushchev	Mukhitdinov	

Candidates:

Pospelov	Kalnberzins	Pervukhin
Korotchenko	Mazurov	
Kirilenko	Mzhavanadze	

Secretariat:

Khrushchev	Kozlov	Mukhitdinov
Suslov	Kuusinen	

(iv) *The Orgburo*

A third body, the Orgburo, was abolished in 1952, when the Secretariat's numbers were raised from five to ten. Its precise composition in 1952 is not known, but in 1946 it consisted of

Stalin
Zhdanov
Malenkov } The Secretaries of the Central Committee.
A. A. Kuznetsov
G. M. Popov

Patolichev
Andrianov
G. F. Aleksandrov } Members of the Central Committee apparatus, representing the Cadres and Agitprop administrations.
Shatalin
Suslov

Bulganin } Minister of Defence and Head of the Armed
Mekhlis   } Forces Political Administration respectively.

Mikhailov.   Head of the Komsomol.
V. V. Kuznetsov. Head of the Trade Unions.
Rodionov.   Prime Minister of the R.S.F.S.R.

The ten-man Secretariat of 1952 — allowing for personnel changes — may be regarded as equivalent to the Ogburo less the five last names listed, who are (except for Mekhlis) peripheral to the Party machine.

(v) *Men no longer at the seat of power — 1960*

    (a) *Living ex-members of the Politburo and small Praesidium:*
Andreyev, Molotov, Kaganovich, Malenkov, Bulganin, Saburov, Zhukov, Kirichenko, Belyaev (full members). Ponomarenko, Melnikov, Shepilov (candidate members).

    (b) *Living ex-members of the large (1952–53) Praesidium (not including the above):*
Andrianov, Chesnokov, Ignatiev, V. V. Kuznetsov,

Mikhailov (full members). Kabanov, Patolichev, Pegov, Puzanov, Yudin, Zverev (candidate members).

(c) *Living ex-members of the Secretariat:*

Molotov, Kaganovich, Andreyev, Malenkov, Ponomarenko, Shepilov, Ignatiev, Shatalin, Patolichev, Pegov, Mikhailov, G. M. Popov, Kirichenko, Belyaev.

INDEX OF THE CENTRAL COMMITTEE
1952 AND 1956

1. *Full Members*

(Those italicised are the probable membership of the Committee at the time of the XXIst Congress 1959.)

			Appointments at time of election (subsequent career in brackets).
Alferov, P. N. *		1956	Sec. Yaroslavl Prov. (Control Com. 1958).
Andreyev, A. A.	1952	1956	Dep. Ch. C. of M. 1952; M. Praes. Sup. Sov. 1956.
Andrianov, V. M.	1952		M. Praes. C.C.; Sec. Leningrad Prov. (rel. Nov. 1953).
Aristov, A. B.	1952	1956	M. Praes. & Sec. C.C. 1952; Sec. C.C. 1956 (M. Praes. C.C. 1957).
Arutinov, G. A.	1952		Sec. Armenia.
Avkhimovich, N. E.		1956	2 Sec. Byelorussia (Ch. C. of M. Byelorussia 1956, rel. April 1959).
Babaev, S.	1952	1956	Sec. Turkmenia 1952 (denounced and dismissed Dec. 1958, expelled 1959).
Bagirov, M. D.	1952		Sec. Azerbaidzhan (denounced July 1953, executed April 1956).
Baibakov, N. K.	1952	1956	Min. Petroleum Ind. 1952; Ch. Gosplan 1956 (Ch. Gosplan R.S.F.S.R. 1957, rel. 1958).
Belyaev, N. I.	1952	1956	Sec. Altai Terr. 1952; Sec. C.C. 1956 (Sec. Kazakhstan & M. Praes. C.C. 1957, dismissed 1960).

Appointments at time of election (subsequent career in brackets).

Benediktov, I. A.	1952	1956	Min. Agric. 1952; Min. State Farms 1956 (Amb. India 1959).
Beria, L. P.	1952		M. Praes. C.C.; Dep. Ch. C. of M. (executed Dec. 1953).
Beshchev, B. P.	1952	1956	Min. Railways 1952 and 1956.
Bobrovnikov, N. I.		1956	Ch. Moscow City Exec. Com.
Boitsov, I. P. *	1952	1956	Sec. Stavropol Terr. 1952 and 1956.
Borkov, G. A.	1952		Sec. Saratov Prov.
Brezhnev, D. D.		1956	2 Sec. Leningrad Prov. (relieved July 1956).
Brezhnev, L. I.	1952	1956	Cand. M. Praes. C.C. 1952; Cand. M. Praes. C.C., and Sec. Kazakhstan 1956.(Sec. C.C. 1956, Ch. Sup. Sov. 1960).
Bulganin, N. A.	1952	1956	M. Praes. C.C. 1952; Ch. C. of M. 1956 (rel. Feb.–Sept. 1958).
Cheplakov, P. F.	1952	(Cand. 1956)	Sec. Sakhalin Prov.
Chernyshev, V. E.	1952	1956	Sec. Kalingrad Prov. 1952 and 1956 (Sec. Maritime Terr. 1959).
Chesnokov, D. I.	1952		M. Praes. C.C.
Daniyalov, A. D.	(Cand. 1952)	1956	Sec. Daghestan Prov. 1952 and 1956.
Dementiev, P. V.	(Cand. 1952)	1956	Dep. M. Aviation Ind. 1952; M. Aviation Ind. 1956 (Ch. State Com. Aviation Tech. 1957).
Denisov, G. A.	1952	1956	Sec. Kurgan Prov. 1952; Sec. Saratov Prov. 1956 (Amb. Bulgaria 1960).
Deryugin, B. I.		1956	Sec. Novosibirsk Prov. (2 Sec. Omsk 1958).
Doronin, P. I.		1956	Sec. Smolensk Prov.
Dudorov, N. P.		1956	Min. Internal Affairs.
Dzhavakhishvili, G. D.		1956	Ch. C. of M. Georgia.

			Appointments at time of election (subsequent career in brackets).
Efimov, A. P.	1952		Sec. Khabarovsk Terr. (rel. 1954).
Efremov, L. N.	1952	1956	Sec. Kursk Prov. 1952 and 1956 (Sec. Gorki Prov. 1958).
Efremov, M. T.		1956	Sec. Kuibyshev Prov. (Head C.C. Party Organs Dept. R.S.F.S.R. 1959).
Egorov, A. N.	1952		Sec. Karelo-Finnia.
Enyutin, G. V.		1956	Sec. Kamensk Prov. (Com. of Sov. Control 1957).
Fadeev, A. A.	1952 (Cand. 1956)		Ch. Union of Writers (suicide 1956).
Furtseva, E. A.	(Cand. 1952)	1956	2 Sec. Moscow City 1952; Cand. M. Praes. & Sec. C.C.; Sec. Moscow City City 1956 (M. Praes. C.C. 1957, Min. Culture 1960).
Gaevoi, A. I.		1956	Sec. Zaporozhe Prov. (Sec. Dnepnopetrovsk Dec. 1957).
Gafurov, B. G.	1952	1956	Sec. Tadzhikistan (rel. 1956).
Goryachev, F. S.	1952	1956	Sec. Tyumen Prov. (Sec. Novosibirsk Prov. 1959).
Grishin, I. T.	1952	1956	Sec. Stalingrad Prov. 1952; Amb. Czechoslovakia 1956 (Dep. M. F. Trade 1960).
Grishin, V. V.	1952	1956	2 Sec. Moscow Prov. 1952; Ch. Trade Unions 1956.
Gromyko, A. A.	(Cand. 1952)	1956	1st Dep. M. F.A. (M. F.A. 1957).
Gusev, M. I.	1952		Sec. Kemerovo Prov.
Ignatiev, S. D.	1952	1956	M. Praes. C.C., Min. of St. Security 1952; Sec. Bashkir Prov. 1956.
Ignatov, N. F.		1956	2 Sec. Moscow Prov. (Ch. Moscow Prov. Exec. Com. 1956, rel. March 1959, Sec. Orel Prov. 1960).

			Appointments at time of election (subsequent career in brackets).
Kiselev, N. V.	1952	1956	Sec. Rostov Prov. 1952 and 1956 (rel. 1960).
Kiselev, V. I.	1952		Sec. Kalinin Prov.
Klimenko, V. K.		1956	Sec. Voroshilovgrad Prov.
Kobelev, B. N.		1956	Sec. Irkutsk Prov.
Kolushchinsky, E. P.		1956	Sec. Omsk Prov.
Konev, I. S.	1952	1956	Marshal, Dep. M. of War 1952; Supreme Commander Warsaw Pact 1956.
Korchagin, P. N.	1952		Sec. Chkalov Prov. (rel. Dec. 1955).
Korneichuk, A. E.	1952	1956	Ch. Praes. Sup. Sov. Ukraine 1952; Writer 1956.
Korotchenko, D. S.	1952	1956	M. Praes. C.C., Ch. C. of M. Ukraine 1952; Ch. Praes. Sup. Sov. Ukraine 1956 (Cand. M. Praes. 1957).
Kosygin, A. N.	1952	1956	Cand. M. Praes. C.C., Dep. Ch. C. of M. 1952; Dep. Ch. C. of M. 1956 (Cand. M. Praes. C.C. 1957; Ch. Gosplan 1959; M. Praes. C.C., 1st Dep. Ch. C. of M. 1960).
Kovrigina, M. D.	1952	1956	Min. Health R.S.F.S.R. 1952; Min. Health 1956 (rel. 1958).
Kozlov, F. R.	1952	1956	2 Sec. Leningrad Prov. 1952; 1st Sec. Leningrad Prov. 1956 (M. Praes. C.C. 1957; Ch. C. of M. R.S.F.S.R. 1957; 1st Dept. Ch. C. of M. 1958; Sec. C.C. 1960).
Kruglov, S. N.	1952		Min. of Internal Affairs (relieved Jan. 1956).
Kucherenko, V. A.		1956	Dep. Ch. C. of M. (Dep. Ch. Gosekon 1956).
Kuliev, T. I.	1952		Ch. C. of M. Azerbaidzhan (relieved March 1954).
Kunaev, D. A.		1956	Ch. C. of M. Kazakhstan (1960 Sec. Kazakhstan).

Appointments at time of election (subsequent careers in brackets).

Kutyrev, A. M.	1952		Sec. Sverdlovsk Prov.
Kuusinen, O. V.	1952	1956	M. Praes. C.C. 1952; Ch. Praes. Sup. Sov. Karelo-Finland 1952 and 1956 (M. Praes. & Sec. C.C. 1957).
Kuznetsov, N. G.	1952		Min. of Navy.
Kuznetsov, V. V.	1952	1956	M. Praes. C.C., Ch. Council of Trade Unions 1952; 1st Dep. Min. F.A. 1956.
Laptev, N. V.		1956	Sec. Chelyabinsk Prov.
Larionov, A. N.	1952	1956	Sec. Ryazan Prov. 1952 and 1956 (died 1960).
Latunov, I. S.	1952	1956	Sec. Archangelsk Prov. 1952; Sec. Vologda Prov. 1956 (rel. 1960).
Lebedev, I. K.	1952	1956	Sec. Omsk Prov. 1952; 1st Dep. Ch. C. of M. R.S.F.S.R. 1956 (Sec. Stavropol Prov. 1957, rel. 1960).
Lubennikov, L. I.		1956	Sec. Karelo-Finland (Sec. Karelian Prov. 1956, Sec. Kemerovo Prov. 1960).
Lukyanov, V. V.	1952		Sec. Yaroslavl. Prov.
Malenkov, G. M.	1952	1956	M. Praes. & Sec. C.C.; Dep. Ch. C. of M. 1952; Dep. Ch. C. of M. 1956 (expelled C.C. June 1957).
Malinovsky, R. Ya.	(Cand. 1952)	1956	Marshal, C.-in-C. Far East 1952 and 1956 (Min. of Defence 1957).
Malyshev, V. A.	1952	1956	M. Praes. C.C., Dep. Ch. C. of M. 1952; Dep. Ch. C. of M. 1956 (died 1957).
Marchenko, I. T.		1956	2 Sec. Moscow City (Sec. Tomsk Prov. 1960).
Marfin, A. I.	1952		?
Markov, V. S.		1956	Sec. Orel Prov. (rel. 1960).
Matskevich, V. V.		1956	Min. Agric.

D D

			Appointments at time of election (subsequent career in brackets).
Mazurov, K. T.		1956	Ch. C. of M. Byelorussia (Sec. C.C. Byelorussia 1956; Cand. M. Praes. C.C. 1957).
Mekhlis, L. Z.	1952		? Head of Political Adm. Armed Forces (died Feb. 1953).
Melnik, D. N.	1952		Sec. Maritime Terr.
Melnikov, L. G.	1952	(Cand. 1956)	M. Praes. C.C.; Sec. Ukraine 1952.
Mgeladze, A. I.	1952		Sec. Georgia.
Mikhailov, N. A.	1952	1956	M. Praes. & Sec. C.C. 1952; Min. Culture 1956 (Amb. Indonesia 1960).
Mikoyan, A. I.	1952	1956	M. Praes. C.C.; Dep. Ch. C. of M. 1952; M. Praes. C.C.; 1st Dep. Ch. C. of M. 1956.
Mitin, M. B.	1952	1956	Ideologist 1952; editor *Cominform Journal* 1956.
Molotov, V. M.	1952	1956	M. Praes. C.C.; Dep. Ch. C. of M. 1952; M. Praes. C.C.; 1st Dep. Ch. C. of M. 1956 (expelled June 1957).
Moskalenko, K. S.		1956	Marshal. G.O.C. Moscow District.
Moskvin, V. A.	1952	1956	Sec. Tomsk Prov. 1952 and 1956 (rel. 1960).
Mukhitdinov, N. A.	1952	1956	Ch. C. of M. Uzbekistan, 1952; Sec. Uzbekistan & Cand. M. Praes. C.C. 1956 (M. Praes. & Sec. C.C. 1957).
Muratov, Z. I.	1952	1956	Sec. Tatar Prov. (resigned 1957).
Mustafaev, I. D.		1956	Sec. Azerbaidzhan (rel. 1959).
Mzhavanadze, V. P.		1956	Sec. Georgia (Cand. M. Praes. C.C. 1957).
Nasriddinova, Ya. S.		1956	Dep. Ch. C. of M. Uzbekistan.
Nedosekin, V. I.	1952		Sec. Tula Prov. (rel. Nov. 1953).
Nikolaev, B. F.	1952		Sec. Smolensk Prov.
Niyazov, A. I.	1952		Sec. Uzbekistan.

Appointments at time of election (subsequent career in brackets).

Prass, F. M.	1952		Sec. Molotov Prov.
Prokofiev, V. A.	1952	1956	Sec. Murmansk 1952 and 1956 (Sec. Novgorod Prov. 1958).
Pronin, V. P.	1952		Min. Labour Reserves.
Puzanov, A. M.	1952	1956	Cand. M. Praes. C.C., Ch. C. of M. R.S.F.S.R. 1952; 1st Dep. Ch. C. of M. R.S.F.S.R. 1956 (Amb. to North Korea 1957).
Pysin, K. G.		1956	Sec. Altai Terr.
Ragimov, S. G.		1956	Ch. C. of M. Azerbaidzhan (relieved July 1958).
Razzakov, I. R.	1952	1956	Sec. Kirghizia.
Rumyantsev, A. M.	1952	1956	Ideologist; Chief Editor *Kommunist* 1956 (Editor *Problems of Peace and Socialism* 1958).
Saburov, M. Z.	1952	1956	M. Praes. C.C., Dep. Ch. C. of M., Ch. Gosplan 1952; M. Praes., 1st Dep. Ch. C. of M. & Ch. Gosplan 1956 (relieved 1957).
Semin, A. V.	1952		Sec. Vologda Prov.
Serdyuk, Z. T.	(Cand. 1952)	1956	Sec. Lvov Prov. 1952; Sec. Moldavia 1956.
Serov, I. A.	(Cand. 1952)	1956	1st Dep. Min. Internal Affairs 1952; Ch. K.G.B. 1956 (relieved Dec. 1958).
Shatalin, N. N.	(Cand. 1952. Full 1953)		Inspector C.C. 1952; Sec. C.C. 1953 (relieved 1955).
Shayakhmetov, Zh.	1952		Sec. Kazakhstan 1952.
Shelepin, A. N.	1952	1956	A Sec. Komsomol 1952; 1st Sec. Komsomol from Nov. 1952 (K.G.B. 1958).

Appointments at time of election (subsequent career in brackets).

Titov, F. E.	1952	1956	Sec. Ivanovo Prov. 1952 and 1956 (2 Sec. Uzbekistan 1959).
Titov, P. I.	1952		Sec. Crimea Prov.
Titov, V. N.		1956	Sec. Kharkov Prov.
Tovmasyan, S. A.		1956	Sec. Armenia.
Ustinov, D. F.	1952	1956	Min. Armaments Ind. 1952; Min. Defence Ind. 1956 (Dep. Ch. C. of M. 1957).
Vagapov, S. A.	1952		Sec. Bashkir Prov.
Vannikov, B. L.	1952	1956	Col. Gen. Engineer & Artillery Services 1952; Dep. Min. Medium Machine Bldg. 1956.
Vasilevsky, A. M.	1952	1956	Min. of Defence 1952; 1st Dep. Min. of Defence 1956 (retired 1958).
Volkov, A. P.		1956	Ch. Moscow Prov. Exec. Com. (Ch. State Com. for Labour & Wages 1957).
Volkov, I. A.	1952		Sec. Orel Prov.
Voronov, G. I.	1952	1956	Sec. Chita Prov. 1952; Dep. Min. Agric. 1956 (Sec. Orenburg 1957).
Voroshilov, K. Ye.	1952	1956	M. Praes. C.C. 1952; M. Praes. C.C. & Ch. Praes. Sup. Sov. 1956 (retired 1960).
Vyshinsky, A. Ya.	1952		Cand. M. Praes. C.C.; Min. F.A. 1952 (died Nov. 1954).
Yakovlev, I. D.	1952	1956	Sec. Novosibirsk Prov. 1952; 2 Sec. Kazakhstan 1956 (Sec. Kazakhstan 1956, Sec. Ulyanovsk Prov. 1958).
Yasnov, M. A.	1952	1956	Ch. Moscow City Exec. Com. 1952; Ch. C. of M., R.S.F.S.R. 1956 (1st Dep. 1958).

			Appointments at time of election (subsequent career in brackets).
Yudin, P. F.	1952	1956	Cand. M. Praes. C.C. 1952; Ambassador to China 1956.
Yusupov, U. Ya.	1952		Min. Cotton Growing 1952.
Zademidko, A. N.		1956	Min. Coal Ind. (Ch. C.N.E. Kemerovo 1957).
Zasyadko, A. F.	1952		Min. Coal Ind. U.S.S.R. (relieved March 1955; Dep. Ch. C. of M. 1958).
Zavenyagin, A. P.	(Cand. 1952)	1956	Dep. Min. Internal Affairs 1952; Dep. Ch. C. of M., U.S.S.R. 1956 (died 1956).
Zhdanov, Yu. A.	1952		Head of Dept. of Science & Culture C.C.
Zhegalin, I. K.	1952	1956	Sec. Grozny Prov. 1952; Sec. Stalingrad Prov. 1956 (Amb. Rumania 1960).
Zhukov, G. K.	(Cand. 1952, full 1953)	1956	Marshal 1952; Min. of Defence & Cand. M. Praes. C.C. 1956 (expelled C.C. Oct. 1957).
Zhukov, K. P.	1952	(Cand.	Sec. Voronezh Prov. 1956)
Zimyanin, M. V.	1952		2 Sec. Byelorussia.
Zverev, A. G.	1952	1956	Cand. M. Praes. C.C., 1952; Min. Finance 1952 and 1956.

The full members elected in 1956 included seventy-nine of the 1952 full members, and thirteen of the candidates. Forty-one were new.

2. Candidate Members

Akhazov, T.A.	1952	Sec. Chuvash Prov.
Aleksandrov, G. F.	1952	Director Institute of Philosophy (Min. Culture 1954, relieved March 1955).
Alekseenko, G. V.	1952	Min. Communications Ind.

			Appointments at time of election (subsequent career in brackets).
Andreyeva, N. N.*		1956	Sec. Baumann Region, Moscow (relieved by Jan. 1957).
Artemyev, P. A.	1952		Col. Gen. G.O.C. Moscow District (relieved 1953).
Bagramyan, I. K.	1952	1956	Marshal.
Bakradze, V. M.	1952		Dep. Ch. C. of M. Georgia (Ch. C. of M. Georgia April 1953, relieved Sept. 1953).
Basisty, N. E.	1952		Admiral, Dep. Min. Navy.
Biryuzov, S. S.		1956	Marshal.
Bogdanov, S. I.	1952		Marshal, C.-in-C. Tank Corps.
Bondarenko, A. D.	1952		Sec. Bryansk Prov.
Borisov, S. Z.	1952	1956	Sec. Yakutsk Prov. 1952 and 1956.
Budenny, S. M.	1952	1956	Marshal (Dep. Min. Agric. 1952).
Butuzov, S. M.	1952	1956	Sec. Penza Prov. 1952 and 1956.
Bubnovsky, N. D.		1956	A Sec. C.C. Ukraine.
Cheplakov, P. F.	(Full 1952)	1956	Sec. Sakhalin Prov.
Chubinidze, M. D.		1956	Ch. Praes. Sup. Sov. Georgia.
Chuikov, V. I.	1952	1956	General 1952; Marshal, G.O.C. Kiev District 1956.
Chumachenko, G. A.	1952		Dep. Min. (Head Political Directorate) Railways.
Churaev, V. M.		1956	Head Dept. of Party Organs. (R.S.F.S.R.) of C.C. (Ditto (Union Republics) 1959).
Daniyalov, A. D.	1952	(Full 1956)	Sec. Daghestan Prov.
Dementiev, P. V.	1952	(Full 1956)	Dep. Min. Aviation Ind.
Dvinsky, B. A.	1952		?
Dygai, N. A.	1952	1956	Min. Constr. of Machine Bldg. Enterprises; Min. Cons. 1956 (Dep. Ch. R.S.F.S.R. Gosplan 1958).

			Appointments at time of election (subsequent career in brackets).
Efremov, D. V.	1952		Min. Electrical Industry.
Elyutin, V. P.		1956	Min. Higher Education.
Epishev, A. A.	1952	1956	Sec. Odessa Prov. 1952; Ambassador to Rumania 1956.
Eremenko, A. I.		1956	Marshal.
Evseenko, M. A.		1956	Min. Petroleum Industry (Dep. Ch. R.S.F.S.R. Gosplan 1957).
Fadeev, A. A.	(Full 1952)	1956	Sec. Union of Writers (suicide 1956).
Fedorov, A. G.	1952		?
Firyubin, N. P.		1956	Ambassador to Yugoslavia (Dep. M.F.A. 1957).
Florentiev, L. Ya.		1956	Sec. Altai Terr. (Sec. Kostroma Prov. 1957).
Furtseva, E. A.	1952	(Full 1956)	2 Sec. Moscow City.
Ganenko, I. P.		1956	Sec. Astrakhan Prov.
Gedvilas, M. A.	1952		Ch. C. of M. Lithuania (relieved Jan. 1956).
Glebovsky, G. N.		1956	Director, Uralmash Works, Sverdlovsk.
Goglidze, S. A.	1952		Col. Gen. of St. Security (executed Dec. 1953).
Gorbatov, A. V.	1952	1956	Col. Gen. G.O.C. Baltic District (relieved 1958).
Gorshenin, K. P.	1952		Min. Justice.
Gorshkov, S. G.		1956	Admiral.
Govorov, L. A.	1952		Marshal, Dep. Min. of Wa (died March 1955).
Grechko, A. A.	1952	1956	Col. Gen. G.O.C. Kiev District 1952; Marshal, C.-in-C. Sov. Forces, Germany 1956.
Grechukha, M. S.		1956	1st Dep. Ch. C. of M. Ukraine.
Grigoryan, V. G.	1952		Dep. Ed. *Cominform Journal* (Head of Press Dept. M.F.A., relieved Sept. 1953).

			Appointments at time of election (subsequent career in brackets).
Grishin, K. N.		1956	Sec. Vladimir Prov.
Grishko, G. E.		1956	Sec. Kiev Prov. (rel. illness, 1957).
Gromov, E. I.		1956	Head Dept. Party Organs. (Union Republics) C.C. (Amb. to Hungary 1957).
Gromyko, A. A.	1952	(Full 1956)	Ambassador to U.K. 1952; 1st Dep. Min. F.A. 1956.
Gureev, N. M.		1956	1st Dep. Ch. C. of M. Ukraine.
Ilichev, L. F.	1952		Chief Editor *Pravda* (Head Press Dept. M.F.A. Sept. 1953).
Ishkov, A. A.		1956	Min. Fish Ind. (Head Dept. Gosplan 1958).
Islyukov, S. M.		1956	Ch. C. of M. Chuvash, A.S.S.R.
Ivashchenko, O. I.		1956	A Sec. Ukraine.
Kairov, I. A.	1952		Min. Education R.S.F.S.R.
Kalchenko, N. T.	1952	(Full 1956)	1st Dep. Ch. C. of M. Ukraine.
Kalmykov, V. D.		1956	Min. Radiotechnical Ind. (Ch. State Con. Radioelectronics 1957).
Kannunikov, M. Ya.	1952	1956	Sec. Pskov Prov.
Karasev, V. Ya.		1956	M. Leningrad Prov. Com.
Kazakov, N. S.	1952		Min. Heavy Machine Bldg.
Kazanets, I. P.		1956	Sec. Stalino Prov.
Khakalov A. U.	1952	1956	Sec. Buryat Mongol Prov.
Khokhlov, I. S.	1952		Ch. Consumers' Cooperatives
Klimov, A. P.		1956	Ch. Consumers' Cooperatives.
Kobulov, B. Z.	1952		Dep. Min. State Security (executed Dec. 1953).
Komarov, P. T.*	1952	1956	Dep. Ch. Party Control Com. 1952 and 1956.
Komyakhov, V. G.		1956	Sec. Crimea Prov.
Konstantinov, F. V.		1956	Head Dept. of Agitation & Propaganda C.C.

Appointments at time of election (subsequent career in brackets).

Korniets, L. R.	1952	1956	Dep. Ch. C. of M. Ukraine 1952; Min. Agric. Procurement 1956 (Ch. State Com. Grain Products 1958).
Kosov, V. V.		1956	Chief Inspector Min. of Agric.
Kostousov, A. I.	1952	1956	Min. Machine Tool Bldg. 1952 and 1956 (Ch. Moscow Prov. C.N.E. 1957).
Koval, K. I.		1956	Head Chief Admin. Econ. Relations with Peoples Democracies (relieved 1957).
Kozlov, A. I.	1952	1956	Head Agric. Dept. C.C. 1952; Min. St. Farms 1953 (dismissed 1955).
Kozlov, V. I.		1956	Ch. Praes. Sup. Sov. Byelorussia (Sec. Chita Prov. 1958, relieved March 1958).
Krakhmalev, M. K.		1956	Sec. Belgorod Prov.
Kulov, K. D.	1952		Sec. N. Ossetian Prov.
Kumykin, P. N.	1952	1956	Min. F. Trade 1952; Dep. Min. F. Trade 1956.
Kuznetsov, F. F.	1952		Head Political Admin. Sov. Army.
Kuznetsova, K. S.	1952		Sec. Trade Unions.
Ladanov, P. F.	1952		Ch. Leningrad Exec. Com.
Latsis, V. T.	1952	1956	Ch. C. of M. Latvia (rel. 1959).
Likhachev, I. A.		1956	Min. Automobile Tpt. & Highways (died 1956).
Lobanov, P. P.		1956	Dep. Ch. C. of M. (relieved 1956).
Loginov, S. P.		1956	2 Sec. Archangel Prov. (Sec. Archangel Prov. 1957, d. 1960).
Lomako, P. F.	1952	1956	Min. Non-ferrous Metallurgy (1952 and 1956); Ch. Krasnoyarsk C.N.E. 1957).

			Appointments at time of election (subsequent career in brackets).
Luchinsky, A. A.	1952	1956	Col. Gen. G.O.C. Leningrad District 1952; Army Gen. G.O.C. Turkestan 1956 (rel. 1957).
Lunev, K. F.		1956	Dep. Ch. K.G.B. (Ch. K.G.B. Kazakhstan 1959).
Lykova, L. P.	1952	1956	2 Sec. Ivanovo Prov. 1952; Sec. Ivanovo Prov. 1956 (2 Sec. Smolensk 1959).
Maksarev, Yu. E.	1952	1956	Min. Tpt. Machine Bldg. 1952; Dep. Min. Tpt & Heavy Machine Bldg. 1956 (Ch. St. Science-Technical Com. 1957, Dep. Ch. 1959).
Malik, Ya. A.	1952	1956	Dep. Min. F.A. 1952; Ambassador in London 1956.
Malinin, M. S.	1952		Col. Gen., Dep. Chief of General Staff (died 1960).
Malinovsky, R. Ya.	1952	(Full 1956)	Marshal.
Mamonov, F. A.	1952		Sec. Astrakhan Prov.
Maslennikov, I. I.	1952		Dep. Min. Internal Affairs.
Melnikov, L. G.	(Full 1952)	1956	Min. Const. of Coal Enterprises (Ch. Kazakhstan Gosplan 1957).
Melnikov, R. E.	1952	1956	2 Sec. Uzbekistan (rel. 1959).
Menshikov, M. A.		1956	Amb. to India (Amb. to Washington 1958).
Meretskov, K. A.	1952		Marshal G.O.C. White Sea District.
Merkulov, V. N.	1952		Min. State Control (executed Dec. 1953).
Mylarshchikov, V. P.		1956	Head Dept. Agric. (R.S.F.S.R.) C.C.
Myuurisep, A. A.	1952	1956	Ch. C. of M. Estonia 1952 and 1956.
Naidek, L. I.		1956	Sec. Odessa Prov. (2 Sec. Ukraine 1957).

Appointments at time of election (subsequent career in brackets).

Popova, N. V.		1956	Ch. Soviet Women's Anti-Fascist Committee.
Postovalov, S. O.	1952	1956	Ch. Crimea Exec. Com. 1952; Sec. Kaluga Prov. 1956.
Raizer, D. Ya.	1952	1956	Min. Constr. Heavy Ind. Enterprises 1952; Min. Constr. Metallurgical & Chemical Enterprises 1956 (Kazakhstan Min. of Constr. 1957, relieved 1958).
Rashidov, Sh. R.		1956	Ch. Praes. Sup. Sov. Uzbekistan (Sec. Uzbekistan 1959).
Rud, G. Ya.		1956	Ch. C. of M. Moldavia (relieved Jan. 1958).
Rudakov, A. P.		1956	M. C.C. Lithuania.
Rudenko, R. A.		1956	Procurator General.
Rumyantsev, S. S.	1952		Sec. Velikie Luki Prov.
Ryabikov, V. M.	1952	1956	Dep. Min. Armaments Ind. 1952 (1958 Dep. Ch. C. of M. R.S.F.S.R.).
Ryasnoy, V. S.	1952		Dep. Min. Internal Affairs.
Semichastny, V. E.		1956	A Sec. Komsomol (Sec. Komsomol 1958; Party Organs Dept. C.C. 1959. 2 Sec. Azerbaidzhan 1959).
Senin, I. S.		1956	1st Dep. Ch. C. of M. Ukraine (Ch. Ukraine Gosplan 1957).
Serdyuk, Z. T.	1952	(Full 1956)	Sec. Lvov Prov.
Serov, I. A.	1952	(Full 1956)	1st Dep. Min. Internal Affairs.
Shaskov, Z. A.	1952	1956	Min. River Fleet 1952, 1956 (ditto R.S.F.S.R. 1956).
Shatalin, N. N.	1952		Inspector C.C.; (full member 1953; Sec. C.C., relieved 1955).
Sheremetiev, A. G.		1956	Min. Ferrous Metallurgy (Ch. Chelyabinsk C.N.E. 1957, relieved 1957).

			Appointments at time of election (subsequent career in brackets).
Shkolnikov, A. M.	1952	(Full 1956)	Sec. Tambov Prov.
Shtemenko, S. M.	1952		Chief of Staff (relieved Feb. 1953).
Shumauskas, M. Yu.		1956	Ch. C. of M. Lithuania.
Simonov, K. M.	1952		Writer.
Sinyagovsky, P. E.		1956	M. C.C. Ukraine.
Sizov, G. F.		1956	Sec. Kurgan Prov.
Skidanenko, I. T.		1956	Min. Electrotechnical Ind. (relieved 1957).
Skulkov, I. P.	1952	1956	Sec. Ulyanovsk Prov. (Ch. Sov. Central Com. R.S.F.S.R. 1958).
Smirnov, N. I.		1956	Ch. Leningrad City Exec. Com.
Sokolov, K. M.	1952		Ch. St. Com. for Constr. (relieved March 1955).
Sokolov, T. I.		1956	Head of Dept. Min. of Agric.
Soloviev, L. N.	1952	1956	Sec. Trade Unions, 1952; Dep. Ch. Trade Unions 1956.
Stepanov, S. A.	1952	1956	Min. Agric. Machine Bld. 1952; Min. Tpt. Machine Bldg. 1956 (Ch. Sverdlovsk C.N.E. 1957).
Stepanova, E. A.	1952		Dep. Director Marx-Engels-Lenin Institute.
Stoletov, V. N.	1952		Min. Higher Education.
Strokin, N. I.		1956	Min. Automobile Ind. (Dep. Ch. Gosplan 1958).
Surganov, F. A.		1956	Sec. Minsk Prov. (A Sec. Byelorussia 1956).
Surkov, A. A.		1956	1st Sec. Union of Writers (relieved 1959).
Tarasov, M. P.		1956	Ch. Praes. Sup. Sov. R.S.F.S.R.
Tashenev, Zh. A.		1956	Ch. Praes. Sup. Sov. Kazakhstan.
Tikhomirov, S. M.	1952	(Full 1956)	Min. Chemical Ind.

			Appointments at time of election (subsequent career in brackets).
Timoshenko, S. K.	1952	1956	Marshal, G.O.C. Byelorussian District 1952 and 1956 (rel. 1960).
Toka, S. K.	1952	1956	Sec. Tuva Prov. 1952 and 1956.
Trofimov, A. S.		1956	Sec. Balashov Prov. (Sec. Chechen Prov. 1959).
Tskhovrebashvili, V. F.	1952		2 Sec. Georgia (Ch. Praes. Sup. Sov. Georgia 1953, relieved Oct. 1953).
Tsyren, V. F.	1952		Head Admin. for Metal Supply (Dep. Ch. Gossnab Jan. 1953).
Tumanova, Z. P.	1952	1956	A Sec. Komsomol.
Tur, I. P.		1956	Sec. Novosibirsk.
Vershinin, K. A.	1952		Marshal of Aviation.
Voronov, F. D.		1956	Factory Director.
Yudin, P. A.	1952	1956	Min. Constr. Materials Ind. 1952 and 1956 (died 1956).
Yumashev, I. S.	1952		Admiral.
Yurkin, T. A.		1956	Min. St. Farms R.S.F.S.R. (R.S.F.S.R. Dep. Min. Agric. 1958).
Zakharov, P. A.	1952		Min. Geology.
Zakharov, S. E.	1952		Admiral. Head Political Directorate Navy.
Zakurdaev, V. I.		1956	Sec. Mordov Prov. (Ch. Com. of Sov. Control 1959).
Zamchevski, I. K.		1956	Sec. Leningrad City (Ambassador to Yugoslavia 1957).
Zarubin, G. N.	1952	1956	Ambassador to Washington 1952 and 1956 (died 1958).
Zavenyagin, A. P.	1952	(Full 1956)	Dep. Min. Internal Affairs (died 1956).
Zhavoronkov, V. G.	1952	1956	Min. Internal Trade 1952; Min. State Control 1956 (Dep. Min. 1956).
Zhigarev, P. F.	1952	1956	Chief Marshal of Aviation.

			Appointments at time of election (subsequent career in brackets).
Zhimerin, D. G.	1952	1956	Min. Electric Power Stations 1952; 1st Dep. Ch. Gosplan 1956 (Dep. Ch. R.S.F.S.R. Gosplan 1957).
Zhukov, G. K.	1952	(Full 1956)	Marshal (full member 1953).
Zhukov, K. P.	(Full 1952)	1956	Sec. Lipetsk Prov. (rel. 1960).
Zhurin, N. I.		1956	Sec. Akmolinsk Prov. (2 Sec. Kazakhstan 1956; Sec. N. Kazakh Prov. 1957).
Zolotukhin, G. S.		1956	Sec. Tambov Prov.
Zorin, V. A.		1956	Dep. Min. F.A. (Amb. to W. Germany).
Zotov, V. P.		1956	Min. Foodstuffs Ind. (Dep. Ch. Gosplan 1957).

The candidate membership elected in 1956 (122) included four demoted from full membership of the 1952 Committee, forty-seven of the 1952 candidate members, and seventy-one new candidate members.

Abbreviations

Admin.	Administration
Agric.	Agriculture
Amb.	Ambassador
Bldg.	Building
C.C.	Central Committee (where not otherwise stated, of the C.P.S.U.)
C. of M.	Council of Ministers (where not otherwise stated, of the U.S.S.R.)
C.N.E.	Council of National Economy
Cand.	Candidate
Ch.	Chairman
Com.	Committee
Constr.	Construction
Dep.	Deputy
Dept.	Department
Econ.	Economic
Exec.	Executive
F.	Foreign

E E

F.A.	Foreign Affairs
Gosekon	State Economic Commission
Gosplan	State Planning Commission
M.	Member, Minister
Min.	Minister
Praes.	Praesidium
Prov.	Provincial Committee of the C.P.S.U.; Province
Rel.	Relations, relieved
Sec.	1st Secretary; Secretariat
2 Sec.	2nd Secretary
A Sec.	A Secretary
Sov.	Soviet
St.	State
Sup. Sov.	Supreme Soviet (where not otherwise stated, of the U.S.S.R.)
Tech.	Technique
Terr.	Territorial Committee; Territory (Krai)
Tpt.	Transport

* Member of the Party Control Committee.

A BREAKDOWN OF THE CENTRAL COMMITTEE, 1952–59

A. *The 1952 Committee*

	Full Members	Candidates
1. Those not re-elected in 1956		
(a) Presumed disgraced by Stalin	V. P. Pronin	G. V. Alekseenko K. D. Kulov V. F. Tsyren P. A. Zakharov
(b) Presumed disgraced or demoted on Stalin's death	D. I. Chesnokov A. I. Mgeladze A. N. Poskrebyshev Yu. A. Zhdanov	V. N. Pavlov M. T. Pomaznev S. M. Shtemenko
(c) Presumed disgraced with Beria	G. A. Arutinov M. D. Bagirov † L. P. Beria † Z. N. Ketskhoveli T. I. Kuliev	P. A. Artemyev V. M. Bakradze S. A. Goglidze † V. G. Grigoryan B. Z. Kobulov † V. N. Merkulov † V. G. Tskhovrebash-vili
(d) Doubtful demotions 1953–54	A. P. Efimov V. V. Lukyanov * V. I. Nedosekin B. F. Nikolayev F. M. Prass E. B. Taibekov P. I. Titov S. A. Vagapov	A. D. Bondarenko I. S. Khokhlov
(e) Presumed demoted in connection with Malenkov	V. M. Andrianov G. A. Borkov A. N. Egorov M. I. Gusev	T. A. Akhazov G. F. Aleksandrov G. A. Chumachenko D. V. Efremov

* Members of the 1956 Revision Committee.   † Executed.

	Full Members	Candidates
1. Those not re-elected in 1956	V. I. Kiselev	M. A. Gedvilas
	P. N. Korchagin	K. P. Gorshenin
	A. M. Kutyrev	N. Z. Kazakov
	D. N. Melnik	F. A. Mamonov
	A. V. Senin	P. I. Parshin
	N. N. Shatalin	S. S. Rumyantsev
	D. G. Smirnov	K. M. Sokolov
	I. A. Volkov	E. A. Stepanova
	A. F. Zasyadko	V. N. Stoletov
(f) Military and military-political demotions	N. G. Kuznetsov	N. E. Basisty
		S. I. Bogdanov
		F. F. Kuznetsov *
		M. S. Malinin *
		K. A. Meretskov *
		K. A. Vershinin
		I. S. Yumashev
		S. E. Zakharov
(g) M.V.D. demotions	S. N. Kruglov	I. I. Maslennikov
		V. S. Ryasnoi
(h) Miscellaneous demotions	A. N. Kidin *	B. A. Dvinsky
	A. I. Marfin	L. F. Kichev *
	Zh. Shayakhmetov	I. A. Kairov
	U. Yu. Yusupov	K. S. Kuznetsova
	M. V. Zimyanin *	A. S. Panyushkin
		M. M. Pidtychenko
		K. M. Simonov *
2. Deaths (except executions)	L. Z. Mekhlis	L. A. Govorov
	M. F. Shkiryatov	
	J. V. Stalin	
	A. Ya. Vyshinsky	
3. Reduced from Member to Candidate	P. F. Cheplakov	
	A. A. Fadeyev	
	L. G. Melnikov	
	K. P. Zhukov	

* Members of the 1956 Revision Committee.

	Full Members	Candidates
4. 1952 Members re-elected in 1956	A. A. Andreev	I. K. Bagramyan
	A. B. Aristov	S. Z. Borisov
	S. Babaev	S. M. Budenny
	N. K. Baibakov	S. M. Butuzov
	N. I. Belyaev	V. I. Chuikov
	I. A. Benediktov	N. A. Dygai
	B. P. Beshchev	A. A. Epishev
	I. P. Boitsov	A. V. Gorbatov
	L. I. Brezhnev	A. A. Grechko
	N. A. Bulganin	M. Ya. Kannunikov
	V. E. Chernyshev	A. U. Khakhalov
	G. A. Denisov	P. T. Komarov
	L. N. Efremov	L. R. Korniets
	B. G. Gafurov	A. I. Kostousov
	F. S. Goryachev	A. I. Kozlov
	I. T. Grishin	P. N. Kumykin
	V. V. Grishin	V. T. Latsis
	S. D. Ignatiev	P. F. Lomako
	N. G. Ignatov	A. A. Luchinsky
	I. G. Kabanov	L. P. Lykova
	L. M. Kaganovich	Yu. E. Maksarev
	Ya. E. Kalnberzins	Ya. E. Malik
	I. V. Kapitonov	R. E. Melnikov
	I. G. Kebin	A. A. Myurisep
	M. V. Khrunichev	M. I. Nedelin
	N. S. Khrushchev	P. V. Nikitin
	A. I. Kirichenko	I. I. Nosenko
	N. V. Kiselev	G. M. Orlov
	I. S. Konev	K. V. Ostrovityanov
	A. E. Korneichuk	Yu. I. Paletskis
	D. S. Korotchenko	D. V. Pavlov
	A. N. Kosygin	A. P. Pchelyakov
	M. D. Kovrigina	S. O. Postovalov
	F. R. Kozlov	D. Ya. Raizer
	O. V. Kuusinen	V. M. Ryabikov
	V. V. Kuznetsov	Z. A. Shashkov
	A. I. Khvorostukhin	I. P. Skulkov
	A. N. Larionov	L. N. Soloviev
	I. K. Lebedev	S. A. Stepanov
	G. M. Malenkov	S. K. Timoshenko
	V. A. Malyshev	S. K. Toka
	N. A. Mikhailov	Z. P. Tumanova

	Full Members	Candidates
4. 1952 Members re-elected in 1956	A. I. Mikoyan	P. A. Yudin
	M. B. Mitin	G. N. Zarubin
	V. M. Molotov	
	V. A. Moskvin	
	N. A. Mukhitdinov	
	Z. I. Muratov	
	N. N. Organov	
	A. M. Pankratova	
	N. S. Patolichev	
	N. M. Pegov	
	M. G. Pervukhin	
	P. K. Ponomarenko	
	P. N. Pospelov	
	V. A. Profofiev	
	A. M. Puzanov	
	I. R. Razzakov	
	A. M. Rumyantsev	
	M. S. Saburov	
	A. N. Shelepin	
	D. T. Shepilov	
	N. M. Shvernik	
	A. Yu. Snechkus	
	V. D. Sokolovsky	
	I. F. Tevosyan	
	F. E. Titov	
	D. F. Ustinov	
	B. L. Vannikov	
	A. M. Vasilevsky	
	G. I. Voronov	
	K. E. Voroshilov	
	I. D. Yakovlev	
	M. A. Yasnov	
	P. F. Yudin	
	I. K. Zhegalin	
	G. K. Zhukov (1953)	
	A. G. Zverev	

B. *The 1956 Committee*
(Those under A4, plus):

1. 1952 Candidates promoted to full membership	A. D. Daniyalov
	P. V. Dementiev
	E. A. Furtseva

	Full Members	Candidates
1. 1952 Candidates promoted to full membership	A. A. Gromyko N. T. Kalchenko R. Ya. Malinovsky B. N. Ponomarev Z. T. Serdyuk I. A. Serov A. M. Shkolnikov S. M. Tikhomirov A. P. Zavenyagin	
2. New Members	P. N. Alferov N. E. Avkhimovich N. I. Bobrovnikov D. D. Brezhnev B. I. Deryugin P. I. Doronin M. P. Dudorov G. D. Dzhavakhishvili M. T. Efremov R. V. Enyutin A. I. Gaevoi N. F. Ignatov A. P. Kirilenko V. K. Klimenko B. N. Kobelev E. P. Kolushchinsky V. A. Kucherenko D. A. Kunaev N. V. Laptev L. I. Lubennikov I. T. Marchenko V. S. Markov V. V. Matskevich K. S. Moskalenko I. G. Mustafaev V. P. Mzhavanadze Ya. S. Nasriddinova N. V. Podgorny D. S. Polyansky K. G. Pysin S. G. Ragimov T. F. Shtykov	N. N. Andreeva S. S. Biryuzov N. D. Bubnovsky M. D. Chubinidze V. D. Churaev V. P. Elyutin A. I. Eremenko M. A. Evseenko N. P. Firyubin L. Ya. Florentiev I. P. Ganenko G. N. Glebovsky S. G. Gorshkov M. S. Grechukha K. N. Grishin G. E. Grishko E. I. Gromov N. M. Gureev A. A. Ishkov S. M. Islyukov O. I. Ivashchenko V. D. Kalmykov V. Ya. Karasev I. P. Kazanets A. P. Klimov V. G. Komyakhov F. V. Konstantinov V. V. Kosov K. I. Koval V. I. Kozlov M. K. Krakhmalev I. A. Likhachev

	Full Members	Candidates
2. New Members	M. M. Stakhursky	P. P. Lobanov
	A. I. Struev	S. P. Loginov
	V. M. Suslov	K. G. Lunev
	V. N. Titov	M. A. Menshikov
	S. A. Tovmasyan	V. P. Mylarshchikov
	A. P. Volkov	L. I. Naidek
	A. N. Zademidko	O. I. Nefedova
		K. P. Orlovsky
		A. U. Petukhov
		S. M. Pilipets
		N. V. Popova
		S. L. Rashidov
		G. Ya. Rud
		A. P. Rudakov
		R. A. Rudenko
		V. E. Semichastny
		A. G. Sheremetiev
		M. Ya. Shumauskas
		P. E. Sinyagorsky
		G. F. Sizov
		I. T. Skidarenko
		N. I. Smirnov
		T. I. Sokolov
		N. I. Strokin
		F. A. Surganov
		A. A. Surkov
		M. P. Tarasov
		Zh. A. Tashenev
		A. S. Trofimov
		I. P. Tur
		F. D. Voronov
		T. A. Yurkin
		I. K. Zamchevski

C. *After 1956*

1. Expelled from the Central Committee June 1957	L. M. Kaganovich
	G. M. Malenkov
	V. M. Molotov
	D. T. Shepilov
2. Expelled October 1957	G. K. Zhukov

	Full Members	Candidates
3. Died 1956–59	V. A. Malyshev	A. A. Fadeev
	A. M. Pankratova	I. A. Likhachev
	I. F. Tevosyan	I. I. Nosenko
	A. P. Zavenyagin	P. A. Yudin
		G. N. Zarubin
4. Expelled from Central Committee 1959	S. Babaev	

RECENT PLENUMS OF THE CENTRAL COMMITTEE, AND PARTY CONGRESSES

Aug.	1952	Calling XIXth Congress.
Oct.	1952	XIXth PARTY CONGRESS.
Oct. 16	1952	Election of Praesidium and Secretariat; Stalin attacks Molotov and Mikoyan.
March 7	1953	First Post-Stalin Settlement (joint session with Praesidium of Supreme Soviet and Council of Ministers).
March 14	1953	Removal of Malenkov and others from Secretariat. Probably decision to repudiate Doctors' Plot.
July	1953	Denunciation of Beria.
Sept. 3–7	1953	Agriculture. Election of Khrushchev as First Secretary. Probably decision on Beria Trial.
Feb. 23–March 2	1954	Agriculture: Virgin Lands. Resolution on Party and State.
June	1954	Agriculture: Probably decision on Ryumin Trial.
Jan. 25–31	1955	Industry. Decision to remove Malenkov from Premiership.
July 4–12	1955	Yugoslavia. Attack on Molotov. Kirichenko and Suslov to Praesidium; Shepilov, Aristov, Belyaev to Secretariat.
Feb.	1956	XXth PARTY CONGRESS.
Feb. 27	1956	Election of new Praesidium and Secretariat.
Dec. 20–24	1956	Five Year Plan amendment. Release of Shepilov from Secretariat.
Feb. 13–14	1957	Industrial decentralisation. Re-election of Shepilov to Secretariat; election of Kozlov as candidate member of Praesidium.
June 22–29	1957	Expulsion of the Anti-Party Group. Election of new Praesidium.

Oct.	1957	Expulsion of Zhukov.
Dec. 16–17	1957	Mukhitdinov to full member of Praesidium. Mukhitdinov, Ignatov, Kirichenko to Secretariat.
Feb. 25–26	1958	Dissolution of M.T.S. Decision to make Khrushchev Prime Minister.
May 6–8	1958	Chemical Industry. Yugoslavia.
June 17–18	1958	Agriculture. Podgorny and Polyansky to candidate membership of Praesidium.
Sept. 5	1958	Calling of XXIst Congress. Removal of Bulganin from Praesidium
Nov. 12	1958	Seven-Year Plan Theses for XXI Congress. Education. Bulganin denounced.
Dec. 15–19	1958	Agriculture. Bulganin confession.
Jan.–Feb.	1959	XXIst (Special) PARTY CONGRESS
June 24–29	1959	Agriculture.
Dec. 22–25	1959	Agriculture.
May 4	1960	Organisational. Removal of Kirichenko and Belyaev. Promotion of Kosygin, Podgorny and Polyansky. Reorganisation of Secretariat.
July 13–16	1960	International Communism. Industry. Resignation of Voroshilov from Praesidium. Brezhnev leaves Secretariat.

Note: V. M. Churaev writes in *World Marxist Review* (English Edition, Vol. 2, No. 6, June 1959) that 'thirteen plenary meetings of the C.C. have been held since the 20th Congress (between Feb. 1956 and Jan. 1959)'. If this is correct one must have taken place without public announcement, perhaps in the period February–December 1956, which is a gap far longer than that permitted by the Party Statutes.

EXTRACTS FROM KHRUSHCHEV'S SECRET
SPEECH, FEBRUARY 1956, RELEVANT TO THE
POST-WAR STRUGGLE FOR POWER

(a)

The Party came out of the war even more united; in the fire of the war, Party cadres were tempered and hardened. Under such conditions nobody could have even thought of the possibility of some plot in the party.

And it was precisely at this time that the so-called 'Leningrad Affair' was born. As we have now proven, this case was fabricated. Those who innocently lost their lives included Comrades Voznesensky, Kuznetsov, Rodionov, Popkov and others.

As is known, Voznesensky and Kuznetsov were talented and eminent leaders. Once they stood very close to Stalin. It is sufficient to mention that Stalin made Voznesensky First Deputy to the Chairman of the Council of Ministers, and Kuznetsov was elected Secretary of the Central Committee. The very fact that Stalin entrusted Kuznetsov with the supervision of the State-security organs shows the trust which he enjoyed.

How did it happen that these persons were branded as enemies of the people and liquidated?

Facts prove that the 'Leningrad Affair' is also the result of wilfulness which Stalin exercised against Party cadres. Had a normal situation existed in the Party's Central Committee and in the Central Committee Political Bureau, affairs of this nature would have been examined there in accordance with Party practice, and all pertinent facts assessed; as a result, such an affair as well as others would not have happened.

We must state that, after the war, the situation became even more complicated. Stalin became even more capricious, irritable and brutal; in particular his suspicion grew. His persecution mania reached unbelievable dimensions. Many workers were becoming enemies before his very eyes. After the war, Stalin separated himself from the collective even more. Everything was decided by him alone, without any consideration for anyone or anything.

This unbelievable suspicion was cleverly taken advantage of by the abject *provocateur* and vile enemy, Beria, who had murdered thousands of Communists and loyal Soviet people. The elevation of Voznesensky and Kuznetsov alarmed Beria. As we have now proven, it had been precisely Beria who had 'suggested' to Stalin the fabrication by him and by his confidants of materials in the form of declarations and anonymous letters, and in the form of various rumours and talks.

The Party's Central Committee has examined this so-called 'Leningrad Affair'; persons who innocently suffered are now rehabilitated and honour has been restored to the glorious Leningrad Party organisation. Abakumov and others who had fabricated this affair were brought before a court; their trial took place in Leningrad and they received what they deserved.

The question arises: Why is it that we see the truth of this affair only now, and why did we not do something earlier, during Stalin's life, in order to prevent the loss of innocent lives? It was because Stalin personally supervised the 'Leningrad Affair', and the majority of the Political Bureau members did not, at that time, know all of the circumstances in these matters and could not therefore intervene.

(b)

Instructive in the same way is the case of the Mingrelian nationalist organisation which supposedly existed in Georgia. As is known, resolutions by the Central Committee, Communist Party of the Soviet Union, were made concerning this case in November 1951 and in March 1952. These resolutions were made without prior discussion with the Political Bureau. Stalin had personally dictated them. They made serious accusations against many loyal Communists. On the basis of falsified documents, it was proven that there existed in Georgia a supposedly nationalistic organisation whose objective was the liquidation of the Soviet power in that republic with the help of imperialistic Powers.

In this connection a number of responsible Party and Soviet workers were arrested in Georgia. As was later proven, this was a slander directed against the Georgian Party organisation . . .

As it developed, there was no nationalistic organisation in Georgia. Thousands of innocent people fell victims to wilfulness and lawlessness. All of this happened under the 'genial' leadership of Stalin, 'the great son of the Georgian nation', as Georgians like to refer to Stalin.

(c)

Let us also recall the 'affair of the doctor-plotters' (animation in the hall). Actually there was no 'affair' outside of the declaration of the woman doctor Timashuk, who was probably influenced or ordered by someone (after all, she was an unofficial collaborator of the organs of state security) to write Stalin a letter in which she declared that doctors were applying supposedly improper methods of medical treatment.

Such a letter was sufficient for Stalin to reach an immediate conclusion that there are doctor-plotters in the Soviet Union. He issued orders to arrest a group of eminent Soviet medical specialists. He personally issued advice on the conduct of the investigation and the method of interrogation of the arrested persons. He said that the academician Vinogradov should be put in chains, another one should be beaten. Present at this Congress as a delegate is the former Minister of State Security, Comrade Ignatiev. Stalin told him curtly, 'If you do not obtain confessions from the doctors we will shorten you by a head.' (Tumult in the hall.)

Stalin personally called the investigative judge, gave him instructions, advised him on which investigative methods should be used; these methods were simple — beat, beat and, once again, beat.

Shortly after the doctors were arrested, we members of the Political Bureau received protocols with the doctors' confessions of guilt. After distributing these protocols, Stalin told us, 'You are blind like young kittens; what will happen without me? The country will perish because you do not know how to recognise enemies.'

The case was so presented that no one could verify the facts on which the investigation was based. There was no possibility of trying to verify facts by contacting those who had made the confessions of guilt.

We felt, however, that the case of the arrested doctors was questionable. We knew some of these people personally because they had once treated us. When we examined this 'case' after Stalin's death, we found it to be fabricated from beginning to end.

This ignominious 'case' was set up by Stalin; he did not, however, have the time in which to bring it to an end (as he conceived that end), and for this reason the doctors are still alive. Now all have been rehabilitated; they are working in the same places they were working in before; they treat top individuals, not excluding members of the Government; they have our full confidence; and they execute their duties honestly, as they did before.

(d)

One of the oldest members of our Party, Klimenti Yefremovich Voroshilov, found himself in an almost impossible situation. For several years he was actually deprived of the right of participation in Political Bureau sessions. Stalin forbade him to attend the Political

Bureau sessions and to receive documents. When the Political Bureau was in session and Comrade Voroshilov heard about it, he telephoned each time and asked whether he would be allowed to attend. Sometimes Stalin permitted it, but always showed his dissatisfaction.

Because of his extreme suspicion, Stalin toyed also with the absurd and ridiculous suspicion that Voroshilov was an English agent (laughter in the hall). It's true — an English agent. A special tapping device was installed in his home to listen to what was said there (indignation in the hall).

By unilateral decision, Stalin had also separated one other man from the work of the Political Bureau — Andrei Andreyevich Andreyev. This was one of the most unbridled acts of wilfulness.

Let us consider the first Central Committee plenum after the XIXth Party Congress when Stalin, in his talk at the plenum, characterised Vyacheslav Mikhailovich Molotov and Anastas Ivanovich Mikoyan and suggested that these old workers of our Party were guilty of some baseless charges. It is not excluded that had Stalin remained at the helm for another several months, Comrades Molotov and Mikoyan would probably have not delivered any speeches at this Congress.

Stalin evidently had plans to finish off the old members of the Political Bureau. He often stated that Political Bureau members should be replaced by new ones.

His proposal, after the XIXth Congress, concerning the election of twenty-five persons to the Central Committee Praesidium, was aimed at the removal of the Political Bureau members and the bringing in of less experienced persons so that these would extol him in all sorts of ways.

We can assume that this was also a design for the future annihilation of the old Political Bureau members and, in this way, a cover for all shameful acts of Stalin, acts which we are now considering.

APPENDIX V

A NOTE ON THE 'CRIMEAN AFFAIR'

Lozovsky (member of the Central Committee and former head of the Soviet Trade Unions) and a number of Yiddish writers seem to have been arrested in December 1948 when the Jewish Anti-Fascist Committee was suddenly dissolved. Nothing was heard of them until the Warsaw Jewish Communist paper *Folkstyme*, on April 4, 1956, named Bergelson and six other leading writers as having been falsely condemned in the U.S.S.R. The New York Communist-line paper *National Guardian* of June 25, 1956, published an account by its correspondent Tabitha Petran of an interview with Ekaterina Furtseva, then candidate member of the Praesidium of the Central Committee. When asked about the Warsaw report she replied that as she had not read *Folkstyme* she could not comment. When L. F. Ilyichev was approached, he spoke of 'slanderous and anti-Soviet' allegations but admitted that Jewish writers had been 'unjustly condemned'.

I. B. Solzberg, a leading Canadian Communist, paid a personal visit to the U.S.S.R. in July 1955. He asked the Central Committee for facts about the fate of the Jewish writers. The Central Committee ordered a Special Committee then investigating such questions to give him the facts. However, the furthest they would go was to admit that writers, not only Jews but of all nationalities, had indeed suffered owing to Beria. No direct answers were given when Solzberg asked what had happened to particular Jewish writers (*Morgn Frayhayt* of November 15, 1956, and the New York *Jewish Life* of February 1957).

On August 29, 1956, an official Canadian Communist Delegation including Solzberg was received by Khrushchev, Suslov and Ponomarev. For two hours they discussed various aspects of the Jewish question. 'Khrushchev said that he agreed with Stalin that the Crimea, which at the end of the anti-Hitlerite war had become depopulated, should not become a centre of Jewish colonisation as in case of war it would have been transformed into a *place d'armes* against the Soviet Union.' He also said 'that the old and tried Comrade Lozovsky had perished guiltlessly, involved in the Crimean affair'. Solzberg, reporting this in *Morgn Frayhayt* of December 12, 1956, adds that he received more information from other Soviet sources: Lozovsky with the group of Jewish writers had perished on

438

August 12, 1952, and one of the Stalinist slanders against them was
that they were working to detach the Crimean province from the
U.S.S.R. When Suslov was asked about the dissolution of the Jewish
Anti-Fascist Committee he said that it had been unjustly dissolved
because people said that it was trying to obtain 'special privileges for
Jews'. He added that the Jewish actor Mikhoels had certainly
worked hard for his compatriots.

The Mikhoels link is, naturally, extremely interesting. For though
he himself died in what was said to be an accident in Minsk in 1949,
he was stated at the time of the Doctors' Plot to have been one of the
main links between the Doctors and the foreign espionage organisations. Dr. Meyer Vovsi, believed to be his brother, was one of the
accused doctors. Mikhoels, the most prominent Jewish actor and
producer in the Soviet Union, was, like the accused writers, a member of the Jewish Anti-Fascist Committee, which therefore provides
a direct link between the Crimean and Doctors' Plots.

OFFICIAL ANNOUNCEMENTS ON THE TRIALS, 1953-56

A. The Beria Case. { 1. Preliminary Investigation.
{ 2. Trial.
B. The Ryumin Case.
C. The Abakumov Case.
D. The Rapava–Rukhadze Case.
E. The Bagirov Case.
F. Article 58 of the Criminal Codex.

A. THE BERIA CASE

1. *Announcement on the Preliminary Investigation*

In U.S.S.R. Procurator General's Office

On June 26, 1953, the Praesidium of the U.S.S.R. Supreme Soviet, having examined the report of the U.S.S.R. Council of Ministers on the criminal activities of L. P. Beria as an agent of foreign capital, directed towards undermining the Soviet State, resolved: to remove L. P. Beria from the post of First Deputy Chairman of the U.S.S.R. Council of Ministers and from the post of U.S.S.R. Minister of Internal Affairs, and to bring Beria to trial. The U.S.S.R. Supreme Soviet on August 8, 1953, approved the Edict of the Praesidium of the U.S.S.R. Supreme Soviet of June 26.

At the present time the U.S.S.R. Procurator-General's Office has finished its inquiry into the case of the traitor to the Motherland, L. P. Beria.

It has been established by the inquiry that Beria, using his position, forged a treacherous group of conspirators, hostile to the Soviet State, with the criminal goal of using the organs of the Ministry of Internal Affairs, both central and local, against the Communist Party and the Government of the U.S.S.R. in the interests of foreign capital, striving in its perfidious schemes to set the Ministry of Internal Affairs above the Party and Government in order to seize power and liquidate the Soviet worker–peasant system for the purpose of restoring capitalism and the domination of the bourgeoisie.

The following accused, linked with Beria for many years by joint criminal activity in the organs of the N.K.V.D.–M.V.D., were active participants in the perfidious group of conspirators: V. N. Merkulov, former Minister of State Security of the U.S.S.R., recently the U.S.S.R. Minister of State Control; V. G. Dekanozov, former chief of one of the administrations of the N.K.V.D. of the U.S.S.R., recently the Minister of Internal Affairs of the Georgian S.S.R.; B. Z. Kobulov, former Deputy People's Commissar of Internal Affairs of the Georgian S.S.R., later Deputy Minister of State Security of the U.S.S.R., and recently Deputy Minister of Internal Affairs of the U.S.S.R.; S. A. Goglidze, former People's Commissar of Internal Affairs of the Georgian S.S.R., and recently chief of one of the administrations of the U.S.S.R. Ministry of Internal Affairs; P. Ya. Meshik, former chief of one of the administrations of the U.S.S.R. N.K.V.D., and recently Minister of Internal Affairs of the Ukranian S.S.R.; and L. E. Vlodzimirsky, former Head of the Section for Investigating Specially Important Cases of the U.S.S.R. Ministry of Internal Affairs.

For many years Beria and his accomplices carefully disguised and concealed their hostile, treacherous activity. After the demise of J. V. Stalin, when reactionary imperialist forces stepped up their subversive activity against the Soviet State, Beria resorted to intensified actions to achieve his criminal goals, first of all by means of using the organs of the Ministry of Internal Affairs to seize power, which soon made it possible to expose the true character of the traitor to the Motherland and to adopt resolute measures to suppress his hostile activity.

Having become U.S.S.R. Minister of Internal Affairs in March 1953, Beria began increasingly to promote the participants in the conspiratorial group to a number of leading posts in the Ministry of Internal Affairs. The conspirators victimised and persecuted honest officials of the Ministry of Internal Affairs who refused to carry out criminal orders of Beria.

For the purpose of undermining the collective-farm system and causing food difficulties in our country, Beria sabotaged by every kind of method and impeded the implementation of most important measures of the Party and Government directed towards an upsurge of the economy of the collective farms and State farms and towards a steady rise in the well-being of the Soviet people.

It has also been established that Beria and his accomplices undertook criminal measures in order to stir up the remains of bourgeois-nationalist elements in the Union Republics, to sow enmity and discord among the peoples of the U.S.S.R. and, in the first place, to undermine the friendship of the peoples of the U.S.S.R. with the great Russian people.

Deprived of any social support within the U.S.S.R., Beria and his accomplices based their criminal calculations on support of the conspiracy by reactionary imperialist forces from abroad.

As has now been established by the inquiry, Beria made contact with foreign Intelligence Services back in the period of the Civil War. In 1919 Beria, who was in Baku, committed treachery by accepting a post as a Secret Agent in the Intelligence Service of the counter-revolutionary Mussavat Government in Azerbaidzhan, which operated under the control of British Intelligence organs. In 1920 Beria, who was in Georgia, again committed a treacherous act by establishing secret contact with the Menshevik Secret Service in Georgia, which was a branch of the British Intelligence Service.

It has been established by the inquiry that in subsequent years also Beria maintained and expanded his secret, criminal contacts with foreign Intelligence Services through spies sent by them, whom he sometimes succeeded in protecting from exposure and deserved punishment.

Acting as a traitor to the Motherland and a spy, Beria, who had sold himself to foreign Intelligence Services, throughout his criminal activity also maintained, with the help of his accomplices, secret contacts with counter-revolutionary, Georgian Menshevik-emi-grants, agents of a number of foreign Intelligence Services.

Carefully concealing and disguising his criminal past and hostile contacts with Intelligence Services of foreign States, Beria chose as his main method, slander, intrigues and various provocations against honest Party and Soviet officials who stood in the way of his schemes, which were hostile to the Soviet State, and hindered him from making his way to power.

Having elbowed their way to responsible posts with the help of these criminal methods in the Transcaucasus and Georgia, and later in the U.S.S.R. Ministry of Internal Affairs, and hatching plans for seizure of power for treacherous purposes, Beria and his accomplices took reprisals against people objectionable to them, not stopping short of acts of high-handedness and illegality, and deceived the Party and State in a base manner.

A whole number of Beria's criminal machinations, directed to-wards achieving careerist goals and preventing exposure of his hostile character, have been established by the inquiry. Thus, it has been established by the inquiry that in order to achieve his treacherous goals, Beria, for a number of years, with the help of his accomplices, waged a criminal struggle of intrigue against the outstanding leader of the Communist Party and Soviet State, Sergo Ordzhonikidze, seeing in him a person who was an obstacle to his further progress and to the realisation of his hostile scheme. As has now been established, Sergo Ordzhonikidze nourished political distrust of Beria. After the demise of Sergo Ordzhonikidze the conspirators continued to take cruel revenge on the members of his family.

Cases have been established by the inquiry of the conspirators committing terroristic murder of persons from which exposure was feared. Thus, M. S. Kedrov — a member of the Communist Party since 1902 and a former member of the Praesidium of the All-Russian Extraordinary Commission for Combating Counter-Revolution and Sabotage and of the collegium of the O.G.P.U. under F. E. Dzerzhinsky — was killed by Beria and his accomplices. The conspirators had grounds to suspect that Kedrov possessed materials on the criminal past of Beria. Other facts have also been established of terroristic murders committed by the conspirators with the criminal purpose of exterminating honourable cadres, devoted to the cause of the Communist Party and of the Soviet regime.

As the inquiry has established, Beria and his accomplices committed a number of treacherous acts, trying to weaken the defence capacity of the Soviet State.

It has been proven by the materials of the inquiry that the participants in the conspiratorial group — the accused Merkulov, Dekanozov, Kobulov, Goglidze, Meshik and Vlodzimirsky — connected with Beria by many years of joint criminal activity, fulfilling many criminal missions of Beria's and helping him conceal and disguise his criminal past, committed a number of the most serious State crimes mentioned above.

Thus, it has been established that the accused Beria, Merkulov, Dekanozov, Kobulov, Goglidze, Meshik and Vlodzimirsky, betraying the Motherland, acted as agents of international imperialism, as mortal enemies of the Soviet people.

Facts of other crimes committed by Beria have also been established by the inquiry, which show his profound moral degeneration and, in addition, facts have also been established by the inquiry of criminal, mercenary actions committed by Beria and of his abuse of power.

Exposed at the inquiry by the testimony of various witnesses and by authentic documentary data, the accused pleaded guilty of committing a number of most serious State crimes.

Beria has been indicted for treason to the Motherland, for organisation of an anti-Soviet conspiracy, for committing terroristic acts, for an active struggle against the working class and the revolutionary working-class movement, manifested by him in his Secret Agent's position in the organs of the Intelligence Service of the counter-revolutionary Mussavat Government during the period of the Civil War, that is for crimes envisaged by articles 58-1b, 58-8, 58-13 and 58-11 of the Criminal Code of the R.S.F.S.R.

Merkulov, Dekanozov, Kobulov, Goglidze, Meshik and Vlodzimirsky have been indicted for treason to the Motherland, for committing terroristic acts and participating in a counter-revolutionary,
treacherous, conspiratorial group — that is, for crimes envisaged by
articles 58-1b, 58-8 and 58-11 of the Criminal Code of the R.S.F.S.R.

In accordance with the Edict of the Praesidium of the U.S.S.R.
Supreme Soviet, the case against Beria, Merkulov, Dekanozov,
Kobulov, Goglidze, Meshik and Vlodzimirsky is subject to examination by a special Court Session of the U.S.S.R. Supreme Soviet in
the manner established by the Law of December 1, 1934.

(*Pravda*, December 17, 1953)

2. *Announcement on the Trial*

In the U.S.S.R. Supreme Court

On December 18–23, 1953, a Special Session of the U.S.S.R.
Supreme Court was held, made up of the following:

Presiding: Marshal of the Soviet Union I. S. Konev, Chairman of
the Special Session. Members of the Session: M. M. Shvernik, Chairman of the All-Union Central Council of Trade Unions; E. L.
Zeidin, First Deputy Chairman of the U.S.S.R. Supreme Court;
General of the Army K. S. Moskalenko; N. A. Mikhailov, Secretary
of the Moscow Provincial Committee of the C.P.S.U.; M. I. Ku-
chava, Chairman of the Council of Trade Unions of Georgia; L. A.
Gromov, Chairman of the Moscow City Court; K. F. Lunev, First
Deputy Minister of Internal Affairs of the U.S.S.R. The Session
examined in camera, in the manner established by the Law of
December 1, 1934, the indictment in the criminal case against L. P.
Beria and others.

In accordance with the indictment, the following were tried: L. P.
Beria, accused of crimes provided for by articles 58-1b, 58-8, 58-13
and 58-11 of the R.S.F.S.R. Criminal Code; V. N. Merkulov, V. G.
Dekanozov, B. Z. Kobulov, S. A. Goglidze, P. Ya. Meshik and L. E.
Vlodzimirsky, accused of crimes provided for by Articles 58-1b, 58-8
and 58-11 of the R.S.F.S.R. Criminal Code.

The Special Session confirmed completely the materials of the
preliminary inquiry and the accusation against all of the accused
which were set forth in the indictment.

It was established by the Court that, betraying the Motherland
and operating in the interests of foreign capital, the accused Beria
forged a treacherous group of conspirators, hostile to the Soviet
State, to which the accused V. N. Merkulov, V. G. Dekanozov, B. Z.
Kobulov, S. A. Goglidze, P. Ya. Meshik and L. E. Vlodzimirsky,
who were connected with Beria for many years by joint criminal

activity, belonged. The conspirators set themselves the criminal goal of using the organs of the Ministry of Internal Affairs against the Communist Party and the Government of the U.S.S.R., of placing the Ministry of Internal Affairs over the Party and Government in order to seize power, liquidate the Soviet worker-peasant system, restore capitalism and the domination of the bourgeoisie.

The Court established that the beginning of the criminal, treacherous activity of L. P. Beria and the establishment by him of secret contacts with foreign Intelligence Services goes back to the time of the Civil War, when in 1919 L. P. Beria, who was in Baku, committed treason by accepting the position of Secret Agent in the Intelligence Service of the counter-revolutionary Mussavat Government in Azerbaidzhan, which operated under control of British Intelligence organs.

In 1920 L. P. Beria, who was in Georgia, again committed treason by establishing secret contact with the Secret Police of the Georgian Menshevik Government, which was also a branch of the British Intelligence Service.

In subsequent years, right up to his arrest, L. P. Beria maintained and expanded his secret contacts with foreign Intelligence Services.

For many years L. P. Beria and his accomplices carefully concealed and disguised their hostile activity.

After the demise of J. V. Stalin, banking on a general increase in the activity of reactionary imperialist forces against the Soviet State, L. P. Beria resorted to intensified actions in order to carry out his anti-Soviet, treacherous designs, which made it possible to expose L. P. Beria and his accomplices in a short time and to suppress their criminal activity.

Having become U.S.S.R. Minister of Internal Affairs in March 1953, the accused L. P. Beria preparing to seize power, began increasingly to promote the participants in the conspiratorial group to leading positions both in the control apparatus of the Ministry of Internal Affairs and in its local organs. L. P. Beria and his accomplices took reprisals against honourable officials of the Ministry of Internal Affairs who refused to carry out criminal orders of the conspirators.

For their anti-Soviet, treacherous purposes, L. P. Beria and his accomplices undertook a number of criminal measures in order to step up the activity of the remnant of bourgeois-nationalistic elements in the Union Republics, to sow enmity and discord between the peoples of the U.S.S.R. and, in the first place, to undermine the friendship of the peoples of the U.S.S.R. with the Great Russian people.

Acting as the mortal enemy of the Soviet people, the accused L. P.

Beria, for the purpose of creating food difficulties in our country, sabotaged and impeded the implementation of most important measures of the Party and Government, directed towards an upsurge of the economy of the collective farms and State farms and towards steady raising of the well-being of the Soviet people.

It has been established that, concealing and disguising their criminal activity, the accused L. P. Beria and his accomplices took terroristic reprisals against people from whom they feared exposure. The conspirators chose as one of the main methods of their criminal activity slander, intrigue and various provocations against honourable Party and Soviet officials who stood in the way of the treacherous schemes, hostile to the Soviet State, of L. P. Beria and his accomplices and who made it difficult for them to elbow their way to power.

It has been established by the Court that the accused L. P. Beria, V. N. Merkulov, V. G. Dekanozov, B. Z. Kobulov, S. A. Goglidze, P. Ya. Meshik and L. E. Vlodzimirsky, using their official positions in the organs of the N.K.V.D.-M.G.B.-M.V.D., committed a number of the most serious crimes for the purpose of exterminating honourable cadres devoted to the cause of the Communist Party and the Soviet regime.

Crimes of L. P. Beria were also established by the Court which show his profound moral corruption, as were instances of criminal, mercenary actions and abuse of power committed by Beria.

The guilt of all the accused in the charges made against them was fully proven in the trial by authentic documents, material evidence, depositions signed by the accused and by the testimony of numerous witnesses.

The accused L. P. Beria, V. N. Merkulov, V. G. Dekanozov, B. Z. Kobulov, S. A. Goglidze, P. Ya. Meshik and L. E. Vlodzimirsky, convicted by the evidence, at the inquiry confirmed the testimony given by them in the preliminary inquiry and pleaded guilty of committing a number of most serious state crimes.

The Special Session of the U.S.S.R. Supreme Court established the guilt of the accused L. P. Beria in betrayal of the Motherland, organisation of an anti-Soviet conspiratorial group for the purpose of seizing power and restoring the domination of the bourgeiosie; in the commission of terroristic acts against political leaders devoted to the Communist Party and the peoples of the Soviet Union; in active struggle against the revolutionary working-class movement in Baku in 1919, when Beria occupied the position of Secret Agent in the Intelligence Service of the counter-revolutionary Mussavat Government in Azerbaidzhan, established contacts there with a foreign Intelligence Service and subsequently maintained and expanded his secret criminal contacts with foreign Intelligence Services up to the moment of exposure and arrest; that is guilt in crimes envisaged by Articles 58-1b, 58-8, 58-13 and 58-11 of the R.S.F.S.R. Criminal Code.

The Court established the guilt of the accused V. N. Merkulov, V. G. Dekanozov, B. Z. Kobulov, S. A. Goglidze, P. Ya, Meshik and L. E. Vlodzimirsky in betrayal of the Motherland, commission of terroristic acts and participation in an anti-Soviet, treacherous group, that is guilt in crimes envisaged by Articles 58-1b, 58-8 and 58-11 of the R.S.F.S.R. Criminal Code.

The Special Session of the U.S.S.R. Supreme Court resolved:

To sentence L. P. Beria, V. N. Merkulov, V. G. Dekanozov, B. Z. Kobulov, S. A. Goglidze, P. Ya. Meshik and L. E. Vlodzimirsky to the highest criminal punishment — death by shooting, with confiscation of the personal property belonging to them and deprivation of military titles and awards.

The sentence is final and not subject to appeal.

Yesterday, December 23, the sentence passed by the Special Session of the U.S.S.R. Supreme Court in the case of those sentenced to the highest form of punishment, death by shooting — L. P. Beria, V. N. Merkulov, V. G. Dekanozov, B. Z. Kobulov, S. A. Goglidze, P. Ya. Meshik and L. E. Vlodzimirsky — was executed.

(Pravda, December 24, 1953)

B. THE RYUMIN CASE

IN THE SUPREME COURT OF THE U.S.S.R.

On July 2–7, 1954, the Military Collegium of the Supreme Court of the U.S.S.R. examined at a court session the case of M. D. Ryumin, accused of a crime envisaged by Article 58-7 of the Criminal Code of the R.S.F.S.R.

It was established by the inquiry that Ryumin during the period of his work in the post of Senior Investigator and then as Head of the Section for Investigating Specially Important Cases of the former Ministry of State Security, acting as a concealed enemy of the Soviet State, engaged for careerist and adventurist purposes on the path of forging investigation materials, on the basis of which provocative cases were engineered and unjustified arrests were carried out of a number of Soviet citizens, including prominent medical workers.

As witnesses testified in court, Ryumin, employing methods of investigation which are forbidden by Soviet law, forced the arrested people to slander themselves and other individuals with the commission of heinous state crimes — treachery, wrecking, espionage, etc.

It was established by a subsequent inquiry that these charges were completely unfounded and the individuals involved in these fabricated cases were fully rehabilitated.

Taking into account the special danger of Ryumin's wrecking work and the seriousness of the consequences of the crimes committed by him, the Military Collegium of the Supreme Court of the U.S.S.R. sentenced Ryumin to the supreme penalty — death by shooting.

The sentence has been carried out.

(Pravda, July 23, 1954)

C. THE ABAKUMOV CASE

IN THE SUPREME COURT OF THE U.S.S.R.

From December 14 to 19, 1954, at an open court session in the city of Leningrad, the Military Collegium of the Supreme Court of the U.S.S.R., composed of Lieut.-General of Justice E. L. Zeidin, First Deputy Chairman of the Supreme Court of the U.S.S.R. and President of the Court; Major-General of Justice V. V. Syuldin, and Colonel of Justice V. V. Borisoglebsky, members of the Court, together with R. A. Rudenko, State Prosecutor, Procurator-General of the U.S.S.R. and State Counsellor of Justice, and for the defence — M. I. Grinev, M. V. Stepanov, N. I. Rogov and L. V. Pavlov, members of the Moscow City Collegium of Lawyers, tried the case on the indictment of the former Minister of State Security of the U.S.S.R. V. S. Abakumov, the former Head of the Section for Investigating Specially Important Cases of the M.G.B. of the U.S.S.R. A. G. Leonov, and V. I. Komarov and M. T. Likhachev, former Deputy Heads of the Section for Investigating Specially Important Cases, and I. A. Chernov and Ya. M. Broverman, ex-officials of the M.G.B. of the U.S.S.R., for crimes envisaged under Articles 58-1-b, 58-7, 58-8 and 58-11 of the Criminal Code of the R.S.F.S.R.

The court inquiry fully confirmed the material of the preliminary inquiry and the indictments made against the accused.

The accused Abakumov, nominated by Beria for the post of Minister of State Security of the U.S.S.R., was a direct acomplice of the criminal conspiratorial group and carried out the hostile tasks of Beria directed against the Communist Party and the Soviet Government.

Committing similar crimes to those of Beria, Abakumov trod the path of adventures and political provocative acts. Abakumov trumped up cases against certain officials of the Party and Soviet apparatus and against representatives of the Soviet intelligentsia, then arrested those persons and, using criminal methods of investigation, forbidden by Soviet law, together with his accomplices Leonov, Komarov and Likhachev extracted from those arrested false evidence and a confession of guilt of serious state crimes.

In this way Abakumov falsified the so-called 'Leningrad Case', in which a number of Party and Soviet officials were arrested without grounds, having been falsely accused of most serious state crimes.

The court inquiry established many other cases of the falsification of trials and criminal violation of Socialist legality by Abakumov and his accomplices.

The persons who were falsely accused by Abakumov and his confederates have now been fully rehabilitated.

In order to cover up the crimes he had committed, Abakumov forbade statements and complaints by the arrested persons, addressed to the Central Committee of the C.P.S.U. and the Soviet Government, to be forwarded.

The Military Collegium of the Supreme Court of the U.S.S.R., recognising the charges made against Abakumov and his accomplices to be fully proven, sentenced the accused I. A. Chernov to be sent to a corrective labour camp for a period of fifteen years; the accused Ya. M. Broverman to be sent to a corrective labour camp for a period of twenty-five years, and the accused V. S. Abakumov, A. G. Leonov, V. I. Komarov and M. T. Likhachev to suffer the highest degree of punishment — death by shooting.

The sentence was met by all those present with great satisfaction. The sentence has been carried out.

(*Pravda*, December 24, 1954)

D. THE RAPAVA–RUKHADZE CASE

In the U.S.S.R. Supreme Court

In September, at an open judicial session in the city of Tbilisi, the Military Collegium of the U.S.S.R. Supreme Court composed of: Lieut.-General of Justice Chertkev, Chairman of the Military Collegium of the U.S.S.R. Supreme Court in the chair; and Colonel of Justice Kostremin and Colonel of Justice Golovtsev, Members of the Military Collegium; with the participation of: As State Counsel for the prosecution: State Councillor of Justice Rudenko, U.S.S.R. Prosecutor-General; and, as counsel for the defence: advocates Gavrilov, Zverov, Galkin, Sannikov, Apraksin, Gugulov and Zorin; considered the criminal case against Rapava, Rukhadze, Tsereteli, Savitsky, Krimyan, Khazani, Paramonov and Nadaraya.

accused of crimes outlined in Articles 58-1b, 58-8 and 58-11 of the Criminal Code: to wit, high treason, terroristic acts and participation in counter-revolutionary organisations.

As a result of the judicial proceedings it has been established that Rapava, formerly Deputy People's Commissar and subsequently People's Commissar of Internal Affairs of the Georgian S.S.R.; Rukhadze, formerly Head of the Interrogation Department of the People's Commissariat of Internal Affairs of the Georgian S.S.R. and subsequently Minister of State Security of the Georgian S.S.R.; Tsereteli, formerly Deputy People's Commissar of Internal Affairs and subsequently Deputy Minister of Internal Affairs of the Georgian S.S.R.; Krimyan, Savitsky, Khazani and Paramonov, formerly interrogators of the People's Commissariat of Internal Affairs of the Georgian S.S.R.; and the accused Nadaraya; actively participated in the anti-Soviet treasonable activity of the enemy of the people, Beria.

Helping Beria to conceal his criminal past and basely deceiving the Party and the State, the accused used their positions in the People's Commissariat of Internal Affairs and subsequently in the Ministry of Internal Affairs and the Ministry of State Security of the Georgian S.S.R. for hostile purposes.

The court established that Beria entrusted the accused with the direct execution of such criminal tasks as were most important to him. With the criminal aim of destroying honest cadres who were loyal to the cause of the Communist Party and the Soviet Government, the accused falsified interrogation proceedings, employing against prisoners criminal methods of interrogation which are strictly forbidden by Soviet law, and resorted to terroristic acts of violence against honest Soviet citizens, falsely accusing them of committing counter-revolutionary crimes.

The accused took an active part in collecting slanderous material and in the struggle of intrigue, which Beria had over a number of years been carrying on against Sergo Ordzhonikidze, the prominent statesman of the Communist Party and of the Soviet State, and subsequently in terroristic acts of violence against members of Ordzhonikidze's family and his close friends who held responsible posts in the State and the Party.

Among the crimes committed by the accused a special place was occupied by their terroristic acts of violence against persons Beria feared might expose him. Such terroristic acts of violence were committed against Mamia Orakhelashvili, former Secretary of the Transcaucasian Party Krai Committee, and his wife, Mariam Orakhelashvili, former People's Commissar of Education of the Georgian S.S.R.; against Division Commander Buachidze, Commander of the Georgian Division; Begiya, Director of the Tbilisi Branch of the Marx–Engels–Lenin Institute; and others.

The Military Collegium of the U.S.S.R. Supreme Court sentenced Rapava, Rukhadze, Tsereteli, Savitsky, Krimyan and Khazani to the supreme criminal penalty — to be shot.

The accused Paramonov was sentenced to twenty-five years' imprisonment, and the accused Nadaraya to ten years' imprisonment.

The verdict was unanimously approved by those present in the court.

The appeals of Rapava, Rukhadze, Tsereteli, Savitsky, Krimyan and Khazani for reprieve by the U.S.S.R. Supreme Soviet Praesidium were dismissed.

The sentence has been carried out.

(Radio Tbilisi, November 22, 1955)

E. THE BAGIROV CASE

IN THE SUPREME COURT OF THE U.S.S.R.

On April 12–26, 1956, in open session in the town of Baku, the Military Collegium of the Supreme Court of the U.S.S.R., composed of A. A. Cheptsov, Lieut.-General of Justice and Chairman of the Military Collegium, who presided, A. A. Kostremin, Colonel of Justice, and G. E. Kovalenko, Colonel of Justice, members of the Collegium, with the participation of the State prosecution — State Councillor of Justice R. A. Rudenko, Prosecutor-General of the U.S.S.R.; and the defence — lawyers V. N. Gavrilov, Ya. M. Nutenko, P. Ya. Bogachev, G. S. Semenovski, K. N. Apraksin and M. I. Grinev — examined the charge brought against M. D. Bagirov, T. M. Borshchev, Kh. I. Grigoryan, R. A. Markaryan, A. S. Atakishiev and S. F. Emelyanov of crimes envisaged by Articles 63-2, 70 and 73 of the Criminal Code of the Azerbaidzhan S.S.R., i.e. high treason, the commission of terrorist acts and participation in a counter-revolutionary organisation.

The court established that the accused Bagirov, being one of the most active and intimate accomplices of the traitor Beria, committed together with him, with the complicity of the other accused persons, a number of extremely grave crimes against the State. Since 1921 Bagirov had been fully informed about Beria's service in the Mussavatist Counter-Intelligence Service and up to the time of Beria's exposure had helped him to evade responsibility, stealing from the archives and handing over to Beria documents concerning his criminal past and also meting out arbitrary treatment to people who could expose Beria. In his turn Beria knew about the criminal past of Bagirov, who was engaged in banditry during the Civil War, he helped Bagirov actively to conceal his criminal past and participated in the elimination of people who could expose Bagirov.

Having set themselves the criminal aim of exterminating honest cadres devoted to the Communist Party and the Soviet regime, Bagirov and Beria involved in their criminal activity the accused Borshchev, Markaryan, Grigoryan, Atakishiev and Emelyanov, appointing them to leading posts in the N.K.V.D., the M.G.B. and the M.V.D. of Azerbaidzhan, and with their active complicity falsified court cases against innocent people. Applying methods of investigation that are most strictly forbidden by Soviet law, the accused extorted from the arrested persons false admissions of counter-revolutionary crimes which they had not in fact committed and also compelled the arrested persons to implicate falsely other people innocent of these crimes. In this way Bagirov and his accomplices, flouting Soviet legality, meted out terroristic arbitrary treatment and created provocational cases against many collective farmers in a number of raions of Azerbaidzhan, workers in the oilfields, the Caspian shipping line, the Party and Soviet aktiv, scientific, art and cultural workers of Azerbaidzhan.

Thus the following were falsely accused of grave crimes against the state and subsequently put to death — Rukhulle Akhundov, Levon Mirzoyan, Ali Geidar Karaev, former Secretaries of the Central Committee of the Communist Party of Azerbaidzhan; Musabekov Gazanfar, former Chairman of the Council of People's Commissars of the Transcaucasian S.F.S.R.; Guseinov Mirza Davud, former Deputy Chairman of the Council of People's Commissars of the Transcaucasian S.F.S.R.; Vezirov Geidar, former People's Commissar for Agriculture of the Azerbaidzhan S.S.R.; Buniat-Zade Dadash, former Chairman of the Council of People's Commissars of the Azerbaidzhan S.S.R.; Sultan Medzhid Efendiev, Chairman of the Azerbaidzhan Central Executive Committee, an old Communist and a member of the Party since 1904; Usein Rakhmanov, Chairman of the Council of People's Commissars of the Azerbaidzhan S.S.R.; Gamid Sulganov, People's Commissar for Public Utilities of Azerbaidzhan, a member of the Communist Party since 1907, and his wife, Aina Sultanova, People's Commissar of Justice of the Azerbaidzhan S.S.R., an old Communist; Khalilov, Deputy Chairman of the Council of People's Commissars of the Azerbaidzhan S.S.R.; Dzhuvarlinski, People's Commissar for Education of the Azerbaidzhan S.S.R.; M. V. Barinov, former Head of the Azerbaidzhan Oil concern and at the moment of his arrest Director of the Chief Administration for Oil, a member of the C.P.S.U. since 1904; Gasan Rakhmanov, Head of the Political Department of the Caspian shipping line; I. Manyailov, Head of the Caspian shipping line; Baba Aliev, former Chairman of the Azerbaidzhan Extraordinary Commission; M. Pleshakov, I. Anashkin, I. Ulyanov, I. Dovlatov, L. Arustanov, old Communists with a pre-revolutionary record of service in the Party, and many other completely innocent Soviet people who have now been rehabilitated by the court.

Bagirov and the other accused took an active part in the intrigues which Beria and his accomplices conducted against Sergo Ordzhonikidze, an outstanding figure in the Communist Party and the Soviet State, compelling the arrested people to give false testimonies against S. Ordzhonikidze.

The materials of the preliminary investigation were fully corroborated during the trial. The guilt of all the accused was established by the testimonies of numerous witnesses cross-examined by the court, by authentic documents and also by the testimonies of the accused who admitted the facts concerning the crimes with which they were charged.

The Military Collegium of the Supreme Court of the U.S.S.R., after finding the accused guilty of high treason, the commission of terroristic acts and participation in a counter-revolutionary organisation and taking into account the particular gravity of the crimes which they committed against the Soviet people, sentenced M. D. Bagirov, T. M. Borshchev, Kh. I. Grigoryan, and R. A. Markaryan to the supreme penalty — death by shooting; and S. F. Emelyanov and A. S. Atakishiev to twenty-five years' imprisonment each.

The sentence was received with great approval by those present in the courtroom.

The appeals of the condemned M. D. Bagirov, T. M. Borshchev, Kh. I. Grigoryan and R. A. Markaryan for clemency were rejected by the Praesidium of the Supreme Soviet of the U.S.S.R.

The sentence has been carried out.

(*Bakinski Rabochy*, May 27, 1956)

ARTICLE 58 OF THE CRIMINAL CODEX OF THE R.S.F.S.R.

(repealed December 1958)

SPECIAL SECTION

Chapter I

1. COUNTER-REVOLUTIONARY CRIMES

Art. 58 i. Any act designed to overthrow, undermine or weaken the authority of the workers' and peasants' Soviets and the workers' and peasants' governments of the Union of Soviet Socialist Republics of the Union and Autonomous Republics, elected by the Soviets on the basis of the Constitution of the U.S.S.R. and the Constitutions of the Union Republics or designed to undermine or weaken the external security of the U.S.S.R. and of the basic economic, political and national achievements of the proletarian revolution, is deemed to be a counter-revolutionary act.

In view of the international solidarity of the interests of all the toilers, such acts are also regarded as counter-revolutionary when they are directed against any other Workers' State, even though not forming part of the U.S.S.R.

Art. 58 i. a. Treason against the homeland, i.e. acts committed by citizens of the U.S.S.R. to the detriment of the military strength of the U.S.S.R., its State independence, or the inviolability of its territory, such as: espionage, betrayal of a military or State secret, desertion to the enemy, flight abroad by land or air are punishable:

> by the supreme measure of criminal punishment — death by shooting and the confiscation of all property; in extenuating circumstances — by deprivation of liberty for a period of ten years and the confiscation of all property.

Art. 58 i. b. These same crimes, if committed by military personnel, are punishable by the supreme measure of criminal punishment — death by shooting and confiscation of all property.

Art. 58 i. c. In the event of flight abroad by land or air or a member of the armed forces, the adult members of his family, if they in any way assisted the preparation or the commission of this act of treason, or even if they knew of it but failed to report it to the authorities, are to be punished: by privation of liberty for a period of from five to ten years and confiscation of all property.

The remaining adult members of the traitor's family, and those living with him or dependent on him at the time of the commission of the crime are liable to deprivation of their electoral rights and to exile to the remote areas of Siberia for a period of five years.

Art. 58 i. d. Failure on the part of a member of the armed forces to report preparations for or the commission of an act of treason entails:

> deprivation of liberty for ten years.

failure on the part of other citizens (not members of the armed forces) to report is punished in accordance with Article 58 xii.

Art. 58 ii. Armed insurrection or incursion of armed bands into Soviet territory, with counter-revolutionary aims, the seizure of power at the centre or in the provinces with the same aims and, in particular, with the aim of forcibly separating from the

U.S.S.R. or from a separate union republic any part of its territory or of violating treaties concluded between the US.S.R. and foreign States, entail:

the supreme measure of social defence — death by shooting, or declaration as an enemy of the labouring masses, and the confiscation of property and deprivation of citizenship of the Union Republic and thereby of the U.S.S.R., and banishment beyond the frontiers of the U.S.S.R. for ever; in extenuating circumstances a reduction of sentence is permitted to deprivation of liberty for a period of not less than three years and the confiscation of all or part of the property.

Art. 58 iii. Maintenance of relations for counter-revolutionary purposes with foreign States or with individual representatives of those States and also assistance, rendered by any means whatsoever, to a foreign State at war with the U.S.S.R. or engaged in fighting the U.S.S.R. by means of intervention or blockade entail:

measures of social defence as indicated in Article 58 ii of the present Code.

Art. 58 iv. The rendering of assistance, by any means whatsoever, to that section of the international bourgeoisie, which, not recognising the equal rights of the communist system which is coming to replace the capitalist system, is endeavouring to overthrow it, and also to public groups and organisations, under the influence of or directly organised by that bourgeoisie in conducing activities hostile to the U.S.S.R. entails:

deprivation of liberty for a period of not less than three years and confiscation of all or part of his property; to be increased in especially grave circumstances to the supreme measure of social defence — death by shooting, or declaration as an enemy of the toiling masses, coupled with deprivation of citizenship of the Union republic and thereby of citizenship of the U.S.S.R., and banishment for ever beyond the frontiers of the U.S.S.R., and the confiscation of property.

Art. 58 v. Influencing a foreign State or any public groups within that State, by maintaining relations with its representatives, use of false documents or by any other means to a declaration of war, to armed intervention in the affairs of the U.S.S.R., or to any other hostile acts, in particular: to blockade, to seize the State property of the U.S.S.R. or its Union Republics, to break off diplomatic relations, to break off agreements concluded with the U.S.S.R., etc., entails:

measures of social defence enumerated in Article 58 ii of this Code.

G G

Art. 58 vi. Espionage, i.e. the transmission, theft or collection, with a view to transmission to foreign States, counter-revolutionary organisations or private persons, of information accounted by reason of its contents an especially guarded State secret is punishable by:

deprivation of liberty for a period of not less than three years, with confiscation of all or part of property; in cases, when espionage has caused, or might have caused, especially grievous consequences to the interests of the U.S.S.R. the supreme measure of social defence — death by shooting, or the declaration to be an enemy of the labouring masses and the deprivation of citizenship of the Union Republic and thereby of the U.S.S.R. and banishment beyond the frontiers of the U.S.S.R. for ever, and confiscation of property.

The transmission, theft or collection with a view to transmission of economic information not constituting by virtue of its contents an especially guarded State secret but not intended for divulgence to the organisations or persons enumerated above, as the result of direct prohibition by law or by order of the heads of departments, establishments or enterprises, either for recompense or gratis is punishable by:

deprivation of liberty for a period not exceeding three years.

Art. 58 vii. The undermining of State industry, transport, trade, monetary exchange or the credit system and also of the co-operative network, committed for counter-revolutionary purposes by means of making use to such ends of State establishments and enterprises, or by means of impeding their normal functioning, and also the utilisation of State establishments and enterprises, or the impeding of their functioning in the interests of their former owners or of capitalist organisations interested in them is punishable by:

the measures of social defence indicated in Article 58 ii of the present Code.

Art. 58 viii. The commission of terrorist acts, directed against representatives of the Soviet regime or members of revolutionary workers' and peasants' organisations, and participation in the commission of such acts, even by persons not belonging to a counter-revolutionary organisation is punishable by:

the measures of social defence, indicated in Article 58 ii of the present Code.

Art. 58 ix. The destruction or damage, for counter-revolutionary purposes, by explosives, arson or other means, of railways or other means of transportation, of the means of public communi-

cation, of water conduits, or public stores and other constructions or of State or public property, is punishable by:

the measures of social defence indicated in Article 58 ii of the
present Code.

Art 58 x. Propaganda or agitation containing an appeal to overthrow, undermine or weaken the Soviet regime, or to commit
individual counter-revolutionary crimes (Articles 58 ii to 58 ix
of the present Code), and also the distribution, the preparation,
or the conservation of literature of this nature, entails:

deprivation of liberty for a period of not less than six months.
Similar actions undertaken under conditions of mass unrest or
involving the exploitation of the religious or national prejudices
of the masses, or under conditions of war, or in localities placed
under martial law are punishable by:

measures of social defence, indicated in Article 58 ii of the
present Code.

Art. 58 xi. Any type of organisational activity, directed towards
the preparation or the commission of crimes provided for in the
present chapter, and also participation in an organisation
formed for the preparation or the commission of one of the
crimes provided for in this chapter, is punishable by:

the measures of social defence, indicated in the relevant
articles of the present chapter.

Art. 58 xii. Failure to report reliable knowledge of preparations
for, or commission of a counter-revolutionary crime entails:

deprivation of liberty for a period of not less than six months.

Art. 58 xiii. Actions or active struggle directed against the working
class and the revolutionary movement, if committed by those in
a responsible or secret (agents') post under the Tsarist regime,
under counter-revolutionary governments during the Civil
War, are punishable by:

the measures of social defence indicated in Article 58 ii of
the present Code.

Art. 58 xiv. Counter-revolutionary sabotage, i.e. deliberate non-
fulfilment by anyone of duties laid down or the wilfully careless
execution of those duties with a view to weakening the authority
of the government, the functioning of the State apparatus,
entails:

deprivation of liberty for a period of not less than one year,
with confiscation of all or part of his property; to be increased
in especially grave circumstances, to the supreme measure of
social defence — death by shooting with confiscation of
property.

(Juridical Publishing House, Moscow, 1949.)

RESOLUTION OF THE CENTRAL COMMITTEE OF THE C.P.S.U. ON THE ANTI-PARTY GROUP: JUNE 1957

At its meetings of June 22–29, 1957, the Plenary Session of the C.C. of the C.P.S.U. considered the question of the anti-Party group of Malenkov, Kaganovich and Molotov which had formed within the Praesidium of the C.C. of the C.P.S.U. At a time when the Party, led by the Central Committee and supported by the people as a whole, is doing enormous work to put into effect the historic decisions of the XXth Congress, designed further to develop the national economy and steadily raise the standard of living of the Soviet people, to re-establish Leninist norms in Party life, to do away with violations of revolutionary law, to extend the links between the Party and the masses, to promote Soviet socialist democracy, to consolidate friendship among the Soviet peoples, to pursue a correct national policy and in the sphere of foreign policy to relax international tension in order to secure a lasting peace, and when notable progress has been made in all these fields, progress well-known to every Soviet citizen, the anti-Party group of Malenkov, Kaganovich and Molotov came out against the Party line. Seeking to change the Party's political line, this group used anti-Party, fractionary, methods in an attempt to change the composition of the Party's leading bodies elected by the plenary meeting of the C.C. of the C.P.S.U.

This was not accidental. In the last three or four years, during which the Party has been steering a resolute course towards rectifying the errors and shortcomings born of the personality cult and waging a successful struggle against the revisionists of Marxism–Leninism, both in the international sphere and inside the country, years during which the Party has done appreciable work to rectify distortions of the Leninist national policy committed in the past, the members of the anti-Party group now laid bare and fully exposed have been offering constant opposition, direct or indirect, to this course approved by the XXth Congress of the C.P.S.U.

The group attempted in effect to oppose the Leninist policy of peaceful co-existence between States with different social systems, of relaxing international tension and establishing friendly relations between the U.S.S.R. and all the peoples of the world. They were against the extension of the rights of the Union republics in the sphere of economic and cultural development and in the sphere of legislation and against enhancing the role of local soviets in the fulfilment of these tasks. Thereby, the anti-Party group resisted the Party's firm course towards a more rapid development of economy and culture in the national Republics, a course ensuring the further promotion of Leninist friendship between all the peoples of our country.

Far from understanding the Party's measures aimed at combating bureaucracy and reducing the inflated State apparatus, the anti-Party group opposed them.

On all these points, it came out against the Leninist principle of democratic centralism being implemented by the Party. The group persistently opposed and sought to frustrate so vastly important a measure as the reorganisation of industrial management and the setting up of Economic Councils in the Economic Areas, approved by the whole of the Party and people. They refused to understand that at the present stage, when progress in Socialist industry has assumed a tremendous scale and continues at a high rate, the development of heavy industry receiving priority, it was indispensable to find new, better forms of industrial management such as would bring out greater reserves and guarantee an even more powerful rise in Soviet industry. The group went so far as to continue its struggle against the reorganisation of industrial management even after the approval of the above measures in the course of the country-wide discussions and the subsequent adoption of a law at the session of the Supreme Soviet of the U.S.S.R.

With regard to agricultural problems, the members of the group showed a lack of understanding of the new, pressing tasks. They would not recognise the necessity of increased material incentives for the collective farm peasantry in expanding output of agricultural products. They objected to the abolition of the old bureaucratic system of planning at the collective farms and the introduction of a new system of planning such as would release the initiative of the collective farms in carrying on their economy, a measure which has already yielded positive results. They drifted so far away from reality as to be unable to see the actual possibility of abolishing at the end of this year obligatory deliveries of farm produce by collective farmers from their individual plots. The implementation of this measure, which is of vital importance for the millions of the working people of the U.S.S.R., was made possible by substantial progress in socially-owned livestock breeding at the collective farms and by the advancement of the State farms.

Instead of supporting this pressing measure, the members of the anti-Party group opposed it. They carried on an entirely unwarranted struggle against the Party's appeal, vigorously supported by the collective farms, regions and Republics, to overtake the U.S.A. in the next few years in per capita output of milk, butter and meat. Thereby, the members of the anti-Party group demonstrated an overbearing attitude to the urgent, vital interests of the broad masses of the people and lack of faith in the enormous potentialities of the socialist economy in the country-wide movement now going on for a speedy increase in milk and meat production.

It cannot be considered accidental that Comrade Molotov, a member of the anti-Party group, who manifested a conservative and narrow-minded attitude, far from realising the necessity of making use of virgin lands, resisted the raising of 35,000,000 ha. of virgin land, an enterprise which acquired such tremendous importance in the economy of our country.

Comrades Malenkov, Kaganovich and Molotov put up a stubborn resistance to the measures which the Central Committee and the whole of our Party were carrying out to do away with the consequences of the personality cult, eliminate the violations of revolutionary law that had been committed and provide such conditions as would preclude their recurrence.

Whereas the workers, collective farmers, our glorious youth, our engineers and technicians, scientific workers, writers and all our intellectuals unanimously supported the measures which the Party was putting into practice in accordance with the decisions of the XXth Congress of the C.P.S.U., whereas the entire Soviet people had joined the vigorous effort to carry those measures into execution, whereas our country is going through a powerful rise in popular activity and a fresh surge of creative energy, the members of the anti-Party group kept turning a deaf ear to this creative movement of the masses.

In the sphere of foreign policy, the group, in particular Comrade Molotov, showed narrow-mindedness and hampered in every way the implementation of the new pressing measures intended to ease international tension and promote universal peace. For a long time, Comrade Molotov in his capacity of Foreign Minister, far from taking through the Ministry of Foreign Affairs measures to improve relations between the U.S.S.R. and Yugoslavia, repeatedly came out against the measures which the Praesidium of the Central Committee was carrying out to improve relations with Yugoslavia. Comrade Molotov's erroneous stand on the Yugoslav issue was unanimously condemned by the Plenary Session of the Central Committee of the C.P.S.U. in July 1955, 'as not being in line with the interests of the Soviet State and the socialist camp and not conforming with the principles of Leninist policy'.

Comrade Molotov raised obstacles to the conclusion of the State Treaty with Austria and the improvement of relations with that country which lies in the centre of Europe. The conclusion of the Austrian Treaty was largely instrumental in lessening international tension in general. He was also against normalisation of relations with Japan, while that normalisation has played an important part in relaxing international tension in the Far East. He opposed the fundamental proposition worked out by the Party on the possibility of preventing war in the present conditions, on the possibility of strengthening contacts between the C.P.S.U. and progressive Parties abroad.

Comrade Molotov repeatedly opposed the Soviet Government's indispensable new steps in defence of peace and the security of nations. In particular he denied the advisability of establishing personal contacts between the Soviet leaders and the statesmen of other countries, which is essential for the achievement of mutual understanding and better international relations.

On many of the above points Comrade Molotov's opinion was supported by Comrade Kaganovich and in a number of cases by Comrade Malenkov. The Praesidium of the Central Committee and the C.C. as a whole patiently corrected them and combated their errors, hoping that they would draw proper lessons from their errors, that they would not persist in them and would fall into step with the whole of the Party's leading body. Nevertheless, they maintained their erroneous anti-Leninist positions.

What underlies the attitude of Comrades Malenkov, Kaganovich and Molotov, which is at variance with the Party line, is the circumstance that they were and still are shackled by old notions and methods, that they have drifted away from the life of the Party and country, fail to see the new conditions, the new situation, take a conservative attitude, stubbornly cling to obsolete forms and methods of work that are no longer in keeping with the interests of the advance towards Communism, rejecting what is born of reality itself and is suggested by the interests of the progress of Soviet society, by the interests of the entire Socialist camp.

Both in internal problems and in matters of foreign policy they are sectarian and dogmatic, and they use a scholastic, inert approach to Marxism–Leninism. They fail to realise that in the present conditions living Marxism–Leninism in action and the struggle for Communism manifest themselves in the execution of the decisions of the XXth Party Congress, in the steady carrying out of the policy of peaceful co-existence, the struggle for friendship among peoples and the policy of the all-round consolidation of the Socialist camp, in better industrial management, in the struggle for the fullest possible advancement of agriculture, for an abundance of food, for large-scale housing construction, for the extension of the rights of the Union Republics, for the flourishing of national cultures, for the all-round encouragement of the initiative of the masses.

Seeing that their erroneous statements and actions were constantly rebuffed in the Praesidium of the Central Committee, which has been consistently putting into practice the line set by the XXth Party Congress, Comrades Malenkov, Kaganovich and Molotov embarked on a group struggle against the Party leadership. Entering into collusion on an anti-Party basis, they set out to change the policy of the Party, to drag the Party back to the erroneous methods of leadership condemned by the XXth Party Congress. They resorted to methods of intrigue and formed a collusion against the Central Committee. The facts revealed at the Plenary Session of the Central Committee show that Comrades Malenkov, Kaganovich and Molotov, as well as Comrade Shepilov, who joined them, having embarked on the path of fractionary struggle, violated the Party Statutes and the decision of the Xth Party Congress 'on Party unity', drafted by Lenin, which says:

'In order to effect strict discipline within the Party and in all Soviet work and to achieve maximum unity in eliminating all fractionary activity, the Congress empowers the Central Committee to apply in cases of breach of discipline or of a revival or toleration of fractionary activity all Party penalties including expulsion from the Party, and in respect of members of the Central Committee their reduction to the status of Alternate Members, or even as an extreme measure, their expulsion from the Party. As a precondition for the application of this extreme measure to Members of the Central Committee, Alternate Members of the Central Committee and Members of the Control Commission shall be the convening of a Plenary Session of the Central Committee to which all Alternate Members of the Central Committee and all members of the Control Commission should be invited. If such a general meeting of the most responsible Party leaders recognises by a two-thirds majority the necessity of reducing a member of the Central Committee to the status of Alternate Member or his expulsion from the Party, then this measure shall be carried out immediately.'

This Lenin resolution makes it obligatory for the Central Committee and all Party organisations tirelessly to consolidate Party unity, to rebuff with determination every evidence of fractionary or group activity, to ensure that the work is indeed carried out by joint effort, that it indeed expresses the unity of will and action of the vanguard of the working class, the Communist Party.

The Plenary Session of the Central Committee notes with great satisfaction the monolithic unity and solidarity of all the Members and Alternate Members of the Central Committee and the Members of the Central Revision Commission of the C.P.S.U., who have unanimously condemned the anti-Party group. Not a single member of the Plenary Session of the Central Committee supported the group. Faced with unanimous condemnation of the anti-Party activities of the group by the Plenary Session of the Central Committee in a situation where the members of the Plenum of the Central Committee unanimously demanded the removal of the members of the group from the Central Committee and their expulsion from the Party, they admitted the existence of a collusion and the harmful nature of their anti-Party activities and committed themselves to complying with the Party decisions and, guided by the interests of all-round consolidation of the Leninist unity of the Party, the Plenary Session of the Central Committee of the C.P.S.U. has resolved:

(1) To condemn as incompatible with the Leninist principles of our Party the fractionary activities of the anti-Party group of Malenkov, Kaganovich and Molotov, and of Shepilov, who joined them.

(2) To exclude Comrades Malenkov, Kaganovich and Molotov from the Praesidium of the Central Committee and from the Central Committee; to remove Comrade Shepilov from the post of Secretary to the Central Committee and to exclude him from Alternate Membership of the Praesidium of the Central Committee and from membership of the Central Committee.

The unanimous condemnation of the fractionary activities of the anti-Party group of Comrades Malenkov, Kaganovich and Molotov by the Central Committee of the Party will serve further to consolidate the unity of the ranks of our Leninist Party, to consolidate its leadership, to promote the struggle for the general line of the Party. The Central Committee of the Party calls on all Communists to rally still more closely around the invincible banner of Marxism–Leninism, to bend all their energies to the successful fulfilment of the tasks of Communist construction.

Adopted on June 29, 1957, by the unanimous vote of all the Members of the Central Committee, the Alternate Members of the Central Committee and the Members of the Central Revision Commission, with one abstention, in the person of Comrade Molotov.

THE CENTRAL COMMITTEE APPARATUS

Extracts from a Report of an Italian Communist Delegation to the

U.S.S.R.

At the headquarters of the Central Committee of the C.P.S.U. the delegation talked to Comrade Yakovlev, deputy head of the 'Party Organs' Department for the Union Republics. . . .

Longo: Which are the working Departments of the Central Committee of the C.P.S.U.?

Reply: The 'Party Organs' Department;

the 'Agitation and Propaganda' Department divided into different sectors (Propaganda; Agitation; Mass work; Central Newspapers; Publications and Reviews);

the 'Culture and Science' Department to which the Department for Higher Institutes and Schools is linked;

the 'Agricultural' Department;

the 'Transport and Communications' Department;

four Departments for the fundamental branches of industry:

Heavy Industry,

Machine Building,

Light Industry,

Construction;

the 'Administrative Organisations' Department;

the 'Commercial and Economic Organisations' Department;

the 'Foreign Affairs' Department;

the Administration Department which deals with the budget, Party Funds and economy. . . .

Longo: What function has the 'Party Organs' Department?

Reply: The Department keeps index cards of Party leaders and officials and prepares statistical data relative to the cadres and to the composition of various organs to suggest eventual modifications to the Central Committee. We follow all questions to do with systematisation and allocation of cadres either for the Party or for Communists working in the Trade Unions, in the Soviets and in social activities generally. . . . Questions referring to the officials in all branches of work of the central Party apparatus also pass through this Department. For example, our Department sanctions the nomination of officials in the 'Agricultural' Department, the 'Transport' Department, etc.

As for the Soviets, our Department gives its opinion on candidates for the more responsible posts down to the level of Chairman and Deputy Chairman of Regional Soviets (lower jobs come under the control of the local Party organs). Moreover, we deal with candidates for ministerial jobs in the Union Republics. . . .

Amadesi: Does this Department deal only with the Party organs of the Union Republics?

Reply: The Union Republics and the Autonomous Republics. For the Russian Federative Republic, which, as you know, does not have its own Central Committee, a special Bureau within the Central Committee of the C.P.S.U. was constituted after the XXth Congress. This Bureau is not controlled by our working Department but is parallel to it and like us is controlled directly by the Central Committee of the C.P.S.U. However, the Bureau for the Russian Federative Republic works in close collaboration with our Department. For example, there is only one office for issuing Party cards. This division of work has proved correct.

Nannuzzi: How is your Department divided and how many functionaries are there?

Reply: The Department is divided into territorial and functional Sectors. There are four territorial Sectors. Each one deals with a group of Union and Autonomous Republics. . . .

There are also four functional Sectors:

Sector for Organisation and Statutary Questions . . .
Membership Sector;
Cadre Sector;
Trade Unions, Youth and Soviet Organs Sector. . . .

The Central Committee of the C.P.S.U. can intervene to correct certain situations which have come about in the Communist Parties of the Union Republics. Through the work of its apparatus, the Central Committee of the C.P.S.U gets to know about local situations, but only in very grave cases are the local directing organs called to the centre to have discussions with the Secretariat.

To give its own indications about work to be done, the Central Committee of the C.P.S.U. largely uses the Party Press: *Pravda*, *Kommunist*, etc.

(*Problemi e Realta dell' U.R.S.S.*
Rome 1958)

EXTRACTS FROM *IMRE NAGY ON COMMUNISM* CONCERNING THE SOVIET LEADERS IN ACTION

As Party Committee members know, since 1953 Matyas Rakosi on countless occasions has tried to revise the June resolution, giving now the Beria case, now international tension, and at other times my alleged errors and excesses, or still other reasons. In this connection Comrade Khrushchev clearly stated:

> In June 1953 we correctly passed judgment on the Hungarian Party's leadership, and that judgment is still entirely correct to-day. They can't hide behind Beria as Rakosi is trying to do. We were there, too, when these errors were ascertained, every one of us! We were right, and what we decided then is also right to-day. This should have been acted on already! (pp. 142–3).

. . . Matyas Rakosi on several occasions tried to shift the responsibility to Beria, with a view to compromising both the June resolution and those who carried out its provisions. For this he has frequently sought Istvan Dobi's backing — whether successfully or not I do not know. However, the fact is that when we expressed some anxiety concerning the question of the farm cooperatives at the June 1953, Moscow conference, Comrade Molotov (and not Beria) reassured us as follows: 'The farm cooperatives must not be disbanded by fiat, but, should they choose to disband voluntarily, they shouldn't be hindered. No harm will come of it.' Thus, and for this reason, did the June resolution provide for the free disbandment of cooperatives which the 'left-wingers' now seek to call right-wing deviation so as to forge a weapon against me (p. 153).

It should further be known that the question of the relation of Party and State was also discussed very sharply in the conference held with the Soviet comrades prior to the June 1953 meeting of the Hungarian Central Committee, and in the spirit represented above. At this conference Comrade Malenkov pointed out that in May 1953 they had discussed with Matyas Rakosi the personal questions also that concerned the separation of Party and State leadership. 'We asked, "Whom do you recommend as your deputy?" He could name no one. He had objections to everyone whose name was mentioned;

he had something against everyone. Everyone was suspect except he alone. This appalled us very much,' said Comrade Malenkov. Comrade Molotov declared that Matyas Rakosi had said that he did want a Premier, 'but he wanted a Premier who would have no voice in the making of decisions'. Comrade Khrushchev noted, 'The matter involved was that the leadership of the Party and the State should not be concentrated in the hands of one man or a few men: this is not desirable' (pp. 250–1).

In his speech at the April meeting of the Central Committee, Matyas Rakosi allegedly said that he felt heavy responsibility for the fact that I had become Premier on July 4, 1953, thereby suggesting that he at least 'recommended' me for Premier. For the sake of truth, it must be stated that it was not Matyas Rakosi, but the Soviet comrades — Comrades Malenkov, Molotov, and Khrushchev — who recommended what Comrade Rakosi and all members of the Hungarian delegation accepted with approbation (p. 252).

It was not without reason that Khrushchev said in June 1953 that 'Matyas Rakosi practised self-criticism so that he would not be criticised any further' (p. 263).

By the end of 1953 and at the beginning of 1954 it had already become evident to the Soviet comrades, too, that there was opposition to the June resolutions, and for this they blamed primarily Matyas Rakosi. Comrade Malenkov said, 'The faults we noted in June are being remedied very slowly. Rakosi had not taken the lead in remedying the faults.' Comrade Khrushchev also noted, 'Gerö has not words of self-criticism or feeling of responsibility for the serious mistakes of the economic policy; at best he admits, "It is possible that Comrade Nagy is right in feeling that I am held back by the old economic policy"' (p. 271).

Our Soviet comrades quite correctly stated that one of the greatest shortcomings of the old leadership was that 'in Hungary, a true collective leadership failed to develop because Rakosi is incapable of working collectively'. 'He has lost the self-confidence required to correct mistakes, and it can happen that proper leadership will come into being over his head, which is a catastrophe for a leader,' said Comrade Khrushchev at the May 1954 conference in Moscow.

Comrade Malenkov, too, found that we were slow in correcting our mistakes in Party leadership and that Rakosi, as Party First Secretary, was not doing the job well. . . .

During our visit preceding the Third Party Congress, the Soviet comrades emphasised:

Comrade Rakosi must take the lead in the fight to correct previous mistakes and to implement the resolutions of the Central

Committee. He must put a final end to the mistakes of the past, bravely, manfully, and like a Bolshevik. He does not have to put the blame on Beria, the international situation, or anything else. Rakosi must promote Party unity by fighting consistently against the mistakes (p. 280).

Comrade Khrushchev, at the first of last year, urged the rehabilitations, saying: 'The detainees are being released slowly. This is Rakosi's fault, because he hasn't taken the matter in hand. Rakosi alludes to the fact that his nerves are bad. Nerves don't count. He has lost self-confidence in the correction of errors.' On the occasion of our Moscow talks prior to the IIIrd Congress, Comrade Khrushchev likewise said the following: 'Rakosi is responsible for the arrests. Therefore he does not want to release these people. He knows that he is guilty and will compromise himself. It is not permissible to denounce men and to throw suspicion on them.' Comrade Khrushchev advised that 'the rehabilitations should be carried out so as not to destroy Rakosi's authority'. But, so that his words would not be misinterpreted, he added, 'We will protect Rakosi's authority only in so far as it is not prejudicial to Party authority.'

'It may happen that on the pretext of protecting Rakosi's authority, the old policy will be reinstated and the freeing of the prisoners will not proceed. Of course, it is difficult for Rakosi to free the prisoners,' Comrade Khrushchev said, 'because he ordered the arrests. Despite that, what happened must be told. Neither silence nor glossing over will increase the authority of the Party; rather it will take frank discussion' (p. 296).

(*Imre Nagy on Communism*,
Thames and Hudson 1957.)

AN EXAMPLE OF SOVIET PROTOCOL

(The Biography of Malenkov in the *Encyclopedic Dictionary*)

(Vol. II)

Version of April 1954

MALENKOV, Georgy Maksimilianovich (born Jan. 8, 1902), outstanding personality of the Communist Party and Soviet State, a true pupil of V. I. Lenin and comrade-in-arms of J. V. Stalin. Member of the Praesidium of the C.C. C.P.S.U. Chairman of the Council of Ministers of the U.S.S.R.; Deputy to the Supreme Soviet of the U.S.S.R. G. M. Malenkov was born in Orenburg (now Chkalov) in the family of an employee. During the Civil War he volunteered for the Red Army. In April 1920 G. M. Malenkov entered the Communist Party. From 1919 until 1921 he was political worker in a squadron, regiment, brigade and the Political Administration of the Eastern and Turkestan Fronts.

After demobilisation in 1921–25 he studied in the Moscow technical college. From 1925 to 1930 G. M. Malenkov performed responsible work in the apparatus of the C.C. of the Communist Party. From 1930 to 1934 he did directing work in the Moscow Committee of the Party. From 1934 to 1939 he was Head of the Department of Leading Party Organs of the C.C. C.P.S.U.(b). In Dec. 1937, during the first election to the Supreme Soviet of the U.S.S.R., G. M. Malenkov was elected a Deputy to the Supreme Soviet of the

Version of February 1955

MALENKOV, Georgy Maksimilian-ovich (born 1902), important personality of the Communist Party and Soviet State.

Member of the C.P.S.U. since 1920. Deputy to the Supreme Soviet of the U.S.S.R.

Born in Orenburg (now Chkalov) in the family of a petty employee. In 1919 he volunteered for the Red Army.

From 1919 until 1921 he was political worker on the Eastern and Turkestan fronts. In 1921–25 he studied in the Moscow technical college. From 1925 to 1930 worked in the apparatus of the C.C. C.P.S.U.(b). From 1930 to 1934 — at work in the Moscow Committee of the C.P.S.U.(b), in 1934–39 he was Head of the Department of Leading Party Organs of the C.C. C.P.S.U.(b).

Version of April 1954

U.S.S.R., and from that time on he has been elected regularly as a Deputy to the Supreme Soviet of the U.S.S.R. and R.S.F.S.R. At the XVIIIth Congress of the C.P.S.U.(b) in March 1939, G. M. Malenkov was elected to the Central Committee, and at the Plenum of the Central Committee in March 1939 was elected Secretary of the C.C. C.P.S.U.(b), a member of the Orgburo of the C.C. C.P.S.U.(b) and appointed Chief of the Administration for Cadres of the C.C. C.P.S.U.(b). At the XVIIIth All-Union Conference of the C.P.S.U.(b) in Feb. 1941 G. M. Malenkov made a speech on the tasks of Party organisations in the sphere of industry and transport. In Feb. 1941 at a Plenum of the C.C. C.P.S.U.(b) G. M. Malenkov was elected a candidate member of the Politburo of the C.C. C.P.S.U.(b).

During the Great Patriotic War from June 30, 1941, to Sept. 4, 1945, G. M. Malenkov was a member of the State Committee. In Aug. 1941 G. M. Malenkov was on the Leningrad Front; in the autumn and winter of 1941 he took an active part in the organisation of operations for the destruction of German fascist troops near Moscow; in March 1942 he went to the Volkhov Front; in July and then in Aug. to Sept. to the Stalingrad and Don Fronts; in March 1943 he was on the Central Front, carrying on everywhere great work in organising forces for the struggle against the German fascist aggressors. As a member of the State Defence Committee G. M. Malenkov directed work for equipping the Soviet Army with new fighting equipment and Soviet aviation with aircraft and engines. For special services

Version of February 1955

At the XVIIIth Congress of the C.P.S.U.(b) (1939) was elected to the C.C. C.P.S.U.(b) and at the Plenum of the C.C. C.P.S.U.(b) — a Secretary of the C.C. C.P.S.U.(b), a member of the Orgburo of the C.C. C.P.S.U.(b) and appointed Chief of the Administration for Cadres of the C.C. C.P.S.U.(b).

In Feb. 1941, at a Plenum of the C.C. C.P.S.U.(b) G. M. Malenkov was elected a candidate member of the Politburo of the C.C. C.P.S.U.(b).

During the Great Patriotic War 1941–45, was a member of the State Defence Committee.

For services in the sphere of

Version of April 1954

in the sphere of increasing production of aircraft and motors in difficult wartime conditions G. M. Malenkov was awarded the title of Hero of Socialist Labour on Sept. 30, 1943. In Nov. 1945 the Praesidium of the Supreme Soviet of the U.S.S.R. awarded the Order of Lenin to G. M. Malenkov for successful work in carrying out the tasks of the Communist Party and Soviet Government. In March 1946 at a Plenum of the C.C. of the Party G. M. Malenkov was elected a member of the Politburo of the C.C. C.P.S.U.(b); he performed at this time work as Secretary of the C.C. of the Party and Deputy Chairman of the Council of Ministers of the U.S.S.R. In Jan. 1952 in connection with his 50th birthday G. M. Malenkov was awarded an Order of Lenin for outstanding services to the Communist Party and Soviet people. In Oct. 1952 at the XIXth Congress of the C.P.S.U. G. M. Malenkov gave the report on the work of the C.C. C.P.S.U.(b).

G. M. Malenkov was elected a member of the C.C. C.P.S.U. by the XIXth Congress of the Party and at the Plenum of the C.C. C.P.S.U. a member of its Praesidium. Until March 1953 he was a Secretary of the C.C. C.P.S.U. On March 15, 1953, the fourth session of the Supreme Soviet of the U.S.S.R. confirmed the appointment of G. M. Malenkov as Chairman of the Council of Ministers of the U.S.S.R.

Version of February 1955

increasing production of aircraft and motors, G. M. Malenkov was awarded the title of Hero of Socialist Labour in 1943.

In March 1946 he was elected a member of the Politburo of the C.C. C.P.S.U.(b); he performed at this time work as Secretary of the C.C. of the Party and Deputy Chairman of the Council of Ministers of the U.S.S.R.

He was elected a member of the C.C. C.P.S.U. by the XIXth Congress of the Party.

From March 1953 until Feb. 1955 he was Chairman of the Council of Ministers of the U.S.S.R. From Feb. 1955 — Minister of Electric Power Stations and Deputy Chairman of the Council of Ministers of the U.S.S.R. Has been awarded three Orders of Lenin.

H H

INDEX

The abbreviations used are those given on pp. 423-4

ABAKUMOV, V. S.: appointed to M.G.B., 87; removed, 187; trial, 97, 100–1, 251, 254, 261, 274, 435, 448–9; other refs., 45, 58, 188, 189, 224
Administration of cadres, 40; *and see* Party Organs Dept.
Administrative Organs Dept., 38–40, 46
Adventurism, 109
Agitprop, 38–40, 464
Agriculture: policies of Stalin, 126, 238–40; Beria, 219; Malenkov, 229–30; Anti-Party Group, 459–60; Khrushchev, 219, 229–43; disputes in 1950–53, 112–28; in 1958, 349; concessions to peasantry, 24, 27; output per hectare, 116; transition to Communism, 361–2; *and see* Virgin Lands Policy.
Agriculture, Dept. of, 38–40
Agrogorod, 28, 120–4
Akhundov, R., 452
Aleksandrov, G. F.: criticised by Zhdanov, 83, 105; and Suslov, 179; M. of Culture, 242, 247–8; dismissed, 258
Alekseenko, G. V., 177
Aliev, B., 452–3
Alsop, Joseph, 298
Ambassadorships, 71
Anashkin, I., 453
Andreyev, A. A.: downfall, 117–19, 157; Malenkovite candidate, 253–4; other refs., 80, 88, 303, 437
Andrianov, V. M.: Sec. Leningrad, 95; Praes., 157–8, 198; dismissed, 231–3; other refs., 40, 83, 162, 290
Andropov, 39
Anti-Party Group: core of, 71–2; linked with Beria, 230; on Virgin Lands policy, 235–41, 460; support State control, 302; opposition to Khrushchev policies, 307–11; voting power in Praes., 313; 'dictator' Khrushchev, 317; how defeated,

318; their policies, 319–20; expulsion, 321, 432; post-fall accusations against, 322–4; dogmatism and bureaucracy of, 326; supported decadent writers, 327; Bulganin added to, 360–1; renewed attacks on, 362–81, 385; C.C. Resolution on, 458–63; other refs., 229, 292–328
Anti-Semitism, 154, 164–5, 172–4, 438–9
Antonov, 133
Antonov-Ovseenko, 99, 281, 286
Apparatchiks, 46
Applause, evidence from, 64
Aprakshin, K. N., 449, 451
Archives, Soviet, 52–3
Aristov, A. B.: in Praes., 157; at XIXth Congress, 159; in Stalin's favour, 179, 181, 209; demoted, 182, 198; fall of, 204–6, 208; protected by Khrushchev, 209; fortunes revive, 234; joins Secretariat, 38, 267, 432; joins R.S.F.S.R. Bureau, 288; on Anti-Party Group, 377; support for Khrushchev, 383; leaves Secretariat, 388; other refs., 40, 70, 161, 162, 190, 203, 347
Aristov, A. P., 181 *n.*
Army: Stalin's purge of, 335, and handling of, 354–5; role in Stalin's last years, 168–70, 331; attitude to Stalin, 330–1; role at Beria's fall, 223, 332; opposed Malenkov, 333; views on nuclear war, 333–4; Zhukov weakens Party influence, 336–8, and Malinovsky strengthens it, 339–44
Army Political Administration, 45
Artel, 22, 82
Artemyev, P. A., 223, 332, 334
Arustanov, L., 453
Arutinov, G. A., 123, 226
Arutyunov, B. N., 184
Atakishiev, A. S., 451–3
Austrian treaty, 265–6

*Printed in Great Britain
by Richard Clay and Company, Ltd.,
Bungay, Suffolk*

Ar